# THE ENLIGHTENMENT
## The Culture of the Eighteenth Century

# The Cultures of Mankind

GREEK CULTURE: The Adventure of the Human Spirit
*Edited by Alice von Hildebrand*

ROMAN CULTURE: Weapons and the Man
*Edited by Garry Wills*

MEDIEVAL CULTURE: The Image and the City
*Edited by Ruth Brantl*

RENAISSANCE CULTURE: A New Sense of Order
*Edited by Julian Mates and Eugene Cantelupe*

THE AGE OF REASON: The Culture of the Seventeenth Century
*Edited by Leo Weinstein*

THE ENLIGHTENMENT: The Culture of the Eighteenth Century
*Edited by Isidor Schneider*

ROMANTICISM: The Culture of the Nineteenth Century
*Edited by Morse Peckham*

TWENTIETH-CENTURY CULTURE: The Breaking Up
*Edited by Robert Phelps*

# The Enlightenment

## The Culture of the Eighteenth Century

Edited by Isidor Schneider

George Braziller · *New York*

## ACKNOWLEDGMENTS

The editor and publisher have made every effort to determine and credit the holders of copyright of the selections in this book. Any errors or omissions may be rectified in future volumes. The editor and publisher wish to thank the following for permission to reprint the material included in this anthology:

Barron's Educational Series, Inc. — for selections from *Emile*, Vol. I, by Jean-Jacques Rousseau, tr. by Rosalie Feltenstein, copyright 1950. Reprinted by permission of the publisher.

Rosica Colin Ltd. — for a selection from *Dangerous Acquaintances*, by Choderlos de Laclos, tr. by Richard Aldington. Copyright by Madame Catherine Guillaume (née Aldington). Reprinted by permission of Rosica Colin Ltd.

Doubleday & Company, Inc. — for selections from *Diderot: Rameau's Nephew and Other Works*, tr. by Jacques Barzun and Ralph H. Bowen. Copyright © 1956 by Jacques Barzun and Ralph H. Bowen. Reprinted by permission of the publisher.

E. P. Dutton & Co., Inc. and J. M. Dent & Sons Ltd. — for selections from *Ethics* by Benedictus de Spinoza, tr. by Andrew Boyle. Everyman's Library. Reprinted by permission of the publishers.

Norbert Guterman — for his translation of Goethe's "An Essay on Granite" from *The Permanent Goethe*, ed. by Thomas Mann. Reprinted by permission of Norbert Guterman.

# Acknowledgments

New Directions — for a selection from "Twelve Dialogues of Fontenelle," tr. by Ezra Pound, from *Pavannes & Divagations* by Ezra Pound, © 1958 by Ezra Pound. Reprinted by permission of the publisher.

Prentice-Hall, Inc. — for selections from *The World of Great Composers,* ed. by David Ewen. © 1962 by Prentice-Hall, Inc., Englewood Cliffs, New Jersey. Reprinted by permission of the publisher.

Princeton University Press — for a selection from "Thoughts on the Imitation of Greek Art in Painting and Sculpture," by Johann J. Winckelmann from *Literary Sources of Art History,* sel. and ed. by Elizabeth Gilmore Holt. Copyright © 1947, 1958 by Princeton University Press. Reprinted by permission of the publisher.

Henry Regnery Company — for selections from *The Social Contract* by Jean-Jacques Rousseau, tr. by Willmoore Kendall. Copyright 1954 by Henry Regnery Company. Reprinted by permission of the publisher.

The Viking Press, Inc. — for a selection from "The Marriage of Figaro" by Beaumarchais, tr. by Crane Brinton, from *The Portable Age of Reason Reader,* ed. by Crane Brinton. Reprinted by permission of the publisher.

The World Publishing Company — for selections from Montesquieu's *The Persian Letters,* tr. by J. Robert Loy. Copyright © 1961 by Meridian Books, Inc. Reprinted by permission of the publisher.

# Preface

The chief associations one brings to the term "The Enlightenment" are expanding scientific knowledge, faith in reason and progress, and morality founded on concepts of natural law rather than on religious commandments and practices. These optimistic attitudes are certainly characteristic of eighteenth-century thinking but skepticism and doubt were never far behind and resistances and countertrends were powerful. In the *philosophes* themselves there were ambivalences and it is possible to view a number of them as both rationalists and romantics and even, in some of their expressions, as reactionaries.

Consequently the sections into which this anthology is divided include antithetical approaches. For example, the middle class which carried out the democratic revolutions also engineered the Industrial Revolution with its scarring of man and nature; and among the selections dealing with it are some protesting voices. Some of the selections also have contents applicable to several of the headings. One of Montesquieu's "Persian Letters," for example, could have been placed under two other headings than the one I finally chose for it.

It was my aim to make my selections as representative as possible of the varied and abundant century of the Enlightenment, but in the inevitable restriction of choices imposed by considerations of space, availability, etc., there are omissions that I regret. On the other hand, to be representative it has been necessary, in some instances, to violate strict chronology. Thus the writings of John Locke, though done in the previous century, so influenced eighteenth-century thinking that it was impossible to do without them.

Omissions within pieces are indicated by three centered dots.

In my long but rewarding reading for this anthology I experienced what I might term a personal enlightenment which clarified my understanding not only of the eighteenth century but of history in general.

7

It is with the hope that the reader will share that experience that I now conclude this undertaking.

There remains for me the pleasant obligation of expressing my gratitude to Mr. George Brantl for his unfailingly perceptive and helpful advice.

*New York City*                                              Isidor Schneider

# Contents

## Part I    Toward a Rational Society

## Part II    Nature as Matrix

9

## *Part* III    The Guidance of Reason

## *Part* IV    Science, the Means

## Part V  The Vision of Progress

## Part VI  Democracy, the Necessary Condition

## Part VII  The Emergence of the Middle Class

## Part VIII    Humanist Morality

## Part IX    Faith Without Dogma

# Contents

## Coda: The Romantic Counterthrust

# List of Illustrations

15

# INTRODUCTION

The Enlightenment, as the eighteenth century is most frequently termed, should be considered, first of all, as a continuation of the preceding century, with its spectacular advances in science and its faith, based on these advances, in the powers of the human mind. On this account the two centuries are often coupled together as the "Age of Reason."

But there are also divergences, and these go deeper than such as may be ascribed simply to different stages of a continuous development. The eighteenth century produced no minds to rank with Newton, Leibniz, or Descartes, and it made no comparable discoveries. Its leading figures turned rather to the application of reason to human behavior and social relations, producing thereby the first formulations of what we call the social sciences.

In the seventeenth century God was still in the foreground and religion retained its place as a major authority, natural law being interpreted as the expression of divine law. In the eighteenth century God receded into the background; the individual, with reason and conscience as his authorities, stepped forward, and human nature became the measure of existence and experience. Among the enlightened, religion was reduced to the easy commitments of deism, which assumed that God was the supreme rationalist who inculcated morals as mathematicians established their postulates. Institutionalized religions were criticized for their dogmas and their residues of superstition.

The eighteenth century took long strides, as we shall see, toward the further secularization of life. Among other manifestations were its wars, in which, unlike the wars of the seventeenth century, the warmakers no longer resorted even to pretended religious motivations. Nationalism began to replace religion, and the French revolutionary wars that closed the century became those of a "nation in arms."

Secularization was reinforced by the Industrial Revolution, which wrought great changes, with the middle class emerging as the dominating class. It was accompanied by a general relaxation of institutional ties.

Man was guided now more than ever before by self-interest; what he liked to believe was his own reason and what he preferred to call his own conscience. The eighteenth century saw the beginnings of rampant individualism. With prospects apparently unlimited and consequences as yet undiscerned, all this was characterized by a euphoric faith in human perfectibility and progress. But instinct and custom, at first viewed as primitive manifestations of reason, were eventually to disclose their incalculable powers. And the romanticism in which the Enlightenment was finally submerged not only marked its concluding and countervailing phase but was its ambivalent companion throughout.

Nevertheless, faith in knowledge and reason and in the progress they were held certain to achieve remained the dominant characteristic of the Enlightenment. This faith was succinctly expressed by the poet Alexander Pope:

> Nature and Nature's laws lay hid in night:
> God said, Let Newton be! and all was light.

Cartesianism, the concept of the mathematical and mechanistic order of the universe, which Newton and Leibnitz elaborated upon after Descartes, was virtually a credo of the eighteenth century. It was generally assumed by the Enlightenment thinkers that all knowledge could be expressed in mathematical terms. Thus, following the example of the political scientist Hobbes, the moralist Spinoza, and other seventeenth-century figures, the theses of Enlightenment thinkers were formulated like geometrical propositions. Further, since heavenly bodies as well as bodies on earth appeared to follow the laws of mechanics established by Newton, everything, from the human body to the universe, was seen as a machine. The most influential work of the French philosopher-physician La Mettrie was entitled "Man, a Machine." It was assumed that God on science, often seen as a return to "natural law," a Utopia could be en- a higher plane and man on a lower could bring the individual human or social machines into perfect working order. Thus, finally, with the aid of visioned. Unlike our time when, under the menace of atomic weaponry, dread is mixed with hope in our attitude toward science, in the eighteenth century science was a source of pure optimism. It was expected to sweep away superstition and provide mechanically perfect models of improved political and economic systems and a richer culture.

No wonder, then, that in no age in European — and perhaps in world — history was such influence wielded by the enlightened, the *philosophes,* those whom we call intellectuals today and who were called the intelligentsia in prerevolutionary Russia. It was the age in which Voltaire, formidable only in the power of the mind, could make his Swiss haven at Ferney, just across the French frontier, virtually an independent court, radiating authority like the court of a monarch. It was the age in which autocrats as powerful as Frederick the Great, Catherine the Great, Joseph II of the haughty Hapsburgs, and other rulers courted the distinction of being "enlightened," and therefore "benevolent" despots, and of entertaining, corresponding with, or extending patronage to the philosophes. It was the age in which man was most confident of the power of reason to dispel confusion, penetrate mysteries, and reorganize society on a rational model. The American and French revolutions toward the end of the century were inspired and sustained by that confidence.

We may view the century of the Enlightenment as part of the five-century European cycle of world history which began with the Portuguese and Spanish maritime expeditions of the 1400's. European exploration, colonization, and conquest continued thereafter until, by the beginning of our century, few areas of the world were free of European domination.

This spatial expansion of Europe was one of the results of the unprecedented release of human energies and expansion of human conciousness set off by the Renaissance. Spain had been the chief gainer, at first, by the European drive overseas and had become the paramount power on the Continent. But she spent the wealth and military prestige she had gained in her conquests in exhausting wars to overthrow Protestantism and, in general, to preserve the old order. In spite of her seemingly overwhelming advantages, the victory went to the irresistible forces of change, and, by the eighteenth century, Spain and Portugal had been reduced to minor powers. The victory was most decisive on the economic front, for the vast booty of the two Indies had precipitated a boom from which the Protestant states, where the new middle class was strongest, profited most.

England and Holland, one threatened by and the other liberated from Spanish rule, having won their mixed religious and political revolutions, now provided enviable examples of a stable political system, a thriving economy notable for its flexibility, and a considerable measure of religious toleration and freedom of thought and expression. The idea of absolute autocratic rule by "divine right" had become so passé that the Stuarts' persistence in it had made them ridiculous as well as intolerable. In the seventeenth century Louis XIV could say, "I am the State!" but in the eighteenth, similar claims by his successors proved empty, and an intelligent autocrat like Frederick the Great, who himself

*1.* Charles Willson Peale, *Benjamin Franklin,* c. 1787.

led his army and himself administered the state and who could therefore have more convincingly asserted the claim, chose rather to characterize himself as the "first servant of the state." England had carried out its second and bloodless "glorious revolution," which advanced the primacy of Parliament over the crown and the middle classes over the nobility by, in effect, hiring William of Orange and, later, the Hanoverians to serve as constitutionally limited monarchs. In return they received decisive English support for their political and military maneuvers in the power struggle on the Continent. By then the leading Protestant nations were past the most dynamic stages of their development. The next phase was to appear in France, when the long, glittering, but finally disastrous reign of Louis XIV came to an end and long-deferred social changes were set into motion.

Chauvinist nostalgia for a past when France dominated the Continent may help to explain why the French call Louis XIV "the Great." All that appears to justify it is that he played the part of absolute monarch with majestic aplomb, that his court set the fashions for European dynastic display, and that, in his reign, French supplanted Latin as the international language, thereby helping to prepare the way for France's intellectual leadership in the Enlightenment. It is illuminating that in a recent French textbook on French civilization the section on the Enlightenment is named "The Century of French Europe."

Otherwise the reign of Louis XIV, the longest in European history, was tragic for France. In his almost incessant wars early victories were overbalanced by later defeats. Their costs drained the national treasury, which was under the additional tap of probably the most extravagant court in history. In the palaces at Versailles a horde of idle nobles, whose chief function was ritualized adulation of the king and whose chief concern was competition for his favor, led the lives of luxurious parasites. Unable to endure the affront to his absolutism which religious tolerance implied, Louis XIV revoked the Edict of Nantes, by which the wise Henry IV had ended the religious civil wars and reunited the people. By that revocation Louis XIV deprived the nation, by forced or voluntary exile, of a considerable number of its most productive citizens and some of its finest minds. Nor did this action succeed in its presumed purpose of consolidating the Catholic religion in France. A new Protestant-tinged sect, the Jansenists, arose to be outlawed in its turn, but to be followed by a wave of skepticism and scorn among the intellectuals toward all institutionalized religion and particularly toward the Catholic Church, against whose continuing persecutions Voltaire could fulminate, "Destroy the infamous thing!" After the death of Louis XIV in 1715 it had become almost fashionable to abjure Church dogma and authority and to avow "deism."

When at last Louis XIV died, the state was insolvent and the trade and taxation policies imbedded in his administrative structure made recovery impossible. All classes knew that change was necessary; that was why the philosophes, who advocated it, could speak with such assurance. But it was destined to come, not through the reforms they agitated for, but through a revolution they would probably have abhorred. Louis XV reigned in the expectation that the foreseen collapse would be deferred beyond his time — which he avowed in his cynical but accurate prophecy, "After me the deluge!"

The anomaly in all this was that France, nevertheless, was charged with irrepressible vitality. Unlike the Iberian nations, where no middle class had emerged to advance national development, in France the dynamism of the rising middle class overcame the blockage of the obsolescent state apparatus which it was eventually to overthrow. This dynamism made itself felt, not only in the French economy, which boomed in spite of the restrictive official mercantilist policies, but in the nation's culture, which expanded and flourished and was carried on mainly by members and spokesmen of the middle class. Their energy and venture proved irresistible. Voltaire, Rousseau, and Diderot and many others suffered imprisonment or exile or both, but they could not be silenced.

In the economic field England continued to advance, initiating the Industrial Revolution in the last decades of the century. But though the contemporary philosophy of England was deeper and its literature richer, intellectually France took, and for many decades held, the lead. Nevertheless, the Enlightenment was a general Occidental phenomenon and the interchange of influences was broad and continuous. The works of English scientists, Newton above all, and of the English philosophers, Locke above all, swayed the French philosophes. The comparatively democratic English institutions were studied and generally overrated by their French admirers. The institutions of the comparatively libertarian Swiss and Dutch were also emulated, and these two small but independent nations provided nearby havens for refugee French savants and for proscribed French ideas. A considerable number of French books were printed abroad or, if secretly printed in France, carried spurious foreign imprints. There was a continent-wide advance in the sciences. In that and other fields Italy's contributions — aside from the the arts, notably music — were the work of the humanitarian Beccaria, the founder of modern penology, and of the philosopher Vico, who posited a conviction of human progress on man's rise from instinctual to conscious understanding. The German states, too, made significant contributions in music, architecture and literature (Goethe and Schiller); in the works of the philosophers (Herder and Kant), archaeology and art history (Winckelmann, whose fervor for classical antiquity was largely responsible for the classical revival that marked the closing decades of the century), and humanism (Lessing, whose *Nathan the Wise* was the first consequential appeal to end the superstition of anti-Semitism). And the American contribution was vital, not only in the works of Franklin, Jefferson, and others, but in providing what seemed a confirmation of the Enlightenment's ideal — or shall we say illusion? — that virtue was proportionate to man's closeness to the state of nature.

What served to emphasize and fix the leading role of the French philosophes in the Enlightenment was its most famous product, the Encyclopedia. Started as a French translation of an existing two-volume English encyclopedia, it was soon carried on as an independent venture of French scholars and became the most ambitious and influential intellectual undertaking of the century, each section being greeted, as it was published, with an avidity hard to conceive of today. Most of the leading French intellectuals were contributors, including Rousseau, who later feuded with the Encyclopedists. In all, thirty-five volumes, counting in separate volumes of illustrative engravings and annotated indices, were printed between the years 1752 and 1784. In spite of government and clerical moves to stop its publication, none of the eager subscribers canceled their subscriptions; and despite its high price, the work went into many editions and was translated into several languages. Its quality was uneven, for, unavoidably, many of the articles were hackwork. Yet general access to information was then so new that the mere availability of knowledge had liberalizing effects on political and social thinking, while the avidity for knowledge was itself a sign of the readiness for change, since for most eighteenth-century minds knowledge and reason were certain means to social betterment.

This quest for knowledge sustained the enormous popularity and influence of the "historical and critical dictionary" of Bayle, which was not a dictionary but a compilation of brief commentaries on various subjects, principally to promote skeptical, pragmatic and critical attitudes toward existing institutions. First persecuted and exiled from France as a Huguenot, Bayle suffered new persecutions at the hands of the exiled Huguenot community and his skepticism was, in part, a product of these persecutions. There were also the popularizations of scientific knowledge by Fontenelle and other writers. And the quest for knowledge stimulated the writing of general histories, by the pious Bossuet at one end and the impious Voltaire at the other, culminating in the most celebrated historical work of the period, Gibbon's *Decline and Fall of the Roman Empire*. It also led to the first scientific organizations of biological data, in the taxonomies of Linnaeus and Buffon. In the prevailing fervor for knowledge even the Tory, Samuel Johnson, was led to the composition of his famous dictionary, after which such reference books became indispensable educational tools.

As editor and chief contributor of the Encyclopedia Denis Diderot deserves to be called its creator. It was almost literally his lifework since it took some thirty of the years of his maturity to complete. In its course he had to cope with governmental and church opposition, temperamental contributors, the financial maneuvers of investors, the sheer lack of reference material, and other obstacles which would have stopped a less resolute and resourceful man. For a considerable number of the articles Diderot had to make personal researches through interviews with craftsmen and visits to workshops, since published information on many entries was not then in existence. Without him, too, the Encyclopedia would not have had its marked libertarian orientation. His article defining "encyclopedia" can be taken as a manifesto of the Enlightenment.

Several times the work was halted by the authorities, and Diderot himself suffered a six-week prison term and subsequent surveillance and harassment. But even merely as a financial investment the Encyclopedia had reached a formidable state involving too many important people; it could not be dealt with arbitrarily. Besides, the Enlightenment had now penetrated into court circles and the elite salons, and it had powerful friends. To appease the officials, the publisher, without the knowledge of Diderot, who reacted with helpless fury, softened certain passages before secretly sending them to press. But such emollients had little effect on the impact of the work as a whole.

That the Encyclopedia was propagandistic in its approach was in character with its century, which, even more than the preceding one, was an age of pamphleteering. Dissident intellectuals — and few intellectuals were not dissenters — were attracted to the Encyclopedia for the opportunity it gave them, however indirectly, to air their discontents and ideas of reform. In that sense they were all Encyclopedists, though the name came to be more narrowly associated with Diderot and his circle, among them the mathematician d'Alembert; the economist-statesman Turgot; the Baron d'Holbach, who was among the few who went to the extreme of avowed atheism; and Helvétius, who was one of the first believers in human equality, holding that all men have equal capacities at birth and it is the environment that prevents equal fulfillment. Rousseau began his career as one of the circle but was soon at odds with it, expressing the romanticism that was always in latent conflict with the rationalism of the Enlightenment and that was eventually to supplant it.

But the French philosophes chiefly associated today with the Enlightenment are Voltaire, Diderot, Montesquieu and, despite his repudiation of rationalism, Rousseau. Voltaire remains pre-eminent among them. Victor Hugo said of him, "To name Voltaire is to characterize the entire eighteenth century"; and the American historian Will Durant wrote, "Italy had a Renaissance, Germany had a Reformation, but France had Voltaire."

It is perhaps not generally known that Voltaire established and maintained his literary reputation by poetic dramas esteemed by his contemporaries as the greatest of their time. Indeed, his culminating literary and personal triumph was the production of a last poetic drama at the age of eighty-four. Visiting Paris from his Swiss refuge at Ferney to attend the performances, there was a bigger crush in the streets for a glimpse of him than for a sight of the king and queen on one of their infrequent visits from Versailles. Today Voltaire's dramas are unactable and even unreadable. It is for other works that he is remembered, chiefly his works in prose.

Just as the content of literature (and of the other arts as well) had changed from the theological to the secular in response to the emergence of the new middle class, which was not associated, as royalty and the aristocracy had been, with the clergy, so the medium of expression was changing to accommodate the expanding audience which the development of printing had brought into being. First had come the substitution of the living vernaculars for the dead classical tongues, and then had come the substitution of prose for verse. Pope could still write his *Essay on Man* as a poem, and Goethe his *Faust,* but other writers of the eighteenth century who sought to influence the public were turning to prose. This accounts for the appearance of the novel, which may be regarded as one of the major inventions of the century. It was therefore no accident that for most of the works in which he sought to sway public opinion Voltaire used prose — for his historical writings, his pamphlets and open letters, and his satirical "romances," which were pamphlets in the guise of fiction, the supreme example of which is his immortal *Candide.*

As in the case of most social reformers, it was the "establishment" that provoked Voltaire into his role as its underminer. In punishment for the spirited reply he made to an insult by a titled fop, Voltaire was imprisoned, then banished. He spent his exile in England, from which he returned an apostle for its relatively democratic institutions, the freedom of its parliamentary debates, its religious toleration and its legal safeguards of individual rights through jury trials, habeas corpus, etc. He was also chiefly instrumental in introducing to France the scientific concepts of Newton and the philosophic concepts of Locke.

Voltaire may be said to be the originator of modern historical writing. Aside from their literary excellence, his histories are distinguished for scientific interest in documented data and the emphasis he places on social forces rather than on dynastic chronicle. His book on "le grand monarque" was called not *Louis XIV* but *The Age of Louis XIV.* His general history was titled *Essays on the Manners and Spirit of Nations.* He used history as a means of judging the present and projecting the future, with reason as its rule and progress as its goal. In his *Age of Louis XIV* he is perhaps too proudly French but even there he strove for the detachment implied in his claim to be a "citizen of the world," and its conclusions triumphantly assert the progress of mankind through reason and knowledge. He used history to condemn slavery, tyranny, superstition, inhumanity, war. He mocked the vanity of military glory and its supposed justifications. "It is forbidden to kill," he wrote, "therefore all murderers are punished unless they kill large numbers to the sound of trumpets."

But the chief objects of his loathing were the hypocrisy, superstition, and particularly the continuing persecutions of the Church of his day. The scornful fury of his denunciation of the drawing and quartering of a Protestant falsely accused of the murder of his son made it impossible to repeat such horrors. Clerical attempts to have the Lisbon earthquake viewed as an act of God for which a merciful intent must be presumed drew from Voltaire a savage poem, immediately banned as blasphemous, which asked where a benign providence could be seen in a disaster in which thirty thousand people, many of them congregated in cathedrals, had lost their lives. It also evoked his ironical *Candide,* in which unremitting calamities befall a youth who follows the counsels of a mentor to whom all is for the best in this best of all possible worlds presided over by a benevolent deity.

It should be added, however, that the concept of an ordered and benevolent destiny was even more a deistic concept. The optimism inherent in the belief in a rational order of nature supervised by a divine mechanic met the problem of evil evasively by the assumption that whatever is is somehow right. Voltaire's attack upon it is one among the various contradictions that marked the thinking of the philosophes.

A few quotations will suggest the power of Voltaire's pen, of which he himself said, "I have no scepter but I have a pen," and which the historian Tallentyre characterized as "the most terrible of all intellectual weapons ever wielded by man."

"If triangles had a God he would have three sides."

"Men enriched by your sweat and misery made you superstitious, not that you might fear God, but that you might fear *them.*"

His feelings for justice and toleration were expressed in such words:

"It is better to risk saving a guilty person than to condemn an innocent one."

"I disapprove of what you say but I will defend to the death your right to say it."

Voltaire died at the end of his triumphant return to Paris. The bishop would not let him be buried in the city that adored him, and his body

2. Jean-Baptiste Pigalle,
*Bust of Diderot.* Bronze.

was rushed outside the walls to find a grave. Thirteen years later a huge procession of Parisians walked to the grave, dug up his remains, and brought them back to Paris. On the hearse hung a placard inscribed, "He prepared us for liberty."

Of Diderot it remains to be said that his importance in French literature does not rest solely on his editorship of the Encyclopedia. His original works, brilliant dialogues, essays and art criticism, figure among his nation's classics. They obviously reflect ambiguities in his life experience and conflicts in his own mind, conflicts more or less perceptible in all the philosophes. A humane man, he could sometimes outdo Voltaire in the savagery of his denunciation. "Men will never be free," he wrote, "until the last king is strangled with the entrails of the last priest." A convinced rationalist, he nevertheless was troubled by the dubious issue of emotions and instincts in their contention with reason. He affirmed his faith in reason and sought and cited evidences of human progress, but the advocates of the irrational in his dialogues were allowed pointed and persuasive arguments.

Most of Diderot's works were not printed in his lifetime and, indeed, were intended for posthumous publication. There were other cases of works written for posthumous circulation, among them the British philosopher David Hume's "Dialogues Concerning Natural Religion." How secure the writers of the Enlightenment must have felt about the value of their work and the prospects of a freer future that they could so confidently and literally write for posterity!

By social origin both Voltaire and Diderot were middle class. Montesquieu, like a number of other philosophes, was a noble. Charles Louis de Secondat, Baron de La Brède and de Montesquieu, to give him all his titles, belonged, however, not to the idle and patrician Nobility of the Blood, but to the Nobility of the Robe, whose titles were earned by public service, generally legal. Through such services the Nobility of the Robe had ties and affinities with the busy middle class. Montesquieu himself served for a number of years as counselor, then as president, of the Parliament of Bordeaux, which mainly functioned as a law court.

His first work, *Persian Letters,* purported to be the observations of an Oriental visitor commenting, with irony or artful naïveté, on the deficiencies, vices, and injustices of life in France under the Bourbons. The book had an enormous international success. It also gave a new and characteristically eighteenth-century turn to the interest in comparative culture that had been set off by the explorations of the preceding centuries and which were continued and extended in the eighteenth. It gave rise to a number of imitations, among them Oliver Goldsmith's *The Citizen of the World,* in which a Chinese sage figures as the amused commentator on Western ways. Montesquieu's second outstanding contribution was his *Considerations on the Causes of the Grandeur and Decadence of the Romans,* which influenced and perhaps inspired Gibbon's *Decline and Fall of the Roman Empire.*

But Montesquieu's most directly influential work was his *The Spirit of Laws,* which rivaled Locke's *Two Treatises on Civil Government* as a guide to the constitution makers of the eighteenth century. Our founding fathers incorporated his principle of the separation of powers — executive, legislative, and judicial — in our Constitution.

For Montesquieu, law was reason in action. As perhaps the first systematic environmentalist, he observed that laws must be adapted to the people, their customs, traditions and religions, and the physical conditions of their countries. Though carried, in some cases, to absurd extremes, such perceptions in Montesquieu's works provided starting points for modern political and social science.

All his writings are charged with the concern for justice, humanity, and progress that characterized the philosophes. Montesquieu attacked slavery and cruel punishments, and the Italian humanitarian Beccaria, whose *Treatise on Crime and Punishment* became the foundation of modern penology, acknowledged Montesquieu as his inspiration. Montesquieu did not underrate the waywardness of the human mind, but he believed that, while in little things man was swayed by his emotions, in big things he was swayed by reason. Rousseau, who had more conflicts and suffered more, had a better understanding of the relations of emotion and behavior. He was intuitively aware that the emotions that moved men in little things were active behind their behavior in big things.

It is one of the ironies of history that Rousseau, who had repudiated the rational principles of the Enlightenment, should have contributed so much to their spread. The other eighteenth-century philosophes made much of nature, natural law, nature's God, etc., and held science to be a revelation of nature and an evidence of its order. In contrast Rousseau identified nature with the instinctual life which he felt that reason, as the fabricator of civilization, repressed. Nevertheless, his apostrophes to nature and his assumption of the moral superiority of "natural man" were, for a considerable time, acceptable to the other philosophes.

In fact there was much common as well as disputed ground between the two sides. Both agreed that European man had been corrupted by his institutions — arbitrary monarchy, parasitic nobility, and superstitious and repressive clergy among them. But where Rousseau held the corruption to be caused by reason's presumptuous attempt to dominate over instinct, with which he identified nature, the other philosophes saw reason as the expression and instrument of natural law by means of which the corruption could be checked and reversed.

Though Rousseau claimed the rank of "citizen," which, in bourgeois Geneva, where he was born, would have made him a member of the better classes, the reduced circumstances of his father gave him a "proletarian" orientation. Bound out to a harsh master engraver, he experienced the virtual slavery of apprenticeship, and it was as a runaway that he began his strange, alienated career. All this conditioned his thinking, and it is probable that the state of nature which he romanticized appealed to him, in part, because it presumed a classless condition. It is likely, further, that his bias against civilization as a departure from the purity of nature derived from his view of civilization as the milieu of the corrupt upper classes.

Rousseau's mother died giving him birth, and this too was part of his conditioning. It probably accounts both for his acute awareness of emotional deprivation and his neurosis, which, in the last decade of his life, appears to have crossed the border line into psychosis. Like other severely neurotic writers, Rousseau put a passion into his work which acted like a psychic contagion upon his readers.

Though he was then one of the Encyclopedists (he wrote chiefly on music, which he also composed creditably in the new homophonic style), Rousseau's first literary work was a challenge to their assumptions. He conceived its ideas in a state of actual or near hallucination, and he reports it in his *Confessions* as a mystic might report a revelation. It was prompted by an announcement of an essay contest, the subject of which was, "Has the Progress of the Arts and Sciences Contributed More to the Corruption or to the Purification of Morals?" With the encouragement of Diderot, who may have deceived himself about its significance and who himself contributed to the eighteenth-century image of the "noble savage," Rousseau's entry upheld the thesis that advancing civilization *did* corrupt morals. It won the prize and made Rousseau famous, though it now holds a negligible place in the Rousseau bibliography.

Among Rousseau's principal works was *Julie, or the New Héloïse,* which established the new convention of romantic love. Actually, the book was a projection of his obsessive attachment to a much younger woman with whom he sought to retain, after being rebuffed, a relationship of "pure friendship." Behind its almost hysterical avowals one can discern both the psychic mechanism of sublimation and the continuing influence of the Calvinist rejection of pleasure as sinful which had pervaded the Geneva of his childhood.

A much more important work was his *Social Contract,* by which he meant the supposed primal agreement of men in the precultural stage to surrender some of their "natural" rights in order to establish social authority and thereby gain security against their own violence and the hazards of nature. This theory was not original. It had been developed in the literary and philosophical polemics preceding and accompanying the parliamentary revolution in England, particularly by Locke, who viewed government as the fulfillment of a primal contract between the people, in whom authority ultimately resided, and the regime they set up. The people had the right to abrogate the contract, by revolution if necessary, when the government became a tyranny and, thereby, itself broke the compact. What gave Rousseau's version its force was, as with all his writings, the passion with which it was charged and its compelling phrasemaking. From it the looming French Revolution was to draw some of its most stirring slogans, such as: "Man is born free yet is everywhere in chains" and "The voice of the people is the voice of God." Yet there was much in this book and in Rousseau's thinking in general that was confused and reactionary. For example, he advocated the right of the rulers of a nation to impose their religion on the ruled; and he spoke out against opening a theater in his native Geneva though he himself had composed and won fame for an opera produced in Paris. Among his political notions were the self-contradictory "forced freedom" and the "general will," the latter a mystical unanimity to which the individual is supposed to submit voluntarily and spontaneously. Both these ideas have been used to justify various types of authoritarianism.

Still more influential was his *Emile, or Treatise on Education.* This account of an imagined experimental rearing of a child became the foundation of modern elementary education. It opened with the birth of the child, and the concept that education begins with birth was in itself revolutionary. It attacked the tight swaddling of infants, urged that mothers nurse their own children even if they could afford wet nurses, emphasized the importance of maternal affection, favored what we should today call "permissive" freedoms for children, and advocated manual training and physical exercise. Above all it preached "learning by doing," which was to become a basic tenet of "progressive education." On this account the only book, other than the Bible, that was allowed a place in Emile's studies was *Robinson Crusoe,* which he regarded as a pre-eminent example of learning by doing, Crusoe having had to reconstruct anew on his desert island the tools and conveniences necessary to civilized life. Crusoe also appealed to Rousseau as an example of the moral regeneration produced in the castaway by his accidental restoration to a state of nature. Today *Emile* is an intellectual curiosity, important chiefly for its place in cultural history; and absurdities in it, ignored or not recognized in its day, stand out, while its contributions, long since assimilated in pedagogical tradition and practice, now sound like truisms.

For incidental antimonarchist comments *Emile* was condemned, and threats of persecution by the Jesuits forced Rousseau into flight, first to Switzerland, then to England. By the time he had returned to France his paranoia had become acute. He now included in his fantasies of conspiracy against him the gentle British philosopher David Hume, whose home had been his haven in England. From then on it was not government officials or Jesuits whom he saw as his persecutors, but his fellow philosophes, particularly Voltaire and the Encyclopedists.

Today it is for his posthumously published *Confessions* that Rousseau is best known and still read. Again he had produced something unprecedented. For perhaps the first time in the literature of biography the importance of childhood as the matrix of personality was perceived. In many of its insights the *Confessions* anticipated the findings of modern depth psychologists. This may be appreciated by a comparison with that other "tell-all" eighteenth-century autobiography, the *Memoirs of Casanova*. There is a desperate candor in the *Confessions* besides which the strutting self-revelations of Casanova appear mere exhibitionism. Yet Rousseau's candor and self-knowledge were not as full as he believed. Much of the book is a recital of his persecution fantasies. Much of it, too, is defensive evasion. Witness his attempts to explain away his treatment of his five children; each, when born, was put by this apostle of freedom and love in a foundling home, making it certain that the child would be deprived of freedom and love.

Rousseau may serve as the most extreme case of the ambivalences which characterized eighteenth-century man, as they do man in every century. No Enlightenment figure can serve as a satisfactory embodiment of reason. In his personal relationships Voltaire was often petty, malicious, and unreasonable. It is clear, too, from their writings, that all the philosophes had to overcome doubts and contradictions. Along with Rousseau, who most influenced them, some, notably the Germans Kant, Herder, Lessing, and Goethe, gave primacy to emotion over reason. In the essentially empiricist philosophy of David Hume, who was influenced by Rousseau, the power of the emotions was acknowledged in statements that put the "passions," as he called them, above reason. "Reason is and ought to be," wrote this British philosopher, "only the slave of the passions and can never pretend to any other office than to obey them." The "enlightened" and "benevolent" despots of the century, whom Voltaire and other philosophes saw as agents of prospective social progress, waged wars as senseless as those of their predecessors and did little to temper their despotism with effective reforms. And alongside the rationalist philosophers and exercising almost comparable influence were mystics and charlatans like Cagliostro, who played a near-Rasputin role at the court at Versailles, and Mesmer, who discovered hypnotism without realizing what it was. Confusing it with the newly discovered force of electricity and naming it, by analogy with Newton's gravitation, "animal magnetism," Mesmer created a furor with it throughout Europe. And finally, France, center of the Enlightenment, met its problems when financial collapse compelled action, not by rationally ordered and progressive change, but by frantic oscillations followed by a political revolution stained by sectarianism and terror, and then by a reversion to absolutism under Napoleon. Revolutions and reactions were to follow alternately in succession for nearly a century before French society achieved a comparatively mature democracy.

For these contradictions and ambivalences the Enlightenment is sometimes scorned and its achievements underrated. But when one reflects on such analogies as the brutalities of the "Age of Chivalry," on the slaughters of Christians by Crusaders, or on the Borgias as eminences of the Renaissance, the contradictions of the eighteenth century seem ordinary. As for the achievements, any representative listing of them is impressive.

Let us begin with the social sciences, which may be considered typical contributions of the age: economics (Adam Smith, the French physiocrats, Quesnay, Du Pont de Nemours, Turgot and others); political science (Locke and Montesquieu, among others); psychology, particularly the "sensationalism" of Condillac, the belief that all the processes of the human mind are derived from sense impressions (a development from Locke's concept that human life begins as a "blank page" immediately inscribed by experience); sociology, particularly the environmentalism of Montesquieu and the Encyclopedists; history, as a record of social and cultural development instead of a dynastic chronicle (Voltaire, Montesquieu, Gibbon, and Hume). Add anthropology, comparative culture, and comparative religion, which had their origins, in part, in the intensified exploration of the eighteenth century, particularly by the great English and French navigators, Cook and Bougainville, and in the expanding trade with the Orient.

A by-product of the Industrial Revolution, which produced greater social changes than the political revolutions of the century, was the new science of geology, born of the observations by the Scottish mining engineer James Hutton of the rock strata his mine borings exposed. Another entirely new field of knowledge, archaeology, was opened by up the discovery, in 1748, of the buried city of Pompeii. It was under the patronage of Mme. Pompadour that the first excavations were carried out. This intensified the interest in the classic past, to which both the American and the French revolutionists turned for heroes to emulate and institutions to follow. Art and decoration were also powerfully influenced by the archaeological discoveries, and Greek decorative motifs -- Pompeii had been a Greek colony absorbed into the Roman Empire — entered into ceramic and furniture design.

But in a curious way, the newly inspired classicism often merged with romanticism. It was romantics like Winckelmann and Schiller who viewed the classical past with uncritical reverence. For the other philo-

3. Maurice Q. de La Tour, *Portrait of Madame de Pompadour.*

sophes the last word was no longer believed to have been said in the classics, nor, for that matter, in the scriptures. Irreverence may be termed a characteristic mood of the Enlightenment, and it was part of its faith in reason and its confidence in progress. The achievements of the seventeenth and eighteenth centuries in mathematics and science were taken as conclusive evidence of man's advance. Among the most influential works of the Enlightenment — and this influence is attested by Swift's satirical use of the same subject in his *The Battle of the Books* — was

Fontenelle's "Digression on the Ancients and the Moderns." In it he makes the sensible point: "Enlightened by the discoveries of the ancients as well as by their mistakes, we need not be surprised that we can surpass them." And in several of his writings Voltaire drew similar conclusions. For such expressions the reactionary opposing side in the controversy blocked Fontenelle's election to the French Academy for many years. But it was a vain victory. Fontenelle was eventually made a member and became the leading figure of the Academy. The triumph of the idea of progress was inevitable.

The existing sciences made notable advances in the eighteenth century. Modern chemistry may be said to have been founded on the discoveries of the Frenchman Antoine Lavoisier, who developed the law of the conservation of mass, and of the Englishmen Henry Cavendish and Joseph Priestley, discoverers, respectively, of hydrogen and oxygen. To physics was added the new branch, electricity, which then evoked awe comparable to that aroused by atomic power in our century. Among the outstanding discoverers in this field were the Italians Luigi Galvani and Alessandro Volta and the American Benjamin Franklin. The systematization of knowledge in the sciences of life, botany and biology, was greatly advanced by the Swede Carolus Linnaeus, whose classifications in botany have survived, little changed, into our time, and the Frenchman the Comte de Buffon, who made parallel classifications in zoology and whose works contain anticipations of the evolutionary concepts of Darwin. "It may be assumed," Buffon wrote, "that all animals have descended from a single living being which, in the course of time, by steady improvement, has brought forth all the forms of other animals." Buffon was also a gifted popularizer, and he furthered the work of the Encyclopedists and of earlier popularizers like Fontenelle who had made astronomy an enthrallment of the salons.

Among other outstanding scientists of the century were the French naturalist and physicist René Antoine de Réaumur, whose inventions included the thermometer named after him; the Italian biologist the Abbé Lazzaro Spallanzani who, by disproving the theory of spontaneous generation, rid his science of a major obstacle to its advance; and the British physician Edward Jenner, whose discovery of vaccination became the basis of the modern science of immunology.

Rousseau's contribution to education has been mentioned. To him should be added Condorcet, who advocated equal education for women and on whose scheme for a national education program the French educational system remains based today.

Through the work of the Dutch scientist Anton van Leeuwenhoek, who discovered protozoa and described, for the first time, human spermatozoa, the incalculable world of microbiology was penetrated. This led to the development of a new branch of medicine: histology, or the anatomy of the microscopic structures of the body. Among other eighteenth-century contributions to medicine were the spread of vaccination, the practice of post-mortem autopsies, the discovery of blood pressure and its significance in diagnosis, and the invention of the stethoscope by the French physician René Laënnec.

Humanitarianism may also be considered largely a product of the Enlightenment. The formulation of a humane penology has already been mentioned. The burning of witches and heretics virtually ceased under the denunciations of the philosophes. So powerful grew the agitation against slavery that, along with the abolition of imprisonment for debt, the freeing of the slaves in the French colonies was one of the first acts of the French Revolution; England was set on the course that led, in 1820, to the emancipation of the slaves in its colonies; and even the American slave states were shamed into ending the open importation of slaves.

Toleration of dissent, whether in religious, political, or other beliefs, became a principle of Western culture. It was to meet with setbacks in the post-Revolutionary reaction, but it was written into American, English, and French constitutional law and was gradually accepted, at least in principle, in other European nations. Toleration was one of the chief goals of the Enlightenment, and in its spread the Freemason, along with the philosophes, played a considerable role. The Freemasons were the most conspicuous of the fraternal orders that developed out of the decay of the guilds. Their advocacy of toleration and other humanist and humane principles probably accounts for the appeal of the Order to the men of the Enlightenment. Among famous Masons of that century were George Washington, Goethe, and Robert Burns. The Masons were not atheists. Indeed some of their lodges were prosecuted for incorporating religious observances in their rituals, and a French lodge that did advocate atheism was repudiated and dissolved. Atheism, in fact, was alien to the Enlightenment concept of a natural order which required a Maker and Regulator of the "machine" of the universe.

But above all these contributions should be put democracy, which, in any significant sense, had appeared only once before in history, more than two thousand years earlier, in Athens. As in Athens, the growth of a trading middle class requiring freedom for its operations proved to be a precondition. It is true that the libertarians of the eighteenth century looked more to the Roman republic in what was assumed to be its greatest and purest phase than to the Athenian demos, which, to some, had the character of a "mobocracy." For Americans, Fabius, Regulus, and Cincinnatus were the models to emulate; for Europeans, with their sense of empire, the conquering consuls. In what ultimately proved to be a speeded-up caricature of Roman history, Napoleon began his reign as Consul and ended it as Imperator. Both in Europe and America there was hesitation over giving direct power to the people, and through indirect representation and property qualifications, attempts were made to institute a new type of rule based on a property-owning middle class. But the drive toward democracy could be slowed, not stopped. In spite of survivals of theocracy, which gradually withered away, and of monarchical and aristocratic institutions, which have been left with no other functions than ceremonials or façades, and of the more active power assumptions of wealth to which countervailing forces have developed, the democracy fostered by the Enlightenment advanced toward maturity.

It should be noted that the emphasis in the democratic developments of the eighteenth century was on the rights of the individual (then thought of, primarily, as the property-owning, middle-class citizen) and on his freedom of action. This stress on the individual citizen is clear not only in the pressure for individual freedoms and for a laissez-faire economy, but in the arts, which now became accessible to the general public and reflected this and other aspects of social change.

It may be seen in literature and the theater arts. The novel, as has already been observed, was practically an eighteenth-century invention. Particularly as developed in England, the best-established of the democracies of that age, its heroes were no longer classical chieftains and demigods, or paladins of feudal chivalry, but plain human beings like Fielding's Tom Jones, Defoe's Moll Flanders, Goldsmith's vicar, etc. Italy's still flourishing and still touring *commedia dell'arte* helped to break down theater convention both by its use of "vulgar" character types and its resourceful improvisations. Ballet, long restricted to the courts, became a public entertainment accessible to the bourgeois.

The emphasis upon and the appeal to the individual may also be seen in eighteenth-century music, particularly in the shift from polyphony to homophony. An individual melody was thereby liberated from the contrapuntal maze like an individual voice from a chorus. Significantly, Rousseau wrote his pieces on music for the Encyclopedia as a partisan of homophony. The same trend may be seen in the movement of the

art out of the churches and into theaters and salons, where it appealed
to the individual as an independent auditor rather than as a member of
a congregation. Following another contemporary trend, reformers like
Gluck tried to rid opera of its artifices and render it more "natural."
For analogous reasons there was a turn to folk melodies and imitation
of sounds in nature. And faith in mathematics and science was carried
over into the work and thinking of some composers, notably Rameau, who
considered himself a philosophe and who attempted, if one may use the
term, to mathematize the structure of music. In any case the rococo music
of the century (the name is taken from its prevailing architectural style)
is now considered, together with the baroque that preceded it, the classical
age of Western music. A listing of its outstanding composers — Bach,
Handel, Haydn, Pergolesi, Corelli, Telemann, Vivaldi, Scarlatti, Cou-
perin, Rameau, Purcell, Mozart, the early Beethoven, Gluck, and many
others — is enough to substantiate it.

The plastic and decorative arts showed analogous trends. Flemish painting carried on at a lower level the genre painting and portraiture of its
burghers that had distinguished it in the previous century. Italian art,
too, had declined, and it is significant that its leading eighteenth-century
painters worked in the merchant republic of Venice. Among them were
Tiepolo, who dominated Italian art of the period with his skyscape fantasies; and Canaletto, Guardi, and Longhi, who painted the city's canals
and its sumptuous mansions. One of Spain's greatest masters, Goya, also
belonged to this century.

The eighteenth was England's great art century with Gainsborough,
Reynolds, Lawrence and Romney, and Blake and Hogarth among its
masters. Though the first four are best-known for their portraiture of
mainly Whig gentry, they shared the enthusiasm for nature of their
French contemporaries and displayed it in the landscapes and green
stretches they used as portrait settings. In their different ways Blake and
Hogarth touched on the darker aspects of their time and their country,
England of the Industrial Revolution, Blake in apocalyptic visions and
Hogarth in his satires, as savage as the hell-fire sermons of the contemporary Methodist revivalists, depicting the miseries and vices of the
slums and the destructive luxuries and vices of the rich.

France was not to reach its apogee in painting till late in the following
century, but its eighteenth-century painting was a graceful expression of
the vogue for nature, with court ladies posing as shepherdesses or
nymphs in idyllic landscapes, or classical scenes. Among the leading artists
were Watteau, Fragonard, Boucher, and Lancret. Popular, too, because
their subjects were from ordinary life, which was taken to be closer to

4. Hubert, *Thirteen Glimpses of Voltaire.*

the life of nature, was the genre painting of Chardin and Greuze. Toward the close of the century, in France, there was a neoclassic revival drawing upon classical history for its themes, with David and his disciple Ingres as the masters.

The century's stress on the individual, already remarked upon, is to be seen in its architecture, interior decoration, faïence, and furniture. The huge baroque palaces at Versailles erected for Louis XIV and filled with massive furniture, which set the style for other European dynasts, were suited to a court life essentially public and ceremonial. But at his death there was an immediate reaction. The new fashions during the Orleans regency and the reign of Louis XV favored lightness and simplicity and grace. For example, the palace built for Mme. Du Barry was the comparatively small Petit Trianon, which is regarded as one of the masterpieces of the later classical style. In their rise the men of the middle classes seldom built castles; they preferred convenient houses ensuring bourgeois comforts and family privacy. They were decorated and furnished, in France, in the Regency and the Louis Quinze fashions, and, in England, in the Hepplewhite, Chippendale, Sheraton, and Adam styles. Examples of these have become the quests and treasures of collectors all over the world.

The new tastes were formed, in part, by diverse social changes. For example, the adoption of the Oriental beverages tea and coffee altered social habits and at the same time influenced the design of table services and other appurtenances.

Contact with the Far East brought in, along with outright *chinoiserie* and other exotics, a taste for ornament, which, along with other influences, led from the baroque of the previous century, itself a decorative elaboration of the classical, to the more fanciful rococo style. In reaction there was a return, toward the end of the century, to a more restrained adaptation of the classical, of which Thomas Jefferson was one of the masters. Some of the finest buildings in this style were those called Georgian in England and Colonial or American Georgian in this country.

Of the five-century European cycle of history, the eighteenth was one of the most dynamic and certainly the most optimistic. It had a fervent, though as it turned out, excessive belief in progress, which was assumed to be an inevitable consequence of increasing scientific knowledge and rational adaptations of newly discovered natural laws. But the progress was not as great as anticipated and had some dubious accompaniments. On that account the Enlightenment has been depreciated as not an Age of Reason, but another Age of Faith — faith in reason. Its expectations of a rational order achieved through scientific knowledge proved no more substantial, it is charged, than those of the medieval City of God. Yet, could as much have been achieved and advanced without the conviction of progress and the faith in reason? In my reading of history Utopia stands as a species of reality, never attainable of course, but necessary to the health of the social organism. Toynbee, I believe, found that what could be called the absence of Utopia was a disease symptom of decaying civilizations.

PART

# I

# Toward a
# Rational Society

It is significant that the Enlightenment produced no
Utopia, no grand plan for a perfect society. What might
be called its Utopias are implied in its satires and arraign-
ments of crumbling feudal, monarchical, and dogmatic
religious institutions. Its thinking, expressed generally in
empirical philosophies, was pragmatic. It looked toward
rational social change, preferably through orderly means,
but if necessary through revolution. Few of the philosophes, however, especially those who felt that they were
influencing "enlightened despots," anticipated the necessity of revolution.

In addition to those that follow, selections under other
section headings reflect the eighteenth-century concepts of
the rational society.

# from *The Encyclopedia*

## DENIS DIDEROT

ENCYCLOPEDIA, noun, feminine gender. (*Philosophy.*) This word signifies *unity of knowledge;* it is made up of the Greek prefix EN, *in,* and the nouns KYKLOS, *circle,* and PAIDEIA, *instruction, science, knowledge.* In truth, the aim of an *encyclopedia* is to collect all the knowledge that now lies scattered over the face of the earth, to make known its general structure to the men among whom we live, and to transmit it to those who will come after us, in order that the labors of past ages may be useful to the ages to come, that our grandsons, as they become better educated, may at the same time become more virtuous and more happy, and that we may not die without having deserved well of the human race.

It would have been difficult to set for oneself a more enormous task than this of dealing with everything that relates to man's curiosity, his duties, his needs and his pleasures. Accordingly, some people, accustomed as they are to judging the feasibility of an enterprise by the poverty of their own resources, have asserted that we would never finish our task. (See the latest edition of the [Jesuits'] *Dictionnaire de Trévoux,* at the word *encyclopédie.*) Our only answer to them will be the following passage from the writings of Chancellor Bacon, which seems to be addressed especially to them: "Those works are possible, which may be accomplished by some person, though not by every one; which may be done by many, though not by one; which may be completed in the succession of ages, though not within the hour-glass of one man's life; and which may be reached by public effort, though not by private endeavor." (*The Advancement of Learning,* Book II, Chapter I)

When one comes to reflect upon the vast subject matter of an encyclopedia, the one thing that can be perceived distinctly is that it cannot be the work of a single man. For how could one man, in the short space of his lifetime, hope to know and describe the universal system of nature and of art, seeing that the numerous and erudite society of academicians of *La Crusca* has taken forty years to compose its dictionary, and that the members of our French Academy worked sixty years on their *Dictionary* before publishing its first edition? Yet what is a linguistic dictionary, what is a compilation of the words of a language, assuming that it is executed as perfectly as possible? It is a very exact résumé of the articles to be included in a systematic encyclopedic dictionary.

.        .        .

All terms must be defined, excepting only the radicals, that is to say, those which refer to simple sensations or to the most abstract general ideas. If any have been left out, the dictionary is incomplete. . . . And who will furnish an exact definition of the word *congruent* unless it be a geometrician? of the word *conjugation* unless it be a grammarian? of the word *azimuth* unless it be an astronomer? of the word *epic* unless it be a man of letters? of the word *exchange* unless it be a merchant? of the word *vice* unless it be a moralist? of the word *hypostasis* unless it be a theologian? of the word *metaphysics* unless it be a philosopher? of the word *gouge,* unless it be a man well-versed in the manual arts? Whence I conclude that if the French Academy did not unite in its assemblies all the various kinds of human knowledge and the most diverse talents, it would be impossible for it not to overlook a large number of expressions which one would search for in vain in its *Dictionary;* or for it not to allow false, incomplete, absurd, or even ridiculous definitions to creep in.

I am fully aware that these views are not shared by those who lecture to us about everything and who nevertheless know nothing; who are not members of our academies and who never will be because they are not worthy to be members; yet who take it upon themselves to decide who should fill vacant places; who, while they presume to set limits to the subjects which the French Academy should consider, are almost indignant to see men like Mairan, Maupertuis, or D'Alembert enter that company; and who do not know that the first time one of these men spoke in the Academy it was to rectify the definition of the word *noon.* One would think, to hear them talk, that they would like to restrict linguistic science and the *Dictionary* of the Academy to those few words which are familiar to them. And, indeed, if they looked a little more closely, they would find a large number of terms even among these — such as tree, animal, plant, flower, vice, virtue, truth, force, laws — for a rigorous definition of which they would have to call the philosopher, the jurist, the historian, or the naturalist to their assistance. In sum, they would need the help of men who know the real or abstract qualities that make a thing what it is and give it its individual or specific character, depending upon whether the thing is unique or one of a class.

.   .   .

In a systematic, universal dictionary, as in any work intended for the general education of mankind, you must begin by contemplating your subject in its most general aspects; you must know the state of mind of your nation, foresee the direction of its future development, hasten to anticipate its progress so that the march of events will not leave your book behind but will rather overtake it along the road; you must be prepared to work solely for the good of future generations because the moment of your own existence quickly passes away, and a great enterprise is not likely to be finished before the present generation ceases to exist. But if you would have your work remain fresh and useful for a long time to come — by virtue of its being far in advance of the national spirit, which marches steadily forward — you must shorten your labors by multiplying the number of your helpers, an expedient that is not, indeed, without its disadvantages, as I shall try to make plain hereafter.

.   .   .

Both the real universe and the world of ideas have an infinite number of aspects by which they may be made comprehensible, and the number of possible "systems of human knowledge" is as large as the number of these points of view. The only system that would be free from all arbitrariness is, as I have said in our "Prospectus," the one that must have existed from all eternity in the mind of God. Hence the plan according to which one would begin with this eternal Being and then descend from Him to all the lesser beings that have emanated from His bosom in the course of time. This plan would resemble the astronomical hypothesis in which the scientist transports himself in imagination to the center of the sun so as to be able to calculate there the behavior of the heavenly bodies that surround him. It is a scheme that has both simplicity and grandeur, but one may discern in it a defect that would be serious in a work composed by men of science and addressed to all men in all ages to come. This is the fault of being too closely tied to our prevailing theology — a sublime science and one that is undoubtedly useful by reason of the knowledge that the Christian receives from it, but even more useful by reason of the sacrifices it demands and the rewards it promises.

As for a general system from which all that is arbitrary would be excluded — something we mortals can never hope to possess — it might not, perhaps, be so great an advantage to possess it. For what would be the difference between reading a book in which all the hidden springs of the universe were laid bare, and direct study of the universe itself? Virtually none: we shall never be capable of understanding more than a certain portion of this great book. To the extent that our impatience and our curiosity — which overmaster us and so often break up the course of our observations — disturb the orderly conduct of our reading, to that extent is our knowledge liable to become disjointed, as it now is. Losing the chain of inductive logic, and ceasing to perceive the connections between one step and those before and after, we would speedily come upon the same lacks and the same uncertainties. We are now busy trying to fill up the voids by means of the study of nature; we would still be busy trying to fill them up if we possessed and could meditate upon that huge book of which I have spoken; but the book would seem no more perfect to our eyes than would the universe itself, and the book would therefore be no less exposed to our presumptuous doubts and objections.

Since an absolutely perfect general plan would in no way supply the deficiencies arising from the weakness of our understanding, let us instead take hold of those things that are bound up with our human condition, being content to make our way upward from them toward some more general notions. The more elevated the point of view from which we approach our subject, the more territory it will reveal to us, the grander and more instructive will be the prospect we shall survey. It follows that the order must be simple, for there is rarely any grandeur without simplicity; it must be clear and easy to grasp, not a tortuous maze in which one goes astray and never sees anything beyond the point where one stands. No, it must rather be a vast, broad avenue extending far into the distance, intersected by other highways laid out with equal care, each leading by the easiest and shortest path to a remote but single goal.

Another consideration must be kept in view. I mean that if one banishes from the face of the earth the thinking and contemplating entity, man, then the sublime and moving spectacle of nature will be but a sad and silent scene; the universe will be hushed; darkness and silence will regain their sway. All will be changed into a vast solitude where unobserved phenomena take their course unseen and unheard. It is only the presence of men that makes the existence of other beings significant. What better plan, then, in writing the history of these beings, than to subordinate oneself to this consideration? Why should we not introduce man into our *Encyclopedia,* giving him the same place that he occupies in the universe? Why should we not make him the center of all that is?

Is there, in all infinite space, any point of origin from which we could more advantageously draw the extended lines which we plan to produce to all the other points? With man at the center, how lively and pleasing will be the ensuing relations between man and other beings, between other beings and man!

For this reason we have decided to seek in man's principal faculties the main divisions within which our work will fall. Another method might be equally satisfactory, provided it did not put a cold, insensitive, silent being in the place of man. For man is the unique starting point, and the end to which everything must finally be related if one wishes to please, to instruct, to move to sympathy, even in the most arid matters and in the driest details. Take away my own existence and that of my fellow men and what does the rest of nature signify?

Although I believe that there is a point beyond which it is dangerous to add further material, I also think that one should not stop until one is very sure that this point has been reached. All the arts and sciences have their metaphysical principles, and this part is always abstract, elevated and difficult. None the less this part must be the main concern of a philosophical dictionary; and one must admit, too, that no matter how much remains to be done in this field, there will still be phenomena that cannot be explained. . . . It happens inevitably that the man of letters, the savant, and the craftsman sometimes walk in darkness. If they make some small amount of progress it is due to pure chance; they reach their goal like a lost traveler who has followed the right path without knowing it. Thus it is of the highest importance to give a clear explanation of the metaphysical basis of phenomena, or of their first, most general principles.

By this means the rest will be made more luminous and more certain in the reader's mind.

.　　.　　.

We have had occasion to learn in the course of our editorial labors that our *Encyclopedia* is a work that could only be attempted in a philosophical century; that this age has indeed dawned; and that posterity, while raising to immortality the names of those who will bring man's knowledge to perfection in the future, will perhaps not disdain to remember our own names. . . .

I have said that it could only belong to a philosophical age to attempt an *Encyclopedia;* and I say so because a work such as this demands more intellectual courage than is commonly to be found in ages of pusillanimous taste. All things must be examined, all must be winnowed and sifted without exception and without sparing anyone's sensibilities. One must dare to see, as we are beginning to do, that the history of literary forms is much the same as that of the first codification of law or the earliest foundation of cities — all owe their origin to some accident, to some odd circumstance, sometimes to a flight of human genius; and those who come after the first inventors are for the most part no more than their slaves. Achievements that ought to have been regarded only as first steps came blindly to be taken for the highest possible degree of development, and so, instead of advancing a branch of art toward perfection, these first triumphs only served to retard its growth by reducing all other artists to the condition of servile imitators. As soon as a name was given to some composition of a particular kind everyone was obliged to model all his productions rigorously after that model, which was perhaps only a sketch. If, from time to time, there appeared men of bold and original genius who, weary under the prevailing yoke, dared to shake it off, to strike out in a new direction away from the beaten path, and to give birth to some work of art to which the conventional labels and the prescribed rules were not exactly applicable, they fell into oblivion and remained for a long time forgotten.

Now, in our own age, we must trample mercilessly upon all these ancient puerilities, overturn the barriers that reason never erected, give back to the arts and sciences the liberty that is so precious to them. . . . The world has long awaited a reasoning age, an age when the rules would be sought no longer in the classical authors but in nature. . . .

# from *Civil Government*

## JOHN LOCKE

123. If man in the state of Nature be so free as has been said, if he be absolute lord of his own person and possessions, equal to the greatest and subject to nobody, why will he part with his freedom, this empire, and subject himself to the dominion and control of any other power?

To which it is obvious to answer, that though in the state of Nature he hath such a right, yet the enjoyment of it is very uncertain and constantly exposed to the invasion of others; for all being kings as much as he, every man his equal, and the greater part no strict observers of equity and justice, the enjoyment of the property he has in this state is very unsafe, very insecure. This makes him willing to quit this condition which, however free, is full of fears and continual dangers; and it is not without reason that he seeks out and is willing to join in society with others, who are already united, or have a mind to unite for the mutual preservation of their lives, liberties and estates, which I call by the general name — property.

124. The great and chief end, therefore, of men uniting into commonwealths, and putting themselves under government, is the preservation of their property; to which in the state of Nature there are many things wanting.

Firstly, there wants an established, settled, known law, received and allowed by common consent to be the standard of right and wrong, and the common measure to decide all controversies between them. For though the law of Nature be plain and intelligible to all rational creatures, yet men, being biased by their interests, as well as ignorant for want of study of it, are not apt to allow of it as a law binding to them in the application of it to their particular cases.

125. Secondly, in the state of Nature there wants a known and indifferent judge, with authority to determine all differences according to the established law. For every one in that state being both judge and executioner of the law of Nature, men being partial to themselves, passion and revenge is very apt to carry them too far, and with too much heat in their own cases, as well as negligence and unconcernedness, make them too remiss in other men's.

126. Thirdly, in the state of Nature there often wants power to back and support the sentence when right, and to give it due execution. They who by any injustice offended will seldom fail where they are able by force to make good their injustice. Such resistance many times makes the punishment dangerous, and frequently destructive to those who attempt it.

127. Thus mankind, notwithstanding all the privileges of the state of Nature, being but in an ill condition while they remain in it are quickly driven into society. Hence it comes to pass, that we seldom find any number of men live any time together in this state. The inconveniencies that they are therein exposed to by the irregular and uncertain exercise of the power every man has of punishing the transgressions of others, make them

take sanctuary under the established laws of government, and therein seek the preservation of their property. It is this makes them so willingly give up every one his single power of punishing to be exercised by such alone as shall be appointed to it amongst them, and by such rules as the community, or those authorised by them to that purpose, shall agree on. And in this we have the original right and rise of both the legislative and executive power as well as of the governments and societies themselves.

128. For in the state of Nature to omit the liberty he has of innocent delights, a man has two powers. The first is to do whatsoever he thinks fit for the preservation of himself and others within the permission of the law of Nature; by which law, common to them all, he and all the rest of mankind are one community, make up one society distinct from all other creatures, and were it not for the corruption and viciousness of degenerate men, there would be no need of any other, no necessity that men should separate from this great and natural community, and associate into lesser combinations. The other power a man has in the state of Nature is the power to punish the crimes committed against that law. Both these he gives up when he joins in a private, if I may so call it, or particular political society, and incorporates into any commonwealth separate from the rest of mankind.

129. The first power — viz., of doing whatsoever he thought fit for the preservation of himself and the rest of mankind, he gives up to be regulated by laws made by the society, so far forth as the preservation of himself and the rest of that society shall require; which laws of the society in many things confine the liberty he had by the law of Nature.

130. Secondly, the power of punishing he wholly gives up, and engages his natural force, which he might before employ in the execution of the law of Nature, by his own single authority, as he thought fit, to assist the executive power of the society as the law thereof shall require. For being now in a new state, wherein he is to enjoy many conveniences from the labour, assistance, and society of others in the same community, as well as protection from its whole strength, he is to part also with as much of his natural liberty, in providing for himself, as the good, prosperity, and safety of the society shall require, which is not only necessary but just, since the other members of the society do the like.

131. But though men when they enter into society give up the equality, liberty, and executive power they had in the state of Nature into the hands of the society, to be so far disposed of by the legislative as the good of the society shall require, yet it being only with an intention in every one the better to preserve himself, his liberty and property (for no rational creature can be supposed to change his condition with an intention

to be worse), the power of the society or legislative constituted by them can never be supposed to extend farther than the common good, but is obliged to secure every one's property by providing against those three defects above mentioned that made the state of Nature so unsafe and uneasy. And so, whoever has the legislative or supreme power of any commonwealth, is bound to govern by established standing laws, promulgated and known to the people, and not by extemporary decrees, by indifferent and upright judges, who are to decide controversies by those laws; and to employ the force of the community at home only in the execution of such laws, or abroad to prevent or redress foreign injuries and secure the community from inroads and invasion. And all this to be directed to no other end but the peace, safety, and public good of the people.

132. The majority having, as has been showed, upon men's first uniting into society, the whole power of the community naturally in them, may employ all that power in making laws for the community from time to time, and executing those laws by officers of their own appointing, and then the form of the government is a perfect democracy; or else may put the power of making laws into the hands of a few select men, and their heirs or successors, and then it is an oligarchy; or else into the hands of one man, and then it is a monarchy; if to him and his heirs, it is a hereditary monarchy; if to him only for life, but upon his death the power only of nominating a successor, to return to them, an elective monarchy. And so accordingly of these make compounded and mixed forms of government, as they think good. And if the legislative power be at first given by the majority to one or more persons only for their lives, or any limited time, and then the supreme power to revert to them again, when it is so reverted the community may dispose of it again anew into what hands they please, and so constitute a new form of government; for the form of government depending upon the placing the supreme power, which is the legislative, it being impossible to conceive that an inferior power should prescribe to a superior, or any but the supreme make laws, according as the power of making laws is placed, such is the form of the commonwealth.

133. By "commonwealth" I must be understood all along to mean not a democracy, or any form of government, but any independent community which the Latins signified by the word *civitas*, to which the word which best answers in our language is "commonwealth," and most properly expresses such a society of men which "community" does not (for there may be subordinate communities in a government), and "city" much less. And therefore, to avoid ambiguity, I crave leave to use the word "commonwealth" in that sense, in which sense I find the word used by King James himself, which I think to be its genuine signification,

which, if anybody dislike, I consent with him to change it for a better.

134. The great end of men's entering into society being the enjoyment of their properties in peace and safety, and the great instrument and means of that being the laws established in that society, the first and fundamental positive law of all commonwealths is the establishing of the legislative power, as the first and fundamental natural law which is to govern even the legislative. Itself is the preservation of the society and (as far as will consist with the public good) of every person in it. This legislative is not only the supreme power of the commonwealth, but sacred and unalterable in the hands where the community have once placed it. Nor can any edict of anybody else, in what form soever conceived, or by what power soever backed, have the force and obligation of a law which has not its sanction from that legislative which the public has chosen and appointed; for without this the law could not have that which is absolutely necessary to its being a law, the consent of the society, over whom nobody can have a power to make laws but by their own consent and by authority received from them; and therefore all the obedience, which by the most solemn ties any one can be obliged to pay, ultimately terminates in this supreme power, and is directed by those laws which it enacts. Nor can any oaths to any foreign power whatsoever, or any domestic subordinate power, discharge any member of the society from his obedience to the legislative, acting pursuant to their trust, nor oblige him to any obedience contrary to the laws so enacted or farther than they do allow, it being ridiculous to imagine one can be tied ultimately to obey any power in the society which is not the supreme.

135. Though the legislative, whether placed in one or more, whether it be always in being or only by intervals, though it be the supreme power in every commonwealth, yet, first, it is not, nor can possibly be, absolutely arbitrary over the lives and fortunes of the people. For it being but the joint power of every member of the society given up to that person or assembly which is legislator, it can be no more than those persons had in a state of Nature before they entered into society, and gave it up to the community. For nobody can transfer to another more power than he has in himself, and nobody has an absolute arbitrary power over himself, or over any other, to destroy his own life, or take away the life or property of another. A man, as has been proved, cannot subject himself to the arbitrary power of another; and having, in the state of Nature, no arbitrary power over the life, liberty, or possession of another, but only so much as the law of Nature gave him for the preservation of himself and the rest of mankind, this is all he doth, or can give up to the commonwealth, and by it to the legislative power, so that the legislative can have

no more than this. Their power in the utmost bounds of it is limited to the public good of the society. It is a power that hath no other end but preservation, and therefore can never have a right to destroy, enslave, or designedly to impoverish the subjects; the obligations of the law of Nature cease not in society, but only in many cases are drawn closer, and have, by human laws, known penalties annexed to them to enforce their observation. Thus the law of Nature stands as an eternal rule to all men, legislators as well as others. The rules that they make for other men's actions must, as well as their own and other men's actions, be conformable to the law of Nature — *i.e.,* to the will of God, of which that is a declaration, and the fundamental law of Nature being the preservation of mankind, no human sanction can be good or valid against it.

136. Secondly, the legislative or supreme authority cannot assume to itself a power to rule by extemporary arbitrary decrees, but is bound to dispense justice and decide the rights of the subject by promulgated standing laws, and known authorised judges. For the law of Nature being unwritten, and so nowhere to be found but in the minds of men, they who, through passion or interest, shall miscite or misapply it, cannot so easily be convinced of their mistake where there is no established judge; and so it serves not as it aught, to determine the rights and fence the properties of those that live under it, especially where every one is judge, interpreter, and executioner of it too, and that in his own case; and he that has right on his side, having ordinarily but his own single strength, hath not force enough to defend himself from injuries or punish delinquents. To avoid these inconveniencies which disorder men's properties in the state of Nature, men unite into societies that they may have the united strength of the whole society to secure and defend their properties, and may have standing rules to bound it by which every one may know what is his. To this end it is that men give up all their natural power to the society they enter into, and the community put the legislative power into such hands as they think fit, with this trust, that they shall be governed by declared laws, or else their peace, quiet, and property will still be at the same uncertainty as it was in the state of Nature.

137. Absolute arbitrary power, or governing without settled standing laws, can neither of them consist with the ends of society and government, which men would not quit the freedom of the state of Nature for, and tie themselves up under, were it not to preserve their lives, liberties, and fortunes, and by stated rules of right and property to secure their peace and quiet. It cannot be supposed that they should intend, had they a power so to do, to give any one or more an absolute arbitrary power over their persons and estates, and put a force into the magistrate's hand to

execute his unlimited will arbitrarily upon them; this were to put themselves into a worse condition than the state of Nature, wherein they had
a liberty to defend their right against the injuries of others, and were
upon equal terms of force to maintain it, whether invaded by a single
man or many in combination. Whereas by supposing they have given up
themselves to the absolute arbitrary power and will of a legislator, they
have disarmed themselves, and armed him to make a prey of them when
he pleases; he being in a much worse condition that is exposed to the
arbitrary power of one man who has the command of a hundred thousand
than he that is exposed to the arbitrary power of a hundred thousand
single men, nobody being secure, that his will who has such a command is
better than that of other men, though his force be a hundred thousand
times stronger. And, therefore, whatever form the commonwealth is
under, the ruling power ought to govern by declared and received laws,
and not by extemporary dictates and undetermined resolutions, for then
mankind will be in a far worse condition than in the state of Nature if
they shall have armed one or a few men with the joint power of a multitude, to force them to obey at pleasure the exorbitant and unlimited decrees of their sudden thoughts, or unrestrained, and till that moment,
unknown wills, without having any measures set down which may guide
and justify their actions. For all the power the government has, being
only for the good of the society, as it ought not to be arbitrary and at
pleasure, so it ought to be exercised by established and promulgated laws,
that both the people may know their duty, and be safe and secure within
the limits of the law, and the rulers, too, kept within their due bounds,
and not be tempted by the power they have in their hands to employ it
to purposes, and by such measures as they would not have known, and
own not willingly.

138. Thirdly, the supreme power cannot take from any man any part
of his property without his own consent. For the preservation of property
being the end of government, and that for which men enter into society,
it necessarily supposes and requires that the people should have property,
without which they must be supposed to lose that by entering into society
which was the end for which they entered into it; too gross an absurdity
for any man to own. Men, therefore, in society having property, they
have such a right to the goods, which by the law of the community are
theirs, that nobody hath a right to take them, or any part of them, from
them without their own consent; without this they have no property at
all. For I have truly no property in that which another can by right take
from me when he pleases against my consent. Hence it is a mistake to
think that the supreme or legislative power of any commonwealth can do

what it will, and dispose of the estates of the subject arbitrarily, or take any part of them at pleasure. This is not much to be feared in governments where the legislative consists wholly or in part in assemblies which are variable, whose members upon the dissolution of the assembly are subjects under the common laws of their country, equally with the rest. But in governments where the legislative is in one lasting assembly, always in being, or in one man as in absolute monarchies, there is danger still, that they will think themselves to have a distinct interest from the rest of the community, and so will be apt to increase their own riches and power by taking what they think fit from the people. For a man's property is not at all secure, though there be good and equitable laws to set the bounds of it between him and his fellow-subjects, if he who commands those subjects have power to take from any private man what part he pleases of his property, and use and dispose of it as he thinks good.

139. But government, into whosesoever hands it is put, being as I have before showed, entrusted with this condition, and for this end, that men might have and secure their properties, the prince or senate, however it may have power to make laws for the regulating of property between the subjects one amongst another, yet can never have a power to take to themselves the whole, or any part of the subjects' property, without their own consent; for this would be in effect to leave them no property at all. And to let us see that even absolute power, where it is necessary, is not arbitrary by being absolute, but is still limited by that reason, and confined to those ends which required it in some cases to be absolute, we need look no farther than the common practice of martial discipline. For the preservation of the army, and in it of the whole commonwealth, requires an absolute obedience to the command of every superior officer, and it is justly death to disobey or dispute the most dangerous or unreasonable of them; but yet we see that neither the sergeant that could command a soldier to march up to the mouth of a cannon, or stand in a breach where he is almost sure to perish, can command that soldier to give him one penny of his money; nor the general that can condemn him to death for deserting his post, or not obeying the most desperate orders, cannot yet with all his absolute power of life and death dispose of one farthing of that soldier's estate, or seize one jot of his goods; whom yet he can command anything, and hang for the least disobedience. Because such a blind obedience is necessary to that end for which the commander has his power — viz., the preservation of the rest, but the disposing of his goods has nothing to do with it.

140. It is true governments cannot be supported without great charge, and it is fit every one who enjoys his share of the protection should pay

out of his estate his proportion for the maintenance of it. But still it must
be with his own consent — *i.e.,* the consent of the majority, giving it either
by themselves or their representatives chosen by them; for if any one shall
claim a power to lay and levy taxes on the people by his own authority,
and without such consent of the people, he thereby invades the fundamental law of property, and subverts the end of government. For what
property have I in that which another may by right take when he pleases
to himself?

141. Fourthly. The legislative cannot transfer the power of making
laws to any other hands, for it being but a delegated power from the
people, they who have it cannot pass it over to others. The people alone
can appoint the form of the commonwealth, which is by constituting the
legislative, and appointing in whose hands that shall be. And when the
people have said, "We will submit, and be governed by laws made by such
men, and in such forms," nobody else can say other men shall make laws
for them; nor can they be bound by any laws but such as are enacted by
those whom they have chosen and authorised to make laws for them.

142. These are the bounds which the trust that is put in them by the
society and the law of God and Nature have set to the legislative power
of every commonwealth, in all forms of government. First: They are to
govern by promulgated established laws, not to be varied in particular
cases, but to have one rule for rich and poor, for the favourite at Court,
and the countryman at plough. Secondly: These laws also ought to be
designed for no other end ultimately but the good of the people. Thirdly:
They must not raise taxes on the property of the people without the consent of the people given by themselves or their deputies. And this property concerns only such governments where the legislative is always in
being, or at least where the people have not reserved any part of the legislative to deputies, to be from time to time chosen by themselves. Fourthly:
Legislative neither must nor can transfer the power of making laws to
anybody else, or place it anywhere but where the people have.

143. The legislative power is that which has a right to direct how
the force of the commonwealth shall be employed for preserving the community and the members of it. Because those laws which are constantly to
be executed, and whose force is always to continue, may be made in a
little time, therefore there is no need that the legislative should be always
in being, not having always business to do. And because it may be too
great temptation to human frailty, apt to grasp at power, for the same
persons who have the power of making laws to have also in their hands
the power to execute them, whereby they may exempt themselves from
obedience to the laws they make, and suit the law, both in its making and

execution, to their own private advantage, and thereby come to have a distinct interest from the rest of the community, contrary to the end of society and government. Therefore in well-ordered commonwealths, where the good of the whole is so considered as it ought, the legislative power is put into the hands of divers persons who, duly assembled, have by themselves, or jointly with others, a power to make laws, which when they have done, being separated again, they are themselves subject to the laws they have made; which is a new and near tie upon them to take care that they make them for the public good.

144. But because the laws that are at once, and in a short time made, have a constant and lasting force, and need a perpetual execution, or an attendance thereunto, therefore it is necessary there should be a power always in being which should see to the execution of the laws that are made, and remain in force. And thus the legislative and executive power come often to be separated.

145. There is another power in every commonwealth which one may call natural, because it is that which answers to the power every man naturally had before he entered into society. For though in a commonwealth the members of it are distinct persons, still, in reference to one another, and, as such, are governed by the laws of the society, yet, in reference to the rest of mankind, they make one body, which is, as every member of it before was, still in the state of Nature with the rest of mankind, so that the controversies that happen between any man of the society with those that are out of it are managed by the public, and an injury done to a member of their body engages the whole in the reparation of it. So that under this consideration the whole community is one body in the state of Nature in respect of all other states or persons out of its community.

146. This, therefore, contains the power of war and peace, leagues and alliances, and all the transactions with all persons and communities without the commonwealth, and may be called federative if any one pleases. So the thing be understood, I am indifferent as to the name.

147. These two powers, executive and federative, though they be really distinct in themselves, yet one comprehending the execution of the municipal laws of the society within itself upon all that are parts of it, the other the management of the security and interest of the public without with all those that it may receive benefit or damage from, yet they are always almost united. And though this federative power in the well or ill management of it be of great moment to the commonwealth, yet it is much less capable to be directed by antecedent, standing, positive laws than the executive, and so must necessarily be left to the prudence and wisdom of those whose hands it is in, to be managed for the public good.

For the laws that concern subjects one amongst another, being to direct their actions, may well enough precede them. But what is to be done in reference to foreigners depending much upon their actions, and the variation of designs and interests, must be left in great part to the prudence of those who have this power committed to them, to be managed by the best of their skill for the advantage of the commonwealth.

148. Though, as I said, the executive and federative power of every community be really distinct in themselves, yet they are hardly to be separated and placed at the same time in the hands of distinct persons. For both of them requiring the force of the society for their exercise, it is almost impracticable to place the force of the commonwealth in distinct and not subordinate hands, or that the executive and federative power should be placed in persons that might act separately, whereby the force of the public would be under different commands, which would be apt some time or other to cause disorder and ruin.

149. Though in a constituted commonwealth standing upon its own basis and acting according to its own nature — that is, acting for the preservation of the community, there can be but one supreme power, which is the legislative, to which all the rest are and must be subordinate, yet the legislative being only a fiduciary power to act for certain ends, there remains still in the people a supreme power to remove or alter the legislative, when they find the legislative act contrary to the trust reposed in them. For all power given with trust for the attaining an end being limited by that end, whenever that end is manifestly neglected or opposed, the trust must necessarily be forfeited, and the power devolve into the hands of those that gave it, who may place it anew where they shall think best for their safety and security. And thus the community perpetually retains a supreme power of saving themselves from the attempts and designs of anybody, even of their legislators, whenever they shall be so foolish or so wicked as to lay and carry on designs against the liberties and properties of the subject. For no man or society of men having a power to deliver up their preservation, or consequently the means of it, to the absolute will and arbitrary dominion of another, whenever any one shall go about to bring them into such a slavish condition, they will always have a right to preserve what they have not a power to part with, and to rid themselves of those who invade this fundamental, sacred, and unalterable law of self-preservation for which they entered into society. And thus the community may be said in this respect to be always the supreme power, but not as considered under any form of government, because this power of the people can never take place till the government be dissolved.

150. In all cases whilst the government subsists, the legislative is the supreme power. For what can give laws to another must needs be superior to him, and since the legislative is no otherwise legislative of the society but by the right it has to make laws for all the parts, and every member of the society prescribing rules to their actions, and giving power of execution where they are transgressed, the legislative must needs be the supreme, and all other powers in any members or parts of the society derived from and subordinate to it.

151. In some commonwealths where the legislative is not always in being, and the executive is vested in a single person who has also a share in the legislative, there that single person, in a very tolerable sense, may also be called supreme; not that he has in himself all the supreme power, which is that of law-making, but because he has in him the supreme execution from whom all inferior magistrates derive all their several subordinate powers, or, at least, the greatest part of them; having also no legislative superior to him, there being no law to be made without his consent, which cannot be expected should ever subject him to the other part of the legislative, he is properly enough in this sense supreme. But yet it is to be observed that though oaths of allegiance and fealty are taken to him, it is not to him as supreme legislator, but as supreme executor of the law made by a joint power of him with others, allegiance being nothing but an obedience according to law, which, when he violates, he has no right to obedience, nor can claim it otherwise than as the public person vested with the power of the law, and so is to be considered as the image, phantom, or representative of the commonwealth, acted by the will of the society declared in its laws, and thus he has no will, no power, but that of the law. But when he quits this representation, this public will, and acts by his own private will, he degrades himself, and is but a single private person without power and without will; the members owing no obedience but to the public will of the society.

152. The executive power placed anywhere but in a person that has also a share in the legislative is visibly subordinate and accountable to it, and may be at pleasure changed and displaced; so that it is not the supreme executive power that is exempt from subordination, but the supreme executive power vested in one, who having a share in the legislative, has no distinct superior legislative to be subordinate and accountable to, farther than he himself shall join and consent, so that he is no more subordinate than he himself shall think fit, which one may certainly conclude will be but very little. Of other ministerial and subordinate powers in a commonwealth we need not speak, they being so multiplied with infinite variety in the different customs and constitutions

of distinct commonwealths, that it is impossible to give a particular account of them all. Only thus much which is necessary to our present purpose we may take notice of concerning them, that they have no manner of authority, any of them, beyond what is by positive grant and commission delegated to them, and are all of them accountable to some other power in the commonwealth.

153. It is not necessary — no, nor so much as convenient — that the legislative should be always in being; but absolutely necessary that the executive power should, because there is not always need of new laws to be made, but always need of execution of the laws that are made. When the legislative hath put the execution of the laws they make into other hands, they have a power still to resume it out of those hands when they find cause, and to punish for any maladministration against the laws. The same holds also in regard of the federative power, that and the executive being both ministerial and subordinate to the legislative, which, as has been shown, in a constituted commonwealth is the supreme, the legislative also in this case being supposed to consist of several persons; for if it be a single person it cannot but be always in being, and so will, as supreme, naturally have the supreme executive power, together with the legislative, may assemble and exercise their legislative at the times that either their original constitution or their own adjournment appoints, or when they please, if neither of these hath appointed any time, or there be no other way prescribed to convoke them. For the supreme power being placed in them by the people, it is always in them, and they may exercise it when they please, unless by their original constitution they are limited to certain seasons, or by an act of their supreme power they have adjourned to a certain time, and when that time comes they have a right to assemble and act again.

154. If the legislative, or any part of it, be of representatives, chosen for that time by the people, which afterwards return into the ordinary state of subjects, and have no share in the legislative but upon a new choice, this power of choosing must also be exercised by the people, either at certain appointed seasons, or else when they are summoned to it; and, in this latter case, the power of convoking the legislative is ordinarily placed in the executive, and has one of these two limitations in respect of time: — that either the original constitution requires their assembling and acting at certain intervals; and then the executive power does nothing but ministerially issue directions for their electing and assembling according to due forms; or else it is left to his prudence to call them by new elections when the occasions or exigencies of the public require the amendment of old or making of new laws, or the redress or prevention of any incon-

veniencies that lie on or threaten the people.

155. It may be demanded here, what if the executive power, being possessed of the force of the commonwealth, shall make use of that force to hinder the meeting and acting of the legislative, when the original constitution or the public exigencies require it? I say, using force upon the people, without authority, and contrary to the trust put in him that does so, is a state of war with the people, who have a right to reinstate their legislative in the exercise of their power. For having erected a legislative with an intent they should exercise the power of making laws, either at certain set times, or when there is need of it, when they are hindered by any force from what is so necessary to the society, and wherein the safety and preservation of the people consists, the people have a right to remove it by force. In all states and conditions the true remedy of force without authority is to oppose force to it. The use of force without authority always puts him that uses it into a state of war as the aggressor, and renders him liable to be treated accordingly.

156. The power of assembling and dismissing the legislative, placed in the executive, gives not the executive a superiority over it, but is a fiduciary trust placed in him for the safety of the people in a case where the uncertainty and variableness of human affairs could not bear a steady fixed rule. For it not being possible that the first framers of the government should by any foresight be so much masters of future events as to be able to prefix so just periods of return and duration to the assemblies of the legislative, in all times to come, that might exactly answer all the exigencies of the commonwealth, the best remedy could be found for this defect was to trust this to the prudence of one who was always to be present, and whose business it was to watch over the public good. Constant, frequent meetings of the legislative, and long continuations of their assemblies, without necessary occasion, could not but be burdensome to the people, and must necessarily in time produce more dangerous inconveniences, and yet the quick turn of affairs might be sometimes such as to need their present help; any delay of their convening might endanger the public; and sometimes, too, their business might be so great that the limited time of their sitting might be too short for their work, and rob the public of that benefit which could be had only from their mature deliberation. What, then, could be done in this case to prevent the community from being exposed some time or other to imminent hazard on one side or the other, by fixed intervals and periods set to the meeting and acting of the legislative, but to entrust it to the prudence of some who, being present and acquainted with the state of public affairs, might make use of this prerogative for the public good? And where else could this be

so well placed as in his hands who was entrusted with the execution of the laws for the same end? Thus, supposing the regulation of times for the assembling and sitting of the legislative not settled by the original constitution, it naturally fell into the hands of the executive; not as an arbitrary power depending on his good pleasure, but with this trust always to have it exercised only for the public weal, as the occurrences of times and change of affairs might require. Whether settled periods of their convening, or a liberty left to the prince for convoking the legislative, or perhaps a mixture of both, hath the least inconvenience attending it, it is not my business here to inquire, but only to show that, though the executive power may have the prerogative of convoking and dissolving such conventions of the legislative, yet it is not thereby superior to it.

157. Things of this world are in so constant a flux that nothing remains long in the same state. Thus people, riches, trade, power, change their stations; flourishing mighty cities come to ruin, and prove in time neglected desolate corners, whilst other unfrequented places grow into populous countries filled with wealth and inhabitants. But things not always changing equally, and private interest often keeping up customs and privileges when the reasons of them are ceased, it often comes to pass that in governments where part of the legislative consists of representatives chosen by the people, that in tract of time this representation becomes very unequal and disproportionate to the reasons it was at first established upon. To what gross absurdities the following of custom when reason has left it may lead, we may be satisfied when we see the bare name of a town, of which there remains not so much as the ruins, where scarce so much housing as a sheepcote, or more inhabitants than a shepherd is to be found, send as many representatives to the grand assembly of law-makers as a whole county numerous in people and powerful in riches. This strangers stand amazed at, and every one must confess needs a remedy; though most think it hard to find one, because the constitution of the legislative being the original and supreme act of the society, antecedent to all positive laws in it, and depending wholly on the people, no inferior power can alter it. And, therefore, the people when the legislative is once constituted, having in such a government as we have been speaking of no power to act as long as the government stands, this inconvenience is thought incapable of a remedy.

158. *Salus populi suprema lex* is certainly so just and fundamental a rule, that he who sincerely follows it cannot dangerously err. If, therefore, the executive who has the power of convoking the legislative, observing rather the true proportion than fashion of representation, regulates not by old custom, but true reason, the number of members in

all places, that have a right to be distinctly represented, which no part of the people, however incorporated, can pretend to, but in proportion to the assistance which it affords to the public, it cannot be judged to have set up a new legislative, but to have restored the old and true one, and to have rectified the disorders which succession of time had insensibly as well as inevitably introduced; for it being the interest as well as intention of the people to have a fair and equal representative, whoever brings it nearest to that is an undoubted friend to and establisher of the government, and cannot miss the consent and approbation of the community; prerogative being nothing but a power in the hands of the prince to provide for the public good in such cases which, depending upon unforeseen and uncertain occurrences, certain and unalterable laws could not safely direct. Whatsoever shall be done manifestly for the good of the people, and establishing the government upon its true foundations is, and always will be, just prerogative. The power of erecting new corporations, and therewith new representatives, carries with it a supposition that in time the measures of representation might vary, and those have a just right to be represented which before had none; and by the same reason, those cease to have a right, and be too inconsiderable for such a privilege, which before had it. It is not a change from the present state which, perhaps, corruption or decay has introduced, that makes an inroad upon the government, but the tendency of it to injure or oppress the people, and to set up one part or party with a distinction from and an unequal subjection of the rest. Whatsoever cannot but be acknowledged to be of advantage to the society and people in general, upon just and lasting measures, will always, when done, justify itself; and whenever the people shall choose their representatives upon just and undeniably equal measures, suitable to the original frame of the government, it cannot be doubted to be the will and act of the society, whoever permitted or proposed to them so to do.

# from *A Letter to Madison*

## THOMAS JEFFERSON

I like much the general idea of framing a government which should go on of itself peaceably, without needing continual recurrence to the state legislatures. I like the organization of the government into Legislative, Judiciary and Executive. I like the power given the Legislature to levy taxes; and for that reason solely approve of the greater house being chosen by the people directly. For tho' I think a house chosen by them will be very illy qualified to legislate for the Union, for foreign nations &c. yet this evil does not weigh against the good of preserving inviolate the fundamental principle that the people are not to be taxed but by representatives chosen immediately by themselves. I am captivated by the compromise of the opposite claims of the great and little states, of the latter to equal, and the former to proportional influence. I am much pleased too with the substitution of the method of voting by persons, instead of that of voting by states: and I like the negative given to the Executive with a third of either house, though I should have liked it better had the Judiciary been associated for that purpose, or invested with a similar and separate power. There are other good things of less moment. I will now add what I do not like. First the omission of a bill of rights providing clearly and without the aid of sophisms for freedom of religion, freedom of the press, protection against standing armies, restriction against monopolies, the eternal and unremitting force of the habeas corpus laws, and trials by jury in all matters of fact triable by the laws of the land and not by the law of Nations. To say, as Mr. Wilson does that a bill of rights was not necessary because all is reserved in the case of the general government which is not given, while in the particular ones all is given which is not reserved might do for the Audience to whom it was addressed, but is surely gratis dictum, opposed by strong inferences from the body of the instrument, as well as from the omission of the clause of our present confederation which had declared that in express terms. It was a hard conclusion to say because there has been no uniformity among the states as to the cases triable by jury, because some have been so incautious as to abandon this mode of trial, therefore the more prudent states shall be reduced to the same level of calamity. It would have been much more just and wise to have concluded the other way that as most of the states had judiciously preserved this palladium, those who had wandered should be brought back to it, and to have established general right instead of general wrong. Let me add that a bill of rights is what the people are entitled to against every government on earth, general or particular, and what no just government should refuse, or rest on inference. The second feature I dislike, and greatly dislike, is the abandonment in every instance of the necessity of rotation in office, and most particularly in the case of the President. Experience concurs with reason in concluding that the first magistrate will always be re-elected if the constitution permits it. He is then an officer for life. . . .

An incapacity to be elected a second time would have been the only effectual preventative. The power of removing him every fourth year by the vote of the people is a power which will not be exercised. The king of Poland is removable every day by the Diet, yet he is never removed. — Smaller objections are the Appeal in fact as well as law, and the binding all persons Legislative, Executive and Judiciary by oath to maintain that constitution. I do not pretend to decide what would be the best method of procuring the establishment of the manifold good things in this constitution, and of getting rid of the bad. Whether by adopting it in hopes of future amendment, or, after it has been duly weighed and canvassed by the people, after seeing the parts they generally dislike, and those they generally approve, to say to them "We see now what you wish. Send together your deputies again, let them frame a constitution for you omitting what you have condemned, and establishing the powers you approve. Even these will be a great addition to the energy of your government." — At all events I hope you will not be discouraged from other trials, if the present one should fail of it's full effect. — I have thus told you freely what I like and dislike: merely as a matter of curiosity for I know your own judgment has been formed on all these points after having heard every thing which could be urged on them. I own I am not a friend to a very energetic government. It is always oppressive. The late rebellion in Massachusets has given more alarm than I think it should have done. Calculate that one rebellion in 13 states in the course of 11 years, is but one for each state in a century and a half. No country should be so long without one. Nor will any degree of power in the hands of government prevent insurrections. France with all it's despotism, and two or three hundred thousand men always in arms has had three insurrections in the three years I have been here in every one of which greater numbers were engaged than in Massachusets and a great deal more blood was spilt. In Turkey, which Montesquieu supposes more despotic, insurrections are the events of every day. In England, where the hand of power is lighter than here, but heavier than with us they happen every half dozen years. Compare again the ferocious depredations of their insurgents with the order, the moderation and the almost self extinguishment of ours. — After all, it is my principle that the will of the Majority should always prevail. If they approve the proposed Convention in all it's parts, I shall concur in it chearfully, in hopes that they will amend it whenever they shall find it work wrong. I think our governments will remain virtuous for many centuries; as long as they are chiefly agricultural; and this will be as long as there shall be vacant lands in any part of America. When they get piled upon one another in large cities, as in Europe, they will become corrupt as in Europe. Above all things I hope the education of the common people will be attended to; convinced that on their good sense we may rely with the most security for the preservation of a due degree of liberty. . . .

# from *Essay on Man*

## ALEXANDER POPE

See him from Nature rising slow to Art!
To copy Instinct then was Reason's part;
Thus then to Man the voice of Nature spake —
"Go, from the Creatures thy instructions take:
"Learn from the birds what food the thickets yield;
"Learn from the beasts the physic of the field;
"Thy arts of building from the bee receive;
"Learn of the mole to plough, the worm to weave;
"Learn of the little Nautilus to sail,
"Spread the thin oar, and catch the driving gale.
"Here too all forms of social union find,
"And hence let Reason, late, instruct Mankind:
"Here subterranean works and cities see;
"There towns aerial on the waving tree.
"Learn each small People's genius, policies,
"The Ant's republic, and the realm of Bees;
"How those in common all their wealth bestow,
"And Anarchy without confusion know;
"And these for ever, tho' a Monarch reign,
"Their sep'rate cells and properties maintain.
"Mark what unvary'd laws preserve each state,
"Laws wise as Nature, and as fix'd as Fate.
"In vain thy Reason finer webs shall draw,
"Entangle Justice in her net of Law.
"And right, too rigid, harden into wrong;
"Still for the strong too weak, the weak too strong.
"Yet go! and thus o'er all the creatures sway,

"Thus let the wiser make the rest obey;
"And, for those Arts mere Instinct could afford,
"Be crown'd as Monarchs, or as Gods ador'd."

Great Nature spoke; observant Men obey'd;
Cities were built, Societies were made:
Here rose one little state; another near
Grew by like means, and join'd, thro' love or fear.
Did here the trees with ruddier burdens bend,
And there the streams in purer rills descend?
What War could ravish, Commerce could bestow,
And he return'd a friend, who came a foe.
Converse and Love mankind might strongly draw,
When Love was Liberty, and Nature Law.
Thus States were form'd; the name of King unknown,
'Till common int'rest plac'd the sway in one.
'Twas VIRTUE ONLY (or in arts or arms,
Diffusing blessings, or averting harms)
The same which in a Sire the Sons obey'd,
A Prince the Father of a People made.

'Till then, by Nature crown'd, each Patriarch sate,
King, priest, and parent of his growing state;
On him, their second Providence, they hung,
Their law his eye, their oracle his tongue.
He from the wond'ring furrow call'd the food,
Taught to command the fire, control the flood,
Draw forth the monsters of th' abyss profound,
Or fetch th' aerial eagle to the ground.
'Till drooping, sick'ning, dying they began
Whom they rever'd as God to mourn as Man:
Then, looking up from sire to sire, explor'd
One great first father, and that first ador'd.
Or plain tradition that this All begun,
Convey'd unbroken faith from sire to son;
The worker from the work distinct was known,
And simple Reason never sought but one:
Ere Wit oblique had broke that steady light,
Man, like his Maker, saw that all was right;
To Virtue, in the paths of Pleasure, trod,
And own'd a Father when he own'd a God.
LOVE all the faith, and all th' allegiance then;

For Nature knew no right divine in Men,
No ill could fear in God; and understood
A sov'reign being but a sov'reign good.
True faith, true policy, united ran,
This was but love of God, and this of Man.

# from *A Treatise of Human Nature*

## DAVID HUME

As the science of man is the only solid foundation for the other sciences, so, the only solid foundation we can give to this science itself must be laid on experience and observation. It is no astonishing reflection to consider that the application of experimental philosophy to moral subjects should come after that to natural, at the distance of above a whole century; since we find in fact that there was about the same interval betwixt the origins of these sciences; and that, reckoning from Thales to Socrates, the space of time is nearly equal to that betwixt my Lord Bacon and some late philosophers in England, who have begun to put the science of man on a new footing, and have engaged the attention, and excited the curiosity, of the public. So true it is, that however other nations may rival us in poetry, and excel us in some other agreeable arts, the improvements in reason and philosophy can only be owing to a land of toleration and of liberty.

Nor ought we to think that this latter improvement in the science of man will do less honour to our native country than the former in natural philosophy, but ought rather to esteem it a greater glory, upon account of the greater importance of that science, as well as the necessity it lay under of such a reformation. For to me it seems evident that the essence of the mind being equally unknown to us with that of external bodies, it must be equally impossible to form any notion of its powers and qualities otherwise than from careful and exact experiments, and the observation of those particular effects which result from its different circumstances and situations. And though we must endeavour to render all our principles as universal as possible, by tracing up our experiments to the utmost, and explaining all effects from the simplest and fewest causes, it is still certain we cannot go beyond experience; and any hypothesis that pretends to discover the ultimate original qualities of human nature ought at first to be rejected as presumptuous and chimerical. . . .

Moral philosophy has, indeed, this peculiar disadvantage, which is not found in natural, that in collecting its experiments it cannot make them purposely, with premeditation, and after such a manner as to satisfy itself concerning every particular difficulty which may arise. When I am at a loss to know the effects of one body upon another in any situation, I need only put them in that situation, and observe what results from it. But should I endeavour to clear up after the same manner any doubt in moral philosophy, by placing myself in the same case with that which I consider, it is evident this reflection and premeditation would so disturb the operation of my natural principles as must render it impossible to form any just conclusion from the phaenomenon. We must, therefore, glean up our experiments in this science from a cautious observation of human life, and take them as they appear in the common course of the world, by men's behaviour in company, in affairs, and in their pleasures. Where experiments of this kind are judiciously collected and compared, we may hope to establish on them a science which will not be inferior in certainty, and will be much superior in utility, to any other of human comprehension.

# The Idea of a Universal History on a Cosmopolitical Plan

## IMMANUEL KANT

Whatsoever difference there may be in our notions of the *freedom of the will* metaphysically considered, it is evident that the manifestations of this will, viz. human actions, are as much under the control of universal laws of nature as any other physical phenomena. It is the province of History to narrate these manifestations; and, let their causes be ever so secret, we know that History, simply by taking its station at a distance and contemplating the agency of the human will upon a large scale, aims at unfolding to our view a regular stream of tendency in the great succession of events — so that the very same course of incidents which, taken separately and individually, would have seemed perplexed, incoherent, and lawless, yet viewed in their connexion and as the actions of the human *species* and not of independent beings, never fail to discover a steady and continuous, though slow, development of certain great predispositions in our nature. Thus, for instance, deaths, births, and marriages, considering how much they are separately dependent on the freedom of the human will, should seem to be subject to no law according to which any calculation could be made beforehand of their amount: and yet the yearly registers of these events in great countries prove that they go on with as much conformity to the laws of nature as the oscillations of the weather. These, again, are events which in detail are so far irregular that we cannot predict them individually; and yet, taken as a whole series, we find that they never fail to support the growth of plants, the currents of rivers, and other arrangements of nature, in a uniform and uninterrupted course. Individual men, and even nations, are little aware that, whilst they are severally pursuing their own peculiar and often contradictory purposes, they are unconsciously following the guidance of a great natural purpose which is wholly unnoticed by themselves, and are thus promoting and making efforts for a great process which, even if they perceived it, they would little regard.

Considering that men, taken collectively as a body, do not proceed, like brute animals, under the law of an instinct, nor yet again, like rational cosmopolites, under the law of a preconcerted plan, one might imagine that no systematic history of their actions (such, for instance, as the history of bees or beavers) could be possible. At the sight of the actions of man displayed on the great stage of the world, it is impossible to escape a certain degree of disgust: with all the occasional indications of wisdom scattered here and there, we cannot but perceive the whole sum of these actions to be a web of folly, childish vanity, and often even of the idlest wickedness and spirit of destruction. Hence, at last, one is puzzled to know what judgment to form of our species, so conceited of its high advantages. In such a perplexity there is no resource for the philosopher but this — that, finding it impossible to presume in the human race any *rational* purpose of its own, he must endeavour to detect some *natural* purpose in such a senseless current of human actions; by means of which a history of creatures that pursue no plan of their own may yet admit a systematic form as the history of creatures that are blindly pursuing a plan of nature. Let us now see whether we can succeed in finding out a clue to such a history, leaving it to nature to produce a man capable of executing it — just as she produced a Kepler who unexpectedly brought the eccentric courses of the planets under determinate laws, and afterwards a Newton who explained these laws out of a universal ground in Nature:

## PROPOSITION THE FIRST

*All tendencies of any creature to which it is predisposed by Nature are destined in the end to develop themselves perfectly and agreeably to their final purpose.*

External as well as internal (or anatomical) examination confirms this remark in all animals. An organ which is not to be used, a natural arrangement that misses its purpose, would be a contradiction in physics. Once departing from this fundamental proposition, we have a Nature no longer tied to laws, but objectless and working at random; and a cheerless reign of Chance steps into the place of Reason.

## PROPOSITION THE SECOND

*In Man, as the sole rational creature upon earth, those tendencies which have to use of his reason for their object are destined to obtain their perfect development in the species only, and not in the individual.*

Reason in a creature is a faculty for extending the rules and purposes of the exercise of all its powers far beyond natural instinct; and it is illimitable in its plans. It works, however, not instinctively, but tentatively, by means of practice, through progress and regress, in order to ascend gradually from one degree of illumination to another. On this account, either it would be necessary for each man to live an inordinate length of time in order to learn how to make a perfect use of his natural tendencies; or else, supposing the actual case that Nature has limited his term of life, she must then require an incalculable series of generations (each delivering its quota of knowledge to its immediate successor) in order to ripen the germs which she has laid in our species to that degree of development which corresponds with her final purpose. And the period of this mature development must exist at least in idea to Man as the object of his efforts: because otherwise his own natural predispositions must of necessity be regarded as objectless; and this would at once take away all *practical* principles, and would expose Nature, the wisdom of whose arrangements must in all other cases be assumed as a fundamental postulate, to the suspicion of capricious dealing in the case of Man only.

## PROPOSITION THE THIRD

*It is the will of Nature that Man should owe to himself alone every-*

*thing which transcends the mere mechanic constitution of his animal existence, and that he should be susceptible of no other happiness or perfection than what he has created for himself, instinct apart, through his own reason.*

Nature does nothing superfluously, and in the use of means to her ends does not play the prodigal. Having given to Man reason, and freedom of the will grounded upon reason, she had hereby sufficiently made known the purpose which governed her in the choice of the furniture and appointments, intellectual and physical, with which she has accoutred him. Thus provided, he had no need for the guidance of instinct, or for knowledge and forethought created to his hand; for these he was to be indebted to himself. The means of providing for his own shelter from the elements, for his own security, and the whole superstructure of delights which add comfort and embellishment to life, were to be the work of his own hands. So far indeed has she pushed this principle that she seems to have been frugal even to niggardliness in the dispensation of her animal endowments to Man, and to have calculated her allowance to the nicest rigour of the demand in the very earliest stage of his existence: as if it had been her intention hereby to proclaim that the highest degree of power, of intellectual perfection, and of happiness to which he should ever toil upwards from a condition utterly savage, must all be wrung and extorted from the difficulties and thwartings of his situation, and the merit therefore be exclusively his own; thus implying that she had at heart his own rational self-estimation rather than his convenience or comfort. She has indeed beset Man with difficulties; and in no way could she have so clearly made known that her purpose with Man was not that he might live in pleasure, but that by a strenuous wrestling with those difficulties he might make himself worthy of living in pleasure. Undoubtedly it seems surprising on this view of the case that the earlier generations appear to exist only for the sake of the latter, viz. for the sake of forwarding that edifice of man's grandeur in which only the latest generations are to dwell, though all have undesignedly taken part in raising it. Mysterious as this appears, it is, however, at the same time necessary, if we once assume a race of rational animals as destined by means of this characteristic reason to a perfect development of their tendencies, and subject to morality in the individual, but immortal in the species.

## PROPOSITION THE FOURTH

*The means which Nature employs to bring about the development of*

*all the tendencies she has laid in Man is the antagonism of these tenden-*
*cies in the social state — no farther, however, than to that point at which*
*this antagonism becomes the cause of social arrangements founded in law.*

By antagonism of this kind I mean the *unsocial sociality* of man — that
is, a tendency to enter the social state, combined with a perpetual resistance to that tendency which is continually threatening to dissolve it. Man
has gregarious inclinations, feeling himself in the social state more than
Man, by means of the development thus given to his natural tendencies.
But he has also strong antigregarious inclinations, prompting him to in-
sulate himself, which arise out of the unsocial desire (existing concur-
rently with his social propensities) to force all things into compliance with
his own humour — a propensity to which he naturally anticipates resistance from his consciousness of a similar spirit of resistance to others
existing in himself. Now, this resistance it is which awakens all the powers
of Man, drives him to master his propensity to indolence, and, in the
shape of ambition, love of honour, or avarice, impels him to procure
distinction for himself amongst his fellows. In this way arise the first
steps from the savage state to the state of culture, which consists peculiarly
in the social worth of Man. Talents of every kind are now unfolded, taste
formed, and by gradual increase of light a preparation is made for such
a mode of thinking as is capable of converting the rude natural tendency
to moral distinctions into determinate practical principles, and finally of
exalting a social concert that had been *pathologically* exorted from the
mere necessities of situation into a *moral* union founded on the reasonable
choice. But for these antisocial propensities, so unamiable in themselves,
which give birth to that resistance which every man meets with in his
own self-interested pretensions, an Arcadian life would arise, of perfect
harmony and mutual love, such as must suffocate and stifle all talents in
their very germs. Men, as gentle as the sheep they fed, would communicate to their existence no higher value than belongs to mere animal life,
and would leave the vacuum of creation, which exists in reference to the
final purpose of man's nature as a rational nature, unfilled. Thanks,
therefore, to Nature for the enmity, for the jealous spirit of envious
competition, for the insatiable thirst after wealth and power! These
wanting, all the admirable tendencies in man's nature would remain for
ever undeveloped. Man, for his own sake as an individual, wishes for
concord; but Nature knows better what is good for Man as a species;
and she ordains discord. He would live in ease and passive content: but
Nature wills that he shall precipitate himself out of this luxury of indolence into labours and hardships, in order that he may devise remedies

against them, and thus raise himself above them by an intellectual conquest, not sink below them by an unambitious evasion. The impulses which she has with this view laid in his moral constitution, the sources of that antisociality and universal antagonism from which so many evils arise, but which again stimulate a fresh reaction of the faculties, and by consequence more and more aid the development of the primitive tendencies, all tend to betray the adjusting hand of a wise Creator, not that of an Evil Spirit that has bungled in the execution of his own designs, or has malevolently sought to perplex them with evil.


## PROPOSITION THE FIFTH

*The highest problem for the Human Species, to the solution of which it is irresistibly urged by natural impulses, is the establishment of a universal Civil Society founded on the empire of political justice.*

Since it is only in the social state that the final purpose of Nature with regard to Man (viz. the development of all his tendencies) can be accomplished — and in such a social state as combines with the utmost possible freedom and consequent antagonism of its members the most rigorous determination of the boundaries of this freedom, in order that the freedom of such individual may coexist with the freedom of others — and since it is the will of Nature that this as well as all other objects of his destination should be the work of men's own efforts: on these accounts a society in which freedom under laws is united with the greatest possible degree of irresistible power — *i.e.* a perfect civil constitution — is the highest problem of Nature for Man: because it is only by the solution of this problem that Nature can accomplish the rest of her purposes with our species. Into this state of restraint Man, who is otherwise so much enamoured of lawless freedom, is compelled to enter by necessity — and that the greatest of all necessity, viz. a necessity self-imposed; his natural inclinations making it impossible for Man to preserve a state of perfect liberty for any length of time in the neighborhood of his fellows. But, under the restraint of a civil community, these very inclinations lead to the best effects: just as trees in a forest, for the very reason that each endeavours to rob the other of air and sun, compel each other to shoot upwards in quest of both, and thus attain a fine erect growth — whereas those which stand aloof from each other under no mutual restraint, and throw out their boughs at pleasure, become crippled and distorted. All the gifts of art and cultivation which adorn the human race — in short, the most beautiful forms of social order — are the fruits of the antisocial principle, which is compelled to discipline itself, and by means won from the very resistance of Man's situation in this world to give perfect development to all the germs of Nature.

## PROPOSITION THE SIXTH

*This problem is at the same time the most difficult of all, and the one which is latest solved by Man.*

The difficulty which is involved in the bare idea of such a problem is this: Man is an animal that, so long as he lives amongst others of his species, stands in need of a master. For he inevitably abuses his freedom in regard to his equals; and, although, as a reasonable creature, he wishes for a law that may set bounds to the liberty of all, yet do his self-interested animal propensities seduce him into making an exception in his own favour whensoever he dares. He requires a master, therefore, to curb his will, and to compel him into submission to a universal will which may secure the possibility of universal freedom. Now, where is he to find this master? Of necessity, amongst the human species. But, as a human being, this master will also be an animal that requires a master. Lodged in one or many, it is impossible that the supreme and irresponsible power can be certainly prevented from abusing its authority. Hence it is that this problem is the most difficult of any; nay, its perfect solution is impossible: out of wood so crooked and perverse as that which man is made of, nothing absolutely straight can ever be wrought. An approximation to this idea is therefore all which Nature enjoins us. That it is also the last of all problems to which the human species addresses itself is clear from this — that it presupposes *just notions* of the nature of a good constitution, great *experience,* and above all a *will* favourably disposed to the adoption of such a constitution: three elements that can hardly, and not until after many fruitless trials, be expected to concur.

## PROPOSITION THE SEVENTH

*The problem of the establishment of a perfect Constitution of Society depends upon the problem of a system of International Relations adjusted to law, and apart from this latter problem cannot be solved.*

To what purpose is labour bestowed upon a civil constitution adjusted to law for individual men, *i.e.* upon the creation of a Commonwealth? The same antisocial impulse which first drove men to such a creation is again the cause that every commonwealth, in its external relations — *i.e.*

as a state in reference to other states — occupies the same ground of lawless and uncontrolled liberty; consequently each must anticipate from the
other the very same evils which compelled individuals to enter the social
state. Nature accordingly avails herself of the spirit of enmity in Man,
as existing even in the great national corporations of that animal, for
the purpose of attaining through the inevitable antagonism of this spirit
a state of rest and security: *i.e.* by wars, by the immoderate exhaustion
of incessant preparations for war, and by the pressure of evil consequences
which war at last entails upon any nation even through the midst of
peace, she drives nations to all sorts of experiments and expedients; and
finally, after infinite devastations, ruin, and universal exhaustion of
energy, to one which reason should have suggested without the cost of
so sad an experience — viz. to quit the barbarous condition of lawless
power, and to enter into a federal league of nations, in which even the
weakest member looks for its rights and for protection noé to its own
power, or its own adjudication, but to this great confederation (*Foedus
Amphictyonum*), to the united power, and the adjudication of the collective will. Visionary as this idea may seem, and as such laughed at in the
Abbé de St. Pierre and in Rousseau (possibly because they deemed it too
near to its accomplishment), it is notwithstanding the inevitable resource
and mode of escape under that pressure of evil which nations reciprocally
inflict; and, hard as it may be to realize such an idea, states must of necessity be driven at last to the very same resolution to which the savage
man of nature was driven with equal reluctance — viz. to sacrifice brutal
liberty, and to seek peace and security in a civil constitution founded
upon law. All wars therefore are so many tentative essays (not in the intention of Man, but in the intention of Nature) to bring about new
relations of states, and by revolutions and dismemberments to form new
political bodies. These again, either from internal defects or external
attacks, cannot support themselves, but must undergo similar revolutions;
until at last, partly by the best possible arrangement of civil government
within, and partly by common concert and legal compact without, a
condition is attained which, like a well-ordered commonwealth, can maintain itself in the way of an automaton.

Now, whether (in the first place) it is to be anticipated from an epi-
curean concourse of efficient causes that states, like atoms, by accidental
shocking together, should go through all sorts of new combinations to
be again dissolved by the fortuitous impulse of fresh shocks, until at
length by pure accident some combination emerges capable of supporting
itself (a case of luck that could hardly be looked for); or whether (in the
second place) we should rather assume that Nature is in this instance

pursuing her regular course of raising our species gradually from the lower steps of animal existence to the very highest of a human existence, and *that* not by any direct interposition in our favour, but through man's own spontaneous and artificial efforts (spontaneous, but yet extorted from him by his situation), and in this apparently wild arrangement of things is developing with perfect regularity the original tendencies she has implanted; or whether (in the third place) it is more reasonable to believe that out of all this action and reaction of the human species upon itself nothing in the shape of a wise result will ever issue — that it will continue to be as it has been, and therefore that it cannot be known beforehand, but that the discord which is so natural to our species will finally prepare for us a hell of evils under the most moral condition of society, such as may swallow up this very moral condition itself and all previous advance in culture by a reflux of the original barbaric spirit of desolation (a fate, by the way, against which it is impossible to be secured under the government of blind chance, with which liberty uncontrolled by law is identical, unless by underlaying this chance with a secret nexus of wisdom): to all this the answer turns upon the following question: Whether it be reasonable to assume a final purpose of all natural processes and arrangements in the parts, and yet a want of purpose in the whole? What therefore the objectless condition of savage life effected in the end — viz. that it checked the development of the natural tendencies in the human species, but then, by the very evils it thus caused, drove man into a state where those tendencies could unfold and mature themselves, namely, the state of civilisation — that same service is performed for states by the barbaric freedom in which they are now existing — viz. that, by causing the dedication of all national energies and resources to war, by the desolations of war, and still more by causing the necessity of standing continually in a state of preparation for war, it checks the full development of the natural tendencies in its progress, but, on the other hand, by these very evils and their consequences, it compels our species at last to discover some law of counterbalance to the principle of antagonism between nations, and, in order to give effect to this law, to introduce a federation of states, and consequently a cosmopolitical condition of security (or police) corresponding to that municipal security which arises out of internal police. This federation will itself not be exempt from danger — else the powers of the human race would go to sleep; it will be sufficient that it contain a principle for restoring the equilibrium between its own action and reaction, and thus checking the two functions from destroying each other. Before this last step is taken, human nature — then about half-way advanced in its progress — is in the deepest abyss of evils under the deceitful semblance of external prosperity; and Rousseau was not so much in the wrong when he preferred the condition of the savage to that of the civilized man at the point where he has reached, but is hesitating to take, the final step of his ascent. We are at this time in a high degree of *culture* as to arts and sciences. We are *civilized* to superfluity in what regards the graces and decorums of life. But to entitle us to consider ourselves *moralized* much is still wanting. Yet the idea of morality belongs even to that of *culture;* but the use of this idea, as it comes forward in mere *civilisation,* is restrained to its influence on manners, as seen in the principle of honour, in respectability of deportment, etc. Nothing indeed of a true moral influence can be expected so long as states direct all their energies to idle plans of aggrandizement by force, and thus incessantly check the slow motions by which the intellect of the species is unfolding and forming itself, to say nothing of their shrinking from all *positive* aid to those motions. But all good that is not engrafted upon moral good is mere show and hollow speciousness — the dust and ashes of mortality. And in this delusive condition will the human race linger, until it shall have toiled upwards in the way I have mentioned from its present chaotic abyss of political relations.

## PROPOSITION THE EIGHTH

*The History of the Human Species as a whole may be regarded as the unravelling of a hidden Plan of Nature for accomplishing a perfect State of Civil Constitution for society in its internal relations (and, as the condition of that, by the last proposition, in its external relations also) as the sole state of society in which the tendencies of human nature can be all and fully developed.*

This proposition is an inference from the preceding. A question arises upon it — whether experience has yet observed any traces of such an unravelling in History? I answer, some little: for the whole period (to speak astronomically) of this unravelling is probably too vast to admit of our collecting even the form of its orbit or the relation of the parts to the whole from the small fraction of it which Man has yet left behind him; just as little as it is possible from the astronomical observations hitherto made to determine the course which our sun together with his whole system of planets pursues amongst the heavenly host; although upon universal grounds derived from the systematic frame of the universe, as well as upon the little stock of observation as yet accumulated, enough is known to warrant us in asserting that there *is* such a course.

Meantime our human nature obliges us to take an interest even in the remotest epoch to which our species is destined, provided we can anticipate it with certainty. So much the less can *we* be indifferent to it, inasmuch as it appears within our power by intellectual arrangements to contribute something towards the acceleration of the species in its advance to this great epoch. On this account the faintest traces of any approximation in such a direction become of importance to us. At present all states are so artificially interconnected that no one can possibly become stationary in its internal culture without retrograding in power and influence with respect to all the rest; and thus, if not the progress, yet the nondeclension, of this purpose of Nature is sufficiently secured through the ambition of nations. Moreover, civil liberty cannot at this day any longer be so arrested in its progress but that all the sources of livelihood, and more immediately trade, must betray a close sympathy with it, and sicken as *that* sickens; and hence a decay of the state in its external relations. Gradually, too, this liberty extends itself. If the citizen be hindered from pursuing his interest in any way most agreeable to himself provided only it can coexist with the liberty of others, in that case the vivacious life of general business is palsied, and in connexion with that again the powers of the whole. Hence it arises that all personal restriction, whether as to commission or omission, is more and more withdrawn; religious liberty is established; and thus, by little and little, with occasional interruptions, arises *Illumination:* a blessing which the human race must win even from the self-interested purposes of its rulers, if they comprehend what is for their own advantage. Now, this Illumination, and with it a certain degree of cordial interest which the enlightened man cannot forbear taking in all the good which he perfectly comprehends, must by degrees mount upwards even to the throne, and exert an influence on the principles of government. At present, for example, our governments have no money disposable for national education, because the estimates for the next war have absorbed the whole by anticipation. The first act, therefore, by which the stage will express its interest in the advancing spirit of the age will be by withdrawing its opposition at least to the feeble and tardy exertions of the people in this direction. Finally, war itself becomes gradually not only so artificial a process, so uncertain in its issue, but also in the afterpains of inextinguishable national debts (a contrivance of modern times) so anxious and burthensome, and, at the same time, the influence which any convulsions of one state exert upon every other state is so remarkable in our quarter of the globe — linked as it is in all parts by the systematic intercourse of trade — that at length those governments which have no immediate participation in the war, under a sense of their own danger, offer themselves as mediators, though as yet without any authentic sanction of law, and thus prepare all things from afar for the formation of a great primary state-body, or Cosmopolitic Areopagus, such as is wholly unprecendented in all preceding ages. Although this body at present exists only in rude outline, yet already a stirring is beginning to be perceptible in all its limbs, each of which is interested in the maintenance of the whole. Even now there is enough to justify a hope that, after many revolutions and remodellings of states, the supreme purpose of Nature will be accomplished in the establishment of a Cosmopolitic State, as the bosom in which all the original tendencies of the human species are to be developed.

# from *Common Sense*

## THOMAS PAINE

### I. ON THE ORIGIN AND DESIGN OF GOVERNMENT IN GENERAL, WITH CONCISE REMARKS ON THE ENGLISH CONSTITUTION

Some writers have so confounded society with government as to leave little or no distinction between them; whereas they are not only different, but have different origins. Society is produced by our wants and governments by our wickedness; the former promotes our happiness *positively* by uniting our affections, the latter *negatively* by restraining our vices. The one encourages intercourse, the other creates distinctions. The first is a patron, the last a punisher.

Society in every state is a blessing, but government, even in its best state, is but a necessary evil; in its worst state an intolerable one; for when we suffer or are exposed to the same miseries *by a government*, which we might expect in an country *without government*, our calamity is heightened by reflecting that we furnish the means by which we suffer. Government, like dress, is the badge of lost innocence; the palaces of kings are built upon the ruins of the bowers of paradise. For were the impulses of conscience clear, uniform, and irresistibly obeyed, man would need no other lawgiver; but that not being the case, he finds it necessary to surrender up a part of his property to furnish means for the protection of the rest; and this he is induced to do by the same prudence which in every other case advises him out of two evils to choose the least. *Wherefore,* security being the true design and end of government, it unanswerably follows that whatever *form* thereof appears most likely to ensure it to us, with the least expense and greatest benefit, is preferable to all others.

In order to gain a clear and just idea of the design and end of government, let us suppose a small number of persons settled in some sequestered part of the earth, unconnected with the rest; they will then represent the first peopling of any country, or of the world. In this state of natural liberty, society will be their first thought. A thousand motives will excite them thereto; the strength of one man is so unequal to his wants, and his mind so unfitted for perpetual solitude, that he is soon obliged to seek assistance and relief of another, who in his turn requires the same. Four or five united would be able to raise a tolerable dwelling in the midst of a wilderness, but *one* man might labor out the common period of life without accomplishing anything; when he had felled his timber he could not remove it, nor erect it after it was removed; hunger in the meantime would urge him to quit his work, and every different want would call him a different way. Disease, nay even misfortune, would be death; for though neither might be mortal, yet either would disable him from living, and reduce him to a state in which he might rather be said to perish than to die.

Thus necessity, like a gravitating power, would soon form our newly arrived emigrants into society, the reciprocal blessings of which would supersede and render the obligations of law and government unnecessary while they remained perfectly just to each other; but as nothing but heaven is impregnable to vice, it will unavoidably happen that in proportion as they surmount the first difficulties of emigration, which bound them together in a common cause, they will begin to relax in their duty and attachment to each other; and this remissness will point out the necessity of establishing some form of government to supply the defect of moral virtue.

Some convenient tree will afford them a statehouse, under the branches of which the whole colony may assemble to deliberate on public matters. It is more than probable that their first laws will have the title only of REGULATIONS and be enforced by no other penalty than public disesteem. In this first parliament every man by natural right will have a seat.

But as the colony increases, the public concerns will increase likewise, and the distance at which the members may be separated will render it too inconvenient for all of them to meet on every occasion as at first, when their number was small, their habitations near, and the public concerns few and trifling. This will point out the convenience of their consenting to leave the legislative part to be managed by a select number chosen from the whole body, who are supposed to have the same concerns at stake which those have who appointed them, and who will act in the same manner as the whole body would act were they present. If the colony continue increasing, it will become necessary to augment the number of representatives, and that the interest of every part of the colony may be attended to, it will be found best to divide the whole into convenient parts, each part sending its proper number; and that the *elected* might never form to themselves an interest separate from the *electors*, prudence will point out the propriety of having elections often, because as the *elected* might by that means return and mix again with the general body of the *electors* in a few months, their fidelity to the public will be secured by the prudent reflection of not making a rod for themselves. And as this frequent interchange will establish a common interest with every part of the community, they will mutually and naturally support each other, and on this (not on the unmeaning name of king) depends the *strength of government and the happiness of the governed.*

Here then is the origin and rise of government; namely, a mode rendered necessary by the inability of moral virtue to govern the world; here too is the design and end of government, viz., freedom and security. And however our eyes may be dazzled with show or our ears deceived by sound; however prejudice may warp our wills or interest darken our understanding, the simple voice of nature and reason will say, it is right.

I draw my idea of the form of government from a principle in nature which no art can overturn, viz. that the more simple anything is, the less liable it is to be disordered, and the easier repaired when disordered; and with this maxim in view, I offer a few remarks on the so much boasted constitution of England. That it was noble for the dark and slavish times in which it was erected, is granted. When the world was overrun with tyranny, the least remove therefrom was a glorious rescue. But that it is imperfect, subject to convulsions, and incapable of producing what it seems to promise, is easily demonstrated.

Absolute governments (though the disgrace of human nature) have this advantage with them, they are simple; if the people suffer, they know the head from which their suffering springs; know likewise the remedy; and are not bewildered by a variety of causes and cures. But the constitution of England is so exceedingly complex that the nation may suffer for years together without being able to discover in which part the fault lies; some will say in one and some in another, and every political physician will advise a different medicine.

I know it is difficult to get over local or long standing prejudices, yet if we will suffer ourselves to examine the component parts of the English constitution, we shall find them to be the base remains of two ancient tyrannies, compounded with some new republican materials.

*First.* — The remains of monarchical tyranny in the person of the King.

*Secondly.* — The remains of aristocratical tyranny in the persons of the Peers.

*Thirdly.* — The new republican materials, in the persons of the Commons, on whose virtue depends the freedom of England.

The two first, by being hereditary, are independent of the people; wherefore in a *constitutional sense* they contribute nothing towards the freedom of the state.

To say that the constitution of England is a *union* of three powers, reciprocally *checking* each other, is farcical; either the words have no meaning, or they are flat contradictions.

To say that the commons is a check upon the king, presupposes two things.

*First.* — That the king is not to be trusted without being looked after; or in other words, that a thirst for absolute power is the natural disease of monarchy.

*Secondly.* — That the commons, by being appointed for that purpose, are either wiser or more worthy of confidence than the crown.

But as the same constitution which gives the commons a power to check the king by withholding the supplies, gives afterwards the king a power to check the commons, by empowering him to reject their other bills; it again supposes that the king is wiser than those whom it has already supposed to be wiser than him. A mere absurdity!

There is something exceedingly ridiculous in the composition of monarchy; it first excludes a man from the means of information, yet empowers him to act in cases where the highest judgment is required. The state of a king shuts him from the world, yet the business of a king requires him to know it thoroughly; wherefore the different parts, by unnaturally opposing and destroying each other, prove the whole character to be absurd and useless.

Some writers have explained the English constitution thus: the king, say they, is one, the people another; the peers are a house in behalf of the king, the commons in behalf of the people; but this hath all the distinctions of a house divided against itself; and though the expressions be pleasantly arranged, yet when examined they appear idle and ambiguous; and it will always happen that the nicest construction that words are capable of, when applied to the description of something which either cannot exist or is too incomprehensible to be within the compass of description, will be words of sound only, and though they may amuse the ear, they cannot inform the mind; for this explanation includes a previous question, viz. *how came the king by a power which the people are afraid to trust, and always obliged to check?* Such a power could not be the gift of a wise people, neither can any power, *which needs checking,* be from God; yet the provision which the constitution makes supposes such a power to exist.

But the provision is unequal to the task; the means either cannot or will not accomplish the end, and the whole affair is a *felo de se;* for as the greater weight will always carry up the less, and as all the wheels of a machine are put in motion by one, it only remains to know which power in the constitution has the most weight, for that will govern; and though the others, or a part of them, may clog, or check the rapidity of its motion, yet so long as they cannot stop it, their endeavors will be ineffectual; the first moving power will at last have its way, and what it wants in speed is supplied by time.

That the crown is this overbearing part in the English constitution needs not be mentioned, and that it derives its whole consequence merely from being the giver of places and pensions is self-evident; wherefore, though we have been wise enough to shut and lock a door against absolute monarchy, we at the same time have been foolish enough to put the crown in possession of the key.

The prejudice of Englishmen in favor of their own government by king, lords, and commons, arises as much or more from national pride than reason. Individuals are undoubtedly safer in England than in some other countries: but the *will* of the king is as much the *law* of the land in Britain as in France, with this difference, that instead of proceeding directly from his mouth, it is handed to the people under the formidable shape of an act of parliament. For the fate of Charles the First hath only made kings more subtle — not more just.

Wherefore, laying aside all national pride and prejudice in favor of modes and forms, the plain truth is that *it is wholly to the constitution of the people, and not to the constitution of the government* that the crown is not as oppressive in England as in Turkey.

7. Thomas Gainsborough,
*Musidora.*

8. Boucher, *Bath of Diana*, 1742.

*9.* Antoine Watteau, *Embarkation for Cythera*, 1717.

*10.* G. B. Tiepolo,
*St. James of Compostela.*

*11.*   Francisco de Goya, *Self-Portrait*, 1783.

*12.* Giovanni Battista Piranesi, *Hadrian's Villa — the Central Room of the Larger Thermae.* Etching, c. 1770. An example of the romantic interest in ruins that marked the late eighteenth century.

13. Canaletto,
*Scene in Venice:
The Piazzetta.*

14. Francesco Guardi,
*Classical Composition —
Ruins and Figures.*
Another example of the
late eighteenth-century
interest in ruins.

# II

# Nature as Matrix

*Newton, Leibnitz, Descartes, and other scientists of the seventeenth century, proceeding mainly along mathematical lines, had established what was held to be a fixed rational order in nature. Relativity and indeterminacy were as yet undreamed of. Reading rational order into every manifestation of nature, the philosophes idealized and, it may even be said in some cases, deified nature. This became one of the sources of the romanticism that eventually displaced rationalism.*

# from *Discourses on Art*

## JOSHUA REYNOLDS

The Third Discourse. . . . The first endeavours of a young Painter, as I have remarked in a former discourse, must be employed in the attainment of mechanical dexterity, and confined to the mere imitation of the object before him. Those who have advanced beyond the rudiments, may, perhaps, find advantage in reflecting on the advice which I have likewise given them, when I recommended the diligent study of the works of our great predecessors; but I at the same time endeavoured to guard them against an implicit submission to the authority of any one master however excellent: or by a strict imitation of his manner, precluding themselves from the abundance and variety of Nature. I will now add that Nature herself is not to be too closely copied. There are excellencies in the art of painting beyond what is commonly called the imitation of nature: and these excellencies I wish to point out. The students who, having passed through the initiatory exercises, are more advanced in the art, and who, sure of their hand, have leisure to exert their understanding, must now be told, that a mere copier of nature can never produce any thing great; can never raise and enlarge the conceptions, or warm the heart of the spectator.

The wish of the genuine painter must be more extensive: instead of endeavouring to amuse mankind with the minute neatness of his imitations, he must endeavour to improve them by the grandeur of his ideas; instead of seeking praise, by deceiving the superficial sense of the spectator, he must strive for fame by captivating the imagination.

The principle now laid down, that the perfection of this art does not consist in mere imitation, is far from being new or singular. It is, indeed, supported by the general opinion of the enlightened part of mankind. The poets, orators, and rhetoricians of antiquity, are continually enforcing this position; that all the arts receive their perfection from an ideal beauty, superior to what is to be found in individual nature. They are ever referring to the practice of the painters and sculptors of their times, particularly Phidias (the favourite artist of antiquity), to illustrate

95

their assertions. As if they could not sufficiently express their admiration of his genius by what they knew, they have recourse to poetical enthusiasm: they call it inspiration; a gift from heaven. The artist is supposed to have ascended the celestial regions, to furnish his mind with this perfect idea of beauty. "He," says Proclus, "who takes for his model such forms as nature produces, and confines himself to an exact imitation of them, will never attain to what is perfectly beautiful. For the works of nature are full of disproportion, and fall very short of the true standard of beauty. So that Phidias, when he formed his Jupiter, did not copy any object ever presented to his sight; but contemplated only that image which he had conceived in his mind from Homer's description." And thus Cicero, speaking of the same Phidias: "Neither did this artist," says he, "when he carved the image of Jupiter or Minerva, set before him any one human figure, as a pattern which he was to copy; but having a more perfect idea of beauty fixed in his mind, this he steadily contemplated, and to the imitation of this all his skill and labour were directed."

The Moderns are no less convinced than the Ancients of this superior power existing in the art; nor less sensible of its effects. Every language has adopted terms expressive of this excellence. The *gusto grande* of the Italians, the *beau ideal* of the French, and the *great style, genius,* and *taste* among the English, are but different appellations of the same thing. It is this intellectual dignity, they say, that ennobles the painter's art; that lays the line between him and the mere mechanick; and produces those great effects in an instant, which eloquence and poetry, by slow and repeated efforts, are scarcely able to attain. . . .

It is not easy to define in what this great style consists; nor to describe, by words, the proper means of acquiring it, if the mind of the student should be at all capable of such an acquisition. Could we teach taste or genius by rules, they would be no longer taste and genius. But though there neither are, nor can be, any precise invariable rules for the exercise, or the acquisition, of these great qualities, yet we may truly say, that they always operate in proportion to our attention in observing the works of nature, to our skill in selecting, and to our care in digesting, methodizing, and comparing our observations. There are many beauties in our art, that seem, at first, to lie without the reach of precept, and yet may easily be reduced to practical principles. Experience is all in all; but it is not every one who profits by experience; and most people err, not so much from want of capacity to find their object, as from not knowing what object to pursue. This great ideal perfection and beauty are not to be sought in the heavens, but upon the earth. They are about us, and upon every side of us. But the power of discovering what is deformed in nature, or in other words, what is particular and uncommon, can be acquired only by experience; and the whole beauty and grandeur of the art consists, in my opinion, in being able to get above all singular forms, local customs, particularities, and details of every kind.

All the objects which are exhibited to our view by nature, upon close examination will be found to have their blemishes and defects. The most beautiful forms have something about them like weakness, minuteness, or imperfection. But it is not every eye that perceives these blemishes. It must be an eye long used to the contemplation and comparison of these forms; and which by a long habit of observing what any set of objects of the same kind have in common, has acquired the power of discerning what each wants in particular. This long laborious comparison should be the first study of the painter, who aims at the greatest style. By this means, he acquires a just idea of beautiful forms; he corrects nature by herself, her imperfect state by her more perfect. His eye being enabled to distinguish the accidental deficiencies, excrescences, and deformities of things, from their general figures, he makes out an abstract idea of their forms more perfect than any one original; and what may seem a paradox, he learns to design naturally by drawing his figures unlike to any one object. This idea of the perfect state of nature, which the Artist calls the Ideal Beauty, is the great leading principle by which works of genius are conducted. By this Phidias acquired his fame. He wrought upon a sober principle what has so much excited the enthusiasm of the world; and by this method you, who have courage to tread the same path, may acquire equal reputation.

This is the idea which has acquired, and which seems to have a right to the epithet of *divine;* as it may be said to preside, like a supreme judge, over all the productions of nature; appearing to be possessed of the will and intention of the Creator, as far as they regard the external form of living beings. When a man once possesses this idea in its perfection, there is no danger, but that he will be sufficiently warmed by it himself, and be able to warm and ravish every one else. . . .

# from *Essay on Man*

## ALEXANDER POPE

Lo, the poor Indian! whose untutor'd mind
Sees God in clouds, or hears him in the wind;
His soul, proud Science never taught to stray
Far as the solar walk, or milky way;
Yet simple Nature to his hope has giv'n,
Behind the cloud-topt hill, an humbler heav'n;
Some safer world in depth of woods embrac'd,
Some happier island in the watry waste,
Where slaves once more their native land behold,
No fiends torment, no Christians thirst for gold.
To Be, contents his natural desire,
He asks no Angel's wing, no Seraph's fire;
But thinks, admitted to that equal sky,
His faithful dog shall bear him company.

.　　.　　.

Vast chain of Being! which from God began,
Natures ethereal, human, angel, man,
Beast, bird, fish, insect, what no eye can see,
No glass can reach; from Infinite to thee,
From thee to Nothing. — On superior pow'rs
Were we to press, inferior might on ours:
Or in the full creation leave a void,
Where, one step broken, the great scale's destroy'd:
From Nature's chain whatever link you strike,
Tenth or ten thousandth, breaks the chain alike.

# from *The Natural History of Selborne*

## GILBERT WHITE

### LETTER LXXXIX

*To the Honourable Daines Barrington*

"Far from all resort of mirth
Save the cricket on the hearth."
MILTON's *Il Penseroso.*

While many other insects must be sought after in fields, and woods, and waters, the *Gryllus domesticus,* or house-cricket, resides altogether within our dwellings, intruding itself upon our notice whether we will or no. This species delights in new-built houses, being, like the spider, pleased with the moisture of the walls; and besides, the softness of the mortar enables them to burrow and mine between the joints of the bricks or stones, and to open communications from one room to another. They are particularly fond of kitchens and bakers' ovens, on account of their perpetual warmth.

Tender insects that live abroad either enjoy only the short period of one summer, or else doze away the cold uncomfortable months in profound slumbers; but these, residing as it were in a torrid zone, are always alert and merry: a good Christmas fire is to them like the heats of the dog-days. Though they are frequently heard by day, yet is their natural time of motion only in the night. As soon as it grows dusk, the chirping increases, and they come running forth, ranging from the size of a flea to that of their full stature. As one should suppose from the burning atmosphere which they inhabit, they are a thirsty race, and show a great propensity for liquids, being found frequently drowned in pans of water, milk, broth, or the like. Whatever is moist they affect; and therefore often gnaw holes in wet woollen stockings and aprons that are hung to the fire: they are the housewife's barometer, foretelling her when it will rain; and they prognosticate sometimes, she thinks, good or ill luck; the death of near relations, or the approach of an absent lover. By being the constant companions of her solitary hours, they naturally become the objects of her superstition. These crickets are not only very thirsty, but very voracious; for they will eat the scummings of pots, and yeast, salt, and crumbs of bread; and any kitchen offal or sweepings. In the summer we have observed them to fly out of the windows when it became dusk, and over the neighbouring roofs. This feat of activity accounts for the sudden manner in which they often leave their haunts, as it does for the method by which they come to houses where they were not known before. It is remarkable, that many sorts of insects seem never to use their wings but when they have a mind to shift their quarters and settle new colonies. When in the air they move *volatu undoso*, in "waves or curves," like woodpeckers, opening and shutting their wings at every stroke, and so are always rising or sinking.

When they increase to a great degree, as they did once in the house where I am now writing, they become noisome pests, flying into the candles, and dashing into people's faces; but may be blasted and destroyed by gunpowder discharged into their crevices and crannies.

[In November, after the servants are gone to bed, the kitchen hearth swarms with minute crickets not so large as fleas, which must have been lately hatched, so that these domestic insects, cherished by the influence of a constant and large fire, regard not the season of the year, but produce their young at a time when their congeners are either dead or laid up for the winter, passing away the uncomfortable months in a state of torpidity.

When house-crickets are out and running about a room in the night, if surprised by a candle, they utter two or three shrill notes, as if it were a signal to their fellows, that they may escape to their crannies and lurking places to avoid danger.]

In families, at such times, they are, like Pharaoh's plague of frogs, — in their bedchambers, and upon their beds, and in their ovens, and in their kneading-troughs. Their shrilling noise is occasioned by a brisk attrition of their wings. Cats catch hearth-crickets, and play with them as they do with mice, and then devour them. Crickets may be destroyed, like wasps, by phials half filled with beer, or any other liquid, and set in their haunts, for, being always eager to drink, they will crowd in till the bottles are full.


## LETTER XC

### To the Honourable Daines Barrington

How diversified are the modes of life not only of incongruous but even of congenerous animals; and yet their specific distinctions are not more various than their propensities. Thus, while the field-cricket delights in sunny dry banks, and the house-cricket rejoices amidst the glowing heat of the kitchen hearth or oven, the *Gryllus gryllo talpa* (the mole-cricket) haunts moist meadows, and frequents the sides of ponds and banks of streams, performing all its functions in a swampy wet soil. With a pair of fore-feet curiously adapted to the purpose, it burrows and works under ground like the mole, raising a ridge as it proceeds, but seldom throwing up hillocks.

As mole-crickets often infest gardens by the sides of canals, they are unwelcome guests to the gardener, raising up ridges in their subterraneous progress, and rendering the walks unsightly. If they take to the kitchen quarters, they occasion great damage among the plants and roots, by destroying whole beds of cabbages, young legumes, and flowers. When dug out they seem very slow and helpless, and make no use of their wings by day; but at night they come abroad, and make long excursions, as I have been convinced by finding stragglers, in a morning, in improbable places. In fine weather, about the middle of April, and just at the close of day, they begin to solace themselves with a low, dull, jarring note, continued for a long time without interruption, and not unlike the chattering of the fern-owl, or goat-sucker, but more inward.

About the beginning of May they lay their eggs, as I was once an eyewitness: for a gardener at a house where I was on a visit, happening to be mowing, on the 6th of that month, by the side of a canal, his scythe struck too deep, pared off a large piece of turf, and laid open to view a curious scene of domestic economy:

> "— — — — ingentem lato dedit ore fenestram:
> Apparet domus intus, et atria longa patescunt:
> Apparent — — — penetralia."
>
> (Virg. Æn. ii. 481–483.)

> "A yawning breach of monstrous size he made:
> The inmost house is now to light displayed:
> The admitted light with sudden lustre falls
> On the long galleries and the splendid halls."
>
> (Dryden.)

There were many caverns and winding passages leading to a kind of chamber, neatly smoothed and rounded, and about the size of a moderate snuff-box. Within this secret nursery were deposited near a hundred eggs of a dirty yellow colour, and enveloped in a tough skin, but too lately excluded to contain any rudiments of young, being full of a viscous substance. The eggs lay but shallow, and within the influence of the sun, just under a little heap of fresh-moved mould, like that which is raised by ants.

When mole-crickets fly they move *cursu undoso,* rising and falling in curves, like the other species mentioned before. In different parts of this kingdom people call them fen-crickets, churr-worms, and eve-churrs, all very apposite names.

Anatomists, who have examined the intestines of these insects, astonish me with their accounts; for they say that, from the structure, position, and number of their stomachs, or maws, there seems to be good reason to suppose that this and the two former species ruminate or chew the cud like many quadrupeds!

# Verses on the Prospect of Planting Arts and Learning in America

## GEORGE BERKELEY

The Muse, disgusted at an age and clime
    Barren of every glorious theme,
In distant lands now waits a better time,
    Producing subjects worthy fame:

In happy climes, where from the genial sun
    And virgin earth such scenes ensue,
The force of art by nature seems outdone,
    And fancied beauties by the true:

In happy climes, the seat of innocence,
    Where nature guides and virtue rules,
Where men shall not impose for truth and sense
    The pedantry of courts and schools:

There shall be sung another golden age,
    The rise of empire and of arts,
The good and great inspiring epic rage,
    The wisest heads, and noblest hearts.

Not such as Europe breeds in her decay;
    Such as she bred when fresh and young,

When heavenly flame did animate her clay,
By future poets shall be sung.

Westward the course of empire takes its way;
The first four acts already past,
A fifth shall close the drama with the day;
Time's noblest offspring is the last.

# Remarks Concerning the Savages of North America

## BENJAMIN FRANKLIN

Savages we call them, because their Manners differ from ours, which we think the Perfection of Civility; they think the same of theirs.

Perhaps, if we could examine the Manners of different Nations with Impartiality, we should find no People so rude, as to be without any Rules of Politeness; nor any so polite, as not to have some Remains of Rudeness.

The Indian Men, when young, are Hunters and Warriors; when old, Counsellors; for all their Government is by Counsel of the Sages; there is no Force, there are no Prisons, no Officers to compel Obedience, or inflict Punishment. Hence they generally study Oratory, the best Speaker having the most Influence. The Indian Women till the Ground, dress the Food, nurse and bring up the Children, and preserve and hand down to Posterity the Memory of public Transactions. These Employments of Men and Women are accounted natural and honourable. Having few artificial Wants, they have abundance of Leisure for Improvement by Conversation. Our laborious Manner of Life, compared with theirs, they esteem slavish and base; and the Learning, on which we value ourselves, they regard as frivolous and useless. An instance of this occurred at the Treaty of Lancaster, in Pennsylvania, *anno* 1744, between the Government of Virginia and the Six Nations. After the principal Business was settled, the Commissioners from Virginia acquainted the Indians by a Speech, that there was at Williamsburg a College, with a Fund for Educating Indian youth; and that, if the Six Nations would send down half a dozen of their young Lads to that College, the Government would take care that they should be well provided for, and instructed in all the Learning of the White People. It is one of the Indian Rules of Politeness not to answer a public Proposition the same day that it is made; they think it would be treating it as a light matter, and that they show it Respect by taking time to consider it, as of a Matter of important. They therefore deferr'd their Answer till the Day following; when their Speaker began, by expressing their deep Sense of the kindness of the Virginia Government, in making them that Offer; "for we know," says he, "that you highly esteem the kind of Learning taught in those Colleges, and that the Maintenance of our young Men, while with you, would be very expensive to you. We are convinc'd, therefore, that you mean to do us Good by your Proposal; and we thank you heartily. But you, who are wise, must know that different Nations have different Conceptions of things; and you will therefore not take it amiss, if our Ideas of this kind of Education happen not to be the same with yours. We have had some Experience of it; Several of our young People were formerly brought up at the Colleges of the Northern Provinces; they were instructed in all your Sciences; but, when they came back to us, they were bad Runners, ignorant of every means of living in the Woods, unable to bear either Cold or Hunger, knew neither how to build a Cabin, take a Deer, or kill an Enemy, spoke our Language imperfectly, were therefore neither fit for Hunters, Warriors, nor Counsellors; they were totally good for nothing. We are however not the less oblig'd by your kind Offer, tho' we decline accepting it; and, to show our grateful Sense of it, if the Gentlemen of Virginia will send us a Dozen of their Sons, we will take great Care of their Education, instruct them in all we know, and make *Men* of them."

Having frequent Occasions to hold public Councils, they have acquired great Order and Decency in conducting them. The old Men sit in the foremost Ranks, the Warriors in the next, and the Women and Children in the hindmost. The Business of the Women is to take exact Notice of what passes, imprint it in their Memories (for they have no writing), and communicate it to their Children. They are the Records of the Council, and they preserve Traditions of the Stipulations in Treaties 100 Years back; which, when we compare with our Writings, we always find exact. He that would speak, rises. The rest observe a profound Silence. When he has finish'd and sits down, they leave him 5 or 6 Minutes to recollect, that, if he has omitted anything he intended to say, or has any thing to add, he may rise again and deliver it. To interrupt another, even in common Conversation, is reckon'd highly indecent. How different this is from the conduct of a polite British House of Commons, where scarce a day passes without some Confusion, that makes the Speaker hoarse in calling *to Order;* and how different from the Mode of Conversation in many polite Companies of Europe, where, if you do not deliver your Sentence with great Rapidity, you are cut off in the middle of it by the Impatient Loquacity of those you converse with, and never suffer'd to finish it!

The Politeness of these Savages in Conversation is indeed carried to Excess, since it does not permit them to contradict or deny the Truth of what is asserted in their Presence. By this means they indeed avoid Disputes; but then it becomes difficult to know their Minds, or what Impression you make upon them. The Missionaries who have attempted to convert them to Christianity, all complain of this as one of the great Difficulties of their Mission. The Indians hear with Patience the Truths of the Gospel explain'd to them, and give their usual Tokens of Assent and Approbation; you would think they were convinc'd. No such matter. It is mere Civility.

A Swedish Minister, having assembled the chiefs of the Susquehanah Indians, made a Sermon to them, acquainting them with the principal historical Facts on which our Religion is founded; such as the Fall of our first Parents by eating an Apple, the coming of Christ to repair the Mischief, his Miracles and Suffering, &c. When he had finished, an Indian Orator stood up to thank him. "What you have told us," says he, "is all very good. It is indeed bad to eat Apples. It is better to make them all into Cyder. We are much oblig'd by your kindness in coming so far, to tell us these Things which you have heard from your Mothers. In return, I will tell you some of those we have heard from ours. In the Beginning, our Fathers had only the Flesh of Animals to subsist on; and if their Hunting was unsuccessful, they were starving. Two of our young Hunters, having kill'd a Deer, made a Fire in the Woods to broil some Part of it. When they were about to satisfy their Hunger, they beheld a beautiful young Woman descend from the Clouds, and seat herself on that Hill, which you see yonder among the Blue Mountains. They said to each other, it is a Spirit that has smelt our broiling Venison, and wishes to eat of it; let us offer some to her. They presented her with the Tongue; she was pleas'd with the Taste of it, and said, 'Your kindness shall be rewarded; come to this Place after thirteen Moons, and you shall find something that will be of great Benefit in nourishing you and your Children to the latest Generation.' They did so, and, to their Surprise, found Plants they had never seen before; but which, from that ancient time, have been constantly cultivated among us, to our great Advantage. Where her right Hand had touched the Ground, they found Maize; where her left hand had touch'd it, they found Kidney-Beans; and where her Backside had sat

on it, they found Tobacco." The good Missionary, disgusted with this idle
Tale, said, "What I delivered to you were sacred Truths; but what you
tell me is mere Fable, Fiction, and Falshood." The Indian, offended, reply'd, "My brother, it seems your Friends have not done you Justice in
your Education; they have not well instructed you in the Rules of Common Civility. You saw that we, who understand and practise those Rules,
believ'd all your stories; why do you refuse to believe ours?" . . .

# An Essay on Granite

## JOHANN WOLFGANG VON GOETHE

Granite is a species of rock that, since times immemorial, has aroused
the interest of men; today this interest is more intense than ever. The
ancients did not know it under this name. They called it syenite, from
Syene, a region on the borders of Ethiopia. The immense masses of this
stone inspired the Egyptians with the idea of creating immense works.
Their kings erected granite obelisks to honor the sun; later they gave this
rock the name of "Fireglow" because of its reddish speckled hue. Granite
sphinxes, statues of Memnon, and columns are still admired by travelers;
and even today, etched against the sky of powerless Rome, stands a crumbling obelisk which the omnipotent rulers of the ancient Empire once
brought intact from a distant continent.

The moderns called this rock "granite" because of its grainy appearance, and in recent times it had to suffer a certain period of humiliation
before it earned the respect in which it is now held by all naturalists. The
immensity of the obelisks and the wondrous pattern of their grain led
an Italian naturalist to believe that the Egyptians artificially solidified
them out of a liquid mass.

But this opinion was quickly discarded, and the dignity of granite was
definitively established by many careful observers. Every journey into
hitherto unexplored mountains confirmed the fact that granite forms
both the lowest and the highest layer, that this species of rock which
began to be the object of close study and could be distinguished from other
minerals, is the foundation of our earth upon which all the other varied
layers rest. In the innermost bowels of the earth, it stands unshaken, its
high ridges soaring, so that the all-enveloping waters never reached the

peaks. This much we know about granite, and little more. Compounded mysteriously from known elements, its origin is no more traceable to fire than to water. Complex, yet simple, its variations are innumerable. The position and relation of its parts, its solidity, and its color, vary with every mountain range, and the masses of each range often differ from one step to another, and yet resemble each other. And so everyone who knows the charm that natural mysteries have for man will not be surprised that I have left my former field of observation and became passionately interested in this one. I do not fear the reproach that it must have been the spirit of contradiction which led me from the consideration and description of the human heart — that most recent, most varied, most mobile, most changeable, most disturbing part of creation — to the study of the oldest, firmest, deepest, most unshakable child of nature. For it will be readily granted that everything in nature is closely connected with everything else, and that the investigating mind does not willingly allow itself to be excluded from anything attainable. I, who have suffered and still suffer a great deal from the changes in men's dispositions, from my own volatility and that of others, should not be begrudged the sublime peace that is the gift of great gentle-tongued nature to those who approach her silently and alone. And let those who have an inkling of this peace follow me.

In this spirit I approach you, most ancient, most dignified monuments of time. Sitting on a high bare peak and suveying a broad landscape, I can say to myself: Here you are resting on a foundation that reaches down to the deepest parts of the earth; not a recent layer, not piled-up fused ruins are interposed between you and the firm ground of the primal world; you do not, as in the fertile beautiful valleys, walk over an ever-fresh grave; these peaks have neither created anything living nor swallowed anything living; they are before all life and above all life. At this moment, when the inner attractive and motive forces of the earth are acting upon me directly, so to speak, when the influences of the sky come closer to me, I am attuned to higher meditations on nature, and since the human mind brings life to everything, a symbol stirs within me, so sublime that I must recognize it as valid. I look down this entirely naked peak where only a scanty patch of moss can be seen in the distance at the foot, and say to myself: So solitary as this is the man who longs to open his soul only to the most ancient, the most primordial, the deepest feelings of truth.

Yes, he can say to himself: Here on the most ancient, the eternal altar, built directly on the foundations of the world, I bring a sacrifice to the being of all beings. I feel the first, the profoundest beginnings of existence; I survey the world, its rugged and its gentle valleys, its distant fertile meadows; my soul rise above itself and above everything else, it longs for the nearer sky. But soon the burning sun brings back thirst and hunger, his human needs. He looks about for those valleys above which his mind had already soared; he envies the inhabitants of those fertile plains, rich in springs, who have built their happy dwellings on the ruins of other men's errors and opinions, who trample the dust of their forefathers, and peacefully gratify the modest needs of their days in a narrow circle. Prepared by these thoughts, the soul penetrates past centuries, evokes all the experiences of careful observers, all the anticipations of visionary minds. These peaks, I say to myself, rose steeper, more jagged, higher in the clouds, when this range still stood as a sea-surrounded island amid the ancient waters; around it soared the spirit that brooded on the waves; and in its vast womb higher mountains formed from the ruins of the primal hills, and the later and more distant mountains formed from their ruins and the remains of their inhabitants. — And now the moss begins first to grow, and the shell-protected creatures of the sea move more rarely, the water recedes, the higher mountains become green, everything begins to teem with life.

However, soon this life is faced with new scenes of destruction. In the distance, raging volcanoes rise that seem to threaten the end of the world; but the ground layer remains unshaken; on it I still safely rest while the people of the distant shores and islands are buried under the shifting soil. I return from this far-ranging meditation and gaze at the rocks themselves; their presence elevates and reassures my soul. I see their mass split by jagged seams, here straight, there leaning upwards, now traced sharply one over the other, now as though thrown over one another in a formless scrawl; and at first sight I might almost exclaim: Here nothing is in its ancient state; here everything is ruins, disorder, and destruction. We shall find this same opinion expressed if we withdraw from the living presence of these mountains, retire into the study, and open the books of our forefathers. One says that the primal rock is entirely whole, as if molded from *one* piece; another, that it was separated into layers and beds by sedimentary formations intersected by many tunnels running in all directions; still another, that these rocks do not form layers but whole masses, separated from each other without an apparent pattern. A different observer, on the contrary, says that he sometimes found sharply defined layers, and then, again, confusion. How can we harmonize all these contradictions and find a guiding thread to further observations?

This is what I at present propose to do; and even if my enterprise is not as successful as I wish and hope, yet my efforts will give others the opportunity to go further; for in observation even errors are useful, since they make one careful and give those who are keen sighted an opportunity to exercise their own vision. One word of warning might not be superfluous at this point, to foreigners if this essay should reach them, even more than to Germans — the observer must learn to distinguish this rock from others. The Italians still confuse a species of lava with small-grained granite, and the French call gneiss, leafy granite or secondary granite; indeed, even we Germans, who are otherwise so meticulous in matters of this kind, have quite recently confused what we call *Totelie-gende,* a mineral fused from quartz and varieties of hornstone, and usually found under beds of slate, and, also, the gray wacke of the Harz, a more homogeneous mixture of quartz and slate fragments, with granite.

# *Beautiful Nature, Beautiful Greeks*

## FRIEDRICH SCHILLER

If we think of that beautiful nature which surrounded the ancient Greeks, if we remember how intimately that people, under its blessed sky, could live with that free nature; how their mode of imagining, and of feeling, and their manners, approached far nearer than ours to the simplicity of nature, how faithfully the works of their poets express this; we must necessarily remark, as a strange fact, that so few traces are met among them of that *sentimental* interest that we moderns ever take in the scenes of nature and in natural characters. I admit that the Greeks are superiorly exact and faithful in their descriptions of nature. They reproduce their details with care, but we see that they take no more interest in them and no more heart in them than in describing a vestment, a shield, armour, a piece of furniture, or any production of the mechanical arts. In their love for the object it seems that they make no difference between what exists in itself and what owes its existence to art, to the human will. It seems that nature interests their minds and their curiosity more than moral feeling. They do not attach themselves to it with that depth of feeling, with that gentle melancholy, that characterise the moderns. Nay, more, by personifying nature in its particular phenomena, by deifying it, by representing its effects as the acts of free being, they take from it that character of calm necessity which is precisely what makes it so attractive to us. Their impatient imagination only traverses nature to pass beyond it to the drama of human life. It only takes pleasure in the spectacle of what is living and free; it requires characters, acts, the accidents of fortune and of manners; and whilst it happens with *us*, at least in certain moral dispositions, to curse our prerogative, this free will, which exposes us to so many combats with ourselves, to so many anxieties and errors, and to wish to exchange it for the condition of beings destitute of reason, for that fatal existence that no longer admits of any choice, but which is so calm in its uniformity, — while we do this, the Greeks, on the contrary, only have their imagination occupied in retracing human nature in the inanimate world, and in giving to the will an influence where blind necessity rules.

Whence can arise this difference between the spirit of the ancients and the modern spirit? How comes it that, being, for all that relates to nature, incomparably below the ancients, we are superior to them precisely on this point, that we render a more complete homage to nature; that we have a closer attachment to it; and that we are capable of embracing even the inanimate world with the most ardent sensibility? It is because nature, in our time, is no longer in man, and that we no longer encounter it in its primitive truth, except out of humanity, in the inanimate world. It is not because we are more *comformable to nature* — quite the contrary; it is because in our social relations, in our mode of existence, in our manners, we are in *opposition with nature*. This is what leads us, when the instinct of truth and of simplicity is awakened — this instinct which, like the moral aptitude from which it proceeds, lives incorruptible and indelible in every human heart — to procure for it in the physical world the satisfaction which there is no hope of finding in the moral order. This is the reason why the feeling that attaches us to nature is connected so closely with that which makes us regret our infancy, for ever flown, and our primitive innocence. Our childhood is all that remains of nature in humanity, such as civilisation has made it, of untouched, unmutilated nature. It is, therefore, not wonderful, when we meet out of us the impress of nature, that we are always brought back to the idea of our childhood. . . .

It is in the fundamental idea of poetry that the poet is everywhere the *guardian* of nature. When he can no longer entirely fill this part, and has already in himself suffered the deleterious influence of arbitrary and factitious forms, or has had to struggle against this influence, he presents himself as the *witness* of nature and as its avenger. The poet will, therefore, be the *expression* of nature itself, or his part will be to *seek* it, if men have lost sight of it. Hence arise two kinds of poetry, which embrace and exhaust the entire field of poetry. All poets — I mean those who are really so — will belong, according to the time when they flourish, according to the accidental circumstances that have influenced their education generally, and the different dispositions of mind through which they pass, will belong, I say, to the order of the *sentimental* poetry or to *simple* poetry.

15.  Jean Baptiste Siméon Chardin, *Saying Grace.*

16.  Jean Baptiste Siméon Chardin, *Still Life with a Jar of Pickled Olives.*

17. Jean Baptiste Siméon Chardin, *The Morning Toilet*.

*18.* Jean Baptiste Siméon Chardin, *Back From Market*.

19. Pietro Longhi,
*The Soirée.*

20. Francisco de Goya,
*Girl With a Water Jug.*

21. Jean Honoré Fragonard, *The Bathers*.

# III

# The Guidance of Reason

*Reason, from its most complex mathematical processes and its most abstruse philosophical formulations to its plainest expressions in common sense, was a guiding principle of the Enlightenment. Involved in the concept of reason was the enlargement of knowledge, particularly knowledge of Nature, whose laws were believed to be contained in the concepts of reason. And the virtues of reason were acclaimed both directly and by implication in satirical thrusts against the irrational in man and his institutions.*

# from *Essay on Man*

## ALEXANDER POPE

Could he, whose rules the rapid Comet bind,
Describe or fix one movement of his Mind?
Who saw its fires here rise, and there descend,
Explain his own beginning, or his end?
Alas what wonder! Man's superior part
Uncheck'd may rise, and climb from art to art;
But when his own great work is but begun,
What Reason weaves, by passion is undone.
　　Trace Science then, with Modesty thy guide;
First strip off all her equipage of Pride;
Deduct what is but Vanity, or Dress,
Or Learning's Luxury, or Idleness;
Or tricks to shew the stretch of human brain,
Mere curious pleasure, or ingenious pain;
Expunge the whole, or lop th' excrescent parts
Of all our Vices have created Arts;
Then see how little the remaining sum,
Which serv'd the past, and must the times to come!

　　Two Principles in human nature reign;
Self-love, to urge, and Reason, to restrain;
Nor this a good, nor that a bad we call,
Each works its end, to move or govern all:
And to their proper operation still,
Ascribe all Good; to their improper, Ill.

# from *The Citizen of the World*

## OLIVER GOLDSMITH

### LETTER THREE

The description of London continued. The luxury of the English.
Its benefits. The fine gentleman. The fine lady.

*From Lien Chi Altangi, to the care of Fipsihi, resident in
Moscow; to be forwarded by the Russian caravan to Fum
Hoam, first president of the ceremonial academy at
Pekin in China.*

Think not, O thou guide of my youth, that absence can impair my
respect, or interposing trackless desarts can blot your reverend figure from
my memory. The farther I travel I feel the pain of separation with more
reluctance; those ties that bind me to my native country, and you, are
still unbroken, while by every remove, I only drag a greater length of
chain.

Could I find aught worth transmitting from so remote a region as this
to which I have wandered, I should gladly send it; but instead of this,
you must be contented with a renewal of my former professions, and an
imperfect account of a people with whom I yet am but superficially
acquainted. The remarks of a man who has been but three days in the
country can only be those obvious circumstances which force themselves
upon the imagination: I consider myself here as a newly created Being
introduced into a new world; every object strikes with wonder and surprise. The imagination, still unsatiated, seems the only active principle
of the mind. The most trifling occurrence gives pleasure, till the gloss of
novelty is worn away. Nor till we have ceased wondering can we possibly grow wise; it is then we call the reasoning principle to our aid, and
compare those objects with each other which we before examined without
reflection.

Behold me then in London, gazing at the strangers, and they at me;
it seems they find somewhat absurd in my figure; and had I been never
from home it is possible I might find an infinite fund of ridicule in

theirs; but by long travelling I am taught to laugh at folly alone, and to find nothing truly ridiculous but [villainy and] vice.

When I had just quitted my native country, and crossed the Chinese wall, I thought every deviation from the customs and manners of China was a departing from nature: I smiled at the blue lips and red foreheads of the Tongusas. I could hardly contain when I saw the Daures dress their heads with horns, the Ostiacs powder their hair with red earth, and the Calmuck beauties trick out in all the finery of sheep-skin. But I soon perceived that the ridicule lay not in them but in me, and that I falsely condemned others for absurdity, because they happened to differ from my standard of perfection, which was founded in prejudice or partiality.

I find no pleasure therefore in taxing the English with departing from nature in their external appearance, which is all I yet know of their character; it is possible they only endeavour to improve her simple plan, since every extravagance in our dress proceeds from a desire of becoming more beautiful than nature made us; this is so harmless a vanity that I not only pardon but approve it. A desire to be more excellent than others is what actually makes us so, and as thousands find a livelihood in society by such appetites, none but the ignorant inveigh against them.

You are not insensible, most reverend Fum Hoam, what numberless trades, even among the Chinese, subsist by the harmless pride of each other. Your nose-borers, feet-swathers, tooth-stainers, eye-brow pluckers, would all want bread, should their neighbours want vanity. Those vanities, however, employ much fewer hands in China than in England; a fine gentleman, or a fine lady, here dressed up to the fashion, seem scarcely to have a single limb or feature as nature has left it. They call in to their assistance fancy on every occasion, and think themselves finest when they most depart from what they really are.

To make a fine gentleman several trades are required, but chiefly a barber; you have undoubtedly heard of the Jewish champion all whose strength lay in his hair. One would think that the English were for placing all wisdom there. In order to appear a wise man, nothing more is requisite than to borrow hair from the heads of all his neighbors and clap it like a bush on his own: the distributors of their laws stick on such quantities that it is almost impossible, even in idea, to distinguish between their heads and their hair.

Those whom I have been now describing affect the gravity of the lion: those I am going to describe more resemble the tricks of the monkey. The barber, who still seems master of the ceremonies, cuts their hair not round the edges as with us, but close to the crown; and then with a composition of meal and hog's lard, plaisters the whole in such a manner as to make it impossible to distinguish whether he wears a cap or a plaister; to make the picture more perfectly striking, conceive the tail of some beast, a pig's tail for instance, appended to the back of his head, and reaching down to that place where other tails are generally seen to begin; thus betailed and bepowdered, he fancies he improves in beauty, dresses up his hard-featured face in smiles, and attempts to look hideously tender. Thus equipped, he is qualified to make love, and hopes for success more from the powder on the outside of his head than the sentiments within.

Yet when you consider what sort of a creature the fine lady is, to whom he pays his addresses, it is not strange to find him thus equipped in order to please her. She is herself every whit as fond of powder, and tails, and ribbands, and hog's lard as he: to speak my secret sentiments, most reverend Fum, the ladies here are horridly ugly; I can hardly endure the sight of them; they no way resemble the beauties of China; the Europeans have a quite different idea of beauty from us; when I reflect on the small footed perfections of thy charming daughter, how is it possible I should have eyes for any other personal excellence. How very broad her face; how very short her nose; how very little her eyes; how very thin her lips; and how very black her teeth; the snow on the tops of Bao is not fairer than her cheek; and her eye-brows are as small as the thread of the finest silk. Here a lady with such perfections would be frightful. The Dutch and Chinese beauties, I own, have some resemblance, but the English ladies are entirely different; red cheeks, big eyes, and teeth of a most odious whiteness are every where to be seen; and then such masculine feet as actually serve *some* of them for walking!

Yet uncivil as nature has been, they seem resolved to outdo her in unkindness; they use white powder, blue powder, and black powder, but never red powder, as among the Tartars, in their hair.

They paint their faces not less than the Calmucks and stick on, with spittle, little black patches on every part of the face, except only the tip of the nose, which I never see with a patch on it. You'll have a better idea of their manner of placing these spots, when I have finished a map of an English face patch'd up to the fashion, which perhaps I shall shortly send to add to your curious collection of beasts, medals, and monsters.

Thus far I have seen, and I have now one of their own authors before me, who tells me something strange and which I can hardly believe. His words are to this effect: "Most ladies in this country have two faces; one face to sleep in, and another to shew in company: the first face is generally reserv'd for the husband and family at home, the other put on to please strangers abroad; [the family face is often indifferent enough, but the outdoor one looks something better;] this last is always made at the toilet, where whim, the looking-glass, and the toad-eater sit in council and settle the complexion of the day."

I can't ascertain the truth of this remark; however, they seem to me to act upon very odd principles upon another occasion, since they wear more cloaths within doors than without; and a lady who seems to shudder at a breeze in her own apartment appears half naked in public. Adieu.

# A Letter to Rousseau

## VOLTAIRE

*August 30, 1755*

Sir, I have received your new book against the human race, and I thank you for it. You will please people by your manner of telling them the truth about themselves, but you will not alter them. The horrors of that human society — from which in our feebleness and ignorance we expect so many consolations — have never been painted in more striking colors: no one has ever been so witty as you are in trying to turn us into brutes: to read your book makes one long to go on all fours. Since, however, it is now some sixty years since I gave up the practice, I feel that it is unfortunately impossible for me to resume it: I leave this natural habit to those more fit for it than are you and I. Nor can I set sail to discover the aborigines of Canada, in the first place because my ill-health ties me to the side of the greatest doctor in Europe, and I should not find the same professional assistance among the Missouris: and secondly because war is going on in that country, and the example of the civilized nations has made the barbarians almost as wicked as we are ourselves. I must confine myself to being a peaceful savage in the retreat I have chosen — close to your country, where you yourself should be.

I agree with you that science and literature have sometimes done a great deal of harm. Tasso's enemies made his life a long series of misfortunes: Galileo's enemies kept him languishing in prison, at seventy years of age, for the crime of understanding the revolution of the earth: and, what is still more shameful, obliged him to forswear his discovery. Since your friends began the *Encyclopædia*, those who dare to be their rivals attack them as *deists, atheists* — even *Jansenists*.

If I might venture to include myself among those whose works have brought them persecution as their sole recompense, I could tell you of men set on ruining me from the day I produced my tragedy *Œdipe:* of a perfect library of absurd calumnies which have been written against me: of an ex-Jesuit priest whom I saved from utter disgrace rewarding me by defamatory libels: of a man yet more contemptible printing my *Age of Louis XIV* with *Notes* in which crass ignorance gave birth to the most abominable falsehoods: of yet another, who sold to a publisher some chapters of a *Universal History* supposed to be by me: of the publisher avaricious enough to print this shapeless mass of blunders, wrong dates, mutilated facts and names: and, finally, of men sufficiently base and craven to assign the production of this farago to me. I could show you all society poisoned by this class of person — a class unknown to the ancients — who, not being able to find any honest occupation — be it manual labor or service — and unluckily knowing how to read and write, become the brokers of literature, live on our works, steal our manuscripts, falsify them, and sell them. I could tell of some loose sheets of a gay trifle which I wrote thirty years ago (on the same subject that Chapelain was stupid enough to treat seriously) which are in circulation now through the breach of faith and the cupidity of those who added their own grossness to my *badinage* and filled in the gaps with a dullness only equalled by their malice; and who, finally, after twenty years, are selling everywhere a manuscript which, in very truth, is theirs and worthy of them only. I may add, last of all, that someone has stolen part of the material I amassed in the public archives to use in my *History of the War of 1741* when I was historiographer of France; that he sold that result of my labors to a bookseller in Paris; and is as set on getting hold of my property as if I were dead and he could turn it into money by putting it up to auction. I could show you ingratitude, imposture, and rapine pursuing me for forty years to the foot of the Alps and the brink of the grave. But what conclusion ought I to draw from all these misfortunes? This only: that I have no right to complain: Pope, Descartes, Bayle, Camoens — a hundred others — have been subjected to the same, or greater, injustice: and my destiny is that of nearly everyone who has loved letters too well.

Confess, sir, that all these things are, after all, but little personal pinpricks, which society scarcely notices. What matter to humankind that a few drones steal the honey of a few bees? Literary men make a great fuss of their petty quarrels: the rest of the world ignores them, or laughs at them.

They are, perhaps, the least serious of all the ills attendant on human life. The thorns inseparable from literature and a modest degree of fame are flowers in comparison with the other evils which from all time have flooded the world. Neither Cicero, Varro, Lucretius, Virgil, or Horace had any part in the proscriptions of Marius, Scylla, that profligate Antony, or that fool Lepidus; while as for that weak tyrant, Octavius Cæsar, cowardly entitled Augustus, he only became an assassin when he was deprived of the society of men of letters.

Confess that Italy owed none of her troubles to Petrarch or to Boccaccio; that Marot's jests were not responsible for the massacre of St. Bartholomew; or the tragedy of the *Cid* for the wars of the Fronde. Great crimes are always committed by great ignoramuses. What makes, and will always make, this world a vale of tears is the insatiable greediness and the indomitable pride of men, from Thamas Kouli-kan, who did not know how to read, to a customhouse officer who can just count. Letters support, refine, and comfort the soul: they are serving you, sir, at the very moment you decry them: you are like Achilles declaiming against fame, and Father Malebranche using his brillant imagination to belittle imagination.

If anyone has a right to complain of letters, I am that person, for in all times and in all places they have led to my being persecuted; still, we must needs love them in spite of the way they are abused — as we cling to society, though the wicked spoil its pleasantness; as we must love our country, though it treats us unjustly; and as we must love and serve the supreme Being, despite the superstition and fanaticism which too often dishonor his service.

M. Chappuis tells me your health is very unsatisfactory; you must come and recover here in your native place, enjoy its freedom, drink with me the milk of its cows, and browse on its grass.

I am yours most philosophically and with the most tender esteem, etc.

# *Of the Encyclopedia*

## VOLTAIRE

A servant of Louis XV told me that while his master, the king, was dining one day at Trianon with a small group, the conversation turned first on hunting and then on gun powder. Someone said that the best powder is made with equal parts of saltpeter, sulphur and coal. The Duke de La Vallière, who knew better, argued that to make a good gun powder all you needed was one part of sulphur and one of coal to five parts of saltpeter that had been well filtered, well evaporated, and well crystallized.

"It is funny," said the Duke de Nivernois, "that we amuse ourselves daily by killing partridges in the park at Versailles, and sometimes by killing men or by being killed ourselves at the frontier, without knowing exactly with what we kill."

"Alas! We are reduced to that state for most things of this world," answered Madame de Pompadour; "I do not know what the rouge I put on my cheeks is made of, and I should be very much embarrassed if someone asked me how the silk hose I am wearing is made."

"It is a pity," the Duke de La Vallière then said, "that His Majesty confiscated our encyclopedic dictionaries, each of which cost us a hundred gold pieces: there we would quickly find the answer to all our questions."

The king justified the confiscation: he had been warned that the twenty-one folio volumes that were found on all the ladies' dressing tables were the most dangerous thing in the world for the French kingdom; and he wanted to know for himself if this were true before allowing anyone to read this work. At the end of the dinner he sent three of his servants for a copy, each of whom returned carrying seven volumes with great difficulty.

They saw at the article "Powder" that the Duke de La Vallière was right; and soon Madame de Pompadour learned the difference between the old Spanish rouge that the ladies of Madrid used to color their cheeks, and the rouge of Parisian ladies. She learned that Greek and Roman ladies were painted with purple that came from seashells, and that consequently our scarlet was the purple of the ancients; she learned that there was more saffron in Spanish rouge, and more cochineal in the French.

She saw how her stockings were manufactured; and the operation of this process delighted her with wonder. "Oh, the fine book!" she exclaimed. "Sire, did you confiscate this storehouse of useful things so as to possess it alone and be the only wise man of your kingdom?"

They all jumped at the volumes like the daughters of Lycomedes at Ulysses' jewels; every one found at once what he was looking for. Those who had lawsuits were surprised to find there the judgment of their cases. The king read all the rights of the crown. "But really," he said, "I don't know why I was told so many bad things about this work."

"Well, don't you see, Sire," said the Duke de Nivernois, "it's because it is very good? Men do not attack the mediocre and the dull of whatever sort. If women try to ridicule a newcomer, it is certain that she is prettier than they."

All the while the others kept leafing through the pages, and the Count de C . . . said aloud: "Sire, you are too fortunate that there should be under your reign men capable of knowing all the arts and of transmitting them to posterity. Everything is here, from how to make a pin to how to make and direct your canons; from the infinitely small to the infinitely great. Thank God for having made men born in your kingdom who have thus served the entire universe. Other nations must either buy the *Encyclopedia* or copy it. Take all my property if you like; but give me back my *Encyclopedia*."

"Yet they say," replied the king, "that there are many faults in this so necessary and so admirable work."

"Sire," rejoined the Count de C . . . , "there were two spoiled sauces at your dinner; we did not eat them, and we ate very well. Would you like to have the whole dinner thrown out the window because of these two sauces?"

The king felt the strength of reason; every one recovered his property: it was a happy day.

Envy and ignorance did not hold themselves beaten; these two immortal sisters continued their outcries, their schemes, their persecutions: ignorance is very learned in these matters.

What happened? Foreigners brought out four editions of this French work, banned in France, and made about eighteen hundred thousand gold pieces.

Frenchmen, try henceforth to understand your interests better.

# Humanity and Reason

## BUFFON

Begotten, some morning, aboard a ship whose departure it never witnessed and whose arrival it will never see, restless traveler over this earth whose course it does not rule, Humanity is not tied to the great external system [of the universe] by any necessary law. Whether it labors down in the hold or up on the bridge, whether it rushes toward the bow or the stern, it alters nothing of the immutable course; in short, humanity is, so to speak, a negligible quantity in the sovereign order of the rest of the universe.

22. *Agriculture,* from *Diderot Pictorial Encyclopedia.* The philosophes were keenly interested in the advances of the Industrial Revolution but believed that agriculture would continue to be the mainstay of national economy. In this engraving some then-modern farming processes are shown.

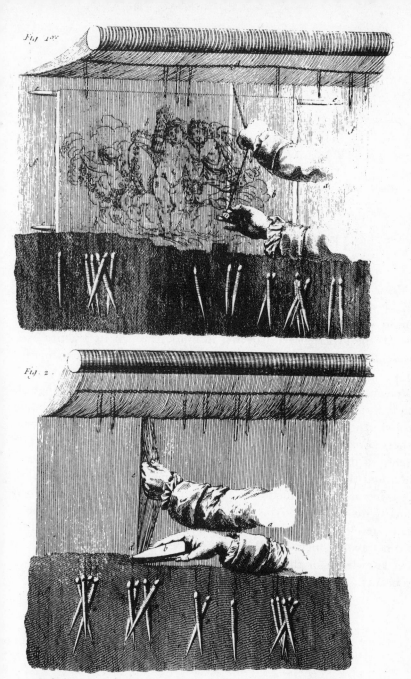

23. *Gobelins Tapestries*, from *Diderot Pictorial Encyclopedia*. One of the most famous French crafts was tapestry making. The engravings show two processes in the making of the famous Gobelins tapestries: the tracing of the design on the warp, and the beating of the weft into the fabric.

# On the Mathematical Principles of Music

## JEAN PHILIPPE RAMEAU

Music is a science which ought to have certain rules. These rules should be derived from a self-evident principle which cannot become known to us without the help of mathematics. I must concede that, despite all the experience I acquired in music through its practice over a considerable period of time, it was only with the help of mathematics that I was able to unravel my ideas, that light replaced an obscurity I had previously not recognized as such. If I had been unable to distinguish principle from rule, the principle soon presented itself to me in a simple and convincing manner. As a result, it then led me to recognize the consequences as many rules related through them to the principle itself. The true sense of these rules, their correct application, their relation to one another, and the order they should observe among themselves (the simplest serving as an introduction to the less simple, and so on by degrees) and finally the choice of terms — all this of which I had previously been ignorant, developed with so much clarity and precision in my mind that I could not avoid concluding that it would be most desirable to have the musical knowledge of this century's composers equal their capacity to create beauty.

# The Moralists

## THE EARL OF SHAFTESBURY

Ye fields and woods, my refuge from the toilsome world of business, receive me in your quiet sanctuaries, and favour my retreat and thoughtful solitude! Ye verdant plains, how gladly I salute ye! Hail all ye blissful mansions! known seats! delightful prospects! Majestic beauties of this earth, and all ye powers and graces! Blessed be ye chaste abodes of happiest mortals, who here in peaceful innocence enjoy a life unenvied, though divine; whilst with blessed tranquility it affords a happy leisure and retreat for man, who, made for contemplation and to search his own and other natures, may here best meditate the causes of things, and, placed amidst the various scenes of Nature, may nearer view her works.

O glorious Nature! supremely fair and sovereign good! all-loving and all lovely, all divine! whose looks are so becoming and of such infinite grace; whose study brings such wisdom, and whose contemplation such delight; whose every single work affords an ampler scene, and is a nobler spectacle than all which ever art presented! O mighty Nature! wise substitute of Providence! impowered creatress! O thou impowering Deity, supreme creator! Thee I invoke and thee alone adore. To thee this solitude, this place, these rural meditations are sacred; whilst thus inspired with harmony of thought, though unconfined by words, and in loose numbers, I sing of Nature's order in created beings, and celebrate the beauties which resolve in thee, the source and principle of all beauty and perfection.

The being is boundless, unsearchable, impenetrable. In thy immensity all thought is lost, fancy gives over its flight, and wearied imagination spends itself in vain, finding no coast nor limit of this ocean, nor, in the widest tract through which it soars, one point yet nearer the circumference than the first centre whence it parted. Thus having oft essayed, thus sallied forth into the wide expanse, when I return again within myself, struck with the sense of this so narrow being and of the fullness of that immense one, I dare no more behold the amazing depths nor sound the abyss of Deity.

Yet since by thee, O sovereign mind, I have been formed such as I am, intelligent and rational, since the peculiar dignity of my nature is to know and contemplate thee, permit that with due freedom I exert those faculties with which thou hast adorned me. Bear with my venturous and bold approach. And since nor vain curiosity, nor fond conceit, nor love of aught save thee alone inspires me with such thoughts as these, be thou my assistant and guide me in this pursuit, while I venture to tread the labyrinth of wide Nature and endeavour to trace thee in thy works.

# from *A Voyage to the Houyhnhnms*

## JONATHAN SWIFT

I HAVE related the Substance of several Conversations I had with my Master, during the greatest Part of the Time I had the Honour to be in his Service; but have indeed for Brevity sake omitted much more than is here set down.

WHEN I had answered all his Questions, and his Curiosity seemed to be fully satisfied; he sent for me one Morning early, and commanding me to sit down at some Distance, (an Honour which he had never before conferred upon me) He said, he had been very seriously considering my whole Story, as far as it related both to my self and my Country: That, he looked upon us as a Sort of Animals to whose Share, by what Accident he could not conjecture, some small Pittance of *Reason* had fallen, whereof we made no other Use than by its Assistance to aggravate our *natural* Corruptions, and to acquire new ones which Nature had not given us. That, we disarmed our selves of the few Abilities she had bestowed; had been very successful in multiplying our original Wants, and seemed to spend our whole Lives in vain Endeavours to supply them by our own Inventions. That, as to myself, it was manifest I had neither the Strength or Agility of a common *Yahoo;* that I walked infirmly on my hinder Feet; had found out a Contrivance to make my Claws of no Use or Defence, and to remove the Hair from my Chin, which was intended as a Shelter from the Sun and the Weather. Lastly, That I could neither run with Speed, nor climb Trees like my *Brethren* (as he called them) the *Yahoos* in this Country.

THAT, our Institutions of *Government* and *Law* were plainly owing to our gross Defects in *Reason,* and by consequence, in *Virtue;* because *Reason* alone is sufficient to govern a *Rational* Creature; which was therefore a Character we had no Pretence to challenge, even from the Account I had given of my own People; although he manifestly perceived, that in order to favour them, I had concealed many Particulars, and often *said the Thing which was not.*

HE was the more confirmed in his Opinion, because he observed, that as I agreed in every Feature of my Body with other *Yahoos,* except where it was to my real Disadvantage in point of Strength, Speed and Activity, the Shortness of my Claws, and some other Particulars where Nature had no Part; so, from the Representation I had given him of our Lives, our Manners, and our Actions, he found as near a Resemblance in the Disposition of our Minds. He said, the *Yahoos* were known to hate one another more than they did any different Species of Animals; and the Reason usually assigned, was, the Odiousness of their own Shapes, which all could see in the rest, but not in themselves. He had therefore begun to think it not unwise in us to *cover* our Bodies, and by that Invention, conceal many of our Deformities from each other, which would else be hardly supportable. But, he now found he had been mistaken; and that the Dissentions of those Brutes in his Country were owing to the same Cause with ours, as I had described them. For, if (said he) you throw among five *Yahoos* as much Food as would be sufficient for fifty, they will, instead of eating peaceably, fall together by the Ears, each single one impatient to *have all to it self;* and therefore a Servant was usually employed to stand by while they were feeding abroad, and those kept at home were tied at a Distance from each other. That, if a Cow died of Age or Accident, before a *Houyhnhnm* could secure it for his own *Yahoos,* those in the Neighbourhood would come in Herds to seize it, and then would ensue such a Battle as I had described, with terrible Wounds made by their Claws on both Sides, although they seldom were able to kill one another, for want of such convenient Instruments of Death as we had invented. At other Times the like Battles have been found between the *Yahoos* of several Neighbourhoods without any visible Cause: Those of one District watching all Opportunities to surprise the next before they are prepared. But if they find their Project hath miscarried, they return home, and for want of Enemies, engage in what I call a *Civil War* among themselves.

THAT, in some Fields of his Country, there are certain *shining Stones* of several Colours, whereof the *Yahoos* are violently fond; and when Part of these *Stones* are fixed in the Earth, as it sometimes happeneth, they will dig with their Claws for whole Days to get them out, and carry them away, and hide them by Heaps in their Kennels; but still looking round with great Caution, for fear their Comrades should find out their Treasure. My Master said, he could never discover the Reason of this unnatural Appetite, or how these *Stones* could be of any Use to a *Yahoo;* but now he believed it might proceed from the same Principle of *Avarice,* which I had ascribed to Mankind. That he had once, by way of Experiment, privately removed a Heap of these *Stones* from the Place where one of his *Yahoos* had buried it: Whereupon, the sordid Animal missing his Treasure, by his loud lamenting brought the whole Herd to the Place, there miserably howled, then fell to biting and tearing the rest; began to pine away, would neither eat nor sleep, nor work, till he ordered a Servant privately to convey the *Stones* into the same Hole, and hide them as before; which when his *Yahoo* had found, he presently recovered his Spirits and good Humour; but took Care to remove them to a better hiding Place; and hath ever since been a very serviceable Brute.

My Master farther assured me, which I also observed my self; That in the Fields where these *shining Stones* abound, the fiercest and most frequent Battles are fought, occasioned by perpetual Inroads of the neighbouring *Yahoos*.

He said, it was common when two *Yahoos* discovered such a *Stone* in a Field, and were contending which of them should be the Proprietor, a third would take the Advantage, and carry it away from them both; which my Master would needs contend to have some Resemblance with our *Suits at Law;* wherein I thought it for our Credit not to undeceive him; since the Decision he mentioned was much more equitable than many Decrees among us: Because the Plaintiff and Defendant there lost nothing beside the *Stone* they contended for; whereas our *Courts of Equity,* would never have dismissed the Cause while either of them had anything left.

My Master continuing his Discourse, said, There was nothing that rendered the *Yahoos* more odious, than their undistinguished Appetite to devour every thing that came in their Way, whether Herbs, Roots, Berries, corrupted Flesh of Animals, or all mingled together: And it was peculiar in their Temper, that they were fonder of what they could get by Rapine or Stealth at a greater Distance, than much better Food provided for them at home. If their Prey held out, they would eat till they were ready to burst, after which Nature had pointed out to them a certain *Root* that gave them a general Evacuation.

There was also another Kind of *Root* very *juicy,* but something rare and difficult to be found, which the *Yahoos* fought for with much Eagerness, and would suck it with great Delight: It produced the same Effects that Wine hath upon us. It would make them sometimes hug, and sometimes tear one another; they would howl and grin, and chatter, and roul and tumble, and then fall asleep in the Mud.

I did indeed observe, that the *Yahoos* were the only Animals in this Country subject to any Diseases; which however, were much fewer than Horses have among us, and contracted not by any ill Treatment they meet with, but by the Nastiness and Greediness of that sordid Brute.

Neither has their Language any more than a general Appellation for those Maladies; which is borrowed from the Name of the Beast, and called *Hnea Yahoo,* or the *Yahoo's-Evil;* and the Cure prescribed is a Mixture of *their own Dung* and *Urine,* forcibly put down the *Yahoo's* Throat. This I have since often known to have been taken with Success: And do here freely recommend it to my Countrymen, for the publick Good, as an admirable Specifick against all Diseases produced by Repletion.

As to Learning, Government, Arts, Manufactures, and the like; my Master confessed he could find little or no Resemblance between the *Yahoos* of that Country and those in ours. For, he only meant to observe what Parity there was in our Natures. He had heard indeed some curious *Houyhnhnms* observe, that in most Herds there was a Sort of ruling *Yahoo,* (as among us there is generally some leading or principal Stag in a Park) who was always more *deformed* in Body, and *mischievous in Disposition,* than any of the rest. That, this *Leader* had usually a Favourite as *like himself* as he could get, whose Employment was to *lick his Master's Feet and Posteriors, and drive the Female* Yahoos *to his Kennel;* for which he was now and then rewarded with a Piece of Ass's Flesh. This *Favourite* is hated by the whole Herd; and therefore to protect himself, keeps always *near the Person of his Leader.* He usually continues in Office till a worse can be found; but the very Moment he is discarded, his Successor, at the Head of all the *Yahoos* in that District, Young and Old, Male and Female, come in a Body, and discharge their Excrements upon him from Head to Foot. But how far this might be applicable to our *Courts* and *Favourites,* and *Ministers of State,* my Master said I could best determine.

# Charles V and Erasmus
## from *Dialogues of the Dead*

### FONTENELLE

ERASMUS. Be in no uncertainty, if there are ranks among the dead, I shall not cede you precedence.

CHARLES. A grammarian! A mere savant, or to push your claims to extremes, a man of wit, who would carry it off over a prince who has been master of the best half of Europe!

ERASMUS. Add also America, and I am not the least more alarmed. Your greatness was a mere conglomeration of chances, as one who should sort out all its parts would make you see clearly. If your grandfather Ferdinand had been a man of his word, you would have had next to nothing in Italy; if other princes had had sense enough to believe in antipodes, Columbus would not have come to him, and America would not have been beneath your dominion; if, after the death of the last Duke of Burgundy, Louis XI had well considered his actions, the heiress of Burgundy would not have married Maximilian, or the Low Countries descended to you; if Henry of Castile, the brother of your grandmother Isabel, had not had a bad name among women, or if his wife had been of an unsuspectable virtue, Henry's daughter would have passed for his daughter and the kingdom of Castile have escaped you.

CHARLES. You alarm me. At this late hour I am to lose Castile, or the Low Lands, or America, or Italy, one or the other.

ERASMUS. You need not laugh. There could not have been a little good sense in one place, or a little good faith in another without its costing you dearly. There was nothing — to your great-uncle's impotence; to the inconstancy of your great-aunt — that you could have done without. How delicate is that edifice whose foundation is such a collection of hazards.

CHARLES. There is no means of bearing so strict an examination as yours. I confess that you sweep away all my greatness and all my titles.

ERASMUS. They were the adornments whereof you boasted, and I have swept them away without trouble. Do you remember having heard said that the Athenian Cimon, having taken prisoner a great number of Persians, put up their clothing and their naked bodies for sale, and since the clothes were greatly magnificent there was great concourse to buy them, but no one would bid for the men? Faith, I think what befell the Persians would happen to a good number of others if one detached their personal merit from that which fortune has given them.

CHARLES. What is personal merit?

ERASMUS. Need one ask that? Everything that is in us, our mind, for example, our knowledge.

CHARLES. And can one reasonably boast of these things?

ERASMUS. Certainly. These are not gifts of chance like high birth and riches.

CHARLES. You surprise me. Does not knowledge come to the savant as wealth comes to most who have it? Is it not by way of inheritance? You receive from the ancients, as we receive from our fathers. If we have been left all we possess, you have been left all that you know, and on this account many scholars regard what they have from the ancients with such respect as certain men regard their ancestral lands and houses, wherein they would hate to have anything changed.

ERASMUS. The great are born heirs of their father's greatness, but the learned are not born inheritors of the ancient learning. Knowledge is not an entail received, it is an wholly new acquisition made by personal effort, or if it is an entail it is so difficult to receive as to be worthy of honour.

CHARLES. Very well. Set the trouble of acquiring mental possessions against that of preserving the goods of fortune, the two things are quite equal; for if difficulty is all that you prize, there is as much in worldly affairs as in the philosopher's study.

ERASMUS. Then set knowledge aside and confine ourselves to the mind, that at least does not depend upon fortune.

CHARLES. Does not depend? The mind consists of a certain formation of cerebrum, is there less luck in being born with a respectable cerebrum than being born son to a king? You were a man of great genius; but ask all the philosophers why you weren't stupid and log-headed; it depended on next to nothing, on a mere disposition of fibres so fine that the most delicate operation of anatomy cannot find it. And after knowing all this the fine wits still dare to tell us that they alone are free from the dominion of chance, and think themselves at liberty to despise the rest of mankind.

ERASMUS. Your argument is that it is as creditable to be rich as to show fine intelligence.

CHARLES. To have fine intelligence is merely a luckier chance, but chance it all is at the bottom.

ERASMUS. You mean that all is chance?

CHARLES. Yes, provided we give that name to an order we do not understand. I leave you to decide whether I have not plucked men cleaner than you have; you merely strip from them certain advantages of birth, I take even those of their understanding. If before being vain of a thing they should try to assure themselves that it really belonged to them, there would be little vanity left in the world.

# IV

# Science, the Means

*The seventeenth-century achievements in the physical sciences gained enormous prestige for scientists and for the scientific approach. In the eighteenth century not only were there further advances in the physical sciences, but conscious applications of the scientific approach in the study of society and man. In these lay the beginnings of the social sciences — sociology, psychology, history as the record of social forces, and the development of archaeology out of "antiquarianism."*

# from *An Essay Concerning the Human Understanding*

## JOHN LOCKE

*All Ideas come from Sensation or Reflection.* — Let us then, suppose the mind to be, as we say, white paper, void of all characters, without any ideas; how comes it to be furnished? Whence comes it by that vast store which the busy and boundless fancy of man has painted on it with an almost endless variety? Whence has it all the materials of reason and knowledge? To this I answer, in one word, from experience; in that all our knowledge is founded, and from that it ultimately derives itself. Our observation, employed either about external sensible objects, or about the internal operations of our minds, perceived and reflected on by ourselves, is that which supplies our understandings with all the materials of thinking. These two are the fountains of knowledge, from whence all the ideas we have, or can naturally have, do spring.

*The Objects of Sensation one Source of Ideas.* — First, our senses, conversant about particular sensible objects, do convey into the mind several distinct perceptions of things, according to those various ways wherein those objects do affect them; and thus we come by those ideas we have, of yellow, white, heat, cold, soft, hard, bitter, sweet, and all those which we call sensible qualities; which when I say the senses convey into the mind, I mean they from external objects convey into the mind what produces there those perceptions. This great source of most of the ideas we have, depending wholly upon our senses, and derived by them to the understanding, I call "sensation."

*The Operations of our Minds, the other Source of them.* — Secondly, the other fountain, from which experience furnisheth the understanding with ideas, is the perception of the operations of our own mind within us, as it is employed about the ideas it has got; which operations, when the soul comes to reflect on and consider, do furnish the understanding with another set of ideas, which could not be had from things without; and such are perception, thinking, doubting, believing, reasoning, knowing, willing, and all the different actings of our own minds; which we being conscious of, and observing in ourselves, do from these receive into our understandings as distinct ideas, as we do from bodies affecting our senses. This source of ideas every man has wholly in himself; and though it be not sense, as having nothing to do with external objects, yet it is very like it, and might properly enough be called "internal sense." But as I call the other "sensation" so I call this "reflection," the ideas it affords being such only as the mind gets by reflecting on its own operations within itself. By reflection, then, in the following part of this discourse, I would be understood to mean that notice which the mind takes of its own operations, and the manner of them; by reason whereof there come to be ideas of these operations in the understanding. These two, I say, viz., external material things, as the objects of sensation, and the operations of our own minds within, as the objects of reflection, are to me the only originals from whence all our ideas take their beginnings. The term "operations" here I use in a large sense, as comprehending not barely the actions of the mind about its ideas, but some sort of passions arising sometimes from them, such as is the satisfaction or uneasiness arising from any thought.

*All our Ideas are of the one or the other of these.* — The understanding seems to me not to have the least glimmering of any ideas which it doth not receive from one of these two. External objects furnish the mind with the ideas of sensible qualities, which are all those different perceptions they produce in us; and the mind furnishes the understanding with ideas of its own operations.

These, when we have taken a full survey of them, and their several modes, combinations, and relations, we shall find to contain all our whole stock of ideas; and that we have nothing in our minds which did not come in one of these two ways. Let any one examine his own thoughts, and thoroughly search into his understanding; and then let him tell me, whether all the original ideas he has there, are any other than of the objects of his senses, or of the operations of his mind, considered as objects of his reflection: and how great a mass of knowledge soever he imagines to be lodged there, he will, upon taking a strict view, see that he has not any idea in his mind but what one of these two hath imprinted; though, perhaps, with infinite variety compounded and enlarged by the understanding, as we shall see hereafter.

*The original of all our Knowledge.* — In time the mind comes to reflect on its own operations about the ideas got by sensation, and thereby stores itself with a new set of ideas, which I call "ideas of reflection." These are the impressions that are made on our senses by outward objects that are extrinsical to the mind, and its own operations, proceeding from powers intrinsical and proper to itself. . . .

# from *Emile*

## JEAN-JACQUES ROUSSEAU

Childhood is not known at all. Concerning the false ideas held about it, the further one goes, the more one is led astray. The wisest are concerned with that which it is important for men to know, without considering that which children are able to learn. They always seek the man in the child, without thinking about what he is before being a man. This is the study to which I have applied myself most, so that if my whole method were chimeric and false, one could always profit from my observations. I may have viewed very wrongly what ought to be done; but I think I have seen clearly the subject upon which one must work. Begin by studying your pupils better, for most assuredly, you do not know them at all; now, if you read this book with this point of view, I do not think it without usefulness for you.

In regard to what is called the systematic part, which is here nothing else but the course of nature, there is what will most disconcert the reader; it is there, doubtless, that I shall be attacked, and perhaps not wrongly. People will think less that they are reading a treatise on education than a visionary's reveries about education. What to do? It is not about another's ideas that I write; it is about my own. I do not see with other men; I have long been reproached for it. But is it up to me to give myself other eyes, and to affect other ideas? No. It is up to me not to be opinionated, not to think myself alone wiser than everyone else; it is up to me, not to change feelings, but to distrust mine; that is all I can do, and what I do. If I sometimes take an affirmative tone, it is not in order to impose it upon the reader; it is in order to speak to him as I think. Why should I propose in the form of a doubt that of which, as far as I am concerned, I have no doubt? I say exactly what goes on in my mind.

While exposing my opinion with freedom, I have so little intention of its being authoritative that I always add my reasons to it, so that they are weighed and I am judged. But though I do not at all wish to be obstinate in defending my ideas, I do not feel myself the less obliged to propose them; for the maxims of which I have an opinion contrary to that of others are not unimportant. They are those whose falsehood or truth is important to know, and which make the happiness or unhappiness of the human race.

"Propose what is feasible," they do not cease to repeat to me. It is as if they said to me, "Propose to do what is done; or at least propose some good which is allied to the existing evil." Such a project, in certain subjects, is much more chimerical than mine; for, in this alliance, the good is spoiled, and the evil is not cured. I should like better to follow the established practice in everything, than to half follow a good one; there would be less contradiction in man; he cannot at the same time tend towards two opposed goals. Fathers and mothers, what is feasible is what you wish to do. Must I answer for your will?

In every sort of project, there are two things to consider: first the absolute excellence of the project; in the second place, the ease of execution.

In the first respect, it suffices, for the project to be admissible and practicable in itself, that what is good about it be in the nature of the thing; here, for example, that the proposed education be suitable to man and well adapted to the human heart.

The second consideration depends upon relations given in certain situations; relationships accidental to the thing, which, consequently, are not at all necessary, and can vary infinitely. Thus such an education can be practicable in Switzerland, and not in France; another can be so among the bourgeois, and another among the nobility. The greater or lesser facility of execution depends upon a thousand circumstances which it is impossible to determine other than by a particular application of the method to such and such a country, to such and such a condition. Now, all these particular applications, not being essential to my subject, do not enter at all into my plan. Others will be able to concern themselves with them, if they wish, each one for the country or the state which he has in mind. It is enough for me that, everywhere that men will be born, one may make of them what I propose; and, having made of them what I propose, what has made what is the best both for themselves and for others. If I do not fulfill this promise, I am doubtless wrong; but if I fulfill it, one would then be wrong to ask more of me; for I promise only that.

Whence comes this unreasonable custom [of swaddling clothes]? from an unnatural custom. Ever since mothers, despising their first duty, have no longer wished to nurse their children, it has been necessary to entrust them to hired women, who, finding themselves thus mothers of strange children for whom [i.e., on whose behalf] nature said nothing to them, have sought only to spare themselves trouble. It would be necessary to watch ceaselessly over a child at liberty; but, when he is well bound, one tosses him in a corner without bothering about his cries. Provided that there are no proofs of negligence by the nurse, provided that the nursling breaks neither arm nor leg, what does it matter, moreover, whether he dies or remains infirm the rest of his days? One preserves his limbs at the expense of his body, and, no matter what happens, the nurse is exonerated.

These sweet mothers, who, rid of their children, gaily give themselves up to the amusements of the town, do they know, however, what treatment the child in swaddling clothes receives in the village? At the least annoyance which arises, he is hung from a nail like a bundle of old clothes; and while, without hurrying, the nurse attends to her business, the unfortunate one remains thus crucified. All those who have been found in this situation had a purple face; the violently compressed chest not allowing the blood to circulate, it mounted to the head, and the patient was believed to be tranquil because he did not have the strength to cry out. I am ignorant of how many hours a child can remain in this state without losing his life, but I doubt if it can go on very long. Here, I think, is one of the greatest conveniences of swaddling clothes.

One pretends that children at liberty could assume bad postures, and indulge themselves in movements capable of harming the good conformation of their limbs. This is one of these foolish reasons of our false wisdom, which no experience has ever confirmed. Of that multitude of children who, among people more sensible than we, are reared with the full liberty of their limbs, not a single one is seen who hurts himself or cripples himself; they do not know how to give their movements the force which can make them dangerous; and when they assume a violent position, pain soon warns them to change it.

But though mothers disdain to nurse their children, customs are going to be reformed of themselves, the feelings of nature are going to reawaken in all hearts. The State is going to be re-peopled; this first point, this point alone, is going to bring everything together again. The charm of domestic life is the best antidote to bad customs. The turmoil of children, which is considered inconvenient, becomes agreeable; it makes the father and the mother more necessary, dearer to one another; it tightens the conjugal bond between them. When the family is lively and animated, domestic cares are the dearest occupation of the wife and the sweetest amusement of the husband. Thus from this corrected abuse alone a general reform will soon result, soon nature will have re-assumed all her rights. Let women become mothers once again, men will soon again become fathers and husbands.

Superfluous words! Even the boredom with the pleasures of the world never leads back to the latter. Women have ceased to be mothers; they will be no more; they do not wish to be any more. When they wished it, they were hardly able to be; today when the contrary custom is established, each one would have to fight against the opposition of all those who approach her, united against an example which some have not given and the others do not wish to follow.

There are sometimes still, however, young persons of a natural goodness who, daring to defy the rule of fashion and the outcries of their sex on this point, fulfill with a virtuous intrepidity this sweet duty which nature imposes upon them. May their number increase through the charm of the blessings destined for those who give themselves up to it! Based upon deductions which the simplest reasoning gives, and upon observations which I have never seen belied, I dare to promise these worthy mothers an attachment both solid and constant on the part of their husbands, a truly filial tenderness on the part of their children, the esteem and respect of the public, happy childbirths without accident or after-effect, strong and vigorous health, finally, the pleasure of seeing themselves imitated by their daughters one day, and pointed out as an example to those of others.

Just as the real nurse is the mother, the real teacher is the father. Let them agree in the regulation of their functions as well as in their system (i.e., of education). Let the child pass from the hands of the one to those of the other. He will be better brought up by a judicious, limited father than by the cleverest teacher in the world, for zeal supplements talent better than talent does zeal.

But business, activities, duties. . . . Ah! of duties, doubtless the last is that of a father! Let us not be astonished that a man whose wife has disdained to nourish the fruit of their union will disdain to rear it. There is no picture more charming than that of the family, but a single missing feature disfigures all the others. If the mother has too little health to be nurse, the father will have too much business to be teacher. The children, sent away, scattered in boarding schools, in convents, in colleges, will take the love of the paternal home elsewhere; or, to put it better, they will bring back to it the habit of being attached to nothing. Brothers and sisters will scarcely know each other. When they are all assembled on ceremonious occasions, they will be able to be quite polite towards each other; they will treat each other as strangers. As soon as there is no longer any intimacy among relatives, as soon as the society of the family no longer creates the sweetness of life, then one must have recourse to bad customs to supplement it. Where is the man stupid enough not to see the chain of all that?

Multitudes of nations wash their new-born children in rivers or in the sea without any other ceremony. But ours, softened before birth by the softness of the fathers and mothers, bring an already spoiled constitution as they enter into life, which ought not at once to be exposed to all the trials which ought to re-establish it. It is only by degrees that one can restore them to their primitive vigor. So begin at first by following the custom, and do not depart from it except little by little. Wash children often; their dirtiness shows the need of it. . . .

No restraining caps, no binders, no swaddling clothes; large, floating infants' clothing, which leaves all the limbs at liberty, and are neither heavy enough to restrain their movements nor warm enough to prevent him from feeling the impressions of the air. Put him in a large, well-padded cradle, in which he can move at ease and without danger. When he begins to grow stronger, let him creep about the room; let him develop, stretch his little limbs; you will see him grow stronger day by day. Compare him with a well-swaddled child of the same age; you will be astonished at the difference in their progress.

When the child begins to distinguish objects, it is important to choose those which one shows him. Naturally all new objects are interesting to man. He feels himself so weak that he fears all that he does not know; the habit of seeing new objects without being affected by them destroys this fear. Children reared in clean houses, where no spiders are allowed, are afraid of spiders, and this fear often remains with them when they are grown up. I have never seen peasants, neither man, woman nor child, afraid of spiders.

Why then would not the child's education begin before he speaks and understands, since simply the choice of objects presented to him is fitted to make him timid or courageous? I want him to become habituated to seeing new objects, ugly, disgusting, bizarre animals, but gradually, until he becomes accustomed to them, and through seeing them handled by others, he finally handles them himself. If, during his childhood, he has seen toads, snakes, lobsters without fright, he will see without horror, when he is older, any animal whatsoever. There are no longer any fright-ful objects for those who see some every day.

All children are afraid of masks. I begin by showing Emile a mask with a pleasant expression; then someone puts this mask over his face before him; I begin to laugh, everyone laughs, and the child laughs with the others. Gradually I accustom him to less pleasant masks, and finally to hideous faces. If I have managed my gradation well, far from being frightened at the last mask, he will laugh as at the first. After that, I have no more fear about his being frightened by masks.

When, in the farewells of Andromache and Hector, little Astyanax, frightened by the plume which floats on his father's helmet, fails to recognize him, throws himself weeping upon his nurse's breast, and wrings a smile, mixed with tears, from his mother, what must be done to cure that fright? Precisely what Hector does. Put the helmet down on the ground, and then caress the child. In a calmer moment, one will not stop at that point. One would approach the helmet, play with the plumes, have the child handle them; finally the nurse would take the helmet and put it laughingly upon her own head, if ever a woman's hand dared to touch Hector's arms.

If there is a question of training Emile to the noise of a fire-arm, I first burn some tinder in a pistol. This quick, fleeting flame, this sort of light delights him. I repeat the same thing with more powder; gradually I add to the pistol a little charge without wadding, then a larger one; finally I accustom him to rifle shots, grapeshot, to cannons, to the most terrible detonations.

I have noticed that children are rarely afraid of thunder, at least if the claps are not frightful and do not really hurt the organ of hearing, otherwise this fear does not come to them except when they have learned that thunder sometimes harms or kills. When reason begins to frighten them, see to it that habit reassures them. With a slow and well-managed gradation, one makes the man and the child fearless in all things.

.          .          .

Inevitably, a child whose body and arms are free will cry less than a child wrapped up in swaddling clothes. He who knows only physical need cries only when he suffers, and this is a very great advantage; for then one knows at the appointed time when he is in need of help, and one should not delay a moment in giving it to him, if possible. But if you cannot console him, keep calm, without coaxing him to soothe him; your caresses will not soothe his colic; he will remember, however, what must be done to be made much of; and if he once knows how to make you busy yourself with him at his will, then he has become your master; all is lost.

Less frustrated in their movements, children will cry less; less plagued by their cries, one will be less tormented to make them keep quiet; threatened or cajoled less often, they will be less fearful or less obstinate, and will remain better in their natural state. It is less by letting children cry than by hurrying to soothe them that one makes them get hernias; and my proof is that the most neglected children are much less subject to it than the others. I am far from wanting them to be neglected on that account; on the contrary, it is important that one anticipate them, and that one does not allow one's self to be warned of their needs by their cries. But neither do I wish that the attentions given them be badly understood. Why should they make crying a rarity, when they see that their cries are good for so many things? Aware of the price put upon their silence, they keep themselves from squandering it. Finally they make it of such value that one can no longer pay for it; it is then that by dint of crying without success, they struggle, exhaust themselves, and become quiet.

The long cries of a child who is neither bound nor sick and who is allowed to want for nothing are only the cries of habit and obstinacy. They are not the work of nature but of the nurse, who, from not knowing how to endure the vexation, increases it, without thinking that by making the child keep quiet today one incites him to cry even more tomorrow.

The only way of curing or of preventing this habit is to pay no attention to it. No one likes to take useless trouble, not even children. They are obstinate in their attempts, but if you have more constancy than they, more determination, they become disheartened and do not come back to it. It is thus that one spares them cries and that one accustoms them to not uttering them except when pain forces them to it.

Moreover, when they cry for a whim or from stubbornness, one sure way to prevent them from continuing is to distract them with some pleasing and striking object which makes them forget that they want to cry. Most nurses excell in this art, and, well handled, it is very useful; but it is of the utmost importance that the child does not perceive the intention of distracting him, and that he amuse himself without knowing that he is being thought of; now this is what all nurses are clumsy about.

Children hear talking from their birth; they are spoken to not only before they can understand what is being said to them, but before they can reproduce the voices which they hear. Their still benumbed organ lends itself only gradually to the limitations of sounds spoken to them, and it is not even certain that at first these sounds carry as distinctly to their ear as to ours. I do not disapprove of the nurse's amusing the child with songs and by very gay and varied expressions; but I disapprove of her constantly deafening him with a multitude of useless words of which he understands nothing but the tone she gives them. I should like the first utterances which one has him hear to be rare, simple, distinct, frequently repeated, and that the words which they express should correspond only to tangible objects which could first be shown to the child. The unfortunate facility which we have of being satisfied with words which we do not understand begins earlier than we think. The schoolboy listens in class to his master's verbiage as he listens in swaddling clothes to the babbling of his nurse. It seems to me that it would be teaching him very usefully to rear him to understand nothing of this.

.        .        .

Nature, to strengthen the body and make it grow, has means which must never be thwarted. A child must not be constrained to stay when he wants to go, nor to go when he wants to remain still. When children's freedom is not spoiled through our fault, they want nothing needlessly. They must jump, run, shout, when they want to. All their movements are needs of their constitution which is seeking to strengthen itself; but one ought to distrust what they desire without being able to do it themselves, and which others are obliged to do for them. The real need, the natural need, must be carefully distinguished from the capricious need which is beginning to appear, or from that which comes only from the overabundance of life of which I have spoken.

I have already said what must be done when a child cries to have this or that. I shall only add that as soon as he can ask for what he wants by speaking, and when, to get it more quickly or to overcome a refusal, he strengthens his request with tears, it ought to be irrevocably refused to him. If need has caused him to speak, you ought to know it, and do at once what he has asked; but to grant something to his tears is to encourage him to pour them out, to teach him to doubt your goodwill, and to believe that importunity has greater effect upon you than goodness. If he does not think you are good, soon he will be bad; if he thinks you weak, soon he will be obstinate. At the first sign it is important to yield what one does not intend to refuse. Do not be lavish with refusals, but never revoke them. . . .

To reason with children was Locke's great maxim; it is the most in fashion today. Its success, however, does not seem to me quite fitted to give it credence; and, as for me, I see nothing more stupid than children who have been reasoned with. Of all man's faculties, reason, which is, so to speak, only a combination of all the others, is that which develops with the greatest difficulty and the latest; and it is that which people want to use to develop the earliest (i.e., faculties)! The master-piece of a good education is to create a reasonable man; and they pretend to rear a child upon reason! It is beginning at the end, it is wanting to make an instrument out of the work. If children understood reason, they would have no need of being brought up; by speaking to them from the earliest age in a language which they do not understand, one accustoms them to being satisfied with words, to discussing everything that is said to them, to believing themselves as wise as their teachers, to becoming argumentative and mutinous; and all that one thinks of obtaining from them through reasonable motives, one never obtains from them except through covetousness, or fear, or vanity, which one is always forced to add to it. . . . (Nature wants children to be children before they are men.) If we wish to pervert this order, we shall produce precocious fruits which will have neither ripeness nor flavor, and which will not be slow to spoil. We shall have young professors and old children. Childhood has ways of seeing, thinking, and feeling which are proper to it; nothing is less sensible than to want to substitute our ways for them, and I should just as well like to ask that a child be five feet tall as that he have judgment at ten years of age. Indeed, what use would reason be to him at that age? It is the bridle of strength, and the child has no need of this bridle.

In trying to convince your pupils of the duty of obedience, you join to this pretended persuasion strength and threats, or, what is worse, flattery and promises. So thus, lured by interest or restrained by force, they pretend to be convinced by reason. They see very well that obedience is advantageous to them, and rebellion harmful, as soon as you are aware of one or the other. But since you demand nothing from them but what is disagreeable to them, and since it is always painful to do another's will, they conceal themselves to do their own, convinced that they do right if their disobedience is unknown; but ready to agree that they do wrong, if they are discovered, from fear of a greater evil. Since the reason for duty does not pertain to their age, there is not a man in the world who succeeds in making them really sensible of it; but the fear of punishment, the hope of pardon, the trouble, the embarrassment of answering, wrings from them all the avowals which one demands; and one thinks them convinced, when one has only bored or intimidated them.

What happens as a result? First, by imposing upon them a duty which they do not feel, you set them against your tyranny, and turn them away from loving you; you teach them to become dissimulators, false, liars, in

24. Antoine Watteau, *L'Enseigne de Gersaint*.

order to extort recompenses or to escape punishments; finally, by
accustoming them always to cover a secret motive by an apparent motive,
you yourself give them the means of abusing you constantly, of taking
from you the knowledge of their real character, and of paying you and
others with vain words as the occasion arises. The laws, you say, although
obligatory to the conscience, also use constraint with grown men. I agree.
But what are these men, if not children spoiled by education? That is
exactly what must be prevented. Use force with children and reason with
men; such is the natural order. The wise man has no need of laws.

Treat your pupil according to his age. First put him in his place, and
keep him there so well that he no longer tries to leave it. Then, before
knowing what wisdom is, he will practice its most important lesson.
Never command him to do anything, no matter what, absolutely nothing.
Never even let him imagine that you pretend to have any authority over
him. Let him know only that he is weak and that you are strong; that,
because of his position and yours, he is necessarily at your mercy; let him
know, let him learn, let him feel; let him feel soon upon his arrogant
head the harsh yoke which nature imposes upon man, the heavy yoke of
the necessity of things, never of the whims of men; let the bridle which
restrains him be force and not authority. Do not forbid him that from
which he ought to abstain; keep him from doing it, without explanations, without reasoning; that which you grant him, grant it at his first

word, without solicitations, without prayers, above all without conditions. Grant with pleasure, refuse only with distaste; but let all your refusals be irrevocable; let no turmoil upset you; let the uttered *no* be an iron wall against which the child will not have exhausted his strength five or six times so that he will no more try to knock it down. It is thus that you will make him patient, equable, resigned, peaceable, even when he does not get what he wants, for it is in man's nature to endure the necessity of things patiently, but not another's ill will. This phrase, "there is no more," is an answer against which a child has never rebelled, unless he thought it a lie. Moreover, there is no middle way here; one must demand nothing at all from him, or bend to him to the most perfect obedience. The worst education is to leave him floating between his wishes and yours, and to dispute ceaselessly between him and you over which of the two will be the master; I should prefer a hundred fold that he would always be.

It is very strange that ever since people have concerned themselves with rearing children, no one has imagined a better instrument than emulation, jealousy, envy, vanity, greed, the vile fear, all the most dangerous passions, the promptest to ferment, the fittest to corrupt the soul, even before the body is formed. With each precocious instruction that one wants to get into their heads, one plants a vice in the depths of their hearts; senseless instructors think of working marvels by making them wicked in order to teach them what goodness is; and then they tell us seriously, "Such is man." Yes, such is the man whom you have made.

All the instruments have been tried, except one, precisely the only one which can succeed: well regulated liberty. One must not concern one's self with rearing a child when one does not know how to lead him where one wishes, according to the laws of the possible and the impossible. The sphere of both being equally unknown to him, one extends it, one closes it in about him as one wishes. He is chained, he is pushed ahead, he is held back, with the single restraint of necessity, without his murmuring against it. He is made supple and docile by the very force of things, without any vice having the opportunity to germinate within him; for the passions never quicken, so that they are of no consequence.

Do not give your pupil any kind of verbal lesson; he ought not to receive any except from experience. Do not inflict any kind of punishment upon him, for he does not know what it is to be at fault. Never make him ask pardon, for he will not know how to offend you. Unaware of all morality in his actions, he can do nothing which is morally bad and which deserves either punishment or reprimand.

I already see the frightened reader judging this child by ours; he is wrong. The perpetual constraint under which you keep your pupils irritates their vivacity; the more they are restrained before your eyes, the more turbulent they are from the moment they escape. They really have to compensate themselves when they can for the harsh constraint in which you keep them. Two schoolboys from the city can wreak more havoc in a country than the youth of an entire village. Shut up a little gentleman and a little peasant in a room; the first will have everything topsy-turvy, everything broken, before the second has left his place. Why so, if not that the one hurries to abuse a moment of license, while the other, always sure of his liberty, never is in a hurry to make use of it? And yet, the children of village folk, flattered or crossed, are still far from the state in which I should like them to be.

Let us state as an incontestable maxim that the first movements of nature are always right; there is no original perversity in the human heart; there is not a single vice in it of which it cannot be said how and where it entered. The only passion natural to man is the love of himself, or self-love taken in a wide sense. This self-love in itself or relative to us is good and useful; and, since it has no necessary connection with any one else, it is naturally indifferent in this respect; it becomes good and evil only by the application which one makes of it and the relations which one forms with it. Until the guide of self-love, which is the reason, can be born, it is important then that a child does nothing because it is seen or heard, nothing, in a word, having bearing upon others, but only that which nature demands of him; and then he will do nothing but good.

.     .     .

The first idea which he must be given is less that of liberty than of property; and, so that he may have this idea, he must have something of his own. To point out to him his clothes, his furniture, his toys, is to tell him nothing, since, although he has the disposal of these things, he does not know how or why he has them. To tell him that he has them because they have been given to him is hardly doing better; for, in order to give, one must have. Behold then a proprietorship anterior to his own; and this is the principle of property which one wishes to explain to him; without counting that the gift is a convention, and that the child cannot yet know what a convention is. Readers, remark, in this example and in a hundred thousand others, how, by stuffing children's heads with words which have no meaning within their comprehension, one thinks, however, that they have been very well taught.

The question is to go back to the origin of property, for it is from thence that the first idea of it ought to arise. The child, living in the country, will have received some idea of rural tasks; one needs for that only eyes, leisure, and he will have both. It is characteristic of every age, especially of his, to wish to create, imitate, produce, to give signs of power and activity. He will not see a garden worked twice, vegetables sown, come up, grow, without his wishing to garden in his turn.

By the principles previously established, I do not oppose his desire; on the contrary, I am in favor of it, I share his taste, I work with him, not for his pleasure but for mine; at least he thinks so. I become his garden boy; waiting until he has the strength of arm, I till the earth for him. He takes possession of it by planting a bean in it; and surely this possession is more sacred and more respectable than that which Nunez Balboa took of southern America in the name of the King of Spain, by planting his standard on the coasts of the Pacific.

One comes to water the beans every day, one sees them come up in transports of joy. I increase this joy by saying to him, "That belongs to you." And then by explaining to him this term, "belong," I make him feel that he has put into it his time, his work, his trouble, his person, finally; that there is in this ground something of himself which he can claim against any one whatsoever, as he could take away his arm from the hand of another man who might want to hold it despite him.

One fine day he arrives in great haste, the watering-can in his hand. O what a sight! O sorrow! all the beans have been torn up, the whole plot is topsy-turvy, the spot itself can no longer be recognized. Ah, what has become of my toil, my work, the sweet fruit of my cares and my sweats? Who has snatched my property from me? Who has taken my beans? This young heart rises up; the first feeling of injustice comes to pour out its sad bitterness; tears run in streams; the desolated child fills the air with groans and cries. One shares his sorrow, his indignation; one seeks, one is informed, one makes searches. Finally one discovers that the gardener has given the blow; he is sent for.

But here we are quite far from what we anticipated. The gardener, learning of what we complain, begins to complain louder than we. "What! gentlemen, it is you who thus spoiled my work! I had sown some Maltese melons there, the seed of which had been given to me as a treasure, and with which I was hoping to delight you when they were ripe; but look, to plant your miserable beans there, you destroyed my melons, which had already come up, and which I shall never replace. You have done me an irreparable wrong, and you yourselves are deprived of the pleasure of eating some exquisite melons."

JEAN-JACQUES. Excuse us, my poor Robert. You put your work, your toil, there. I do indeed see that we did wrong to spoil your work; but we will get you some other seed from Malta, and we shall no longer till the soil without knowing whether some one has laid hand to it before us.

ROBERT. Well, then, gentlemen, you can rest, for there is no more fallow land. I myself work that which my father improved; each one does as much on his land, and all the lands which you see have been occupied for a long time.

EMILE. Mr. Robert, then there is often melon seed lost?

ROBERT. Excuse me, my young fellow, for we do not often have young gentlemen as thoughtless as you among us. No one touches his neighbor's garden; each one respects the work of others so that his own may be safe.

EMILE. But I have no garden.

ROBERT. What does that matter to me? If you spoil mine, I shall no longer let you walk in it, for, you see, I do not want to waste my pains.

JEAN-JACQUES. Couldn't we make an arrangement with good Robert? Let him grant to us, to my little friend and me, a corner of his garden to cultivate, on the condition that he will have half of the produce.

ROBERT. I grant it to you without the condition. But remember that I shall come to cultivate your beans, if you touch my melons.

In this attempt at the way to inculcate primitive ideas in children, one sees how the idea of property goes back naturally to the right of the first occupant through work.

# from *An Essay on the Manners and Spirit of Nations*

## VOLTAIRE

You are at length resolved, then, to surmount your disgust from reading modern history since the decline of the Roman Empire, and to gain a general idea of the nations which inhabit and ravage the face of the earth. All that you seek to learn in this immensity of matter, is only that which deserves to be known; the spirit, the manners and customs of the principal nations, supported by facts which one cannot ignore. The aim of this work is not to know the precise year in which the brutal

25. *Chemistry Laboratory,* from *Diderot Pictorial Encyclopedia.*

sovereign of a barbarous people was succeeded by a prince unworthy of being known. If a man could have the misfortune to encumber his head with the chronological series of all the dynasties which have existed, all his knowledge would be a jumble of words. As it is laudable to know the great actions of those sovereigns who have made their peoples better and happier, so is it reasonable to ignore vulgar reigns, which serve only to burden the memory. What advantage can you derive from the minute details of a number of petty interests and connections which no longer survive; of families long extinct that contested the possession of provinces now swallowed up in mighty kingdoms? Almost every city now has its own particular history, whether true or false, more voluminous and more detailed than that of Alexander the Great. There is more writing in the archives of a single convent, than in the annals of the Roman Empire.

A reader must limit himself and select from these immense collections which serve only to confuse. They constitute a vast store-house, from which you take what is necessary for your own occasions.

The illustrious Bossuet, who, in his discourse on a phase of universal history has seized its true spirit, at least in what he says of the Roman Empire, left off at the reign of Charlemagne. Your design is by beginning with this era, to make a picture of mankind; but you must often go back to earlier times. That eloquent writer, in briefly mentioning the Arabians, who founded such a mighty empire, and established such a flourishing religion, speaks of them only as a deluge of barbarians. He seems to have written solely to insinuate that everything in the world was made for the Jewish nation; that if God gave the Asian Empire to the Babylonians, it was to punish the Jews; if God made Cyrus reign, it was to avenge them; if God sent forth the Romans, it was again to chastise these Jews. This may be; but the greatness of Cyrus and the Romans have still other causes, and Bossuet himself did not omit them in speaking of the spirit of nations.

It might well be wished that he did not completely forget the ancient peoples of the Orient, like the Indians and Chinese, who were so important before the other nations were formed.

Fed as we are by the produce of ther country, clothed with their materials, amused by the games which they invented, even instructed by their old moral fables, why should we neglect to know the spirit of those nations which our European traders have constantly visited, ever since they first found the way to their coasts?

In your philosophical inquiries concerning this globe, you naturally direct your first attention to the East, the cradle of the arts, to which the western world owes everything.

The oriental and southern climes owe everything to nature; whereas we, in these northern regions, owe all to time, to commerce, and to belated industry. The old countries of the Celts, Allobroges, Picts, Germans, Sarmatians, and Scythians, produced nothing but wild fruits, rocks, and forests. Sicily, indeed, is said to have produced a small quantity of oats; but as for wheat, rice, and delicious fruits, they grew on the borders of the Euphrates, in China, and in India. The most fertile countries were the first inhabited, and the first regulated by police. The whole Levant, from Greece to the extremities of our hemisphere, was famous long before we knew so much of it as to realize that we were savages. If we want to know anything of our ancestors, the Celts, we must have recourse to the Greeks and Romans, nations of a much later date than the Asiatics.

For example, although the Gauls bordering on the Alps, along with the inhabitants of these mountains, settled on the banks of the Po, from where they penetrated to Rome three hundred and sixty-one years after the founding of that city, and even besieged the capital, we should never have known of this expedition but for the Romans. Though other Gauls, about one hundred years later, invaded Thessaly and Macedonia, and advanced to the coast of the Euxine Sea, all the information we have of this adventure, is from the Greek; and they have neither told us who those Gauls were, nor what route they followed. In our own country there is not the slighest trace of these migrations, which resemble those of the Tartars: they only prove that we were a numerous but not a civilized people. The Grecian colony that founded Marseilles six hundred years before the Christian era, could not polish Gaul: the Greek language did not extend beyond their own territory.

Gauls, Germans, Spaniards, Britons, Sarmatians, we know nothing about ourselves that happened over eighteen centuries ago, except for the little we learn from the records of conquerors. We do not even have fables, we have not dared to invent an origin. The vain idea that all the West was peopled by Gomer, the son of Japhet, is a fiction of the East.

If the ancient Tuscans, who instructed the first inhabitants of Rome, knew something more than the other peoples of the West, they either owed that knowledge to the Greek colonies that settled among them, or rather, because it has always been the peculiar property of that soil to produce men of genius, just as the territory of Athens was more suitable for the arts than those of Thebes and Lacedæmon. But what monuments do we have of ancient Tuscany? None at all. We exhaust ourselves in vague conjectures on some unintelligible inscriptions which have escaped the injuries of time, and which probably belong to the first centuries of the Roman republic. As for the other nations of Europe, we have nothing in their old language anterior to the Christian era.

Maritime Spain was discovered by the Phœnicians, as the Spaniards have since discovered America. The Tyrians, the Carthaginians, and the Romans were in turn enriched by the treasures of the earth which that country produced. The Carthaginians benefited from mines, but they were less rich than those of Mexico and Peru; time had exhausted them as it will exhaust those of the new world. Pliny declares that the Romans, in the space of nine years, drew from these mines eight thousand marks of gold, and about twenty-four thousand of silver. It must be admitted that those pretended descendants of Gomer made a very bad use of the various advantages which their country produced, for they were subjugated by the Carthaginians, the Romans, the Vandals, the Goths, and the Arabs.

What we learn of the Gauls from Julius Cæsar and other Roman authors, gives us the idea of a people in need of being subdued by an enlightened nation. The dialects of the Celtic language were frightful. The emperor Julian, in whose reign it was still spoken, says in his *Misopogon* that they resembled the croaking of ravens. In Cæsar's time, their manners were as barbarous as their language. The druids, gross impostors made for the people whom they governed, sacrificed human victims, whom they burned in large and hideous statues of straw. The female druids plunged their knives into the hearts of prisoners, and predicted future events from the flowing of their blood. The vast stones, a little hollowed, found on the confines of Gaul and Germany, are said to be the altars on which those sacrifices were made. These are the only monuments of ancient Gaul. Those who inhabited the coasts of Biscay and Gascony sometimes fed on human flesh. We must turn our eyes with horror from these savage times, which are the shame of human nature.

Let us count among the follies of the human imagination, the notion entertained in our days, that the Celts were descended from the Hebrews. They sacrificed their own species, it is said, because Jephthah sacrificed his daughter. The druids were clad in white, in imitation of the Jewish priests: like these, they had a high priest. The female druids were representatives of Moses' sister and Deborah. The poor wretch pampered at Marseilles, and offered as a sacrifice, crowned with flowers, and loaded with curses, originated from the scape-goat. They go so far as to find some resemblance between a few Celtic and Hebrew words, equally ill pronounced; and thence conclude that the Jews and the Celts are of the same family. Thus reason is insulted in our universal histories, and the little knowledge we might have of antiquity stifled under a heap of forced conjectures.

The Germans nearly resembled the Gauls in their morals: like them they sacrificed human victims; like them they decided their private disputes by single combat; the only difference was, that the Germans were coarser and less industrious than their neighbors. Cæsar, in his memoirs, tells us that their magicians always fixed the day of combat. He states that when one of their kings, Ariovistus, brought a hundred thousand of his wandering Germans to pillage the Gauls, he who wished to enslave them and not pillage them sent two Roman officers to enter into conference with this barbarian: Ariovistus put them in irons. He adds that the two officers were destined to be sacrificed to the Germans' gods and were about to be, when he delivered them by his victory.

The families of all these savages had, in Germany, as their only domicile, wretched cottages, at one end of which the father, mother, sisters, brothers, and children lay huddled together, naked, upon straw; while at the other end was their cattle. These, however, are the same people whom we shall soon see in possession of Rome! Tacitus praises the manners of the Germans, but in the same way as Horace extolls the savages known as Getae; neither one knew anything about those they were praising, and wanted only to satirize Rome. The same Tacitus, in the midst of his éloges, admits that everyone knows that the Germans would rather live on plunder than cultivate the earth; and after pillaging their neighbors, they return to their homes to eat and sleep. It is the life of our present-day highway men and cut-purses, whom we punish with the wheel and the rope; and this is what Tacitus had the nerve to praise in order to make the court of the Roman emperors detested, through contrast with Germanic virtue! A mind so just as yours should regard Tacitus as an ingenious satirist, as profound in his ideas as he is concise in his expressions, who wrote the criticism rather than the history of his country, and who would deserve our admiration had he been impartial.

When Cæsar invaded Britain, he found that island still more savage than Germany: the natives scarcely took the trouble to cover their nakedness with skins. The women belonged in common to all the men of the same district. The habitations were willow cabins; and the ornaments of both sexes were figures painted on their bodies, by pricking the skin and pouring the juice of herbs over it, an art still practiced by the savages in America.

That human nature was for a long series of ages plunged in this state so nearly resembling that of brutes, and even inferior to it in many respects, is only too true. The reason, as has been said, is that it is not in human nature for man *to desire what he does not know*. He has always needed not only a prodigious space of time but also lucky circumstances in order to raise himself above the level of animal life.

You have, therefore, great reason for resolving to go at once to those nations which were first civilized. Long before the empires of China and India commenced, perhaps the world produced nations that were learned, polished, and powerful; and these were, perhaps, plunged again, by deluges of barbarians, into that first state of ignorance and brutality which is called the state of nature.

The taking of Constantinople was alone sufficient to annhilate the spirit of ancient Greece. The Goths destroyed the genius of the Romans. The coast of Africa, formerly so rich and flourishing, is nothing now but the haunt of bandits. Changes still more extraordinary must have happened in less favorable climates. Physical and moral causes must have joined; for although the ocean cannot have entirely changed its bed, it is certain that vast tracts of lands have been by turns overflowed and forsaken by the sea. Nature must have been exposed to many scourges and vicissitudes. The most beautiful and most fertile soils of western Europe, all of the low lands watered by the rivers of the Rhine, the Meuse, the Seine, the Loire, have been covered by the ocean for a prodigious number of centuries; you have already seen this in the *Philosophy of History*.

We will say again that it is not so certain that the mountains which cross the old and new world were formerly plains covered by the seas, because:

1. Many of these mountains are fifteen thousand feet and more above sea level.

2. If there had been a time when these mountains did not exist, where would the streams have come from which are so necessary to animal life? These mountains are the waters' reservoirs. In the two hemispheres they move in different directions: they are, as Plato says, the bones of this great animal called *the earth*. We observe that the slightest plants have an invariable structure; why should the earth be exempt from the general law?

3. If the mountains were thought to have carried the seas, it would be a contradiction in the order of nature, a violation of the laws of gravitation and hydrostatics.

4. The ocean's bed is hollow and in its crest one finds no chains of mountains from one end to the other or from east to west, as we see on earth. Hence we must not conclude that this globe was long a sea just because several parts of the globe were water. We must not conclude that water covered the Alps and the Andes just because it covered lower Gaul, Greece, Germany, Africa and India. We can hardly assert that Mount Taurus was navigable because the Philippine archipelago and the Moluccas were a continent. It is very likely that high mountains have always been very much as they are. How many books do not state that a ship's anchor has been found on the summit of the Swiss mountains? Yet this is as false as all the stories found in these books.

Let us admit in physics only that which is proven, and in history, that which is of the greatest and most recognized probability. It may well be that mountainous countries have undergone, through volcanoes and earthquakes, as many changes as the low countries; but wherever rivers have their sources, there have been mountains. A thousand local revolutions have certainly changed a part of the globe, both physically and morally, but we do not know them; and men have decided to write history so late that the human race, old though it is, seems new to us.

Besides, you begin your investigations at an age when the chaos of our Europe begins to take a form, after the fall of the Roman empire. Let us survey the world together; let us see in what condition it was then, by studying it in the same way in which it seems to have been civilized: that is, from the oriental countries to our own, and let us direct our first attention to a people who had a continuous history in a language already fixed, when we did not even possess writing.

# On Man

## CLAUDE-ADRIEN HELVÉTIUS

The understanding is nothing more than the assemblage of our ideas. Our ideas, says Locke, come to us by the senses; and from this principle, as from mine, it may be concluded that our understanding is nothing more than an acquisition.

To regard it as a mere gift of nature, or the effect of a particular organization, without being able to name the organ by which it is produced, is to bring back to philosophy the occult qualities; it is to believe without proof, and judge at a venture.

History and experience equally inform us that the understanding is independent of the greater or less acuteness of the senses; that men of different constitutions are susceptible of the same passions and the same ideas.

The principles of Locke, far from contradicting this opinion, confirm it; they prove that education makes us what we are; that men the more resemble each other as their instructions are more similar; and consequently that a German resembles a Frenchman more than an Asiatic; and another German more than a Frenchman; and in short, if the understandings of men be very different, it is because none of them have the same education.

.    .    .

What is a science? A series of propositions which all relate to one general and original principle. Is morality a science? Yes; if in corporeal sensation I have discovered the sole principle of which all the precepts of morality are the necessary consequences. It is an evident proof of the truth of this principle, that it explains all the modes of being of mankind, that it developes the causes of their understanding, their stupidity, their love, their hatred, their errors and contradictions. This principle ought to be the more easily and universally adopted, as the existence of corporeal sensibility is a fact allowed by all, as the idea of it is clear, the notion distinct, the expression determinate, and, lastly, as no error can mix itself with so simple an axiom.

26. *Cross section of Newcomen steam engine in operation.*

Corporeal sensibility seems to have been given to men as a tutelar angel, charged to watch incessantly over their preservation. Let men be happy; this perhaps is the sole view of nature, and the sole principle of morality. When the laws are good, private interest will never be destructive of that of the public: every one will be employed in pursuing his felicity; every one will be fortunate and just; because every one will perceive that his happiness depends upon that of his neighbour.

.     .     .

If it be true that the talents and the virtues of a people determine their power and their happiness, no question can be more important than this: *are the talents and virtues of each individual, the effect of his organisation, or of the education he receives?*

I am of the latter opinion. . . . If I can demonstrate that man is, in fact, nothing more than the product of his education, I shall doubtless reveal an important truth to mankind. They will learn, that they have in their own hands the instrument of their greatness and their felicity, and that to be happy and powerful nothing more is requisite than to perfect the science of education. . . .

Man is born ignorant; he is not born a fool; and it is not even without labour that he is made one. To be such, and to be able to extinguish in himself his natural lights, art and method must be used; instruction must heap on him error upon error; the more he reads, the more numerous must be the prejudices he contracts.

.    .    .

Two opinions concerning this subject divide the learned of the present age. Some maintain that, *The understanding is the effect of a certain sort of interior temperament and organisation.* But no one has, by a series of observations, yet determined the sort or organs, temperament, or nourishment that produces the understanding. This assertion being vague and destitute of proof, is then reduced to this, *The understanding is the effect of an unknown cause, or occult quality, to which is given the name of temperament or organisation.*

Quintilian, Locke, and I, say:

*The inequality in minds or understandings, is the effect of a known cause, and this cause is the difference of education.* . . .

Experience then proves that the character and spirit of a people change with the form of government; and that a different government gives by turns, to the same nation, a character noble or base, firm or fickle, courageous or cowardly. Men therefore are endowed at their birth, either with no disposition, or with dispositions to all vices and all virtues; they are therefore nothing more than the produce of their education. If the Persian have no idea of liberty, and the savage no idea of servitude, it is the effect of their different instruction. . . .

Whoever says that men do not easily change their characters by constraint, only says that habits long established are not to be destroyed in an instant.

The man of ill humour preserves his character, because he has always some inferior on whom he can exercise his ill nature. But let him be kept a long time in the presence of a lion or a tyrant, and there is no doubt but a continued restraint, transformed into a habit, will soften his character. In general, as long as we are young enough to contract new habits, the only incurable faults, and vices, are those that we cannot correct without employing means of which morals, laws, or customs do not allow the practice. There is nothing impossible to education; it makes the bear dance. . . .

Man is born without ideas and without passions, but he is born an imitator and docile to example; consequently it is to instruction he owes his habits and his character. Now I ask, why habits contracted during a certain time, cannot at length be effaced by contrary habits. How many people do we see change their character with their rank, according to the different place they occupy at court, and in the ministry; in short, according to the change that happens in their situation.

# from *The Spirit of Laws*

## MONTESQUIEU

Laws, in their most general signification, are the necessary relations arising from the nature of things. In this sense all beings have their laws; the Deity His laws, the material world its laws, the intelligences superior to man their laws, the beasts their laws, man his laws.

They who assert that a blind fatality produced the various effects we behold in this world talk very absurdly; for can anything be more unreasonable than to pretend that a blind fatality could be productive of intelligent beings?

There is, then, a prime reason; and laws are the relations subsisting between it and different beings, and the relations of these to one another.

God is related to the universe, as Creator and Preserver; the laws by which He created all things are those by which He preserves them. He acts according to these rules, because He knows them; He knows them, because He made them; and He made them because they are in relation to His wisdom and power.

Since we observe that the world, though formed by the motion of matter, and void of understanding, subsists through so long a succession of ages, its motions must certainly be directed by invariable laws; and could we imagine another world, it must also have constant rules, or it would inevitably perish.

Thus the creation, which seems an arbitrary act, supposes laws as invariable as those of the fatality of the atheists. It would be absurd to say that the Creator might govern the world without those rules, since without them it could not subsist.

These rules are a fixed and invariable relation. In bodies moved, the motion is received, increased, diminished, or lost, according to the relations of the quantity of matter and velocity; each diversity is uniformity, each change is constancy. . . .

Man, as a physical being, is like other bodies governed by invariable laws. As an intelligent being, he incessantly transgresses the laws established by God, and changes those of his own instituting. He is left to his private direction, though a limited being, and subject, like all finite intelligences, to ignorance and error: even in imperfect knowledge he loses; and as a sensible creature, he is hurried away by a thousand impetuous passions. Such a being might every instant forget his Creator; God has therefore reminded him of his duty by the laws of religion. Such a being is liable every moment to forget himself; philosophy has provided against this by the laws of morality. Formed to live in society, he might forget his fellow creatures; legislators have therefore by political and civil laws confined him to his duty. . . .

As soon as man enters into a state of society he loses the sense of his weaknesses; equality ceases, and then commences the state of war.

Each particular society begins to feel its strength, whence arises a state of war between different nations. The individuals likewise of each society become sensible of their force; hence the principal advantages of this society they endeavor to convert to their own emolument, which constitutes a state of war between individuals.

These two different kinds of states give rise to human laws. Considered as inhabitants of so great a planet, which necessarily contains a variety of nations, they have laws relating to their mutual intercourse, which is what we call the law of nations. As members of a society that must be properly supported, they have laws relating to the governors and the governed, and this we distinguish by the name of politic law. They have also another sort of laws, as they stand in relation to each other; by which is understood civil law.

The law of nations is naturally founded on this principle, that different nations ought in time of peace to do one another all the good they can, and in time of war as little injury as possible, without prejudicing their real interests.

The object of war is victory; that of victory is conquest; and that of conquest preservation. From this and the preceding principle all those rules are derived which constitute the law of nations.

All countries have a law of nations, no excepting the Iroquois themselves, though they devour their prisoners: for they send and receive ambassadors, and understand the rights of war and peace. The mischief is that their law of nations is not founded on true principles.

Besides the law of nations relating to all societies, there is a polity or civil constitution for each particularly concerned. No society can subsist without a form of government. "The united strength of individuals," as Gravina [Italian poet and jurist, 1664–1718] well observes, "constitutes what we call the body politic."

The general force may be in the hands of a single person, or of many. Some think that Nature having established paternal authority, the most natural government was that of a single person. But the example of paternal authority proves nothing. For if the power of a father relates to a single government, that of brothers after the death of a father, and that of cousin-germans after the decease of brothers, refer to a government of many. The political power necessarily comprehends the union of several families.

Better is it to say that the government most conformable to Nature is that which best agrees with the humor and disposition of the people in whose favor it is established.

The strength of individuals cannot be united without a conjunction of their wills. "The conjunction of those wills," as Gravina again very justly observes, "is what we call the civil state."

Law in general is human reason, inasmuch as it governs all the inhabitants of the earth; the political and civil laws of each nation ought to be only the particular cases in which human reason is applied.

They should be adapted in such a manner to the people for whom they are framed that it should be a great chance if those of one nation suit another.

They should be in relation to the nature and principle of each government; whether they form it, as may be said of politic laws; or whether they support it, as in the case of civil institutions.

They should be in relation to the climate of each country, to the quality of its soil, to its situation and extent, to the principal occupation of the natives, whether husbandmen, huntsmen, or shepherds: they should have relation to the degree of liberty which the constitution will bear; to the religion of the inhabitants, to their inclinations, riches, numbers, commerce, manners, and customs. In fine, they have relations to each other, as also to their origin, to the intent of the legislator, and to the order of things on which they are established; in all of which different lights they ought to be considered.

# from *The Autobiography*

## BENJAMIN FRANKLIN

Before I proceed in relating the part I had in public affairs under this new governor's administration, it may not be amiss here to give some account of the rise and progress of my philosophical reputation.

In 1746, being at Boston, I met there with a Dr Spence, who was lately arrived from Scotland, and show'd me some electric experiments. They were imperfectly perform'd, as he was not very expert; but, being on a subject quite new to me, they equally surpris'd and pleased me. Soon after my return to Philadelphia, our library company receiv'd from Mr P. Collinson, Fellow of the Royal Society of London, a present of a glass tube, with some account of the use of it in making such experiments. I eagerly seized the opportunity of repeating what I had seen at Boston; and, by much practice, acquir'd great readiness in performing those, also, which we had an account of from England, adding a number of new ones. I say much practice, for my house was continually full, for some time, with people who came to see these new wonders.

To divide a little this incumbrance among my friends, I caused a number of similar tubes to be blown at our glass-house, with which they furnish'd themselves, so that we had at length several performers. Among these, the principal was Mr Kinnersley, an ingenious neighbor, who, being out of business, I encouraged to undertake showing the experiments for money, and drew up for him two lectures, in which the experiments were rang'd in such order, and accompanied with such explanations in such method, as that the foregoing should assist in comprehending the following. He procur'd an elegant apparatus for the purpose, in which all the little machines that I had roughly made for myself were nicely form'd by instrument-makers. His lectures were well attended, and gave great satisfaction; and after some time he went thro' the colonies, exhibiting them in every capital town, and pick'd up some money. In the West India islands, indeed, it was with difficulty the experiments could be made, from the general moisture of the air.

Oblig'd as we were to Mr Collinson for his present of the tube, etc., I thought it right he should be inform'd of our success in using it, and wrote him several letters containing accounts of our experiments. He got them read in the Royal Society, where they were not at first thought worth so much notice as to be printed in their Transactions. One paper, which I wrote for Mr Kinnersley, on the sameness of lightning with electricity, I sent Dr Mitchel, an acquaintance of mine, and one of the members also of that society, who wrote me word that it had been read, but was laughed at by the connoisseurs. The papers, however, being shown to Dr Fothergill, he thought them of too much value to be stifled, and advis'd the printing of them. Mr Collinson then gave them to Cave for publication in his Gentleman's Magazine; but he chose to print them separately in a pamphlet, and Dr Fothergill wrote the preface. Cave, it seems, judged rightly for his profit, for by the additions that arrived afterward they swell'd, to a quarto volume, which has had five editions, and cost him nothing for copy-money.

It was, however, some time before those papers were much taken notice of in England. A copy of them happening to fall into the hands of the Count de Buffon, a philosopher deservedly of great reputation in France, and, indeed, all over Europe, he prevailed with M. Dalibard to translate them into French, and they were printed at Paris. The publication offended the Abbé Nollet, preceptor in Natural Philosophy to the royal family, and an able experimenter, who had form'd and publish'd a theory of electricity, which then had the general vogue. He could not at first believe that such a work came from America, and said it must have been fabricated by his enemies at Paris, to decry his system. Afterwards, having been assur'd that there really existed such a person as Franklin at Philadelphia, which he had doubted, he wrote and published a volume of Letters, chiefly address'd to me, defending his theory, and denying the verity of my experiments, and of the positions deduc'd from them.

I once purpos'd answering the abbé, and actually began the answer; but, on consideration that my writings contain'd a description of experiments which any one might repeat and verify, and if not to be verifi'd, could not be defended; or of observations offer'd as conjectures, and not delivered dogmatically, therefore not laying me under any obligation to defend them; and reflecting that a dispute between two persons, writing in different languages, might be lengthened greatly by mistranslations, and thence misconceptions of one another's meaning, much of one of the abbé's letters being founded on an error in the translation, I concluded to let my papers shift for themselves, believing it was better to spend what time I could spare from public business in making new experiments, than in disputing about those already made. I therefore never answered M.

27. *Uranographic Machine.*

Nollet, and the event gave me no cause to repent my silence; for my friend M. le Roy, of the Royal Academy of Sciences, took up my cause and refuted him; my book was translated into the Italian, German, and Latin languages; and the doctrine it contain'd was by degrees universally adopted by the philosophers of Europe, in preference to that of the abbé; so that he lived to see himself the last of his sect, except Monsieur B———, of Paris, his *élève* and immediate disciple.

What gave my book the more sudden and general celebrity, was the success of one of its proposed experiments, made by Messrs Dalibard and de Lor at Marly, for drawing lightning from the clouds. This engag'd the public attention everywhere. M. de Lor, who had an apparatus for experimental philosophy, and lectur'd in that branch of science, undertook to repeat what he called the *Philadelphia Experiments*; and, after they were performed before the king and court, all the curious of Paris flocked to see them. I will not swell this narrative with an account of that capital experiment, nor of the infinite pleasure I receiv'd in the success of a similar one I made soon after with a kite at Philadelphia, as both are to be found in the histories of electricity.

Dr Wright, an English physician, when at Paris, wrote to a friend, who was of the Royal Society, an account of the high esteem my experiments were in among the learned abroad, and of their wonder that my writings had been so little noticed in England. The society, on this, resum'd the consideration of the letters that had been read to them; and the celebrated Dr Watson drew up a summary account of them, and of all I had afterwards sent to England on the subject, which he accompanied with some praise of the writer. This summary was then printed in their Transactions; and some members of the society in London, particularly the very ingenious Mr Canton, having verified the experiment of procuring lightning from the clouds by a pointed rod, and acquainting them with the success, they soon made me more than amends for the slight with which they had before treated me. Without my having made any application for that honor, they chose me a member, and voted that I should be excus'd the customary payments, which would have amounted to twenty-five guineas; and ever since have given me their Transactions gratis. They also presented me with the gold medal of Sir Godfrey Copley for the year 1753, the delivery of which was accompanied by a very handsome speech of the president, Lord Macclesfield, wherein I was highly honored.

# On Inoculation

## VOLTAIRE

The rest of Europe, that is, the Christian part of it, very gravely assert that the English are fools and madmen; fools, because they give smallpox to their children, in order to keep them from getting it; madmen, because with perfect ease they give their children a dreadful disease, with the aim of preventing a possible evil. The English, on their side, call the rest of Europe unnatural and cowardly; unnatural, in leaving their children exposed to death from smallpox; and cowardly, in fearing to give their children a trifling pain. In order to determine which of the two is in the right, I shall now relate the history of this famous practice, which is discussed outside of England with so much dread.

The women of Circassia have from time immemorial been accustomed to giving their children smallpox, even as early as at six months of age, by making an incision in the arm, and afterward inserting in this incision a pustule carefully taken from the body of some other child. This pustule so insinuated produces in the body of the patient the same effect that leaven does in a piece of dough; that is, it ferments in it, and communicates to the mass of blood the qualities with which it is impregnated. The pustules of the child infected in this manner with smallpox serve to convey the same disease to others. It is perpetually circulating through the different parts of Circassia; and when, unluckily, there is no infection of smallpox in the country, it creates the same uneasiness as an unhealthy season would have occasioned.

What has given rise to this custom in Circassia, and which seems so strange to other nations, is, however, a cause common to all the nations on the face of the earth; that is, the tenderness of mothers, and motives of interest.

The Circassians are poor, and their daughters are beautiful; hence, they are the principal article of their foreign commerce. It is they who supply beauties for the harems of the grand seigneur, the sufi of Persia, and others who are rich enough to purchase and to maintain these precious commodities. These people train their children in the complete art of dancing lasciviously and of arousing by the most voluptuous artifices, the desire of those haughty lords to whom they are destined. These poor creatures repeat their lesson every day with their mothers, in the same manner as our girls do their catechism; that is, without understanding a thing about it.

Now it often happened that a father and mother, after having taken great pains in giving their children a good education, suddenly see their hopes frustrated. Smallpox getting into the family, one daughter perhaps died; another lost an eye; a third recovered, but with a disfigured nose; so that the poor folk were hopelessly ruined. Often, too, when there was an epidemic, commerce was interrupted for several years which caused notable decline in the seraglios of Turkey and Persia.

A commercial people are always very much alert to their interests, and never neglect knowledge that may be of use in the carrying on of their trade. The Circassians found that of a thousand persons there was hardly one that was ever twice infected by smallpox completely formed; that there had been instances of a person's having had a slight touch of it, or something resembling it, but there never were any two cases known to be dangerous; in short, never has the same person been known to have been twice infected with this disorder. They also noticed that when the disease is mild, and the eruption has only to pierce through a thin and delicate skin, it leaves no mark on the face. From these natural observations they concluded, that if a child of six months or a year old was to have a mild kind of smallpox, not only would the child certainly survive, but it would get better without bearing any marks of it, and would be immune during the rest of its life.

Hence it followed, that to save the life and beauty of their children, their only method would be to give them the disease early, which they did, by inserting into the child's body a pustule taken from the body of one infected with smallpox, the most completely formed, and at the same time the most favorable kind that could be found. The experiment could hardly fail. The Turks, a very sensible people, soon adopted this practice; and, at this day, there is scarcely a pasha in Constantinople who does not inoculate his children while they are at the breast.

There are some who pretend that the Circassians formerly learned this custom from the Arabians. We will leave this point in history to be elucidated by some learned Benedictine, who will not fail to compose several large volumes upon the subject, together with the necessary proof. All I have to say of the matter is that, in the beginning of the reign of George I, Lady Mary Wortley Montagu, one of the most celebrated ladies in England for her strong and solid good sense, happening to be with her husband at Constantinople, resolved to give smallpox to a child she had had in that country. In vain did her chaplain remonstrate that this practice was not Christian, and could only be expected to succeed with infidels; my lady Wortley's son recovered, and was presently as well as could be wished. This lady, on her return to London, communicated the experiment she had made to the princess of Wales, now queen of Great Britain. It must be admitted that, setting crowns and titles aside, this princess is certainly born for the encouragement of arts, and for the good of the human race. She is an amiable philosopher seated on a throne, who has improved every opportunity of instruction, and has never lost any occasion of showing her generosity. It is she who, on hearing that a daughter of Milton was still living, and in extreme misery, immediately sent her a valuable present; she it is who encourages the celebrated Father Courayer; in a word, it is she who deigned to become the mediator between Dr. Clarke and Mr. Leibnitz. As soon as she heard of inoculation for smallpox, she had it tried on four criminals under sentence of death, who were thus doubly indebted to her for their lives: for she not only rescued them from the gallows, but, by means of this artificial attack of smallpox, prevented them from having it in the natural way, which in all probability they would have had, and of which they might have died at a more advanced age.

The princess, thus assured of the utility of this proof, had her own children inoculated. All England followed her example; and from that time at least ten thousand children are indebted for their lives to Lady Mary Wortley Montagu, as are all the girls for their beauty.

Out of every hundred persons, at least sixty contract smallpox; of these sixty, twenty die, in the most favorable times, and twenty more wear disagreeable marks of this cruel disease as long as they live. Here is then a fifth part of the human race killed, or, at least, horribly disfigured. Among the vast numbers inoculated in Great Britain, or in Turkey, none are ever known to die, except such as were in a very ill state of health, and doomed to die in any case. No one is marked by it; no one is ever infected a second time, supposing the inoculation to be perfect. It is, therefore, certain that, had some French lady imported this secret from Constantinople into Paris, she would have rendered an everlasting service to the nation. The duke de Villequier, father of the present duke d'Aumont, a nobleman of the most robust constitution, would not have been cut off in the flower of his age.

The prince de Soubise, who enjoyed the most remarkable state of good health ever known, would not have been carried off at twenty-five; nor would the grandfather of Louis XV have been laid in his grave by it in his fiftieth year. The twenty thousand persons who died at Paris in 1723 would have been now alive. What shall we say then? Is it that the French do not love life? Are they indifferent to beauty? It is true that we are a very odd kind of people! It is possible that in ten years we may think of adopting this British custom, provided the doctors and curates allow it; or, perhaps, the French will inoculate their children, out of sheer whim, should those islanders leave it off, out of natural inconstancy.

I learn that the Chinese have practised this custom for a hundred years; the example of a nation that is considered the wisest and the best governed in the universe, is a strong prejudice in its favor. It is true, the Chinese follow a method peculiar to themselves; they make no incision, but take smallpox up the nose in powder, just as we do a pinch of snuff: this method is more pleasant, but amounts to much the same thing, and serves equally to prove that had inoculation been practised in France, it would have saved the lives of thousands.

# from *Essay on Man*

## ALEXANDER POPE

Know then thyself, presume not God to scan;
The proper study of Mankind is Man.
Plac'd on this isthmus of a middle state,
A Being darkly wise, and rudely great:
With too much knowledge for the Sceptic side,
With too much weakness for the Stoic's pride,
He hangs between; in doubt to act, or rest;
In doubt to deem himself a God, or Beast;
In doubt his Mind or Body to prefer;
Born but to die, and reas'ning but to err;
Alike in ignorance, his reason such,
Whether he thinks too little, or too much:
Chaos of Thought and Passion, all confus'd;
Still by himself abus'd, or disabus'd;
Created half to rise, and half to fall;
Great lord of all things, yet a prey to all;
Sole judge of Truth, in endless Error hurl'd:
The glory, jest, and riddle of the world!
    Go, wond'rous creature! mount where Science guides,
Go, measure earth, weigh air, and state the tides;
Instruct the planets in what orbs to run,
Correct old Time, and regulate the Sun;
Go, soar with Plato to th' empyreal sphere,
To the first good, first perfect, and first fair;
Or tread the mazy round his follow'rs trod,
And quitting sense call imitating God;
As Eastern priests in giddy circles run,
And turn their heads to imitate the Sun.
Go, teach Eternal Wisdom how to rule —
Then drop into thyself, and be a fool!

Superior beings, when of late they saw
A mortal Man unfold all Nature's law,
Admir'd such wisdom in an earthly shape,
And shew'd a NEWTON as we shew an Ape.

# On the Association of Ideas

## DAVID HUME

As all simple ideas may be separated by the imagination, and may be united again in what form it pleases, nothing would be more unaccountable than the operations of that faculty, were it not guided by some universal principles, which render it, in some measure, uniform with itself in all times and places. Were ideas entirely loose and unconnected, chance alone would join them; and it is impossible the same simple ideas should fall regularly into complex ones (as they commonly do), without some bond of union among them, some associating quality, by which one idea naturally introduces another. This uniting principle among ideas is not to be considered as an inseparable connexion; for that has been already excluded from the imagination: nor yet are we to conclude that without it the mind cannot join two ideas; for nothing is more free than that faculty: but we are only to regard it as a gentle force, which commonly prevails, and is the cause why, among other things, languages so nearly correspond to each other; nature, in a manner, pointing out to every one those simple ideas which are most proper to be united into a complex one. The qualities from which this association arises, and by which the mind is, after this manner, conveyed from one idea to another, are three, viz., Resemblance, Contiguity in time or place, and Cause and Effect.

I believe it will not be very necessary to prove that these qualities produce an association among ideas, and upon the appearance of one idea naturally introduce another. It is plain, that, in the course of our thinking, and in the constant revolution of our ideas, our imagination runs easily from one idea to any other that *resembles* it, and that this quality alone is to the fancy a sufficient bond and association. It is likewise evident that as the senses in changing their objects are necessitated to change them regularly, and take them as they lie *contiguous* to each other, the imagination must, by long custom, acquire the same method of thinking, and run along the parts of space and time in conceiving its objects. As to the connexion that is made by the relation of *cause and effect*, we shall have occasion afterwards to examine it to the bottom, and therefore shall not at present insist upon it. It is sufficient to observe that there is no relation which produces a stronger connexion in the fancy, and makes one idea more readily recall another, than the relation of cause and effect betwixt their objects.

That we may understand the full extent of these relations, we must consider that two objects are connected together in the imagination, not only when the one is immediately resembling, contiguous to, or the cause of, the other, but also when there is interposed betwixt them a third object which bears to both of them any of these relations. This may be carried on to a great length; though at the same time we may observe that each remove considerably weakens the relation. Cousins in the fourth degree are connected by *causation*, if I may be allowed to use that term; but not so closely as brothers, much less as child and parent. In general, we may observe that all the relations of blood depend upon cause and effect, and are esteemed near or remote, according to the number of connecting causes interposed betwixt the persons.

Of the three relations above-mentioned, this of causation is the most extensive. Two objects may be considered as placed in this relation, as well when one is the cause of any of the actions or motions of the other, as when the former is the cause of the existence of the later. For as that action or motion is nothing but the object itself, considered in a certain light, and as the object continues the same in all its different situations, it is easy to imagine how such an influence of objects upon one another may connect them in the imagination.

We may carry this farther, and remark not only that two objects are connected by the relation of cause and effect when the one produces a motion or any action in the other, but also when it has a power of producing it. And this we may observe to be the source of all the relations of interest and duty, by which men influence each other in society, and are placed in the ties of government and subordination. A master is such a one as, by his situation, arising either from force or agreement, has a power of directing in certain particulars the actions of another, whom we call servant. A judge is one who, in all disputed cases, can fix by his opinion the possession or property of anything betwixt any members of the society. When a person is possessed of any power there is no more required to convert it into action, but the exertion of the will; and *that* in every case is considered as possible, and in many as probable; especially in the case of authority, where the obedience of the subject is a pleasure and advantage to the superior.

These are, therefore, the principles of union or cohesion among our simple ideas, and in the imagination supply the place of that inseparable connexion, by which they are united in our memory. Here is a kind of Attraction, which in the mental world will be found to have as extraordinary effects as in the natural, and to show itself in as many and as various forms. Its effects are everywhere conspicuous; but, as to its causes, they are mostly unknown, and must be resolved into *original* qualities of human nature, which I pretend not to explain. Nothing is more requisite for a true philosopher than to restrain the intemperate desire of searching into causes, and, having established any doctrine upon a sufficient number of experiments, rest contented with that, when he sees a farther examination would lead him into obscure and uncertain speculations. In that case his inquiry would be much better employed in examining the effects than the causes of his principle.

Amongst the effects of this union or association of ideas, there are none more remarkable than those complex ideas which are the common subjects of our thoughts and reasoning, and generally arise from some principle of union among our simple ideas. These complex ideas may be divided into *Relations, Modes,* and *Substances.* We shall briefly examine each of these in order, and shall subjoin some considerations concerning our *general* and *particular* ideas, before we leave the present subject, which may be considered as the elements of this philosophy.

# from *The Life and Opinions of Tristram Shandy, Gent.*

## LAURENCE STERNE

I wish either my father or my mother, or indeed both of them, as they were in duty both equally bound to it, had minded what they were about when they begot me; had they duly considered how much depended upon what they were then doing; — that not only the production of a rational Being was concerned in it, but that possibly the happy formation and temperature of his body, perhaps his genius and the very cast of his mind; — and, for aught they knew to the contrary, even the fortunes of his whole house might take their turn from the humours and dispositions which were then uppermost; —— Had they duly weighed and considered all this, and proceeded accordingly, —— I am verily persuaded I should have made a quite different figure in the world, from that in which the reader is likely to see me. — Believe me, good folks, this is not so inconsiderable a thing as many of you may think it; — you have all, I dare say, heard of the animal spirits, as how they are transfused from father to son, etc. etc. — and a great deal to that purpose: — Well, you may take my word, that nine parts in ten of a man's sense or his nonsense, his successes and miscarriages in this world depend upon their motions and activity, and the different tracts and trains you put them into, so that when they are once set a-going, whether right or wrong, 'tis not a halfpenny matter, — away they go cluttering like hey-go mad; and by treading the same steps over and over again, they presently make a road of it, as plain and as smooth as a garden-walk, which, when they are once used to, the Devil himself sometimes shall not be able to drive them off it.

"Pray, my Dear," quoth my mother, "have you not forgot to wind up the clock?" —— "Good G — !" cried my father, making an exclamation, but taking care to moderate his voice at the same time, —— "Did ever woman, since the creation of the world, interrupt a man with such a silly question?" Pray, what was your father saying? —— Nothing.

—— Then, positively, there is nothing in the question that I can see, either good or bad. —— Then, let me tell you, Sir, it was a very unseasonable question at least, — because it scattered and dispersed the animal spirits, whose business it was to have escorted and gone hand in hand with the HOMUNCULUS, and conducted him safe to the place destined for his reception.

The Homunculus, Sir, in however low and ludicrous a light he may appear, in this age of levity, to the eye of folly or prejudice; — to the eye of reason in scientific research, he stands confessed — a Being guarded and circumscribed with rights. —— The minutest philosophers, who, by the bye, have the most enlarged understandings, (their souls being inversely as their enquiries) shew us incontestably, that the Homunculus is created by the same hand, — engendered in the same course of nature, — endowed with the same locomotive powers and faculties with us: — That he consists as we do, of skin, hair, fat, flesh, veins, arteries, ligaments, nerves, cartilages, bones, marrow, brains, glands, genitals, humours and articulations; — is a Being of as much activity, — and, in all senses of the word, as

much and as truly our fellow-creature as my Lord Chancellor of England.
— He may be benefited, — he may be injured, — he may obtain redress; —
in a word, he has all the claims and rights of humanity, which Tully,
Puffendorf, or the best ethic writers allow to arise out of that state and
relation.

Now, dear Sir, what if any accident had befallen him in his way alone!
— or that, through terror of it, natural to so young a traveller, my little
Gentleman had got to his journey's end miserably spent; — his muscular
strength and virility worn down to a thread; — his own animal spirits
ruffled beyond description, — and that in this sad disordered state of
nerves, he had lain down a prey to sudden starts, or a series of melancholy
dreams and fancies, for nine long, long months together. — I tremble to
think what a foundation had been laid for a thousand weaknesses both
of body and mind, which no skill of the physician or the philosopher
could ever afterwards have set thoroughly to rights.

To my uncle Mr. Toby Shandy do I stand indebted for the preceding
anecdote, to whom my father, who was an excellent natural philosopher,
and much given to close reasoning upon the smallest matters, had oft,
and heavily complained of the injury; but once more particularly, as my
uncle Toby well remembered, upon his observing a most unaccountable
obliquity, (as he called it) in my manner of setting up my top, and justi-
fying the principles upon which I had done it, — the old gentleman shook
his head, and in a tone more expressive by half of sorrow than reproach,
— he said his heart all along foreboded, and he saw it verified in this, and
from a thousand other observations he had made upon me, That I should
neither think nor act like any other man's child: — "But alas!" continued
he, shaking his head a second time, and wiping away a tear which was
trickling down his cheeks, "My Tristram's misfortunes began nine months
before ever he came into the world."

— My mother, who was sitting by, looked up, — but she knew no more
than her backside what my father meant, — but my uncle, Mr. Toby
Shandy, who had been often informed of the affair, — understood him
very well.

I know there are readers in the world, as well as many other good
people in it, who are no readers at all, — who find themselves ill at ease,
unless they are let into the whole secret from first to last, of everything
which concerns you.

It is in pure compliance with this humour of theirs, and from a back-
wardness in my nature to disappoint any one soul living, that I have been

so very particular already. As my life and opinions are likely to make some noise in the world, and, if I conjecture right, will take in all ranks, professions, and denominations of men whatever, — be no less read than the *Pilgrim's Progress* itself — and in the end, prove the very thing which Montaigne dreaded his Essays should turn out, that is, a book for a parlour-window; — I find it necessary to consult every one a little in his turn; and therefore must beg pardon for going on a little further in the same way: For which cause, right glad I am, that I have begun the history of myself in the way I have done; and that I am able to go on, tracing every thing in it, as Horace says, *ab Ovo*.

Horace, I know does not recommend this fashion altogether: But that gentleman is speaking only of an epic poem or a tragedy; — (I forget which,) — besides, if it was not so, I should beg Mr. Horace's pardon; — for in writing what I have set about, I shall confine myself neither to his rules, nor to any man's rules that ever lived.

To such, however, as do not choose to go so far back into these things, I can give no better advice, than that they skip over the remaining part of this chapter; for I declare beforehand, 'tis wrote only for the curious and inquisitive.

———————————————— Shut the door ————————————————

I was begot in the night, betwixt the first Sunday and the first Monday in the month of March, in the year of our Lord one thousand seven hundred and eighteen. I am positive I was, — But how I came to be so very particular in my account of a thing which happened before I was born, is owing to another small anecdote known only in our own family, but now made public for the better clearing up this point.

My father, you must know, who was originally a Turkey merchant, but had left off business for some years, in order to retire to, and die upon, his paternal estate in the county of ———, was, I believe, one of the most regular men in everything he did, whether 'twas matter of business, or matter of amusement, that ever lived. As a small specimen of this extreme exactness of his, to which he was in truth a slave, — he had made it a rule for many years of his life — on the first Sunday-night of every month throughout the whole year, — as certain as ever the Sunday-night came, —— to wind up a large house-clock, which we had standing on the backstairs head, with his own hands: — And being somewhere between fifty and sixty years of age at the time I have been speaking of, — he had likewise gradually brought some other little family concernments to the same period, in order, as he would often say to my uncle Toby, to get them all out of the way at one time, and be no more plagued and pestered with them the rest of the month.

It was attended with but one misfortune, which, in a great measure, fell upon myself, and the effects of which I fear I shall carry with me to my grave; namely, that from an unhappy association of ideas, which have no connection in nature, it so fell out at length, that my poor mother could never hear the said clock wound up, — but the thoughts of some other things unavoidably popped into her head — and *vice versâ:* —— Which strange combination of ideas, the sagacious Locke, who certainly understood the nature of these things better than most men, affirms to have produced more wry actions than all other sources of prejudice whatsoever.

But this by the bye.

Now it appears by a memorandum in my father's pocket-book, which now lies upon the table, "That on Lady-day, which was on the 25th of the same month in which I date my geniture, — my father set out upon his journey to London, with my eldest brother Bobby, to fix him at Westminster school"; and, as it appears from the same authority, "That he did not get down to his wife and family till the second week in May following," — it brings the thing almost to a certainty. However, what follows in the beginning of the next chapter, puts it beyond all possibility of doubt.

—— But pray, Sir, What was your father doing all December, — January, and February? —— Why, Madam, — he was all that time afflicted with a Sciatica.

On the fifth day of November, 1718, which to the era fixed on, was as near nine calendar months as any husband could in reason have expected, — was I Tristram Shandy, Gentleman, brought forth into this scurvy and disastrous world of ours. —— I wish I had been born in the Moon, or in any of the planets, (except Jupiter or Saturn, because I never could bear cold weather) for it could not well have fared worse with me in any of them (though I will not answer for Venus) than it has in this vile, dirty planet of ours, — which, o' my conscience, with reverence be it spoken, I take to be made up of the shreds and clippings of the rest; —— not but the planet is well enough, provided a man could be born in it to a great title or to a great estate; or could any how contrive to be called up to public charges, and employments of dignity or power; —— but that is not my case; —— and therefore every man will speak of the fair as his own market has gone in it; —— for which cause I affirm it over again to be one of the vilest worlds that ever was made; — for I can truly say, that from the first hour I drew my breath in it, to this, that I can now scarce draw it at all, for an asthma I got in skating against the wind in Flanders; — I have been the continual sport of what the world calls Fortune; and though I will not wrong her by saying, She has ever made me feel the weight of any great or signal evil; —— yet with all the good temper in the world, I affirm it of her, that in every stage of my life, and at every turn and corner where she could get fairly at me, the ungracious duchess has pelted me with a set of as pitiful misadventures and cross accidents as ever small Hero sustained.

In the beginning of the last chapter, I informed you exactly when I was born; but I did not inform you how, No, that particular was reserved entirely for a chapter by itself; — besides, Sir, as you and I are in a manner perfect strangers to each other, it would not have been proper to have let you into too many circumstances relating to myself all at once. — You must have a little patience. I have undertaken, you see, to write not only my life, but my opinions also; hoping and expecting that your knowledge of my character, and of what kind of a mortal I am, by the one, would give you a better relish for the other: As you proceed farther with me, the slight acquaintance, which is now beginning betwixt us, will grow into familiarity; and that, unless one of us is in fault, will terminate in friendship. — *O diem praeclarum!* — then nothing which has touched me will be thought trifling in its nature, or tedious in its telling. Therefore, my dear friend and companion, if you should think me somewhat sparing of my narrative on my first setting out — bear with me, — and let me go on, and tell my story my own way: — Or, if I should seem now and then to trifle upon the road, — or should sometimes put on a fool's cap with a bell to it, for a moment or two as we pass along, — don't fly off, — but rather courteously give me credit for a little more wisdom than appears upon my outside; — and as we jog on, either laugh with me, or at me, or in short, do anything, — only keep your temper.

In the same village where my father and my mother dwelt, dwelt also a thin, upright, motherly, notable, good old body of a midwife, who with the help of a little plain good sense, and some years' full employment in her business, in which she had all along trusted little to her own efforts, and a great deal to those of dame Nature, — had acquired, in her way, no small degree of reputation in the world: —— by which the word *world,* need I in this place inform your worship, that I would be understood to mean no more of it, than a small circle described upon the circle of the great world, of four English miles diameter, or thereabouts, of which the cottage where the good old woman lived, is supposed to be the centre? — She had been left, it seems, a widow in great distress, with three or four small children, in her forty-seventh year; and as she was at that time a person of decent carriage, — grave deportment, — a woman moreover of few words, and withal an object of compassion, whose distress, and silence under it, called out the louder for a friendly lift: the wife of the parson of the parish was touched with pity; and having often lamented an inconvenience, to which her husband's flock had for many years been exposed, inasmuch as there was no such thing as a midwife, of any kind or degree, to be got at, let the case have been never so urgent, within less than six or seven long miles riding; which said seven long miles in dark nights and dismal roads, the country thereabouts being nothing but a deep clay, was almost equal to fourteen; and that in effect was sometimes next to having no midwife at all; it came into her head, that it would be doing as seasonable a kindness to the whole parish, as to the poor creature herself, to get her a little instructed in some of the plain principles of the business, in order to set her up in it. As no woman thereabouts was better qualified to execute the plan she had formed than herself, the gentlewoman very charitably undertook it; and having great influence over the female part of the parish, she found no difficulty in effecting it to the utmost of her wishes. In truth, the parson joined his interest with his wife's in the whole affair; and in order to do things as they should be, and give the poor soul as good a title by law to practice, as his wife had given by institution, — he cheerfully paid the fees for the ordinary's licence himself, amounting in the whole, to the sum of eighteen shillings and four pence; so that betwixt them both, the good woman was fully invested in the real and corporal possession of her office, together with all its rights, members, and appurtenances whatsoever.

These last words, you must know, were not according to the old form in which such licences, faculties, and powers usually ran, which in like cases had heretofore been granted to the sisterhood. But it was according to a neat Formula of Didius his own devising, who having a particular turn for taking to pieces, and new framing over again, all kinds of instruments in that way, not only hit upon this dainty amendment, but coaxed many of the old licensed matrons in the neighbourhood, to open their faculties afresh, in order to have this wham-wham of his inserted.

I own I never could envy Didius in these kinds of fancies of his: — But every man to his own taste. — Did not Dr. Kunastrokius, that great man, at his leisure hours, take the greatest delight imaginable in combing of asses tails, and plucking the dead hairs out with his teeth, though he had tweezers always in his pocket? Nay, if you come to that, Sir, have not the wisest of men in all ages, not excepting Solomon himself, — have they not had their Hobby-Horses; — their running horses, — their coins and their

cockle-shells, their drums and their trumpets, their fiddles, their pallets, —
their maggots and their butterflies? — and so long as a man rides his Hobby-
Horse peaceably and quietly along the King's highway, and neither compels you or me to get up behind him, — pray, Sir, what have either you
or I to do with it?

— *De gustibus non est disputandum;* — that is, there is no disputing
against Hobby-Horses; and for my part, I seldom do; nor could I with
any sort of grace, had I been an enemy to them at the bottom; for happening, at certain intervals and changes of the moon, to be both fiddler
and painter, according as the fly stings: — Be it known to you, that I keep
a couple of pads myself, upon which, in their turns, (nor do I care who
knows it) I frequently ride out and take the air; — though sometimes, to
my shame be it spoken, I take somewhat longer journeys than what a
wise man would think altogether right. — But the truth is, — I am not a
wise man; — and besides am a mortal of so little consequence in the world,
it is not much matter what I do: so I seldom fret or fume at all about it:
Nor does it much disturb my rest, when I see such great Lords and tall
Personages as hereafter follow: — such, for instance, as my Lord A, B, C,
D, E, F, G, H, I, K, L, M, N, O, P, Q, and so on, all of a row, mounted
upon their several horses, some with large stirrups, getting on in a more
grave and sober pace; — — others on the contrary, tucked up to their very
chins, with whips across their mouths, scouring and scampering it away
like so many little party-coloured devils astride a mortgage, — and as if
some of them were resolved to break their necks. — — So much the better —
say I to myself; — for in case the worst should happen, the world will
make a shift to do excellently well without them; and for the rest, — — why
— — God speed them — — e'en let them ride on without opposition from me;
for were their lordships unhorsed this very night — 'tis ten to one but that
many of them would be worse mounted by one half before to-morrow
morning.

Not one of these instances therefore can be said to break in upon my
rest. — — But there is an instance, which I own puts me off my guard, and
that is, when I see one born for great actions, and what is still more for
his honour, whose nature ever inclines him to good ones; — when I behold
such a one, my Lord, like yourself, whose principles and conduct are as
generous and noble as his blood, and whom, for that reason, a corrupt
world cannot spare one moment; — when I see such a one, my Lord,
mounted, though it is but for a minute beyond the time which my love
to my country has prescribed to him, and my zeal for his glory wishes, —
then, my Lord, I cease to be a philosopher, and in the first transport of
an honest impatience, I wish the Hobby-Horse, with all his fraternity,

at the Devil.

"MY LORD,

"I maintain this to be a dedication, notwithstanding its singularity in the three great essentials of matter, form, and place: I beg, therefore, you will accept it as such, and that you will permit me to lay it, with the most respectful humility, at your Lordship's feet, — when you are upon them, — which you can be when you please; — and that is, my Lord, whenever there is occasion for it, and I will add, to the best purposes too. I have the honour to be,

"*My Lord,*
*Your Lordship's most obedient,*
*and most devoted,*
*and most humble servant,*
Tristram Shandy."

I solemnly declare to all mankind, that the above dedication was made for no one Prince, Prelate, Pope, or Potentate, — Duke, Marquis, Earl, Viscount, or Baron, of this, or any other Realm in Christendom; — nor has it yet been hawked about, or offered publicly or privately, directly or indirectly, to any one person or personage, great or small; but is honestly a true Virgin-Dedication untried on, upon any soul living.

I labour this point so particularly, merely to remove any offence or objection which might arise against it from the manner in which I propose to make the most of it; — which is the putting it up fairly to public sale; which I now do.

—— Every author has a way of his own in bringing his points to bear; — for my own part, as I hate chaffering and higgling for a few guineas in a dark entry; — I resolved within myself, from the very beginning, to deal squarely and openly with your Great Folks in this affair, and try whether I should not come off the better by it.

If therefore there is any one Duke, Marquis, Earl, Viscount, or Baron, in these his Majesty's dominions, who stands in need of a tight, genteel dedication, and whom the above will suit, (for by the bye, unless it suits in some degree I will not part with it) —— it is much at his service for fifty guineas; —— which I am positive is twenty guineas less than it ought to be afforded for, by any man of genius.

My Lord, if you examine it over again, it is far from being a gross piece of daubing, as some dedications are. The design, your Lordship sees, is good, — the colouring transparent, — the drawing not amiss; — or to speak more like a man of science, — and measure my piece in the painter's scale, divided into 20, — I believe, my Lord, the outlines will turn out as 12, — the composition as 9, — the colouring as 6, — the expression 13 and a half, — and the design, — if I may be allowed, my Lord, to understand my own design, and supposing absolute perfection in designing, to be as 20, — I think it cannot well fall short of 19. Besides all this, — there is keeping in it, and the dark strokes in the Hobby-Horse, (which is a secondary figure, and a kind of back-ground to the whole) give great force to the principal lights in your own figure, and make it come off wonderfully; — and besides, there is an air of originality in the *tout ensemble.*

Be pleased, my good Lord, to order the sum to be paid into the hands of Mr. Dodsley, for the benefit of the author, and in the next edition care shall be taken that this chapter be expunged, and your Lordship's titles, distinctions, arms, and good actions, be placed at the front of the preceding chapter: All which, from the words, *De gustibus non est disputandum,* and whatever else in this book relates to Hobby-Horses, but no more, shall stand dedicated to your Lordship. — The rest I dedicate to the Moon, who, by the bye, of all the Patrons or Matrons I can think of, has most power to set my book a-going, and make the world run mad after it.

Bright Goddess,

If thou art not too busy with Candid and Miss Cunegund's affairs, — take Tristram Shandy's under thy protection also.

# V

# The Vision of Progress

*In all fields progress became an article of Enlightenment faith. Late in the preceding century Fontenelle had argued that, with the achievements of the Ancients as their starting points, it was inevitable for the Moderns to advance beyond them. Debate over the standing of the Ancients and the Moderns was so frequent in the eighteenth century that Swift made it the subject of one of his satires,* The Battle of the Books. *Toward the end of the century the balance began to shift back to the Ancients, particularly in the idolization of the Greeks, which, with the German archaeologist Winckelmann, became part of the romantic movement.*

# from *The Progress of the Human Mind*

## THE MARQUIS DE CONDORCET

Man is born with the faculty of receiving sensations. In those which he receives, he is capable of perceiving and of distinguishing the simple sensations of which they are composed. He can retain, recognize, combine them. He can preserve or recall them to his memory; he can compare their different combinations; he can ascertain what they possess in common, and what characterizes each; lastly, he can affix signs to all these objects, the better to know them, and the more easily to form from them new combinations.

This faculty is developed in him by the action of external objects, that is, by the presence of certain complex sensations, the constancy of which, whether in their identical whole, or in the laws of their change, is independent of himself. It is also exercised by communication with other similarly organized individuals, and by all the artificial means which, from the first development of this faculty, men have succeeded in inventing.

Sensations are accompanied with pleasure or pain, and man has the further faculty of converting these momentary impressions into durable sentiments of a corresponding nature, and of experiencing these sentiments either at the sight or recollection of the pleasure or pain of beings sensitive like himself. And from this faculty, united with that of forming and combining ideas, arise, between him and his fellow creatures, the ties of interest and duty, to which nature has affixed the most exquisite portion of our felicity, and the most poignant of our sufferings.

Were we to confine our observations to an enquiry into the general facts and unvarying laws which the development of these faculties presents to us, in what is common to the different individuals of the human species, our enquiry would bear the name of metaphysics.

But if we consider this development in its results, relative to the mass of individuals coexisting at the same time on a given space, and follow it from generation to generation, it then exhibits a picture of the progress of the human intellect. This progress is subject to the same general laws, observable in the individual development of our faculties; being the result of that very development considered at once in a great number of individuals united in society. But the result which every instant presents, depends upon that of the preceeding instants, and has an influence on the instants which follow.

This picture, therefore, is historical; since, subjected as it will be to perpetual variations, it is formed by the successive observation of human societies at the different eras through which they have passed. It will accordingly exhibit the order in which the changes have taken place, explain the influence of every past period upon that which follows it, and thus show, by the modifications which the human species has experienced, in its incessant renovation through the immensity of ages, the course which it has pursued, and the steps which it has advanced towards knowledge and happiness. From these observations on what man has heretofore been, and what he is at present, we shall be led to the means of securing and of accelerating the still further progress, of which, from his nature, we may indulge the hope.

Such is the object of the work I have undertaken; the result of which will be to show, from reasoning and from facts, that no bounds have been fixed to the improvement of the human faculties; that the perfectibility of man is absolutely indefinite; that the progress of this perfectibility, henceforth above the control of every power that would impede it, has no other limit than the duration of the globe upon which nature has placed us. The course of this progress may doubtless be more or less rapid, but it can never be retrograde; at least while the earth retains its situation in the system of the universe, and the laws of this system shall neither effect upon the globe a general overthrow, nor introduce such changes as would no longer permit the human race to preserve and exercise therein the same faculties, and find the same resources.

The first state of civilization observable in the human species, is that of a society of men, few in number, subsisting by means of hunting and fishing, unacquainted with every art but the imperfect one of fabricating in an uncouth manner their arms and some household utensils, and of constructing or digging for themselves an habitation; yet already in possession of a language for the communication of their wants, and a small number of moral ideas, from which are deduced their common rules of conduct, living in families, conforming themselves to general customs that serve instead of laws, and having even a rude form of government.

In this state it is apparent that the uncertainty and difficulty of procuring subsistence, and the unavoidable alternative of extreme fatigue or an absolute repose, leave not to man the leisure in which, by resigning himself to meditation, he might enrich his mind with new combinations. The means of satisfying his wants are even too dependent upon chance and the seasons, usefully to excite an industry, the progressive improvement of which might be transmitted to his progeny; and accordingly the attention of each is confined to the improvement of his individual skill and address.

For this reason, the progress of the human species must in this stage have been extremely slow; it could make no advance but at distant intervals, and when favored by extraordinary circumstances. Meanwhile, to the subsistence derived from hunting and fishing, or from the fruits which the earth spontaneously offered, succeeds the sustenance afforded by the animals which man has tamed, and which he knows how to preserve and multiply. To these means is afterwards added an imperfect agriculture; he is no longer content with the fruit or the plants which chance throws in his way; he learns to form a stock of them, to collect them around him, to sow or to plant them, to favour their reproduction by the labor of culture.

Property, which, in the first state, was confined to his household utensils, his arms, his nets, and the animals he killed, is now extended to his flock, and next to the land which he has cleared and cultivated. Upon the death of its head, this property naturally devolves to the family. Some individuals possess a superfluity capable of being preserved. If it be absolute, it gives rise to new wants. If confined to a single article, while the proprietor feels the want of other articles, this want suggests the idea of exchange. Hence moral relations multiply, and become complicate. A greater security, a more certain and more constant leisure, afford time for meditation, or at least for a continued series of observations. The custom is introduced, as to some individuals, of giving a part of their superfluity in exchange for labor, by which they might be exempt from labor themselves. There accordingly exists a class of men whose time is not engrossed by corporeal exertions, and whose desires extend beyond their simple wants. Industry awakes; the arts already known, expand and improve; the facts which chance presents to the observation of the most attentive and best cultivated minds, bring to light new arts; as the means of living become less dangerous and less precarious, population increases; agriculture, which can provide for a greater number of individuals upon the same space of ground, supplies the place of the other sources of subsistence; it favors the multiplication of the species, by which it is favored in its turn; in a society become more sedentary, more connected, more intimate, ideas that have been acquired communicate themselves more quickly, and are perpetuated with more certainty. And now the dawn of the sciences begins to appear; man exhibits an appearance distinct from the other classes of animals, and is no longer like them confined to an improvement purely individual.

The more extensive, more numerous and more complicated relations which men now form with each other, cause them to feel the necessity of having a mode of communicating their ideas to the absent, of preserving the remembrance of a fact with more precision than by oral tradition, of fixing the conditions of an agreement more securely than by the memory of witnesses, of stating, in a way less liable to change, those respected customs to which the members of any society agree to submit their conduct.

Accordingly the want of writing is felt, and the art invented. It appears at first to have been an absolute painting, to which succeeded a conventional painting, preserving such traits only as were characteristic of the objects. Afterwards, by a kind of metaphor analogous to that which was already introduced into their language, the image of a physical object became expressive of moral ideas. The origin of those signs, like the origin of words, was liable in time to be forgotten; and writing became the art of affixing signs of convention to every idea, every word, and of consequence to every combination of ideas and words.

There was now a language that was written, and a language that was spoken, which it was necessary equally to learn, between which there must be established a reciprocal correspondence.

Some men of genius, the eternal benefactors of the human race, but whose names and even country are for ever buried in oblivion, observed that all the words of a language were only the combinations of a very limited number of primitive articulations; but that this number, small as it was, was sufficient to form a quantity almost infinite of different combinations. Hence they conceived the idea of representing by visible signs, not the ideas or the words that answered to them, but those simple elements of which the words are composed.

Alphabetical writing was then introduced. A small number of signs served to express every thing in this mode, as a small number of sounds sufficed to express every thing orally. The language written and the language spoken were the same; all that was necessary was to be able to know, and to form, the few given signs; and this last step secured for ever the progress of the human race.

It would perhaps be desirable at the present day, to institute a written language, which, devoted to the sole use of the sciences, expressing only such combinations of simple ideas as are found to be exactly the same in every mind, employed only upon reasonings of logical strictness, upon operations of the mind precise and determinate, might be understood by men of every country, and be translated into all their idioms, without being, like those idioms, liable to corruption, by passing into common use.

Then, singular as it may appear, this kind of writing, the preservation of which would only have served to prolong ignorance, would become, in the hands of philosophy, an useful instrument for the speedy propagation of knowledge, and advancement of the sciences.

It is between this degree of civilization and that in which we still find the savage tribes, that we must place every people whose history has been handed down to us, and who, sometimes making new advancements, sometimes plunging themselves again into ignorance, sometimes floating between the two alternatives or stopping at a certain limit, sometimes totally disappearing from the earth under the sword of conquerors, mixing with those conquerors, or living in slavery; lastly, sometimes receiving knowledge from a more enlightened people, to transmit it to other nations, form an unbroken chain of connection between the earliest periods of history and the age in which we live, between the first people known to us, and the present nations of Europe.

In the picture then which I mean to sketch, three distinct parts are perceptible.

In the first, in which the relations of travelers exhibit to us the condition of mankind in the least civilized nations, we are obliged to guess by what steps man in an isolated state, or rather confined to the society necessary for the propagation of the species, was able to acquire those first degrees of improvement, the last term of which is the use of an articulate language: and acquisition that presents the most striking feature, and indeed the only one, a few more extensive moral ideas and a slight commencement of social order excepted, which distinguishes him from animals living like himself in regular and permanent society. In this part of our picture, then, we can have no other guide than an investigation of the development of our faculties.

To this first guide, in order to follow man to the point in which he exercises arts, in which the rays of science begin to enlighten him, in which nations are united by commercial intercourse; in which, in fine, alphabetical writing is invented, we may add the history of the several societies that have been observed in almost every intermediate state: though we can follow no individual one through all the space which separates these two grand epochs of the human race.

Here the picture begins to take its colouring in great measure from the series of facts transmitted to us by history: but it is necessary to select these facts from that of different nations, and at the same time compare and combine them, to form the supposed history of a single people, and delineate its progress.

From the period that alphabetical writing was known in Greece, history is connected by an uninterrupted series of facts and observations, with the period in which we live, with the present state of mankind in the most enlightened countries of Europe; and the picture of the progress and advancement of the human mind becomes strictly historical. Philosophy has no longer any thing to guess, has no more supposititious combinations to form; all it has to do is to collect and arrange facts, and exhibit the useful truths which arise from them as a whole, and from the different bearings of their several parts.

There remains only a third picture to form, — that of our hopes, or the progress reserved for future generations, which the constancy of the laws of nature seems to secure to mankind. And here it will be necessary to shew by what steps this progress, which at present may appear chimerical, is gradually to be rendered possible, and even easy; how truth, in spite of the transient success of prejudices, and the support they receive from the corruption of governments or of the people, must in the end obtain a durable triumph; by what ties nature has indissolubly united the advancement of knowledge with the progress of liberty, virtue, and respect for the natural rights of man; how these blessings, the only real ones, though so frequently seen apart as to be thought incompatible, must necessarily amalgamate and become inseparable, the moment knowledge shall have arrived at a certain pitch in a great number of nations at once, the moment it shall have penetrated the whole mass of a great people, whose language shall have become universal, and whose commercial intercourse shall embrace the whole extent of the globe. This union having once taken place in the whole enlightened class of men, this class will be considered as the friends of human kind, exerting themselves in concert to advance the improvement and happiness of the species.

We shall expose the origin and trace the history of general errors, which have more or less contributed to retard or suspend the advance of reason, and sometimes even, as much as political events, have been the cause of man's taking a retrograde course towards ignorance.

Those operations of the mind that lead to or retain us in error, from the subtle paralogism, by which the most penetrating mind may be deceived, to the mad reveries of enthusiasts, belong equally, with that just mode of reasoning that conducts us to truth, to the theory of the development of our individual faculties; and for the same reason, the manner in which general errors are introduced, propagated, transmitted, and rendered permanent among nations, forms a part of the picture of the progress of the human mind. Like truths which improve and enlighten it, they are the consequence of its activity, and of the disproportion that always exists between what it actually knows, what it has the desire to know, and what it conceives there is a necessity of acquiring.

It is even apparent, that, from the general laws of the development of our faculties, certain prejudices must necessarily spring up in each stage of our progress, and extend their seductive influence beyond that stage; because men retain the errors of their infancy, their country, and the age in which they live, long after the truths necessary to the removal of those errors are acknowledged.

In short, there exist, at all times and in all countries, different prejudices, according to the degree of illumination of the different classes of men, and according to their professions. If the prejudices of philosophers be impediments to new acquisition of truth, those of the less enlightened classes retard the propagation of truths already known, and those of esteemed and powerful professions oppose like obstacles. These are the three kinds of enemies which reason is continually obliged to encounter, and over which she frequently does not triumph till after a long and painful struggle. The history of these contests, together with that of the rise, triumph, and fall of prejudice, will occupy a considerable place in this work, and will by no means form the least important or least useful part of it.

If there be really such an art as that of foreseeing the future improvement of the human race, and of directing and hastening that improvement, the history of the progress it has already made must form the principal basis of this art. Philosophy, no doubt, ought to proscribe the superstitious idea, which supposes no rules of conduct are to be found but in the history of past ages, and no truths but in the study of the opinions of antiquity. But ought it not to include in the proscription, the prejudice that would proudly reject the lessons of experience? Certainly it is meditation alone that can, by happy combinations, conduct us to the general principles of the science of man. But if the study of individuals of the human species be of use to the metaphysician and moralist, why should that of societies be less useful to them? And why not of use to the political philosopher? If it be advantageous to observe the societies that exist at one and the same period, and to trace their connection and resemblance, why not to observe them in a succession of periods? Even supposing that such observation might be neglected in the investigation of speculative truths, ought it to be neglected when the question is to apply those truths to practice, and to deduce from science the art that should be the useful result? Do not our prejudices, and the evils that are the consequence of them, derive their source from the prejudices of our ancestors? And will it not be the surest way of undeceiving us respecting the one, and of preventing the other, to develop their origin and effects?

Are we not arrived at the point when there is no longer any thing to fear, either from new errors, or the return of old ones; when no corrupt institution can be introduced by hypocrisy, and adopted by ignorance or enthusiasm; when no vicious combination can effect the infelicity of a great people? Accordingly would it not be of advantage to know how nations have been deceived, corrupted, and plunged in misery.

Every thing tells us that we are approaching the era of one of the grand revolutions of the human race. What can better enlighten us as to what we may expect, what can be a surer guide to us, amidst its commotions, than the picture of the revolutions that have preceded and prepared the way for it? The present state of knowledge assures us that it will be happy. But is it not upon condition that we know how to assist it with all our strength? And, that the happiness it promises may be less dearly bought, that it may spread with more rapidity over a greater space, that it may be more complete in its effects, is it not requisite to study, in the history of the human mind, what obstacles remain to be feared, and by what means those obstacles are to be surmounted?

# A Letter on Human Progress

## THOMAS JEFFERSON

I am among those who think well of the human character generally. I consider man as formed for society, and endowed by nature with those dispositions which fit him for society. I believe also, with Condorcet, as mentioned in your letter, that his mind is perfectible to a degree of which we cannot as yet form any conception. It is impossible for a man who takes a survey of what is already known, not to see what an immensity in every branch of science yet remains to be discovered, and that too of articles to which our faculties seem adequate. In geometry and calculation we know a great deal. Yet there are some desiderata. In anatomy great progress has been made; but much is still to be acquired. In natural history we possess knowledge; but we want a great deal. In chemistry we are not yet sure of the first elements. Our natural philosophy is in a very infantine state; perhaps for great advances in it, a further progress in chemistry is necessary. Surgery is well advanced; but prodigiously short of what may be. The state of medecine is worse than that of total ignorance. Could we divest ourselves of every thing we suppose we know in it, we should start from a higher ground and with fairer prospects. From Hippocrates to Brown we have had nothing but a succession of hypothetical systems each having it's day of vogue, like the fashions and fancies of caps and gowns, and yielding in turn to the next caprice. Yet the human frame, which is to be the subject of suffering and torture under these learned modes, does not change. We have a few medecines, as the bark, opium, mercury, which in a few well defined diseases are of unquestionable virtue: but the residuary list of the materia medica, long as it is, contains but the charlataneries of the art; and of the diseases of doubtful form, physicians have ever had a false knowledge, worse than ignorance. Yet surely the list of unequivocal diseases and remedies is capable of enlargement; and it is still more certain that in the other branches of science, great fields are yet to be explored to which our faculties are equal, and that to an extent of which we cannot fix the limits. I join you therefore in branding as cowardly the idea that the human mind is incapable of further advances. This is precisely the doctrine which the present despots of the earth are inculcating, and their friends here re-echoing; and applying especially to religion and politics; "that it is not probable that any thing better will be discovered than what was known to our fathers." We are to look backwards then and not forwards for the improvement of science, and to find it amidst feudal barbarians and the fires of Spital-fields. But thank heaven the American mind is already too much opened, to listen to these impostures; and while the art of printing is left to us, science can never be retrograde; what is once acquired of real knowlege can never be lost. To preserve the freedom of the human mind then and freedom of the press, every spirit should be ready to devote itself to martyrdom; for as long as we may think as we will, and speak as we think, the condition of man will proceed in improvement. The generation which is going off the stage has deserved well of mankind for the struggles it has made, and for having arrested that course of despotism which had overwhelmed the world for thousands and thousands of years. If there seems to be danger that the ground they have gained will be lost again, that danger comes from the generation your cotemporary. But that the enthusiasm which characterises youth should lift it's parricide hands against freedom and science, would be such a monstrous phænomenon as I cannot place among possible things in this age and this country.

# On Classic Art

## JOHANN J. WINCKELMANN

To those who know and study the works of the Greeks, their master-pieces reveal not only nature in its greatest beauty, but something more than that; namely, certain ideal beauties of nature which, as an old commentator of Plato teaches us, exist only in the intellect.

The most beautiful bodies found among us today might, perhaps not be more similar to the Greek bodies than Iphicles was to Hercules, his brother. The influence of a mild clear climate determined the earliest development of the Greeks, but physical exercise from infancy gave this development its noble form. Take a young Spartan, bred, by a hero and heroine, never bound by swaddling clothes, who has slept on the bare ground from the age of seven and has been trained in wrestling and swimming from earliest infancy; put him beside a young Sybarite of our day and then decide which one the artist would choose as a model for a youthful Theseus, and Achilles, or even a Bacchus. Were he to choose a Sybarite, the result would be a "Theseus raised on rose petals" while the young Spartan would make a "Theseus raised on meat," as one Greek painter phrased the difference between two possible concepts of that hero.

The Greek youths were spurred to athletic prowess by the great Olympic games; and the laws demanded for these ten months' training to take place at Elis where the games themselves were held. The largest prizes were not always awarded to mature men, but often to youths, as we know from Pindar's odes. The highest ambition of Greek youth was to resemble the divine Diagoras.

Look at the swift Indian, as he hunts the stag on foot: how easily the blood courses through his veins; how supple and swift will be his nerves and muscles, how lithe his whole body! Thus Homer depicts his heroes, and his Achilles is characterized especially by his fleetness.

Through these exercises the bodies, free from superfluous fat, acquired the noble and manly contours that the Greek masters gave to their statues.

Every ten days the young Spartans had to show themselves naked before the Ephores, and those who showed signs of fat, had to follow a stricter diet. Indeed, one of the laws of Pythagoras was to beware of all excess weight. Perhaps this was the reason why the Greek youths of the earliest times were permitted only dairy dishes while they were in training for wrestling contests. Everything that disfigured the body was carefully avoided; Alcibiades refused to play the flute in his youth because it might distort his face, and the Athenian youths followed his example. Furthermore, the clothing of the Greeks was so designed as not to interfere with the natural growth of the body, while today our tight and binding dress makes the natural beauty of our bodies suffer, especially at the neck, waist, and thighs. Even the fair sex of the Greeks refused any restricting fashions. The young Spartan girls were so lightly and scantily clothed that they were called "hip-revealers."

It is also well known what great care the Greeks took to have beautiful offspring. Even Quillet, in his *Callipaedia,* knows of fewer ways to achieve this than the Greeks did. They went so far as to try changing the color of the eyes from blue to black. Another means of furthering this aim was the establishment of beauty contests. They were held at Elis and the prizes consisted of weapons that were displayed in the temple of Minerva. There could be no lack of thorough and expert judges for these contests, since the Greeks, as Aristotle relates, had all their children taught how to draw, for they believed this would help them to appreciate physical beauty.

Even today the inhabitants of most Greek islands, and especially the women of the island of Scios, are a beautiful race despite the fact they are mixed with various foreign strains. Thus they strongly suggest the beauty of their forebears, who claimed to be of a race more ancient than the moon.

Even today there are whole peoples among whom beauty is no distinction because everyone is beautiful. All travelers relate this of the Georgians, and also of the Kabardinski, a nation in the Crimean Tartary.

The diseases that destroy so much beauty and spoil even the noblest countenance were still unknown among the Greeks. In none of the writings of the Greek physicians do we find a mention of smallpox. The literary descriptions of Greeks, as Homer so frequently gives them in the most minute detail, never refer to such obvious blemishes as smallpox scars. The venereal diseases, and their result, the English *malaise,* did not devastate the beautiful bodies of the Greeks. Generally speaking everything that nature and knowledge could contribute to the growth and development of a beautiful body was used to full advantage by the Greeks, from the moment of birth to full physical maturity. The superior beauty of their bodies as compared to ours, then, is a fact that can be maintained with the greatest assurance.

In a country where the work of nature was hampered by strict laws, as in Egypt, which was the original home of the arts and of science, nature's most perfect products were likely, for the most part, to remain unknown to the artists. In Greece, however, where people devoted themselves to joy and pleasure from infancy, and where the prosperity of the citizens never affected the freedom of their customs, nature revealed itself in all its beauty, to the great benefit of the artist.

The school of the artist was the gymnasium, where the youths, ordinarily clothed because of modesty, exercised quite naked. It was the gathering place of philosophers as well as artists: Socrates visited it to teach Charmides, Artolycus and Lysis; Phidias went there to enrich his art with these magnificent figures. There one learned the movement of muscles, and studied the contours of the body, or the impressions the young wrestlers had made in the sand. The most beautiful aspects of the nude revealed themselves here in many varied and noble poses unattainable by hired models such as are used in our academies.

Only the inner sensation brings forth the essence of truth; the draftsman who wants truth in his figures will not even grasp a shadow of it unless he interpolates those elements that the soul of an indifferent model cannot possibly experience or express through passionate gestures. The introductions to many of Plato's dialogues are placed in the gymnasium of Athens and give us a conception of the noble souls of Greek youth. They permit us to assume equally harmonious actions and poses in their exercises. The most beautiful young people danced nude on the stage, and the great Sophocles in his youth was the first to do so. At the Eleusinian games, Phyrene bathed nude in public, and, rising from the waters, became to the artists the model for a Venus Anadyomene. It is also well known that at certain celebrations the Spartan girls danced naked in front of the young people. Strange as this may seem, one only has to recall that among the early Christians, men and women were baptized naked by simultaneous immersion in the same font. Thus every celebration in Greece became an opportunity for the artists to study beautiful natural forms in detail. Their generous human nature prevented the Greeks from introducing brutal spectacles. If it is true, as some say, that such entertainments were common in Ionic Asia, they must have been abolished at an early date. When Antiochus Epiphanes, king of Syria, imported Roman gladiators, the Greeks at first were filled with horror at these miserable creatures. Gradually, however, human compassion waned and these spectacles, too, became subjects for artists. From them Etesilas modelled his dying warrior, "in which one could see how much of his soul yet remained in his body."

These frequent opportunities for observing nature caused the Greek artists to go even further: they began to form general concepts of beauty for the individual parts of the body as well as for its proportions: concepts that were meant to rise above nature, being taken from a spiritual realm that existed only in the mind.

In this way Raphael formed his Galathea. As he says in his letter to Count Balthasar Castiglione, "Since beauty is rare among women, I follow a certain idea formed in my imagination."

According to such concepts, the Greeks made their gods and human beings superior to the ordinary form of material things. With gods and goddesses, the forehead and nose formed an almost straight line. The portraits of famous women on Greek coins show the same type of profile, although in these cases ideal concepts did not readily offer themselves. Or should one surmise that this was as typical a feature among the Greeks as the flat nose among the Calmucks (Tartars) or the small eyes among the Chinese? The large eyes of Greek heads on reliefs and coins might support this assumption. The Roman empresses were portrayed on Greek coins in exactly the same manner. The profiles of Livia and Agrippina resemble those of Artemisia and Cleopatra.

Nevertheless, one finds that Greek artists generally observed the law that the Thebans had made for their artists: namely, to follow nature as best they knew under threat of punishment. Where they could not employ the graceful Greek profile without prejudicing the likeness, the Greeks followed nature without modification, as can be seen in the beautiful head of Julia, daughter of the Emperor Titus, by Evodus. However, the law "to achieve portrait likeness and beauty at the same time" was always the highest rule recognized by the Greek artist and presupposed, of necessity, his intention of achieving something more beautiful and more perfect than nature. Polygnotus always observed this law. Thus I do not believe that Praxiteles deviated from this general precept of art when he fashioned the Cnidian Venus after his mistress, Cratina, nor did other masters when they took Lais as a model for the Three Graces. Work of this kind mirrors the sensuous beauty of the model while it retains the grandeur inspired by the artist's lofty concept of perfection; its human aspect derives from the first, its divine from the second source.

Anyone sufficiently enlightened to contemplate the essence of art will discover many new beauties by comparing the structure of Greek figures with that of modern works, especially when they follow nature rather than the old style. In most modern statutes, one finds many small and altogether too minute wrinkles in places where the skin is pinched. On the other hand, the analogous parts of Greek statutes show these wrinkles merging into each other in gentle, wavy curves that unify the whole area. The skin of these masterpieces shows no strains but only gentle tension: it is supported by healthy flesh without bulges. Thus it follows even the fullest contours with perfect smoothness and never produces those particular, willful little wrinkles that we observe on our bodies. Similarly, modern works display too many and too sensuous dimples, while in ancient statuary dimples are used with subtlety and wisdom, reflecting the physical perfection of the Greeks. Often only the trained eye can discover them.

Here, again, it appears probable that the bodies of the Greeks possessed more regularity, nobler proportions, and a fuller contour, without the drawn tensions and hollows found in our own bodies. Certainly, in these matters, it is impossible to go beyond the realm of probability. However, even the probability merits the attention of our artists and connoisseurs, especially since it is necessary to remove the prejudice with which many regard those who admire these monuments, and to avoid the impression that we value them as models because of their age only.

The opinions of artists vary on this subject; it demands more thorough treatment than it can receive in this context. The great Bernini is known to have been one of those who wanted to deny that the Greeks had the advantage of a more beautiful body, as well as a higher ideal of beauty. He thought that nature endowed all things with beauty; that it was the function of art to discover it. He prided himself on having lost his preconceived opinion of the superiority of the Greeks, which he had originally held because of the beauty of the Medicean Venus, when after thorough study he discovered the same beauty in nature itself.

It was, then, the statue of Venus that suggested to Bernini the appreciation of those beauties that he at first had perceived only in it and for which he would not otherwise have sought in the realm of nature. Does this not prove that it is easier to recognize the beauty of Greek statues than the beauty of nature, and that consequently the beauty of Greek statues is more moving, less diffused, and more unified? Therefore, the study of nature is a more troublesome and tortuous approach to beauty than the study of antique statuary, and Bernini did not show his students the most direct way.

# from *The Age of Louis XIV*

## VOLTAIRE

I would gladly have it in my power to do justice to all the great men who, like Newton, gave luster to their country during the last hundred years. I have called that period the age of Louis XIV, not only because that monarch gave greater encouragement to the arts than all his fellow-kings together, but also because in his lifetime he outlived three generations of the kings of Europe. I have set the limits of this epoch at some years before Louis XIV and some years after him; for it was during this space of time that the human spirit has made most progress.

From 1660 to the present day the English have made greater progress in all the arts than in all preceding ages. I will not here repeat what I have said elsewhere of Milton. It is true that some critics disapprove of his fantastic descriptions, his paradise of fools, his alabaster walls which encircle the earthly paradise; his devils, who transform themselves from giants into pygmies that they may take less room in council, seated in a vast hall of gold erected in hell; his cannons fired from heaven, his mountains hurled at the heads of foes; his angels on horseback, angels who are cut in two and their dissevered bodies as quickly joined together again. His long descriptions and repetitions are considered tedious; it is said that he has equalled neither Ovid nor Hesiod in his long description of the way in which the earth, the animals and mankind were created. His dissertations on astronomy are condemned as too dry and the creations of his fancy as being extravagant, rather than marvelous, and more disgusting than impressive; such is a long passage upon chaos; the love of Sin and Death and the children of their incest; and Death, "who turns up his nose to scent across the immensity of chaos the change that has come over the earth, like a crow scenting a corpse" — Death, who smells out the odor of the Fall, who strikes with his petrifying hammer on cold and dry; and cold and dry with hot and moist, transformed into four fine army generals, lead into battle their embryonic atoms like light-armed infantry. Criticism indeed exhausts itself, but never praise. Milton remains at once the glory and wonder of England; he is compared to Homer, whose defects are as great, and he is preferred to Dante, whose conceptions are yet more fantastic.

Among the large number of pleasing poets who graced the reign of Charles II, such as Waller, the Earl of Dorset and the Earl of Rochester, the Duke of Buckingham and many others, we must single out Dryden, who distinguished himself in every branch of poetry; his works are full of details both brilliant and true to nature, lively, vigorous, bold and passionate, merits in which none of his own nation equals him nor any of the ancients surpass him. If Pope, who succeeded him, had not written late in life his *Essay on Man,* he could not be compared to Dryden.

No other nation has treated moral subjects in poetry with greater depth and vigor than the English; there lies, it seems to me, the greatest merit of her poets.

There is another kind of elegant writing which requires at once a mind more cultured and more universal; such was Addison's; he achieved immortal fame with his *Cato,* the only English tragedy written from beginning to end in an elegant and lofty style, and his other moral and critical works breathe a perfect taste; in all he wrote, sound sense appears adorned by a lively fancy, and his manner of writing is an excellent model for any country. Dean Swift left several passages whose like is not to be found among the writers of antiquity — a Rabelais made perfect.

The English have hardly any examples of funeral orations; it is not their custom to praise their kings and queens in churches; but pulpit oratory, which was in London coarse before the reign of Charles II, suddenly improved. Bishop Burnet admits in his *Memoirs* that it was brought about by imitating the French. Perhaps they have surpassed their masters; their sermons are less formal, less pretentious and less declamatory than those of the French.

It is, moreover, remarkable that this insular people, separated from the rest of the world and so lately cultured, should have acquired at least as much knowledge of antiquity as the Italians have been able to gather in Rome, which was for so long the meeting-place of the nations. Marsham penetrated the mysteries of ancient Egypt. No Persian had such a knowledge of the Zoroastrian religion as the scholar Hyde. The Turks were unacquainted with the history of Mahomet and the preceding centuries, and its interpretation was left to the Englishman Sale, who turned his travels in Arabia to such good profit.

There is no other country in the world where the Christian religion has been so vigorously attacked and so ably defended as in England. From Henry VII to Cromwell men argued and fought, like that ancient breed of gladiators who descended into the arena sword in hand and a bandage on their eyes. A few slight differences in creed and dogma were sufficient to cause frightful wars, but from the Restoration to the present day when every Christian tenet has been almost annually attacked, such disputes have not aroused the least disturbance; science has taken the place of fire and sword to silence every argument.

It is above all in philosophy that the English have become the teachers of other nations. It is no mere question of ingenious systems. The false myths of the Greeks should have disappeared long ago and modern myths should never have appeared at all. Roger Bacon broke fresh ground by declaring that Nature must be studied in a new way, that experiments must be made; Boyle devoted his life to making them. This is no place for a dissertation on physics; it is enough to say that after three thousand years of fruitless research, Newton was the first to find and demonstrate the great natural law by which all elements of matter are mutually attracted, the law by which all the stars are held in their courses. He was indeed the first to see the light; before him it was unknown.

His principles of mathematics, which include a system of physics at once new and true, are based on the discovery of the calculus, incorrectly called *infinitesimal,* a supreme effort of geometry, and one which he made at the age of twenty-four. It was a great philosopher, the learned Halley, who said of him "that it is not permitted to any mortal to approach nearer to divinity."

A host of expert geometricians and physicists were enlightened by his discoveries and inspired by his genius. Bradley discovered the aberration of the light of fixed stars, distant at least twelve billion leagues from our small globe.

Halley, whom I have quoted above, though but an astronomer, received the command of one of the king's ships in 1698. It was on this ship that he determined the position of the stars of the Antarctic Pole, and noted the variations of the compass in all parts of the known globe. The voyage of the Argonauts was in comparison but the crossing of a bark from one side of a river to the other. Yet Halley's voyage has been hardly spoken of in Europe.

The indifference we display towards great events become too familiar, and our admiration of the ancient Greeks for trivial ones, is yet another proof of the wonderful superiority of our age over that of the ancients. Boileau in France and Sir William Temple in England obstinately refused to acknowledge such a superiority; they were eager to disparage their own age, in order to place themselves above it: but the dispute between the ancients and the moderns has been at last decided, at any rate in the field of philosophy. There is not a single ancient philosopher whose works are taught today to the youth of any enlightened nation.

Locke alone should serve as a good example of the advantage of our age over the most illustrious ages of Greece. From Plato to Locke there is indeed nothing; no one in that interval developed the operations of the human mind, and a man who knew the whole of Plato and only Plato, would know little and that not well.

Plato was indeed an eloquent Greek; his *Apologia of Socrates* stands a service rendered to philosophers of every nation; he should be respected, as having represented ill-fortuned virtue in so honorable a light and its persecutors in one so odious. It was long thought that ethics so admirable could not be associated with metaphysics so false; he was almost made a Father of the Church for his *Ternaire,* which no one has ever understood. But what would be thought today of a philosopher who should tell us that one substance is the same as *any other;* that the world is a figure of twelve pentagons; that fire is a pyramid which is connected with the earth by numbers? Would it be thought convincing to prove the immortality and transmigration of the soul by saying that sleep is born of wakefulness and wakefulness of sleep, the living from the dead and the dead from the living? Such reasonings as these have been admired for many centuries, and still more fantastic ideas have since been employed in the education of mankind.

Locke alone has developed the *human understanding* in a book where there is naught but truths, a book made perfect by the fact that these truths are stated clearly.

To complete our review of the superiority of the past century over all others, we may cast our eyes towards Germany and the North. Hevelius of Danzig was the first astronomer to study deeply the planet of the moon; no man before him surveyed the heavens with greater care: and of all the great men that the age produced, none showed more plainly why it should be justly called the age of Louis XIV. A magnificent library that he possessed was destroyed by fire; upon which the King of France bestowed on the astronomer of Danzig a present which more than compensated him for the loss.

Mercator of Holstein was the forerunner of Newton in geometry; and the Bernouillis in Switzerland were worthy pupils of that great man. Leibnitz was for some time regarded as his rival.

The celebrated Leibnitz was born at Leipzig; and died, full of learning, in the town of Hanover; like Newton, worshiping a god, and seeking counsel of no man. He was perhaps the most universal genius in Europe: a historian assiduous in research; a sagacious lawyer, enlightening the study of law with science, foreign to that subject though it seem; a metaphysician sufficiently open-minded to endeavor to reconcile theology with metaphysics; even a Latin poet, and finally a mathematician of sufficient caliber to dispute with the great Newton the invention of the infinitesimal calculus, so that for some time the issue remained uncertain.

It was the golden age of goemetry; mathematicians frequently challenged one another, that is to say, they sent each other problems to be solved, almost as the ancient kings of Asia and Egypt are reported to have sent each other riddles to divine. The problems propounded by the geometricians were more difficult than the ancient riddles; and in Germany, England, Italy and France, not one of them was left unsolved. Never was intercourse between philosophers more universal; Leibnitz did much to encourage it. A republic of letters was being gradually established in Europe, in spite of different religions. Every science, every art, was mutually assisted in this way, and it was the academies which formed this republic. Italy and Russia were allied by literature. The Englishman, the German and the Frenchman went to Leyden to study. The celebrated physician Boerhaave was consulted both by the Pope and by the Czar. His greatest pupils attracted the notice of foreigners and thus became to some extent the physicians of the nation; true scholars in every branch drew closer the bonds of this great fellowship of intellect, spread everywhere and everywhere independent. This intercourse still obtains, and is indeed one of the consolations for those ills which political ambition scatters throughout the earth.

Italy throughout this century preserved her ancient glory, though she produced no new Tassos nor Raphaels; it is enough to have produced them once. Men like Chiabrera, and later Zappi and Filicaia, showed that refinement is still a characteristic of that nation. Maffei's *Merope* and the dramatic works of Metastasio are worthy monuments of the age.

# Freedom in Music

## GEORGE FREDERICK HANDEL

I believe the question can be reduced to this: whether one should prefer an easy and more perfect method to another which is accompanied by great difficulties capable not only of disgusting pupils with music, but also of wasting precious time that could be better utilized in probing more deeply into this art and in developing one's talent. It is not that

I should like to declare that one can draw no benefit from solmization, but since one can acquire the same knowledge in much less time by the method used so successfully at present, I do not see why one should not take the road that leads more rapidly and easily to the desired end. As regards the Greek modes . . . no doubt knowledge of them is necessary to those who would study and play ancient music, which was composed according to those modes, but since we have freed ourselves from the narrow limits of ancient music, I do not see what use can be made of Greek modes in modern music.

# Progress in Opera

## CHRISTOPH WILLIBALD VON GLUCK

When I undertook to set the opera *Alceste* to music, I resolved to avoid all those abuses which had crept into Italian opera through the mistaken vanity of singers and the unwise compliance of composers, and which had rendered it wearisome and ridiculous, instead of being, as it once was, the grandest and most imposing stage work of modern times. I endeavored to reduce music to its proper function, that of seconding poetry by enforcing the expression of the sentiment, and the interest of the situations, without interrupting the action, or weakening it by superfluous ornament. My idea was that the relation of music to poetry was much the same as that of harmonious coloring and well-disposed light and shade to an accurate drawing, which animates the figures without altering their outlines. I have therefore been very careful never to interrupt a singer in the heat of a dialogue in order to introduce a tedious ritornelle, nor to stop him in the middle of a piece either for the purpose of displaying the flexibility of his voice on some favorable vowel, or that the orchestra might give him time to take breath before a long sustained note. Furthermore, I have not thought it right to hurry through the second part of a song if the words happened to be the most important of the whole, in order to repeat the first part regularly four times over; or to finish the air where the sense does not end in order to allow the singer to exhibit his power of varying the passage at pleasure. In fact, my object was to put an end to abuses against which good taste and good sense have long protested in vain.

My idea was that the overture ought to indicate the subject and prepare the spectators for the character of the piece they are about to see; that the instruments ought to be introduced in proportion to the degree of interest and passion in the words; and that it was necessary above all to avoid making too great a disparity between the recitative and the air of a dialogue, so as not to break the sense of a period or awkwardly interrupt the movement and animation of a scene.

I also thought that my chief endeavor should be to attain a grand simplicity, and consequently I have avoided making a parade of difficulties at the cost of clearness; I have set no value on novelty as such, unless it was naturally suggested by the situation and suited to the expression. In short, there was no rule which I did not consider myself bound to sacrifice for the sake of effect.

*28.* C. Marchioni, *Caffé Haus, Villa Albani,* Rome. Example of neoclassicism.

29. *Christ Church,* Cambridge, Mass.

*30. Monticello* (Residence of Jefferson).

*31. St. Michael's Church,*
Charleston, South Carolina.

32. *University of Virginia, Rotunda.*

33. *Redwood Library,* Newport, Rhode Island.

34. Jacques Ange Gabriel, *Petit Trianon, Versailles.* Garden façade.

35. Johann Bernhard Fischer von Erlach, *Karlskirche,* Vienna. Exterior.

36. *Ford Mansion, Palladian Doorway* (Washington's Headquarters).

37. James Gibbs, *St. Martin-in-the-Fields,* London. Façade.

38. Giovanni Battista Piranesi, *S. Maria del Priorato,* Rome. View of façade from southwest.

# VI

# Democracy, the Necessary Condition

*Although a number of the leading philosophes thought that social advance would be directed from the top through voluntary acts of enlightened rulers, belief in democracy as the ultimate and necessary condition for progress was implied even when it was not outrightly advocated. And the idea of democracy was given a wide diversity of expression, from political manifestos to poetry acclaiming the common man.*

# from *Persian Letters*

## MONTESQUIEU

Do not expect me to be able just now to talk to you seriously about European usages and customs. I have only a faint idea of them myself and have barely had time to be amazed by them.

The King of France is the most powerful prince of Europe. Unlike his neighbor the King of Spain, he has no gold mines. Yet he possesses greater riches, for he draws from the vanity of his subjects a wealth more inexhaustible than mines. He has been known to undertake and wage great wars with no other funds than honorary titles to sell, and by reason of this miracle of human pride, his troops are paid, his fortresses armed, and his navies fitted out.

Moreover, this king is a great magician. He exercises his empire over the very minds of his subjects and makes them think as he likes. If he has only one million crowns in his treasury and he needs two million, he has only to convince them that one crown equals two, and they believe him. If he is involved in a war that is difficult in the waging and finds himself short of money, he has only to put into their heads the notion that a slip of paper is money, and they are immediately convinced. He even goes so far as to make them believe that he can cure them of all manner of disease by touching them, so great is his strength and dominion over their minds.

What I am telling you about this prince ought not astonish you. For there is another magician even more powerful than the first and who has no less dominion over the mind of the first than that one has over the minds of others. This magician is called the Pope. Sometimes he has the King believing that three are only one, sometimes that the bread he eats is not bread and the wine he drinks not wine, and a thousand other things of the sort.

And, in order to keep up his second wind and not let the prince lose the habit of believing, this magician occasionally gives him certain articles of faith for exercise. Two years ago, he sent him a great writ, which he called the *Constitution*,[1] and at all costs, wanted to make the prince and all his subjects believe everything that was contained therein. He succeeded with the prince, who submitted immediately and gave a good example to his subjects. But some of them rebelled and said they weren't going to believe a single word of what was in the writ. Women were behind this revolt, which divided the whole court, the whole kingdom, and every family. This Constitution forbids the people to read a book that all the Christians claim was brought down from heaven; it is, properly speaking, their Koran. The women, outraged at this insult to their sex, aroused everyone and everything against the Constitution. They have managed to bring the men around to their side, and in this case, the men do not choose to exercise their prerogative. It must be admitted, all the same, that this mufti does not reason badly, and, by the great Ali, he must have been instructed in the principles of our holy law. For, since women are inferior to us by creation and since our prophets tell us that they won't enter into paradise, why should they get involved with reading a book that was written solely to teach the way to paradise?

I have heard stories that sound miraculous, told about the King, and I have no doubt you will hesitate to believe them.

They say that while he was making war on his neighbors, all allied against him, he was surrounded in his own kingdom by a countless number of invisible enemies. They add that he had been seeking them out for thirty years and that in spite of the untiring efforts of certain dervishes in his trust, he could not find a single one of them. They are living with him, they are at his court, in his capital city, in his armies, in his law courts, and yet it is said that he will suffer the vexation of dying without having found them out. One might say that they exist in general and yet no longer have any identity in particular. They form a body with no members. No doubt heaven chooses to punish the prince for not having been moderate enough against his conquered enemies, for it provides him with invisible ones whose jinni and destiny are superior to his own.

I shall continue to write to you, and I shall teach you things far removed from Persian character and spirit. It is certainly the same earth carrying both countries, but the men of this country where I am and those of the country where you are are quite different.

---

1. [A reference to the papal bull "Unigenitus" which condemned "101 errors" in a popular book by the Jansenist, Père Quesnel.]

# Rules by Which a Great Empire May Be Reduced to a Small One

## BENJAMIN FRANKLIN

PRESENTED TO A LATE MINISTER, WHEN HE ENTERED
UPON HIS ADMINISTRATION

An ancient Sage boasted, that, tho' he could not fiddle, he knew how to make a *great city* of a *little one*. The science that I, a modern simpleton, am about to communicate, is the very reverse.

I address myself to all ministers who have the management of extensive dominions, which from their very greatness are become troublesome to govern, because the multiplicity of their affairs leaves no time for *fiddling*.

I. In the first place, gentlemen, you are to consider, that a great empire, like a great cake, is most easily diminished at the edges. Turn your attention, therefore, first to your *remotest* provinces; that, as you get rid of them, the next may follow in order.

II. That the possibility of this separation may always exist, take special care the provinces are never incorporated with the mother country; that they do not enjoy the same common rights, the same privileges in commerce; and that they are governed by *severer* laws, all of *your enacting,* without allowing them any share in the choice of the legislators. By carefully making and preserving such distinctions, you will (to keep to my simile of the cake) act like a wise ginger-bread-baker, who, to facilitate a division, cuts his dough half through in those places where, when baked, he would have it *broken to pieces*.

III. Those remote provinces have perhaps been acquired, purchased, or conquered, at the *sole expence* of the settlers, or their ancestors, without the aid of the mother country. If this should happen to increase her *strength,* by their growing numbers, ready to join in her wars; her *commerce,* by their growing demand for her manufactures; or her *naval*

*power,* by greater employment for her ships and seamen, they may prob-
bly suppose some merit in this, and that it entitles them to some favour;
you are therefore to *forget it all, or resent it,* as if they had done you injury. If they happen to be zealous whigs, friends of liberty, nurtured in
revolution principles, *remember all that* to their prejudice, and resolve to
punish it; for such principles, after a revolution is thoroughly established,
are of *no more use;* they are even *odious* and *abominable.*

IV. However peaceably your colonies have submitted to your government, shewn their affection to your interests, and patiently borne their
grievances; you are to *suppose* them always inclined to revolt, and treat
them accordingly. Quarter troops among them, who by their insolence
may *provoke* the rising of mobs, and by their bullets and bayonets *suppress* them. By this means, like the husband who uses his wife ill *from
suspicion,* you may in time convert your *suspicions* into *realities.*

V. Remote provinces must have *Governors* and *Judges,* to represent
the Royal Person, and execute everywhere the delegated parts of his
office and authority. You ministers know, that much of the strength of
government depends on the *opinion* of the people; and much of that
opinion on the *choice of rulers* placed immediately over them. If you send
them wise and good men for governors, who study the interest of the
colonists, and advance their prosperity, they will think their King wise
and good, and that he wishes the welfare of his subjects. If you send
them learned and upright men for Judges, they will think him a lover of
justice. This may attach your provinces more to his government. You are
therefore to be careful whom you recommend for those offices. If you can
find prodigals, who have ruined their fortunes, broken gamesters or stock-
jobbers, these may do well as *governors;* for they will probably be rapa-
cious, and provoke the people by their extortion. Wrangling proctors and
pettifogging lawyers, too, are not amiss; for they will be for ever disputing
and quarrelling with their little parliaments. If withal they should be
ignorant, wrong-headed, and insolent, so much the better. Attornies'
clerks and Newgate solicitors will do for *Chief Justices,* especially if they
hold their places *during your pleasure;* and all will contribute to impress
those ideas of your government, that are proper for a people *you would
wish to renounce it.*

VI. To confirm these impressions, and strike them deeper, whenever
the injured come to the capital with complaints of maladministration,
oppression, or injustice, punish such suitors with long delay, enormous
expence, and a final judgment in favour of the oppressor. This will have
an admirable effect every way. The trouble of future complaints will be

prevented, and Governors and Judges will be encouraged to farther acts of oppression and injustice; and thence the people may become more disaffected, and at length desperate.

VII. When such Governors have crammed their rich coffers, and made themselves so odious to the people that they can no longer remain among them, with safety to their persons, *recall and reward* them with pensions. You may make them *baronets* too, if that respectable order should not think fit to resent it. All will contribute to encourage new governors in the same practice, and make the supreme government, *detestable.*

VIII. If, when you are engaged in war, your colonies should vie in liberal aids of men and money against the common enemy, upon your simple requisition, and give far beyond their abilities, reflect that a penny taken from them by your power is more honourable to you, than a pound presented by their benevolence; despise therefore their voluntary grants, and resolve to harass them with novel taxes. They will probably complain to your parliaments, that they are taxed by a body in which they have no representative, and that this is contrary to common right. They will petition for redress. Let the Parliaments flout their claims, reject their petitions, refuse even to suffer the reading of them, and treat the petitioners with the utmost contempt. Nothing can have a better effect in producing the alienation proposed; for though many can forgive injuries, *none ever forgave contempt.*

IX. In laying these taxes, never regard the heavy burthens those remote people already undergo, in defending their own frontiers, supporting their own provincial governments, making new roads, building bridges, churches, and other public edifices, which in old countries have been done to your hands by your ancestors, but which occasion constant calls and demands on the purses of a new people. Forget the *restraints* you lay on their trade for *your own* benefit, and the advantage a *monopoly* of this trade gives your exacting merchants. Think nothing of the wealth those merchants and your manufacturers acquire by the colony commerce; their encreased ability thereby to pay taxes at home; their accumulating, in the price of their commodities, most of those taxes, and so levying them from their consuming customers; all this, and the employment and support of thousands of your poor by the colonist, you are *intirely to forget.* But remember to make your arbitrary tax more grievous to your provinces, by public declarations importing that your power of taxing them has *no limits;* so that when you take from them without their consent one shilling in the pound, you have a clear right to the other nineteen. This will probably weaken every idea of *security in their property,* and convince them, that under such a government they *have nothing they can call their own;* which can scarce fail of producing the *happiest consequences!*

X. Possibly, indeed, some of them might still comfort themselves, and say, "Though we have no property, we have yet *something* left that is valuable; we have constitutional *liberty,* both of person and of conscience. This King, these Lords, and these Commons, who it seems are too remote from us to know us, and feel for us, cannot take from us our *Habeas Corpus* right, or our right of trial *by a jury of our neighbours;* they cannot deprive us of the exercise of our religion, alter our ecclesiastical constitution, and compel us to be Papists, if they please, or Mahometans." To annihilate this comfort, begin by laws to perplex their commerce with infinite regulations, impossible to be remembered and observed; ordain seizures of their property for every failure; take away the trial of such property by Jury, and give it to arbitrary Judges of your own appointing, and of the lowest characters in the country, whose salaries and emoluments are to arise out of the duties or condemnations, and whose appointments are *during pleasure.* Then let there be a formal declaration of both Houses, that opposition to your edicts is *treason,* and that any person suspected of treason in the provinces may, according to some obsolete law, be seized and sent to the metropolis of the empire for trial; and pass an act, that those there charged with certain other offences, shall be sent away in chains from their friends and country to be tried in the same manner for felony. Then erect a new Court of Inquisition among them, accompanied by an armed force, with instructions to transport all such suspected persons; to be ruined by the expence, if they bring over evidences to prove their innocence, or be found guilty and hanged, if they cannot afford it. And, lest the people should think you cannot possibly go any farther, pass another solemn declaratory act, "that King, Lords, Commons had, hath, and of right ought to have, full power and authority to make statutes of sufficient force and validity to bind the unrepresented provinces IN ALL CASES WHATSOEVER." This will include *spiritual* with temporal, and, taken together, must operate wonderfully to your purpose; by convincing them, that they are at present under a power something like that spoken of in the scriptures, which can not only *kill their bodies,* but *damn their souls* to all eternity, by compelling them, if it pleases, *to worship the Devil.*

XI. To make your taxes more odious, and more likely to procure resistance, send from the capital a board of officers to superintend the collection, composed of the most *indiscreet, ill-bred,* and *insolent* you can find. Let these have large salaries out of the extorted revenue, and live in open, grating luxury upon the sweat and blood of the industrious; whom they are to worry continually with groundless and expensive prosecutions before the abovementioned arbitrary revenue Judges; *all at the cost of the party prosecuted,* tho' acquitted, because *the King is to pay no costs.* Let these men, *by your order,* be exempted from all the common taxes and burthens of the province, though they and their property are protected by its laws. If any revenue officers are *suspected* of the least tenderness for the people, discard them. If others are justly complained of, protect and reward them. If any of the under officers behave so as to provoke the people to drub them, promote those to better offices: this will encourage others to procure for themselves such profitable drubbings, by multiplying and enlarging such provocations, and *all will work toward the end you aim at.*

XII. Another way to make your tax odious, is to misapply the produce of it. If it was originally appropriated for the *defence* of the provinces, the better support of government, and the administration of justice, where it may be *necessary,* then apply none of it to that *defence,* but bestow it where it is *not necessary,* in augmented salaries or pensions to every governor, who has distinguished himself by his enmity to the people, and by calumniating them to their sovereign. This will make them pay it more unwillingly, and be more apt to quarrel with those that collect it and those that imposed it, who will quarrel again with them, and all shall contribute to your *main purpose,* of making them *weary of your government.*

XIII. If the people of any province have been accustomed to support their own Governors and Judges to satisfaction, you are to apprehend that such Governors and Judges may be thereby influenced to treat the people kindly, and to do them justice. This is another reason for applying part of that revenue in larger salaries to such Governors and Judges, given, as their commissions are, *during your pleasure* only; forbidding them to take any salaries from their provinces; that thus the people may no longer hope any kindness from their Governors, or (in Crown cases) any justice from their Judges. And, as the money thus misapplied in one province is extorted from all, probably *all will resent the misapplication.*

XIV. If the parliaments of your provinces should dare to claim rights, or complain of your administration, order them to be harassed with *repeated dissolutions.* If the same men are continually returned by new elections, adjourn their meetings to some country village, where they cannot be accommodated, and there keep them *during pleasure;* for this, you know, is your PREROGATIVE; and an excellent one it is, as you may manage it to promote discontents among the people, diminish their respect, and *increase their disaffection.*

XV. Convert the brave, honest officers of your *navy* into pimping tide-waiters and colony officers of the *customs.* Let those, who in time of war fought gallantly in defence of the commerce of their countrymen, in peace be taught to prey upon it. Let them learn to be corrupted by great and real smugglers; but (to shew their diligence) scour with armed boats every bay, harbour, river, creek, cove, or nook throughout the coast of your colonies; stop and detain every coaster, every wood-boat, every fisherman, tumble their cargoes and even their ballast inside out and upside down; and, if a penn'orth of pins is found unentered, let the whole be seized and confiscated. Thus shall the trade of your colonists suffer more from their friends in time of peace, than it did from their enemies in war. Then let these boat crews land upon every farm in their way, rob the orchards, steal the pigs and the poultry, and insult the inhabitants. If the injured and exasperated farmers, unable to procure other justice, should attack the aggressors, drub them, and burn their boats; you are to call this *high treason and rebellion,* order fleets and armies into their country, and threaten to carry all the offenders three thousand miles to be hanged, drawn, and quartered. *O! this will work admirably!*

XVI. If you are told of discontents in your colonies, never believe that they are general, or that you have given occasion for them; therefore do not think of applying any remedy, or of changing any offensive measure. Redress no grievance, lest they should be encouraged to demand the redress of some other grievance. Grant no request that is just and reasonable, lest they should make another that is unreasonable. Take all your informations of the state of the colonies from your Governors and officers in enmity with them. Encourage and reward these *leasing-makers;* secrete their lying accusations, lest they should be confuted; but act upon them as the clearest evidence; and believe nothing you hear from the friends of the people: suppose all *their* complaints to be invented and promoted by a few factious demagogues, whom if you could catch and hang, all would be quiet. Catch and hang a few of them accordingly; and the *blood of the Martyrs* shall *work* miracles in favour of your purpose.

XVII. If you see *rival nations* rejoicing at the prospect of your disunion with your provinces, and endeavouring to promote it; if they translate, publish, and applaud all the complaints of your discontented colonists, at the same time privately stimulating you to severer measures, let not that *alarm* or offend you. Why should it, since you all mean *the same thing?*

XVIII. If any colony should at their own charge erect a fortress to secure their port against the fleets of a foreign enemy, get your Governors to betray that fortress into your hands. Never think of paying what it cost the country, for that would look, at least, like some regard for justice; but turn it into a citadel to awe the inhabitants and curb their commerce. If they should have lodged in such fortress the very arms they bought and used to aid you in your conquests, seize them all; it will provoke like *ingratitude* added to *robbery*. One admirable effect of these operations will be, to discourage every other colony from erecting such defences, and so your enemies may more easily invade them; to the great disgrace of your government, and of course *the furtherance of your project.*

XIX. Send armies into their country under pretence of protecting the inhabitants; but, instead of garrisoning the forts on their frontiers with those troops, to prevent incursions, demolish those forts, and order the troops into the heart of the country, that the savages may be encouraged to attack the frontiers, and that the troops may be protected by the inhabitants. This will seem to proceed from your ill will or your ignorance, and contribute farther to produce and strengthen an opinion among them, *that you are no longer fit to govern them.*

XX. Lastly, invest the General of your army in the provinces, with great and unconstitutional powers, and free him from the controul of even your own Civil Governors. Let him have troops enow under his command, with all the fortresses in his possession; and who knows but (like some provincial Generals in the Roman empire, and encouraged by the universal discontent you have produced) he may take it into his head to set up for himself? If he should, and you have carefully practiced these few *excellent rules* of mine, take my word for it, all the provinces will immediately join him; and you will that day (if you have not done it sooner) get rid of the trouble of governing them, and all the *plagues* attending their *commerce* and connection from henceforth and for ever.

Q.E.D.

# A Man's a Man for A' That

## ROBERT BURNS

Is there for honest poverty
   That hings his head, an' a' that;
The coward slave—we pass him by,
   We dare be poor for a' that!
For a' that, an' a' that,
   Our toils obscure an' a' that,
The rank is but the guinea's stamp,
   The man's the gowd for a' that.

What though on hamely fare we dine,
   Wear hoddin grey, an' a' that?
Gie fools their silks, and knaves their wine,
   A man's a man for a' that.
For a' that, an' a' that,
   Their tinsel show an' a' that,
The honest man, tho' e'er sae poor,
   Is king o' men for a' that.

Ye see yon birkie ca'd a lord,
   Wha struts, an' stares, an' a' that;
Tho' hundreds worship at his word,
   He's but a coof for a' that.
For a 'that, an' a' that,
   His ribband, star, an' a' that,
The man o' independent mind
   He looks an' laughs at a' that.

A prince can mak a belted knight,
   A marquis, duke, an' a' that;
But an honest man's aboon his might,
   Gude faith, he maunna fa' that!
For a' that, an' a' that,

Their dignities an' a' that,
The pith o' sense, an' pride o' worth,
Are higher rank than a' that.

Then let us pray that come it may,
(As come it will for a' that,)
That Sense and Worth, o'er a' the earth,
Shall bear the gree, an' a' that.
For a' that, an' a' that,
It's coming yet for a' that,
That man to man, the world o'er,
Shall brithers be for a' that.

# On Economic Inequality

## CLAUDE-ADRIEN HELVÉTIUS

The almost universal unhappiness of man, and of nations, arises from the imperfections of their laws, and the too unequal partition of their riches. There are in most kingdoms only two classes of citizens, one of which want necessaries, and the other riot in superfluities.

The former cannot gratify their wants but by excessive labour: such labour is a natural evil for all; and to some it is a punishment.

The second class live in abundance, but at the same time in the anguish of discontent. Now discontent is an evil almost as much to be dreaded as indigence.

Most countries, therefore, must be peopled by the unfortunate. What would be done to make them happy? Diminish the riches of some; augment that of others; put the poor in such a state of ease, that they may by seven or eight hours' labour abundantly provide for the wants of themselves and their families. It is then, that a people will become as happy as they can be.

. . .

There are few good patriots; few citizens that are always just: Why? Because men are not educated to be just; because the present morality, as I have just said, is nothing more than a jumble of gross errors and contradictions; because to be just a man must have discernment, and they obscure in children the most obvious conceptions of the natural law.

But are children capable of conceiving adequate ideas of justice? This I know, that if by the aid of a religious catechism we can engrave on the memory of a child articles of faith that are frequently the most absurd, we might consequently, by the aid of a moral catechism, there engrave the precepts of an equity, which daily experience would prove to be at once useful and true. . . .

# from *The Social Contract*

## JEAN-JACQUES ROUSSEAU

### THE SUBJECT OF THIS FIRST BOOK

Man was born free, but is everywhere in bondage. This or that man believes himself the master of his fellow men, but is nevertheless more of a slave than they. How did this change *from freedom into bondage* come about? I do not know. Under what conditions can it be rendered legitimate? This problem I believe I can solve.

Were I to consider only force, and the results that it produces, I should say: As long as a people is constrained to obey, and does obey, it is acting rightly; *but* once that people is capable of shaking off its yoke, and does shake it off, it is acting even more rightly—for the following reason: Since in recovering its freedom it exercises the self-same right as the man that took it away, either it is justified in recovering it, or whoever took it away was not justified in doing so.

In any case, social order is a right — a sacred right, which serves as the basis for all other rights; *it does not, that is to say, flow from force.* Yet it does not flow from nature *either.* It therefore rests upon agreements.

Our task here is to find out what those agreements are. But before going into that, I must demonstrate what I have just asserted.

### CONCERNING THE EARLIEST SOCIETIES

The oldest of societies, and the only society that is *in any sense* natural, is the family. Yet *we must not overlook the rôle of agreements even here:* the children do not remain tied to the father beyond the period during which they have need of him in order to preserve themselves. Once that need disappears, the natural bond is dissolved: *i.e.,* the children are exempted from the obedience they have hitherto owed to the father, the father is exempted from the duties that he has hitherto owed to the children, and father and children alike resume their independence. If they continue together, they no longer do so out of natural necessity but rather out of choice, so that *thenceforth* even the family keeps itself alive only by agreement.

The freedom that they *subsequently* enjoy in common derives from the nature of man, whose first law is to look to his self-preservation, just as his first duties are those he owes to himself — man being, once he has attained the age of reason, the sole judge as to the means of preserving himself, and by that very token his own master.

The family, on this showing, is, if you like, the earliest model of political societies: the ruler in the one corresponds to the father in the other, the people in the one to the children in the other; all, in both cases, have been born free and equal to one another, and alienate their freedom only as it is to their advantage to do so. The only difference is this: In the family, the father has his reward for the care he bestows upon his children in the love he bears them. In the state, the pleasure of giving orders takes the place of love, which the ruler does not have for the people.

Grotius denies that all power among men is instituted in the interest of the governed, and cites slavery as an example proving his point. His most characteristic mode of reasoning is to argue from fact to right. A man might use a more logical mode of reasoning, but none more favorable to tyrants.

"Learned studies of public law are often merely histories of ancient abuses; and those who take the trouble to devote hard study to them are misdirecting their energies." (From the unpublished "Treatise on the Interests of France vis-à-vis its Neighbors," by the Marquis d'Argenson. That is just what Grotius does.)

If we are to believe Grotius, then, it is an open question whether the entire human race belongs to five-score individuals or the five-score individuals to the entire human race. Grotius seems, throughout his book, to lean toward the first of these views. Hobbes takes the same position. You end up, on such a showing, with mankind divided into so many herds of cattle — each with its drover, tending it in order to devour it.

Just as the shepherd belongs to a higher order of being than his flock, so the drovers of men, *i.e.,* their rulers, belong to a higher order of being than their peoples. That, according to Philo, is what the Emperor Caligula argued, drawing from the analogy either of two fairly safe inferences: that kings are gods, and that peoples are animals.

This fellow Caligula's argument parallels Hobbes' and Grotius'. Aristotle also — and at an earlier date than either of them — held that men are by no means equal by nature — that, rather, some are born to be slaves and some to be masters.

Aristotle was right, but he mistook effect for cause. Nothing is more certain than that every man born in slavery is born to be a slave. Men in shackles lose everything — even the desire to shake them off: They cherish their bondage as Ulysses' companions cherished being brutes. If, then, there are slaves by nature, that is because *previously* there were slaves against nature: force made the first slaves, and the latter's own cowardice kept them in slavery.

## ALL ROADS LEAD BACK TO AN ORIGINAL AGREEMENT

Even if I conceded everything I have refuted in the foregoing pages, the apologists of despotism would be no better off.

There is a great difference between establishing order in a society and gaining mastery over a multitude. Let as many separate individuals as you please be bound, one after another, to one man: I see only a master and some slaves, not a people and its ruler — an aggregation, if you like, but not an association. There is no public good, and *thus* no body politic. Let the one man gain mastery over half the world: he is still a mere individual; his interest, distinct as it is from that of the other individuals, remains merely a private interest. Let him die and the empire he leaves behind — like an oak tree that breaks asunder and falls into a heap of ashes after being consumed by fire — at once disintegrates, and has nothing to draw it together.

A people, says Grotius, can give itself to a king. On his own showing, then, it is *already* a people before it gives itself to a king: *for* the gift is itself a civil act, calling for prior public discussion. In that case, *however,* it would seem a good idea to examine the act by which a people becomes a people before we examine the act by which it elects a king. For this act, which necessarily precedes the other, is for that reason the true basis of society.

In short: unless the king has been elected by unanimous vote, what, failing a prior agreement, is the source of the minority's obligation to submit to the choice of the majority? Whence the right of the hundred who do wish a master to speak for the ten who do not? The majority principle is itself a product of agreement, and presupposes unanimity on at least one occasion.

## CONCERNING THE SOCIAL PACT

This is my premise: men have reached a point where the obstacles hindering their preservation in the state of nature are so obstructive as to defy the resources each individual, while in that state, can devote to his preservation. This being the case, that primitive condition cannot continue: humankind would perish if it did not change its way of life.

Now: unable as they are to add to their resources, men can only combine and channel those that are at hand. Thus their sole means of preserving themselves from now on is to create a pool of resources capable of surmounting the obstacles, to set those resources to work in response to one and the same purpose, and to see to it that they act in concert.

Such a pool of resources can arise only out of the coming together of several men. Since, however, each man's power and freedom are the chief instruments *he uses* for his self-preservation, *the following question presents itself:* How is he to pledge them without doing himself hurt, *i.e.*, without neglecting the duties he owes himself?

This difficult question may be restated, in terms appropriate to my inquiry, as follows: "Is a method of associating discoverable which will defend and protect, with all the collective might, the person and property of each associate, and in virtue of which each associate, though he becomes a member of the group, nevertheless obeys only himself, and remains as free as before?" This is the problem, a basic one, for which the social contract provides the solution.

The terms of this contract are dictated by the nature of the transaction, and in such fashion that modifying them in any way would render them nugatory and without effect: they are, therefore, everywhere the same, everywhere tacitly accepted and recognized, though nowhere perhaps have they been systematically formulated. Whence it follows that each individual immediately resumes his primitive rights, surprising as this may seem, when any violation of the social pact occurs; *i.e.*, he recovers his natural freedom, and thereby loses the contractual freedom for which he renounced it.

The contract's terms reduce themselves, when clearly grasped, to a single stipulation, namely: the total alienation to the whole community of each associate, together with every last one of his rights. The reasons for this are as follows: each gives himself completely, so that, in the first place, this stipulation places an equal burden upon everybody; and nobody, for that very reason, has any interest in making it burdensome for others.

The alienation is made without reservations, so that, in the second place, no more perfect union is possible, and no associate has any subsequent demand to make *upon the others*. For if the individual retained any rights whatever, this is what would happen: There being no common superior able to say the last word on any issue between him and the public, he would be his own judge on this or that point, and so would try before long to be his own judge on all points. The state of nature would thus persist; and the association would necessarily become useless, if not tyrannical.

Each gives himself to everybody, so that, in the third place, he gives himself to nobody; and since every associate acquires over every associate the same power he grants to every associate over himself, each gains an equivalent for all that he loses, together with greater power to protect what he possesses.

If, then, we exclude from the social contract everything not essential to it, we shall find that it reduces itself to the following terms: "Each of us puts into the common pool, and under the sovereign control of the general will, his person and all his power. And we, as a community, take each member unto ourselves as an indivisible part of the whole."

This act of association forthwith produces, in lieu of the individual persons of the several contracting parties, a collective moral body. The latter is made up of as many members as there are voices in the assembly, and it acquires, through the said act of association, its unity, its collective self, its life, and its will.

A public person formed by other persons uniting in the manner just described was in the past called a city; nowadays it is called a republic, or body politic. (We moderns have almost completely lost sight of the true meaning of the word "city." For most people, nowadays, a town is a city, a burgher a citizen. People fail to grasp the fact that a town is made up of houses, a city of citizens — a mistake that once cost the Carthaginians very dearly indeed. I have read of no instance in which the title "cives" was conferred upon the subjects of a prince — not even, in days gone by, upon the Macedonians, or, in our day, upon the English, though they come closer to being free than any other subjects. The French are alone in making everyday use of the title "citizens," and they *merely* because they have no real grasp of its meaning — as one can see from their dictionaries; otherwise they would be guilty, in appropriating it, of the crime of lèse majesté. For them, *be it noted*, the word denotes a virtue rather than a right. When Bodin made bold to speak of our citizens and burghers, thus failing to draw any distinction between them, he blundered enormously. M. d'Alembert did not make this mistake: he carefully distinguished, in his article on Geneva, the four classes — or even five, counting out-and-out foreigners as a separate class — in our town, of which just two make up the republic. No other French author, so far as I know, has understood the true meaning of the word "citizen.")

The members of a body politic call it "the state" when it is passive, "the sovereign" when it is active, and "a power" when they compare it with others of its kind. Collectively they use the title "people," and they refer to one another individually as "citizens" when speaking of their participation in the authority of the sovereign, and as "subjects" when speaking of their subordination to the laws of the state. These terms, however, are often confused, *i.e.,* mistaken for one another, and it is enough to know how to tell them apart when they are used with maximum precision.

## CONCERNING THE SOVEREIGN

The act of association, as the above formula makes clear, entails a reciprocal obligation between the public and *certain* individuals. The formula further makes it clear that each individual, since in a manner of speaking he *also* enters into a contract with himself, finds himself with two sets of obligations, namely: those toward individuals, which attach to his membership in the sovereign; and those toward the sovereign, which attach to his membership in the state. The civil law maxim that a man is not bound by engagements entered into with himself is, however, not applicable here: there is a great deal of difference between an obligation entered into with oneself and an obligation entered into with a whole of which one is a part.

We must further notice this: because of the dual capacity in which the several subjects can be regarded, collective decisions can create obligations on the part of each of them toward the sovereign, but cannot, for the opposite reason, create obligations on the part of the sovereign toward itself. It is, therefore, contrary to the nature of the body politic for the sovereign to impose upon itself a law that it cannot subsequently set aside. Since the sovereign can be regarded only in a single capacity, its position in this regard is precisely that of an individual entering into a contract with himself. Evidently, then, there is — and can be — no type of fundamental law that is binding upon the people as a body — not even the social contract.

This does not mean that the body politic is not quite free to enter into engagements with another such body as regards something that does not impair the contract. For, with respect to the outside world, it is a mere person, an individual. But *it does mean that* the body politic, or the sovereign, because it owes its very existence to the sanctity of the contract, can in no circumstances obligate itself, even vis-à-vis another body politic, to anything that impairs that original agreement — it cannot, for example, alienate a portion of itself, or subordinate itself to another sovereign. At the moment when it violates the agreement in virtue of which it exists it annihilates itself. And out of *that which has become* nothing comes nothing.

Once such a multitude as we have assumed is thus united in a body politic, no one can offend one of its members without attacking it; still less can anyone offend it without its members' being injured. Not only duty, that is to say, but interest equally, obligates the two contracting parties to be of mutual assistance; *i.e.,* the several individuals should try, under their joint auspices, to maximize the advantages the latter hold out to them.

As for the sovereign, since it consists exclusively of the individuals who are its members, it has no interest that goes against theirs, and cannot possibly have such an interest. The sovereign power therefore has no need to offer guarantees to the subjects *collectively,* it being impossible for a body to will to injure all of its members. Nor, as we shall see later, can it injure them individually either. The sovereign needs only to exist in order to be what it ought to be.

It is, however, quite otherwise with the subjects over against the sovereign: if it did not take steps to assure itself of their fidelity, it could not count on them, despite the interest they have in common, to discharge their commitments.

The facts of the matter are these: It is possible for each individual, qua man, to have a private will contrary to, or *at least* other than, the general will that he has qua citizen. It is *also* possible for the urgings of that private interest to be quite different from those of the common interest; *i.e.,* his independent and absolute natural self may lead him to regard what he owes to the common cause as a gratuitous contribution, *that is,* a contribution the making of which will burden him more than the loss of it will hurt the others. And he may, deeming the moral person that constitutes the state a fiction because not a man, successfully claim the rights of the citizen while unwilling to perform the obligations of the subject. If this sort of thing, inequitable as it is, were to become general, it would accomplish the ruin of the body politic.

To the end, therefore, that the social pact shall not be a meaningless formality, it includes, by implication, the following undertaking, in the absence of which the other undertakings it includes would have no binding force: Whoever refuses to obey the general will shall be constrained to do so by the entire body politic, which is only another way of saying that his fellows shall force him to be free. For this is the undertaking that dedicates each citizen to the fatherland, and thus insures each citizen against personal dependence of any kind. *In a word:* This undertaking is the king-pin of the political machine: None other can legitimize the *other* undertakings involved in civil society. Take it away, and these *other* undertakings would be absurd and tyrannical — a potential breeding-ground for the most enormous abuses.

# from *The Marriage of Figaro*

## BEAUMARCHAIS

FIGARO (*Alone, walking in the darkness, speaks in sombre tones*). . . . No, Monsieur le Comte, you shan't have her! You shan't have her. Because you are a great noble, you think you are a great genius! Nobility, a fortune, a rank, appointments to office: all this makes a man so proud! What did you do to earn all this? You took the trouble to get born — nothing more. Moreover, you're really a pretty ordinary fellow! While as for me, lost in the crowd, I've had to use more knowledge, more brains, just to keep alive than your likes have had to spend on governing Spain and the Empire for a century. And you want to contest with me — Someone's coming, it's she — no, nobody — The night is black as the devil, and here I am plying the silly trade of husband, though I'm only half a husband. (*He sits down on a bench*) Is there anything stranger than my fate? Son of I don't know whom, kidnapped by robbers, brought up in their ways, I got disgusted with them, and tried to follow an honest career; and everywhere I met with rebuffs. I learned chemistry, pharmacy, surgery, and all the credit of a great noble barely succeeded in putting a veterinary's lancet in my hand! Tired of making sick beasts sadder, I turned to a very different trade, and threw myself into the life of the theatre. What a stone I hung around my neck that time! I sketched a comedy about harem life; being a Spanish writer, I assumed I could be irreverent towards Mohammed without any scruples: but at once an

Envoy from somewhere complained that my verses offended the Sublime Porte, Persia, a part of India, all Egypt, the kingdoms of Barca, Tripoli, Tunis, Algiers and Morocco; and there was my comedy burned, to please some Mohammedan princes not one of whom I suppose knows how to read, and who keep cursing away at us all as "Christian dogs" — not being able to degrade the human spirit, they take revenge by abusing it. A question came up about the nature of wealth: and since it isn't necessary to own a thing to reason about it, I, penniless, wrote on the value of money and the *produit net:* at once I saw, from the inside of a cab, the lowered drawbridge of a fortress prison at the entrance to which I left hope and liberty! (*He gets up*) How I'd love to get one of these powerful men of four days' standing, so ready with such penalties, just after some good disgrace had fermented his pride! I'd tell him — that printed fool-ishness has no importance, except for those who try to suppress it; that without freedom to blame, there can be no flattering eulogies; and that only little men fear little writings. (*He sits down again*) Tired of feeding an obscure boarder, they let me out of prison. I was told that during my economic retreat, there had been established in Madrid a system of free sale of products which included even the press. To profit by this sweet liberty, I announced a periodical, and, thinking to offend no one, I called it *The Useless Journal.* Whew! I had a thousand poor devils of scribblers rise up against me: I was suppressed; and there I was once more among the unemployed. I began almost to despair; I was thought of for a gov-ernment post, but unfortunately I was qualified for it. They needed an accountant: a dancer got the job. All that was left for me was stealing; I set up a faro game; and now, good folk, I supped in society, and people known as *comme il faut* opened their houses to me politely, on condition they kept three-quarters of the profits. I might have gone pretty far, for I was beginning to understand that to gain wealth it is better to have know-how [*savoir-faire*] than to have knowledge [*savoir*]. But as every-body about me stole, while insisting I stay honest, I should have failed once more. I should have left this world and put a watery grave between me and it, but a kindly God recalled me to my first condition. I took up once more my barber's case and my English leather strop. I travelled about, shaving, from town to town, living at last a carefree life.

# from *Dangerous Acquaintances*

## CHODERLOS DE LACLOS

*Letter from the Vicomte de Valmont to the Marquise de Merteuil*

She is conquered, that proud woman who dared to think she could resist me! Yes, my friend, she is mine, entirely mine; after yesterday she has nothing left to grant me.

I am still too full of my happiness to be able to appreciate it, but I am astonished by the unsuspected charm I felt. Is it true then that virtue increases a woman's value even in her moment of weakness? But let me put that puerile idea away with old woman's tales. Does one not meet almost everywhere a more or less well-feigned resistance to the first triumph? And have I not found elsewhere the charm of which I speak? But yet it is not the charm of love; for after all, if I have some-times had surprising moments of weakness with this woman resembling that pusillanimous passion, I have always been able to overcome them and return to my principles. Even if yesterday's scene carried me, as I now think, a little further than I intended; even if I shared for a moment the agitation and ecstasy I created; that passing illusion would now have disappeared, and yet the same charm remains. I confess I should even feel a considerable pleasure in yielding to it, if it did not cause me some anxiety. Shall I, at my age, be mastered like a schoolboy, by an involun-tary and unsuspected sentiment? No; before everything else, I must combat and thoroughly examine it.

And perhaps I have already a glimpse of the cause of it! At least the idea pleases me and I should like it to be true.

Among the crowd of women for whom I have hitherto filled the part and functions of a lover, I had never met one who had not at least as much desire to yield to me as I had to bring her to doing so; I had even accustomed myself to call "prudes" those who only came halfway to meet me, in opposition to so many others whose provocative defence never covers but imperfectly the first advances they have made.

Here on the contrary I found a first unfavourable prejudice, supported

241

afterwards by the advice and reports of a woman who hated me but who was clear-sighted; I found a natural and extreme timidity strengthened by an enlightened modesty; I found an attachment to virtue, controlled by religion, able to count two years of triumph already, and then remarkable behaviour inspired by different motives but all with the object of avoiding my pursuit.

It was not then, as in my other adventures, a merely more or less advantageous capitulation which it is more easy to profit by than to feel proud of; it was a complete victory, achieved by a hard campaign and decided by expert manœuvres. It is therefore not surprising that this success, which I owe to myself alone, should become more valuable to me; and the excess of pleasure I feel even yet is only the soft impression of the feeling of glory. I cling to this view which saves me from the humiliation of thinking I might depend in any way upon the very slave I have enslaved myself; that I do not contain the plenitude of my happiness in myself; and that the faculty of enjoying it in all its energy should be reserved to such or such a woman, exclusive of all others.

These sensible reflections shall guide my conduct in this important occasion; and you may be sure I shall not allow myself to be so enchained that I cannot break these new ties at any time, by playing with them, and at my will. But I am already talking to you of breaking off and you still do not know the methods by which I acquired the right to do so; read then, and see what wisdom is exposed to in trying to help folly. I observed my words and the replies I obtained so carefully that I hope to be able to report both with an exactness which will content you.

You will see by the copies of the two enclosed letters who was the mediator I chose to bring me back to my fair one and what zeal the holy person used to unite us. What I must still inform you of — a thing I learned from a letter intercepted as usual — is that the fear and little humiliation of being abandoned had rather upset the austere devotee's prudence and had filled her heart and head with sentiments and ideas which, though they lacked common sense, were none the less important. It was after these preliminaries, necessary for you to know, that yesterday, Thursday, the 28th, a day fixed beforehand by the ungrateful person herself, that I presented myself before her as a timid and repentant slave, and left a crowned conqueror.

It was six o'clock in the evening when I arrived at the fair recluse's house, for, since her return, her doors have been shut to everyone. She tried to rise when I was announced; but her trembling knees did not allow her to remain in that position: she sat down at once. As the servant who had brought me in had some duty to perform in the room, she seemed to be made impatient by it. We filled up this interval with the customary compliments. But not to lose any time, every moment of which was precious, I carefully examined the locality; and there and then I noted with my eyes the theatre of my victory. I might have chosen a more convenient one, for there was an ottoman in the same room. But I noticed that opposite it there was a portrait of the husband; and I confess I was afraid that with such a singular woman one glance accidentally directed that way might destroy in a moment the work of so many exertions. At last we were left alone and I began.

After having pointed out in a few words that Father Anselme must have informed her of the reasons for my visit, I complained of the rigorous treatment I had received from her; and I particularly dwelt upon the "contempt" which had been shown me. She defended herself, as I expected; and as you would have expected too, I founded the proofs of it on the suspicion and fear I had inspired, on the scandalous flight which had followed upon them, the refusal to answer my letters, and even the refusal to receive them, etc., etc. As she was beginning a justification (which would have been very easy) I thought I had better interrupt; and to obtain forgiveness for this brusque manner I covered it immediately by a flattery: "If so many charms have made an impression on my heart," I went on, "so many virtues have made no less a mark upon my soul. Seduced no doubt by the idea of approaching them I dared to think myself worthy of doing so. I do not reproach you for having thought otherwise; but I am punished for my error." As she remained in an embarrassed silence, I continued: "I desired, Madame, either to justify myself in your eyes or to obtain from you forgiveness for the wrongs you think I have committed, so that at least I can end in some peace the days to which I no longer attach any value since you have refused to embellish them."

Here she tried to reply, however: "My duty did not permit me." And the difficulty of finishing the lie which duty exacted did not permit her to finish the phrase. I therefore went on in the most tender tones: "It is true then that it was from me you fled?" "My departure was necessary." "And what took you away from me?" "It was necessary." "And forever?" "It must be so." I do not need to tell you that during this short dialogue the tender prude was in a state of oppression and her eyes were not raised to me.

I felt I ought to animate this languishing scene a little; so, getting up with an air of pique, I said: "Your firmness restores me all of my own. Yes, Madame, we shall be separated, separated even more than you think; and you shall congratulate yourself upon your handiwork at leisure." She was a little surprised by this tone of reproach and tried to answer. "The resolution you have taken . . ." said she. "Is only the result of my despair," I replied with vehemence. "It is your will that I should be unhappy; I will prove to you that you have succeeded even beyond your wishes." "I desire your happiness," she answered. And the tone of her voice began to show a rather strong emotion. So, throwing myself at her feet, I exclaimed in that dramatic tone of mine you know: "Ah! cruel woman, can there exist any happiness for me which you do not share? Ah! Never! Never!" I confess that at this point I had greatly been relying on the aid of tears; but either from a wrong disposition or perhaps only from the painful and continual attention I was giving to everything, it was impossible for me to weep.

Fortunately I remembered that any method is equally good in subjugating a woman, and that it sufficed to astonish her with a great emotion for the impression to remain both deep and favourable. I made up therefore by terror for the sensibility I found lacking; and with that purpose, only changing the inflection of my voice and remaining in the same position, I continued: "Yes, I make an oath at your feet, to possess you or die." As I spoke the last words our eyes met. I do not know what the timid person saw or thought she saw in mine, but she rose with a terrified air, and escaped from my arms, which I had thrown round her. It is true I did nothing to detain her; for I have several times noticed that scenes of despair carried out too vividly become ridiculous as soon as they become long, or leave nothing but really tragic resources which I was very far from desiring to adopt. However, as she escaped from me, I added in a low and sinister tone, but loud enough for her to hear: "Well, then! Death!"

I then got up; and after a moment of silence I cast wild glances upon her which, however much they seemed to wander, were none the less clear-sighted and observant. Her ill-assured bearing, her quick breathing, the contraction of all her muscles, her trembling half-raised arms, all proved to me that the result was such as I had desired to produce; but, since in love nothing is concluded except at very close quarters, and we were rather far apart, it was above all things necessary to get closer together. To achieve this, I passed as quickly as possible to an apparent tranquillity, likely to calm the effects of this violent state, without weakening its impression.

My transition was: "I am very unfortunate. I wished to live for your happiness, and I have disturbed it. I sacrifice myself for your tranquillity, and I disturb it again." Then in a composed but constrained way: "Forgive me, Madame; I am little accustomed to the storms of passions and can repress their emotions but ill. If I am wrong to yield to them, remember at least that it is for the last time. Ah! Calm yourself, calm yourself, I beseech you." And during this long speech, I came gradually nearer. "If you wish me to be calm," said the startled beauty, "you must yourself be more tranquil." "Well, then, I promise it," said I. And I added in a weaker voice: "If the effort is great, at least it will not be for long. But," I went on immediately in a distraught way, "I came, did I not, to return you your letters? I beg you, deign to receive them back. This painful sacrifice remained for me to accomplish; leave me nothing that can weaken my courage." And taking the precious collection from my pocket, I said: "There it is, that deceitful collection of assurances of your friendship! It attached me to life," I went on. "So give the signal yourself which must separate me from you forever."

Here the frightened Mistress yielded entirely to her tender anxiety. "But, M. de Valmont, what is the matter, and what do you mean? Is not the step you are taking today a voluntary one? Is it not the fruit of your own reflections? And are they not those which have made you yourself approve the necessary course I adopted from a sense of duty?" "Well," I replied, "that course decided mine." "And what is that?" "The only one which, in separating me from you, can put an end to my own." "But tell me, what is it?" Then I clasped her in my arms, without her defending herself in the least; and, judging from this forgetfulness of conventions, how strong and powerful her emotion was, I said, risking a tone of enthusiasm: "Adorable woman, you have no idea of the love you inspire; you will never know to what extent you were adored, and how much this sentiment is dearer to me than my existence! May all your days be fortunate and tranquil; may they be embellished by all the happiness of which you have deprived me! At least reward this sincere wish with a regret, with a tear; and believe that the last of my sacrifices will not be the most difficult for my heart. Farewell."

While I was speaking, I felt her heart beating violently; I observed the change in her face; I saw above all that she was suffocated by tears but that only a few painful ones flowed. It was at that moment only that I feigned to go away; but, detaining me by force, she said quickly: "No, listen to me." "Let me go," I answered. "You will listen to me, I wish it." "I must fly from you, I must." "No," she cried. At this last word she rushed or rather fell into my arms in a swoon. As I still doubted of so lucky a success, I feigned a great terror; but with all my terror I guided, or rather, carried her towards the place designed beforehand as the field of my glory; and indeed she only came to her senses submissive and already yielded to her happy conqueror.

Hitherto, my fair friend, I think you will find I adopted a purity of method which will please you; and you will see that I departed in no respect from the true principles of this war, which we have often remarked is so like the other. Judge me then as you would Frederic of Turenne. I forced the enemy to fight when she wished only to refuse battle; by clever manœuvres I obtained the choice of battlefield and of dispositions; I inspired the enemy with confidence, to overtake her more easily in her retreat; I was able to make terror succeed confidence before joining battle; I left nothing to chance except from consideration of a great advantage in case of success and from the certainty of other resources in case of defeat; finally, I only joined action when I had an assured retreat by which I could cover and retain all I had conquered before. I think that is everything that can be done; but now I am afraid of growing softened in the delights of Capua, like Hannibal. This is what happened afterwards.

I expected so great an event would not take place without the usual tears and despair; and if I noticed at first a little more confusion, and a kind of interior meditation, I attributed both to her prudishness; so, without troubling about these slight differences which I thought were purely local, I simply followed the high-road of consolations; being well persuaded that, as usually happens, sensations would aid sentiment, and that a single action would do more than all the words in the world, which, however, I did not neglect. But I found a really frightening resistance, less from its excess than from the manner in which it showed itself.

Imagine a woman seated, immovably still and with an unchanging face, appearing neither to think, hear, nor listen; a woman whose fixed eyes flowed with quite continual tears which came without effort. Such was Madame de Tourvel while I was speaking; but if I tried to recall her attention to me by a caress, even by the most innocent gesture, immediately there succeeded to this apparent apathy, terror, suffocation, convulsions, sobs, and at intervals a cry, but all without one word articulated.

These crises returned several times and always with more strength; the last was so violent that I was entirely discouraged and for a moment feared I had gained a useless victory. I fell back on the usual commonplaces, and among them was this: "Are you in despair because you have made me happy?" At these words the adorable woman turned towards me; and her face, although still a little distraught, had yet regained its heavenly expression. "Your happiness!" said she. You can guess my reply. "You are happy then?" I redoubled my protestations. "And happy through me?" I added praises and tender words. While she was speaking, all her limbs relaxed; she fell back limply, resting on her armchair; and abandoning to me a hand which I had dared to take, she said: "I feel that idea console and relieve me."

You may suppose that having found my path thus, I did not leave it again; it was really the right, and perhaps the only, one. So when I wished to attempt a second victory I found some resistance at first, and what had passed before made me circumspect; but having called to my aid that same idea of happiness I soon found its results favourable. "You are right," said the tender creature, "I cannot endure my existence except as it may serve to make you happy. I give myself wholly up to it; from this moment I give myself to you and you will experience neither refusals nor regrets from me."

It was with this naïve or sublime candour that she surrendered to me her person and her charms, and that she increased my happiness by sharing it. The ecstasy was complete and mutual; and, for the first time, my own outlasted the pleasure. I only left her arms to fall at her knees, to swear an eternal love to her; and, I must admit it, I believed what I said. Even when we separated, the idea of her did not leave me and I had to make an effort to distract myself.

Ah! Why are you not here to balance the charm of this action by that of its reward? But I shall lose nothing by waiting, shall I? And I hope I can consider as a thing agreed on between us the pleasant arrangement I proposed to you in my last letter. You see I carry things out and that, as I promised you, my affairs have gone well enough for me to be able to give you part of my time. Make haste then to get rid of your heavy Belleroche, abandon the whining Danceny, and concern yourself with me. What can you be doing in the country that you do not even reply to me? Do you know I should like to scold you for it? But happiness inclines us to indulgence. And then I do not forget that by returning to my place among your numerous suitors I must again submit to your little caprices. But remember, the new lover wishes to lose none of his old rights as a friend.

Good-bye, as of old. . . . Yes, good-bye, my angel! I send you all love's kisses.

P.S. Do you know that Prévan, after a month's imprisonment, has been forced to leave his Corps? It is the news of all Paris today. Really, he is cruelly punished for a fault he did not commit, and your success is complete!

*Paris, the 29th of October, 17 —.*

# London

## WILLIAM BLAKE

I wander thro' each charter'd street,
Near where the charter'd Thames doth flow,
And mark in every face I meet
Marks of weakness, marks of woe.

In ev'ry cry of every Man,
In ev'ry Infant's cry of fear,
In every voice, in every ban,
The mind-forg'd manacles I hear.

How the Chimney-sweeper's cry
Every black'ning Church appalls;
And the hapless Soldier's sigh
Runs in blood down Palace walls.

But most thro' midnight streets I hear
How the youthful Harlot's curse
Blasts the new born Infant's tear
And blights with plagues the Marriage hearse.

# from *Elegy Written in a Country Churchyard*

## THOMAS GRAY

Perhaps in this neglected spot is laid
Some heart once pregnant with celestial fire;

Hands, that the rod of empire might have swayed,
   Or waked to ecstasy the living lyre.

But Knowledge to their eyes her ample page,
   Rich with the spoils of Time, did ne'er unroll;
Chill poverty repressed their noble rage,
   And froze the genial current of the soul.

Full many a gem of purest ray serene
   The dark unfathomed caves of ocean bear;
Full many a flower is born to blush unseen,
   And waste its sweetness on the desert air.

Some village Hampden, that with dauntless breast
   The little tyrant of his fields withstood,
Some mute inglorious Milton here may rest,
   Some Cromwell, guiltless of his country's blood.

Th' applause of listening senates to command,
   The threats of pain and ruin to despise,
To scatter plenty o'er a smiling land,
   And read their history in a nation's eyes,

Their lot forbade: nor circumscribed alone
   Their growing virtues, but their crimes confined;
Forbade to wade through slaughter to a throne,
   And shut the gates of Mercy on mankind,

The struggling pangs of conscious truth to hide,
   To quench the blushes of ingenuous shame,
Or heap the shrine of luxury and pride
   With incense kindled at the Muse's flame.

# VII

# The Emergence
# of the Middle Class

*In the eighteenth century the middle class, already becoming dominant in England, America, and the Low Countries, emerged in France. Where its rise was successfully checked, as in the Iberian Peninsula and eastern Europe, society stagnated. The emergence of the middle class was reflected in the philosophy, the nascent social sciences, and the literature of the period. But its incipient evils, already visible in the industrially scarred or abandoned countryside and, socially, in the growing sycophancy toward the new rich, became the subjects of denunciation and satire.*

# Art and the Bourgeois

from *Persian Letters*

## MONTESQUIEU

Either you are not thinking about what you say, or your actions are better than your thinking. You left your country for an education, and yet you scorn all instruction. To educate yourself, you have come to a country where the arts are cultivated, and yet you consider them harmful. Shall I say what I think, Rhedi? I am more in agreement with you than you are with yourself.

Have you ever reflected upon the unhappy and savage condition into which the loss of the arts would drag us? You don't need to imagine it; you can see it. There still exists on earth peoples among whom a passably instructed monkey could live in honor. He would find that he was about on the same level with the other inhabitants. Nobody would find that he had an unusual mind or a strange character. He would be accepted like anyone else, and would even stand out by his gentleness.

You write that founders of empires have almost all been ignorant of the arts. I cannot deny that barbarous peoples have been able to spread over the earth like impetuous torrents and to cover the best-organized kingdoms with their armies. But note attentively that from the conquered nations they have learned the arts and how to use them. Without that their power would have passed like the noise of thunder and storm.

You fear, you say, that some crueler method of destruction than that now used will be invented. No. If a fatal invention were to be made, it would soon be outlawed by international law, and unanimous agreement among nations would bury the discovery. Princes have no interest in conquering by such means. They have to be on the lookout for additional subjects, not territory.

You commiserate on the invention of gunpowder and shells, and you find it strange that there should no longer be an impregnable fortress —

that is to say, you find it strange that wars should be ended sooner today than they used to be before.

You must have noticed in your readings in history, that since the invention of gunpowder, battles are much less bloody than they were before, because there is practically no direct engagement now.

And even if some particular case where one of the arts was harmful were to be found, should it for that reason be abandoned? Do you believe, Rhedi, that religion, which our Holy Prophet brought down from heaven, is harmful because it will one day serve to confound the perfidious Christians?

You think that arts soften a people and are thereby the cause for the fall of empires. You speak of the destruction of the empire of the ancient Persians as the effect of their softness. But that example is far from decisive, since the Greeks who conquered and subjugated them so many times, cultivated the arts with infinitely more care than they.

When people say that the arts make men effeminate, they are not in any case talking of the people who practice them, for these people are never idle, and of all vices, idleness is the one that most softens courage.

The whole question reduces to those who appreciate the arts. But in every organized society, those who enjoy the commodities of one art are obliged to cultivate another unless they want to be brought to shameful poverty, and therefore, it follows that softness and idleness are incompatible with the arts.

Paris is perhaps the most sensual city in the world, the city where pleasures are most highly refined. Yet it is the city where people lead the hardest life. So that one man can live in delight, a hundred others must labor ceaselessly. A woman has taken it into her head that she must appear at a gathering in a certain attire. From that moment on, fifty workers get no more sleep and are without time to drink and eat. She orders and is obeyed more promptly than our monarch would be, because personal profit is the greatest monarch on earth.

This ardor for work, this passion for growing rich, passes along from social class to social class, from the artisans right up to the nobles. No one likes to be poorer than the one he has just noticed directly below him. You will see in Paris a man who has the wherewithal to live until Judgment Day, and yet he works ceaselessly and risks shortening his life in piling up, as he puts it, the necessities of life.

The same spirit is caught by the nation. Work and industry are everywhere. Where then is this effeminate people you talk so much of?

I shall suppose, Rhedi, that a kingdom sanctions only those arts — already quite a few — that are absolutely necessary to the tilling of the soil, and that it banishes all those that serve only delight and fancy. I maintain that this state will be one of the most miserable ever to exist in the world.

If the inhabitants were courageous enough to give up so many things they need, that people would grow weaker each day and the state would become so enfeebled that no power would be too small to conquer it.

It would be easy for me to go into great detail and to demonstrate to you that the incomes of individuals, and consequently, that of the prince, would cease almost completely. There would be almost no more balance of professional skill between citizens. You would see the end of that circulation of wealth and progression of income proper to the interdependence of the arts. Each individual would live from his land and would derive from it just exactly what he needed to keep from dying of hunger. But since this is often not even a twentieth of the state income, the number of inhabitants would have to diminish proportionately until there remained only a twentieth part of them.

Study carefully where the income from industry goes. A fund of capital produces each year for its owner only the twentieth part of its value. Yet from a pistole's worth of color, a painter will paint a canvas worth fifty. The same can be said for goldsmiths, woolworkers, silkworkers, and all other kinds of artisans.

From all this, you must conclude, Rhedi, that to keep a prince powerful, his subjects must live in pleasure. He must work to secure all manner of superfluity for them, devoting to this as much attention as he turns to the necessities of life.

# *Preface to Poor Richard Improved*

## BENJAMIN FRANKLIN

Courteous Reader,

I have heard that nothing gives an Author so great Pleasure, as to find his Works respectfully quoted by other learned Authors. This Pleasure I have seldom enjoyed; for tho' I have been, if may say it without Vanity, an *eminent Author* of Almanacks annually now a full Quarter of a Century, my Brother Authors in the same Way, for what Reason I know not, have ever been very sparing in their Applauses; and no other Author has taken the least Notice of me, so that did not my Writings produce me some solid *Pudding,* the great Deficiency of *Praise* would have quite discouraged me.

I concluded at length, that the People were the best Judges of my Merit; for they buy my Works; and besides, in my Rambles, where I am not personally known, I have frequently heard one or other of my Adages repeated, with, *as Poor Richard says,* at the End on't; this give me some Satisfaction, as it showed not only that my Instructions were regarded, but discovered likewise some Respect for my Authority; and I own, that to encourage the Practice of remembering and repeating those wise Sentences, I have sometimes *quoted myself* with great Gravity.

Judge then how much I must have been gratified by an Incident I am going to relate to you. I stopt my Horse lately where a great Number of People were collected at a Vendue of Merchant Goods. The Hour of Sale not being come, they were conversing on the Badness of the Times, and one of the Company call'd to a plain clean old Man, with white Locks, *Pray, Father* Abraham, *what think you of the Times? Won't these heavy Taxes quite ruin the Country? How shall we ever be able to pay them? What would you advise us to?* —— Father *Abraham* stood up, and reply'd, If you'd have my Advice, I'll give it you in short, for a *Word to the Wise is enough,* and *many Words won't fill a Bushel,* as *Poor Richard* says. They join'd in desiring him to speak his Mind, and gathering round him, he proceeded as follows;

"Friends, says he, and Neighbours, the Taxes are indeed very heavy, and if those laid on by the Government were the only Ones we had to pay, we might more easily discharge them; but we have many others, and much more grievous to some of us. We are taxed twice as much by our *Idleness,* three times as much by our *Pride,* and four times as much by our *Folly,* and from these Taxes the Commissioners cannot ease or deliver us by allowing an Abatement. However let us hearken to good Advice, and something may be done for us; *God helps them that help themselves,* as *Poor Richard* says, in his Almanack of 1733.

It would be thought a hard Government that should tax its People one tenth Part of their *Time,* to be employed in its Service. But *Idleness* taxes many of us much more, if we reckon all that is spent in absolute *Sloth,* or doing of nothing, with that which is spent in idle Employments or Amusements, that amount to nothing. *Sloth,* by bringing on Diseases, absolutely shortens Life. *Sloth, like Rust, consumes faster than Labour wears, while the used Key is always bright,* as *Poor Richard* says. But *dost thou love Life, then do not squander Time, for that's the Stuff Life is made of,* as *Poor Richard* says. — How much more than is necessary do

39. William Hogarth, *The Harlot's Progress, Plate I. The Innocent Country Girl Ensnared by a Procuress.*

we spend in Sleep! forgetting that *The sleeping Fox catches no Poultry,* and that *there will be sleeping enough in the Grave,* as *Poor Richard* says. If Time be of all Things the most precious, *wasting Time* must be, as *Poor Richard* says, *the greatest Prodigality,* since, as he elsewhere tells us, *Lost Time is never found again;* and what we call *Time-enough, always proves little enough:* Let us then up and be doing, and doing to the Purpose; so by Diligence shall we do more with less Perplexity. *Sloth makes all Things difficult, but Industry all easy,* as *Poor Richard* says; and *He that riseth late, must trot all Day, and shall scarce overtake his Business at Night.* While *Laziness travels so slowly, that Poverty soon overtakes him,* as we read in *Poor Richard,* who adds, *Drive thy Business, let not that drive thee;* and *Early to Bed, and early to rise, makes a Man healthy, wealthy and wise.*

So what signifies *wishing* and *hoping* for better Times. We may make these Times better if we bestir ourselves. *Industry need not wish,* as *Poor Richard* says, and *He that lives upon Hope will die fasting. There are no Gains, without Pains;* then *Help Hands, for I have no Lands,* or if I have, they are smartly taxed. And, as *Poor Richard* likewise observes, *He that hath a Trade hath an Estate, and He that hath a Calling, hath an Office of Profit and Honour;* but then the *Trade* must be worked at, and the *Calling* well followed, or neither the *Estate,* nor the *Office,* will enable us to pay our Taxes. — If we are industrious we shall never starve; for, as *Poor Richard* says, *At the Working Man's House* Hunger *looks in, but dares not enter.* Nor will the Bailiff or the Constable enter, for *Industry pays Debts, while Despair encreaseth them,* says *Poor Richard.* — What though you have found no Treasure, nor has any rich Relation left you a Legacy, *Diligence is the Mother of Good luck, as Poor Richard says, and God gives all Things to Industry.* Then *plough deep, while Sluggards sleep, and you shall have Corn to sell and to keep,* says *Poor Dick.* . . .

# On Commerce

## VOLTAIRE

Commerce, which has enriched the citizens of England, has helped make them free, and this freedom has in turn extended commerce; hence the greatness of the state. It is commerce which gradually established the naval forces that have made the English the masters of the sea. They have now close to two hundred war ships. Posterity will perhaps be surprised to learn that a little island which has but a small quantity of lead, tin, clay and wool became so powerful through its commerce that it could send in 1723 three fleets to three extremities of the world at the same time, one to Gibraltar, conquered and maintained by its arms; another to Porto-Bello, to deprive the king of Spain of the enjoyment of the treasures of the Indies; and the third to the Baltic Sea to prevent the powers of the north from fighting.

When Louis XIV made Italy tremble, and his armies, already in possession of Savoy and Piedmont, were on the point of taking Turin, Prince Eugene had to march from the remotest parts of Germany to the assistance of the duke of Savoy. He had no money, without which cities can neither be taken nor defended. He had recourse to the English merchants. In half an hour's time they lent him fifty millions, with which he liberated Turin, beat the French, and wrote this short note to those who had lent him the money: "Gentlemen, I have received your money, and flatter myself I have employed it to your satisfaction."

All this gives an English merchant a just pride, and causes him, not without reason, to compare himself to a citizen of Rome. Thus the younger son of a peer of the realm does not disdain trade. Lord Townshend, secretary of state, has a brother who is satisfied with being a merchant in the city. At the time when Lord Oxford ruled all England, his younger brother was a merchant at Aleppo, whence he would not depart, and where he died.

This custom, which is now unhappily dying out, appears monstrous to a German, whose head is full of the hereditary privilege of his family. They can never conceive how it is possible that the son of an English peer should be no more than a rich and powerful bourgeois, while in Germany everyone is a prince. I have known more than thirty highnesses of the same name, whose whole fortunes and estate put together amounted to a few coats of arms and their pride.

In France anybody is a marquis who wants to be; and whoever comes from the obscurity of some remote province with money in his pocket and a name that ends with *"ac"* or *"ille,"* can say "A man of my quality and rank"; and hold merchants in the most sovereign contempt. The merchant hears his profession spoken of scornfully so often, that he is foolish enough to blush because of it. I do not know, however, which is the most useful to his country, a powdered lord, who knows to a minute when the king rises or goes to bed, perhaps to stool, and who gives himself airs of importance in playing the part of a slave in the antechamber of some minister; or a merchant, who enriches his country, and from his office sends his orders to Surat or Cairo, thereby contributing to the happiness of the world.

# from *The Wealth of Nations*

## ADAM SMITH

### OF THE PRINCIPLE WHICH GIVES OCCASION TO THE DIVISION OF LABOR

The division of labor, from which so many advantages are derived, is not originally the effect of any human wisdom, which foresees and intends

*40.* Bibiena, *Design for Stage Setting with Perspectives.*

that general opulence to which it gives occasion. It is the necessary, though very slow and gradual consequence of a certain propensity in human nature which has in view no such extensive utility; the propensity to truck, barter, and exchange one thing for another.

Whether this propensity be one of those original principles in human nature of which no further account can be given; or whether, as seems more probable, it be the necessary consequence of the faculties of reason and speech, it belongs not to our present subject to inquire. It is common to all men, and to be found in no other race of animals, which seem to know neither this nor any other species of contracts. Two greyhounds, in running down the same hare, have sometimes the appearance of acting in some sort of concert. Each turns her towards his companion, or endeavors to intercept her when his companion turns her towards himself. This, however, is not the effect of any contract, but of the accidental concurrence of their passions in the same object at that particular time. Nobody ever saw a dog make a fair and deliberate exchange of one bone for another with another dog. Nobody ever saw one animal by its gestures and natural cries signify to another, this is mine, that yours; I am willing to give this for that. When an animal wants to obtain something either of a man or of another animal, it has no other means of persuasion but to gain the favor of those whose service it requires. A puppy fawns upon its dam, and a spaniel endeavors by a thousand attractions to engage the attention of its master who is at dinner, when it wants to be fed by him. Man sometimes uses the same arts with his brethren, and when he has no other means of engaging them to act according to his inclinations, endeavors by every servile and fawning attention to obtain their good will. He has not time, however, to do this upon every occasion. In civilized society he stands at all times in need for the cooperation and assistance of great multitudes, while his whole life is scarce sufficient to gain the friendship of a few persons. In almost every other race of animals each individual, when it is grown up to maturity, is entirely independent, and in its natural state has occasion for the assistance of no other living creature. But man has almost constant occasion for the help of his brethren, and it is in vain for him to expect it from their benevolence only. He will be more likely to prevail if he can interest their self-love in his favor, and show them that it is for their own advantage to do for him what he requires of them. Whoever offers to another a bargain of any kind, proposes to do this. Give me that which I want, and you shall have this which you want, is the meaning of every such offer; and it is in this manner that we obtain from one another the far greater part of those good offices which we stand in need of. It is not from the benevolence of the butcher, the brewer, or the baker that we expect our dinner, but from their regard to their own interest. We address ourselves, not to their humanity but to their self-love, and never talk to them of our own necessities but of their advantages. Nobody but a beggar chooses to depend chiefly upon the benevolence of his fellow citizens. Even a beggar does not depend upon it entirely. The charity of well disposed people, indeed, supplies him with the whole fund of his subsistence. But though this principle ultimately provides him with all the necessaries of life which he has occasion for, it neither does nor can provide him with them as he has occasion for them. The greater part of his occasional wants are supplied in the same manner as those of other people, by treaty, by barter, and by purchase. With the money which one man gives him he purchases food. The old clothes which another bestows upon him he exchanges for other old clothes which suit him better, or for lodging, or for food, or for money, with which he can buy either food, clothes, or lodging, as he has occasion.

As it is by treaty, by barter, and by purchase that we obtain from one another the greater part of those mutual good offices which we stand in need of, so it is this same trucking disposition which originally gives occasion to the division of labor. In a tribe of hunters or shepherds a particular person makes bows and arrows, for example, with more readiness and dexterity than any other. He frequently exchanges them for cattle or for venison with his companions; and he finds at last that he can in this manner get more cattle and venison that if he himself went to the field to catch them. From a regard to his own interest, therefore, the making of bows and arrows grows to be his chief business, and he becomes a sort of armourer. Another excels in making the frames and covers of their little huts or movable houses. He is accustomed to be of use in this way to his neighbors, who reward him in the same manner with cattle and with venison, till at last he finds it his interest to dedicate himself entirely to this employment, and to become a sort of house carpenter. In the same manner a third becomes a smith or a brazier, a fourth a tanner or dresser of hides or skins, the principal part of the clothing of savages. And thus the certainty of being able to exchange all that surplus part of the produce of his own labor, which is over and above his own consumption, for such parts of the produce of other men's labor as he may have occasion for, encourages every man to apply himself to a particular occupation, and to cultivate and bring to perfection whatever talent or genius he may possess for that particular species of business.

The difference of natural talents in different men is, in reality, much less than we are aware of; and the very different genius which appears to distinguish men of different professions, when grown up to maturity, is not upon many occasions so much the cause as the effect of the division of labor. The difference between the most dissimilar characters, between a philosopher and a common street porter, for example, seems to arise not so much from nature as from habit, custom, and education. When they came into the world, and for the first six or eight years of their existence, they were perhaps very much alike, and neither their parents nor play fellows could perceive any remarkable difference. About that age, or soon after, they come to be employed in very different occupations. The difference of talents comes then to be taken notice of, and widens by degrees, till at last the vanity of the philosopher is willing to acknowledge scarce any resemblance. But without the disposition to truck, barter, and exchange, every man must have procured to himself every necessary and conveniency of life which he wanted. All must have had the same duties to perform, and the same work to do, and there could have been no such difference of employment as could alone give occasion to any great difference of talents.

41. Antoine Watteau, *Italian Comedians.*

42. Nicolas Lancret, *Italian Comedians.*

As it is this disposition which forms that difference of talents, so remarkable among men of different professions, so it is this same disposition which renders that difference useful. Many tribes of animals acknowledged to be all of the same species derive from nature a much more remarkable distinction of genius, than what, antecedent to custom and education, appears to take place among men. By nature a philosopher is not in genius and disposition half so different from a street porter, as a mastiff is from a greyhound, or a greyhound from a spaniel, or this last from a shepherd's dog. Those different tribes of animals, however, though all of the same species, are of scarce any use to one another. The strength of the mastiff is not, in the least, supported either by the swiftness of the greyhound, or by the sagacity of the spaniel, or by the docility of the shepherd's dog. The effects of those different geniuses and talents, for want of the power or disposition to barter and exchange, cannot be brought into a common stock, and do not in the least contribute to the better accommodation and conveniency of the species. Each animal is still obliged to support and defend itself, separately and independently, and derives no sort of advantage from that variety of talents with which nature has distinguished its fellows. Among men, on the contrary, the most dissimilar geniuses are of use to one another; the different produces of their respective talents, by the general disposition to truck, barter, and exchange, being brought, as it were, into a common stock, where every man may purchase whatever part of the produce of other men's talents he has occasion for.

# from *Robinson Crusoe*

## DANIEL DEFOE

Being the third son of the family, and not bred to any trade, my head began to be filled very early with rambling thoughts: my father, who was very ancient, had given me a competent share of learning, as far as house-education and a country free-school generally go, and designed me for the law; but I would be satisfied with nothing but going to sea; and my inclination to this led me so strongly against the will, nay, the commands of my father, and against all the entreaties and persuasions of my mother and other friends, that there seemed to be something fatal in that propension of nature, tending directly to the life of misery which was to befall me.

My father, a wise and grave man, gave me serious and excellent counsel against what he foresaw was my design. He called me one morning into his chamber, where he was confined by the gout, and expostulated very warmly with me upon this subject: he asked me what reasons more than a mere wandering inclination I had for leaving my father's house and my native country, where I might be well introduced, and had a prospect of raising my fortune by application and industry, with a life of ease and pleasure. He told me it was men of desperate fortunes on one hand, or of aspiring, superior fortunes on the other, and who went abroad upon adventures, to rise by enterprise, and make themselves famous in undertakings of a nature out of the common road; that these things were all either too far above me, or too far below me; that mine was the middle state, or what might be called the upper station of low life, which he had found, by long experience, was the best state in the world, the most suited to human happiness, not exposed to the miseries and hardships, the labour and sufferings of the mechanic part of mankind, and not embarrassed with the pride, luxury, ambition, and envy of the upper part of mankind. He told me, I might judge of the happiness of this state by this one thing, viz., that this was the state of life which all other people envied; that kings have frequently lamented the miserable consequences of being born to great things, and wished they had been placed in the middle of the two extremes, between the mean and the great; that the wise man gave his testimony to this, as the just standard of true felicity, when he prayed to have neither poverty nor riches.

He bade me observe it, and I should always find, that the calamities of life were shared among the upper and lower part of mankind; but that the middle station had the fewest disasters, and was not exposed to so many vicissitudes as the higher or lower part of mankind! nay, they were not subjected to so many distempers and uneasiness, either of body or mind, as those were, who, by vicious living, luxury, and extravagances, on one hand, or by hard labour, want of necessaries, and mean or insufficient diet, on the other hand, bring distempers upon themselves by the natural consequences of their way of living; that the middle station of life was calculated for all kind of virtues and all kind of enjoyments; that peace and plenty were the handmaids of a middle fortune; that temperance, moderation, quietness, health, society, all agreeable diversions, and all desirable pleasures, were the blessings attending the middle station of life; that this way men went silently and smoothly through the world, and comfortably out of it, not embarrassed with the labours of the hands or of the head, not sold to a life of slavery for daily bread, or harassed with perplexed circumstances, which rob the soul of peace, and the body of rest; nor enraged with the passion of envy, or the secret burning lust of ambition for great things; but, in easy circumstances, sliding gently through the world, and sensibly tasting the sweets of living, without the bitter; feeling that they are happy, and learning by every day's experience to know it more sensibly.

.     .     .

The rainy season sometimes held longer or shorter as the winds happened to blow, but this was the general observation I made. After I had found by experience the ill consequences of being abroad in the rain, I took care to furnish myself with provisions beforehand, that I might not be obliged to go out; and I sat within doors as much as possible during the wet months. This time I found much employment, and very suitable also to the time, for I found great occasion for many things which I had no way to furnish myself with but by hard labour and constant application; particularly, I tried many ways to make myself a basket, but all the twigs I could get for the purpose proved so brittle, that they would do nothing. It proved of excellent advantage to me now, that when I was a boy, I used to take great delight in standing at a basket-maker's in the town where my father lived, to see them make their wicker-ware; and being, as boys usually are, very officious to help, and a great observer of the manner how they worked those things, and sometimes lending a hand, I had by these means full knowledge of the methods of it, that I wanted nothing but the materials; when it came into my mind that the twigs of that tree from whence I cut my stakes that grew, might possibly be as tough as the sallows, willows, and osiers in England, and I resolved to try. Accordingly, the next day, I went to my country house, as I called it, and cutting some of the smaller twigs, I found them to my purpose as much as I could desire; whereupon I came the next time prepared with a hatchet to cut down a quantity, which I soon found, for there was great plenty of them. These I set up to dry within my circle or hedge, and when they were fit for use, I carried them to my cave; and here, during the next season, I employed myself in making, as well as I could, a great many baskets, both to carry earth, or to carry or lay up anything, as I had occasion; and though I did not finish them very handsomely, yet I made them sufficiently serviceable for my purpose; and thus, afterwards, I took care never to be without them; and as my wicker-ware decayed, I made more, especially strong deep baskets to place my corn in, instead of sacks, when I should come to have any quantity of it.

Having mastered this difficulty, and employed a world of time about it, I bestirred myself to see, if possible, how to supply two wants. I had no vessel to hold anything that was liquid, except two runlets, which were almost full of rum, and some glass bottles, some of the common size, and others which were case-bottles-square, for the holding of waters, spirits, &c. I had not so much as a pot to boil anything, except a great kettle, which I saved out of the ship, and which was too big for such use as I desired it, viz., to make broth, and stew a bit of meat by itself. The second thing I fain would have had was a tobacco-pipe; but it was impossible to me to make one; however, I found a contrivance for that too at last. I employed myself in planting my second rows of stakes or piles and in this wicker-working all the summer or dry season, when another business took me up more time than it could be imagined I could spare.

.    .    .

My case was this, it was to be a large tree which was to be cut down, because my board was to be a broad one. This tree I was three days a cutting down, and two more cutting off the boughs, and reducing it to a log, or piece of timber. With inexpressible hacking and hewing, I reduced both the sides of it into chips till it began to be light enough to move, then I turned it, and made one side of it smooth and flat as a board from end to end; then turning that side downward, cut the other side, till I brought the plank to be about three inches thick, and smooth on both sides. Any one may judge the labour of my hands in such a piece of work, but labour and patience carried me through that and many other things; I only observe this in particular, to show the reason why so much of my time went away with so little work, viz., that what might be a little to be done with help and tools, was a vast labour, and required a prodigious time to do alone, and by hand. But notwithstanding this, with patience and labour I went through many things, and, indeed, everything that my circumstances made necessary to me to do, as will appear by what follows.

I was now in the months of November and December, expecting my crop of barley and rice. The ground I had manured or dug up for them was not great, for as I observed, my seed of each was not above the quantity of half a peck, for I had lost one whole crop by sowing in the dry season; but now my crop promised very well, when, on a sudden, I found

I was in danger of losing it all again by enemies of several sorts, which it was scarce possible to keep from it; as, first the goats, and wild creatures which I called hares, who, tasting the sweetness of the blade, lay in it night and day, as soon as it came up, and eat it so close, that it could get no time to shoot up into stalk.

This I saw no remedy for, but by making an enclosure about it with a hedge, which I did with a great deal of toil, and the more, because it required speed. However, as my arable land was but small, suited to my crop, I got it totally well fenced, in about three weeks' time, and shooting some of the creatures in the day-time, I set my dog to guard it in the night, tying him up to a stake at the gate, where he would stand and bark all night long; so in a little time the enemies forsook the place, and the corn grew very strong and well, and began to ripen apace.

But as the beasts ruined me before, while my corn was in the blade, so the birds were as likely to ruin me now, when it was in the ear; for going along by the place to see how it throve, I saw my little crop surrounded with fowls, of I know not how many sorts, who stood, as it were, watching till I should be gone. I immediately let fly among them, for I always had my gun with me: I had no sooner shot, but there rose up a little cloud of fowls, which I had not seen at all, from among the corn itself.

This touched me sensibly, for I foresaw that in a few days they would devour all my hopes, that I should be starved, and never be able to raise a crop at all, and what to do I could not tell; however, I resolved not to lose my corn, if possible, though I should watch it night and day. In the first place, I went among it, to see what damage was already done, and found they had spoiled a good deal of it, but that as it was yet too green for them, the loss was not so great, but that the remainder was like to be a good crop, if it could be saved.

I staid by it to load my gun, and then coming away, I could easily see the thieves sitting upon all the trees about me, as if they only waited till I was gone away, and the event proved it to be so; for as I walked off, as if I was gone, I was no sooner out of their sight, than they dropt down, one by one, into the corn again. I was so provoked, that I could not have patience to stay till more came on, knowing that every grain that they eat now was, as it might be said, a peck-loaf to me in the consequence; but coming up to the hedge, I fired again, and killed three of them. This was what I wished for; so I took them up, and served them as we serve notorious thieves in England, viz., hanged them in chains, for a terror to others. It is impossible to imagine almost that this should have such an effect as it had, for the fowls would not only not come at the corn, but, in short, they forsook all that part of the island, and I could never see a bird near the place as long as my scare-crows hung there. This I was very glad of, you may be sure, and about the latter end of December, which was our second harvest of the year, I reaped my corn.

I was sadly put to it for a scythe or sickle to cut it down, and all I could do was to make one as well as I could, out of one of the broadswords, or cutlasses, which I saved among the arms out of the ship. However, as my first crop was but small, I had no great difficulty to cut it down; in short, I reaped it my way, for I cut nothing off but the ears, and carried it away in a great basket which I had made, and so rubbed it out with my hands, and at the end of all my harvesting, I found that out of my half-peck of seed I had near two bushels of rice, and above two bushels and a half of barley, that is to say, by my guess, for I had no measure at that time.

However, this was a great encouragement to me, and I foresaw that, in time, it would please God to supply me with bread: and yet here I was perplexed again, for I neither knew how to grind, or make meal of my corn, or indeed how to clean it and part it; nor if made into meal, how to make bread of it, and if how to make it, yet I knew not how to bake it; these things being added to my desire of having a good quantity for store, and to secure a constant supply, I resolved not to taste any of this crop, but to preserve it all for seed against the next season, and, in the meantime, to employ all my study and hours of working to accomplish this great work of providing myself with corn and bread.

It might be truly said, that now I worked for my bread. 'Tis a little wonderful, and what I believe few people have thought much upon, viz., the strange multitude of little things necessary in the providing, producing, curing, dressing, making, and finishing this one article of bread.

# from *Tom Jones*

## HENRY FIELDING

An author ought to consider himself, not as a gentleman who gives a private or eleemosynary treat, but rather as one who keeps a public ordinary, at which all persons are welcome for their money. In the former case, it is well known that the entertainer provides what fare he pleases; and though this should be very indifferent, and utterly disagreeable to

the taste of his company, they must not find any fault; nay, on the contrary, good breeding forces them outwardly to approve and commend
whatever is set before them. Now the contrary of this happens to the
master of an ordinary. Men who pay for what they eat will insist on
gratifying their palates, however nice and whimsical these may prove;
and if everything is not agreeable to their taste, will challenge a right to
censure, to abuse, and to d — n their dinner without control.

To prevent, therefore, giving offense to their customers by any such
disappointment, it hath been usual with the honest and well-meaning
host to provide a bill of fare which all persons may peruse at their first
entrance into the house; and having thence acquainted them with the
entertainment they may expect, may either stay and regale with what
is provided for them, or may depart to some other ordinary better accommodated to their taste.

As we do not disdain to borrow wit or wisdom from any man who is
capable of lending us either, we have condescended to take a hint from
these honest victualers, and shall prefix not only a general bill of fare
to our whole entertainment, but shall likewise give the reader particular
bills to every course which is to be served up in this and ensuing volumes.

The provision, then, which we have made here is no other than *Human
Nature*. Nor do I fear that my sensible reader, though most luxurious
in his taste, will start, cavil or be offended, because I have named but
one article. The tortoise, — as the alderman of Bristol, well learned in
eating, knows by much experience, — besides the delicious calibash and
calipee, contains many different kinds of food; nor can the learned reader
be ignorant, that in human nature, though here collected under one
general name, is such a prodigious variety, that a cook will sooner have
gone through all the several species of animal and vegetable food in the
world, than an author will be able to exhaust so extensive a subject.

An objection may perhaps be apprehended from the more delicate,
that this dish is too common and vulgar; for what else is the subject of
all the romances, novels, plays and poems, with which the stalls abound?
Many exquisite viands might be rejected by the epicure, if it was a
sufficient cause for his contemning of them as common and vulgar, that
something was to be found in the most paltry alleys under the same name.
In reality, true nature is as difficult to be met with in authors, as the
Bayonne ham, or Bologna sausage, is to be found in the shops.

But the whole, to continue the same metaphor, consists in the cookery
of the author; for, as Mr. Pope tells us,

> True wit is nature to advantage drest;
> What oft was thought, but ne'er so well exprest.

The same animal which hath the honor to have some part of his flesh eaten at the table of a duke, may perhaps be degraded in another part, and some of his limbs gibbeted, as it were, in the vilest stall in town. Where, then, lies the difference between the food of the nobleman and the porter, if both are at dinner on the same ox or calf, but in the seasoning, the dressing, the garnishing, and the setting forth? Hence the one provokes and incites the most languid appetite, and the other turns and palls that which is the sharpest and keenest.

In like manner, the excellence of the mental entertainment consists less in the subject than in the author's skill in well dressing it up. How pleased, therefore, will the reader be to find that we have, in the following work, adhered closely to one of the highest principles of the best cook which the present age, or perhaps that of Heliogabalus, hath produced. This great man, as is well known to all polite lovers of eating, begins at first by setting plain things before his hungry guests, rising afterward by degrees as their stomachs might be supposed to decrease, to the very quintessence of sauce and spices. In like manner, we shall represent human nature at first to the keen appetite of the reader, in that more plain and simple manner in which it is found in the country, and shall thereafter hash and ragoo it with all the high French and Italian seasoning of affectation and vice which courts and cities afford. By these means, we doubt not but our reader may be rendered desirous to read on forever, as the great person just above-mentioned is supposed to have made some persons eat.

Having promised this much, we will now detain those who like our bill of fare, no longer from their diet, and shall proceed directly to serve up the first course of our history for their entertainment.

# from *Rameau's Nephew*

## DENIS DIDEROT

*Vertumnis, quotquot sunt, natus iniquis.*[1]
Horace

Rain or shine, it is my regular habit every day about five to go and take a walk around the Palais-Royal. I can be seen, all by myself, dreaming on D'Argenson's bench. I discuss with myself questions of politics, love, taste, or philosophy. I let my mind rove wantonly, give it free rein to follow any idea, wise or mad, that may come uppermost; I chase it as do our young libertines along Foy's Walk, when they are on the track of a courtesan whose mien is giddy and face smiling, whose nose turns up. The youth drops one and picks up another, pursuing all and clinging to none: my ideas are my trollops.

If the weather is too cold or rainy, I take shelter in the Regency Café, where I entertain myself by watching chess being played. Paris is the world center, and this café is the Paris center, for the finest skill at this game. It is there that one sees the clash of the profound Legal, the subtle Philidor, the staunch Mayot; that one sees the most surprising strokes and that one hears the stupidest remarks. For although one may be a wit and a great chess player, like Legal, one may also be a great chess player and a fool, like Foubert and Mayot.

One day I was there after dinner, looking hard, saying little, and listening the least amount possible, when I was accosted by one of the oddest characters in this country, where God has not stinted us. The fellow is a compound of elevation and abjectness, of good sense and lunacy. The ideas of decency and depravity must be strangely scrambled in his head, for he shows without ostentation the good qualities that nature has bestowed upon him, just as he does the bad ones without shame. Apart from this, he is endowed with a strong constitution, a special warmth of imagination, and an unusual power of lung. If you ever meet him and are not put off by his originality, you will either stuff your fingers into your ears or run away. Lord, what lungs!

He has no greater opposite than himself. Sometimes he is thin and wan like a patient in the last stages of consumption; you could count his teeth through his skin; he looks as if he had been days without food or had just come out of a Trappist monastery. The next month, he is sleek and fat as if he ate regularly at a banker's or had shut himself up in a Bernardine convent. Today his linen is filthy, his clothes torn to rags, he is virtually barefoot, and he hangs his head furtively; one is tempted to hail him and toss him a coin. Tomorrow he is powdered, curled, well dressed: he holds his head high, shows himself off — you would almost take him for a man of quality. He lives from day to day, sad or cheerful according to luck. His first care on arising in the morning is to ascertain where he will dine; after dinner he ponders supper. Night brings its own worries — whether to return on foot to the garret where he sleeps (unless the landlady has taken back the key from impatience at receiving no rent); or whether to repair to a suburban tavern and await the dawn over a crust of bread and a mug of beer. When he hasn't as much as sixpence in his pocket, as sometimes happens, he falls back on a cab-driving friend of his, or the coachman of a noble lord, who gives him a shakedown in a stable, alongside the horses. The next morning he still has bits of his mattress in his hair. If the weather is mild, he perambulates all night up and down the Cours-la-reine or the Champs-Elysées. Daybreak sees him back in town, all dressed from yesterday for today and from today perhaps for the remainder of the week.

I have no great esteem for such eccentrics. Some people take them on as regular acquaintances or even friends. But for my part it is only once a year that I stop and fall in with them, largely because their character stands out from the rest and breaks that tedious uniformity which our education, our social conventions, and our customary good manners have brought about. If such a character makes his appearance in some circle, he is like a grain of yeast that ferments and restores to each of us a part of his native individuality. He shakes and stirs us up, makes us praise or blame, smokes out the truth, discloses the worthy and unmasks the rascals. It is then that the sensible man keeps his ears open and sorts out his company.

I knew my man from quite a while back. He used to frequent a house to which his talent had given him entrée. There was an only daughter; he swore to the father and mother that he would marry her. They shrugged it off, laughed in his face, told him he was crazy. But I lived to see it happen. He asked me for a little money, which I gave him. He had somehow made his way into a few good families, where he could always dine provided he would not speak without asking permission first.

He kept quiet and ate with fury. He was remarkable to see under that restraint. If he had the inclination to break the treaty and open his mouth, at the first word all the guests would shout "Why, Rameau!" Then rage would blaze in his eyes and he fell to eating with greater fury still. You wanted to know his name and now you know it. He is the nephew of the famous musician who delivered us from the plainsong of Lully that we had intoned for over a century, and who wrote so much visionary gibberish and apocalyptic truth about the theory of music — writings that neither he nor anyone else ever understood. We have from him a number of operas in which one finds harmony, snatches of song, disconnected ideas, clatter, flights, triumphal processions, spears, apotheoses, murmurings, endless victories, and dance tunes that will last for all time. Having eliminated "the Florentine," [Lully] in public favor, he will be eliminated by the Italian virtuosos—as he himself foresaw with grief, rancor, and depression of spirits. For no one, not even a pretty woman who wakes up to find a pimple on her nose, feels so vexed as an author who threatens to survive his own reputation — witness Marivaux and the younger Crébillon.

He accosts me: Ha ha! So there you are, master Philosopher! And what are you up to among all these idlers? Do you waste your time, too, pushing wood? (That is the contemptuous way of describing chess and checkers.)

MYSELF. No, but when I have nothing better to do, I enjoy watching those who push well.

HE. In that case you don't enjoy yourself very often. Apart from Legal and Philidor, the others don't know what they're doing.

MYSELF. What of M. de Bissy?

HE. Oh that one is to chess what Mlle. Clairon is to acting: they know about their respective playing all that can be *learned*.

MYSELF. I see you're hard to please. You forgive nothing but sublime genius.

HE. True: in chess, checkers, poetry, eloquence, music and other nonsense of that kind, what's the use of mediocrity?

MYSELF. Not much use, I admit. But it takes a crowd to cultivate the game before one man of genius emerges. He is one out of many. But let it go. It's an age since I've seen you. I don't think about you very much when I don't see you but I'm always glad when I do. What have you been doing?

HE. What you and I and the rest do, namely, good and evil, and also nothing. And then I was hungry and I ate when I had the chance. After eating I was thirsty and I have occasionally drunk. Meanwhile my beard grew and when grown I had it shaved.

MYSELF. There you did wrong. A beard is all you lack to be a sage.

HE. Right you are. My forehead is broad and wrinkled; I have a glowing eye, a beaky nose, spacious cheeks, thick black brows, a clean-cut mouth, curved-out lips and a square jaw. Cover this ample chin with a flowing beard and I assure you it would look splendid in bronze or marble.

MYSELF. Side by side with Caesar, Marcus Aurelius, and Socrates.

HE. No. I should like it better between Diogenes and Phryne. I am as cheeky as the one and often visit the sisters of the other.

MYSELF. And you are still in good health?

HE. Usually, yes, but not so well today.

MYSELF. How is that? You have a paunch like Silenus and a face like ——

HE. A face like its counterpart behind. That's because the spleen which is wasting my dear uncle seems to fatten his dear nephew.

MYSELF. Speaking of the uncle, do you ever see him?

HE. I see him pass in the street.

MYSELF. Doesn't he do anything for you?

HE. If he ever has done anything for anybody, it must be without knowing it. He is a philosopher after a fashion: he thinks of no one but himself; the rest of the universe doesn't matter a tinker's dam to him. His wife, his daughter, may die as soon as they please. Provided the parish bells that toll for them continue to sound the intervals of the twelfth and the seventeenth, all will be well. It's lucky for him and that's what I envy especially in men of genius. They are good for only one thing – apart from that, zero. They don't know what it is to be citizens, fathers, mothers, cousins, friends. Between you and me, one should try to be like them in every way, but without multiplying the breed. The world needs men, but men of genius, no; I say, no! No need of them. They are the ones who change the face of the earth. Even in small things stupidity is so common and powerful that it is not changed without fracas. What results is partly the reformer's vision, partly the old status quo — whence two gospels, a parti-colored world. The wisdom of the monk Rabelais is the true wisdom for his own peace of mind and other people's too: to do one's duty, more or less, always speak well of the father superior, and let the world wag. It must be all right since the majority is content with it. If I knew history, I could prove to you that evil has always come here below through a few men of genius; but I don't know any history because I don't know anything at all. The devil take me if I've ever learnt a single thing and if, having learnt nothing, I am worse off. One day I was at table with one of the King's Ministers who has brains enough

for ten. Well, he showed us as plain as two and two make four that
nothing is more useful to the nations of the earth than lies, nothing more
harmful than the truth. I don't quite recall his proof but it followed very
clearly that men of genius are poisonous and that if at birth a child bore
the mark of this dangerous gift of nature, he should be either smothered
or thrown to the dogs.

MYSELF. And yet those people who are so down on genius all pretend
to have some.

HE. I'm sure they think so inside, but they don't dare admit it.

MYSELF. From modesty! So you developed from then on an undying
hatred of genius?

HE. Which I'll never get over.

MYSELF. But I remember the time when you were in despair at the
thought of being a common man. You'll never be happy if the pros and
cons weigh with you equally. You should make up your mind and stick
to it. I agree with you that men of genius are usually odd, or — as the
saying goes, "great wits are sure to madness near allied"; but that doesn't
change the truth that ages without genius are despised. Men will continue to honor the nations where genius thrived. Sooner or later they put
up statues to them and call them benefactors of the race. With all due
respect to the sublime minister you were quoting, I believe that although
a lie may serve for a while, it is harmful in the long run; and, contrari-
wise, truth necessarily is best in the long run, even though it may do
harm at the moment. From which I incline to think that the man of
genius who denounces a common error or who establishes a general truth
always deserves our veneration. Such a man may fall a victim to prejudice
or existing law; but there are two kinds of laws — those based on equity,
which are universally true, and those based on whim, which owe their
force only to blindness or local necessity. These last cast odium on their
violator for only a brief moment, an odium which time casts back upon
the judges and the peoples who carried out the law. Which of the two,
Socrates or the judge who made him drink hemlock, is today the dis-
honored man?

HE. A great comfort to Socrates! Was he any the less convicted? any
the less put to death? Was he less of an agitator? In violating a bad law,
did he not encourage fools to despise the good ones? Wasn't he in any
case a queer and troublesome citizen? A while ago you yourself were
not far from marking down the man of genius too!

MYSELF. Listen, my dear fellow. A society should not tolerate any bad
laws, and if it had only good ones it would never find itself persecuting
men of genius. I never said that genius went with evil nor evil with genius.

A fool is more often a knave than a genius is. And even if the latter is difficult to get on with, irritating and irritable — add wicked, if you like — what do you infer from it?

HE. That he should be drowned.

MYSELF. Gently, dear fellow. Look and tell me — I shan't take your uncle as an example. He is a hard man, brutal, inhuman, miserly, a bad father, bad husband, and bad uncle. And it is by no means sure that he is a genius who has advanced his art to such a point that ten years from now we shall still discuss his works. Take Racine instead — there was a genius, and his reputation as a man was none too good. Take Voltaire ——

HE. Don't press the point too far: I am a man to argue with you.

MYSELF. Well, which would you prefer — that he should have been a good soul, at one with his ledger, like Briasson, or with his yardstick, like Barbier; legitimately getting his wife with child annually — a good husband, good father, good uncle, good neighbor, fair trader and nothing more; or that he should have been deceitful, disloyal, ambitious, envious, and mean, but also the creator of *Andromaque, Britannicus, Iphigénie, Phèdre,* and *Athalie?*

HE. For himself I daresay it would have been better to be the former.

MYSELF. That is infinitely truer than you think.

HE. There you go, you fellows! If we say anything good, it's like lunatics or people possessed — by accident. It's only people like you who really know what they're saying. I tell you, Master Philosopher, I know what I say and know it as well as you know what you say.

MYSELF. Let's find out: why better for Racine?

HE. Because all those mighty works of his did not bring him in twenty thousand francs, and if he had been a good silk merchant of rue St. Denis or St. Honoré, a good grocer or apothecary in a large way of business, he would have amassed a huge fortune, in the course of doing which there is no pleasure he would have failed to enjoy. From time to time he would have given a dollar to a poor buffoon like me and I would have made him laugh, besides procuring for him an occasional young girl to distract him a little from eternally living with his wife. We would have eaten excellent meals at his table, played high, drunk excellent wines, coffee, liqueurs; we would have had delightful picnics — you can see I knew perfectly well what I was saying — you laugh, but let me finish — it would have been better for those around him.

MYSELF. Unquestionably. Provided he hadn't used unworthily the riches acquired in legitimate trade, and had kept from his house all the gamblers, parasites, sycophants, idlers, and debauchees, as well as ordered his shopboys to beat up the officious gentlemen who would help husbands to a little distraction from habitually living with their wives.

HE. Beat up, my good sir, beat up! No one is beaten up in a well-ordered city. The profession is respectable; many people, even persons of title, are in it. And what in hell do you think money is for, if not to have good board, good company, pretty women, every kind of pleasure and every sort of amusement? I'd rather be a beggar than own a fortune without these enjoyments. But to come back to Racine. The fellow was of use only to people he didn't know, at a time when he had ceased to live.

MYSELF. Granted. But compare the good and the evil. A thousand years from now he will draw tears, will be admired by men all over the earth, will inspire compassion, human kindness, love. People will wonder who he was, from what country, and France will be envied. As against this, he brought suffering on a few persons who are dead and in whom we take no interest. We have nothing more to fear from his vices or his errors. It would no doubt have been preferable if nature had bestowed upon him the virtues of a good man as well as the talents of a great one. He is a tree which has stunted a few trees in his vicinage and blighted the plants growing at his feet; but his topmost branch reached the sky and his boughs spread afar. He has afforded shade to those past, present, and future who come to rest close to his majestic trunk. He bore fruit of exquisite savor and that will not perish. Again, it would be desirable if Voltaire had the sweetness of Duclos, the ingenuity of Abbé Trublet, the rectitude of Abbé d'Olivet; [2] but as that cannot be, consider the really interesting side of the problem; forget for a moment the point we occupy in time and space, and project your vision into centuries to come, into the most remote places, and nations yet unborn. Think of the welfare of our species and, supposing that we ourselves are not generous enough, let us thank nature for knowing her business better than we. . . .

.        .        .

HE. And think of poverty! The voice of conscience and honor is pretty feeble when the guts cry out. Isn't it enough that if I ever get rich I shall be bound to make restitution? I am prepared to do this in every conceivable way — through gorging, through gambling, through guzzling, and through wenching.

MYSELF. But I'm afraid you will never get rich.

HE. I suspect it too.

MYSELF. Suppose it did work out, what then?

HE. I would act like all beggars on horseback. I'd be the most insolent ruffian ever seen. I'd remember every last thing they made me go through and pay them back with slings and arrows. I love bossing people and I will boss them. I love being praised and they will praise me. I'll have the whole troop of Villemorien's bootlickers on salary, and I'll say to them what's been said to me: "Come on, dogs, entertain me." And they will. "I want decent people pulled to pieces." And they will be — if any can be found. Then too, we'll have women, and when drunk we'll thee-and-thou one another. We will drink and make up tales and develop all sorts of whims and vices. It will be delightful. We'll prove that Voltaire has no genius; that Buffon is always up on stilts like the turgid declaimer he is; that Montesquieu was only a wit. We'll tell D'Alembert to stick to his ciphering and we'll kick behind and before all the little stoics like you who despise us from sour grapes, whose modesty is the prop of pride, and whose good conduct springs from lack of means. Ah, what music you'll hear from us!

MYSELF. Knowing what worthy use you would make of wealth, I see how deplorable it is that you are poor. You would certainly be doing honor to human nature, good to your compatriots and credit to yourself.

HE. I almost think you're making fun of me, Master Philosopher. But you don't even suspect with whom you're tangling; you don't seem to know that at this very moment I represent the most important part of Town and Court. The well-to-do of every description have either said or not said to themselves the words I've just confided to you; the fact remains that the life I would lead in their position is precisely theirs. That's where you fellows are behind the times. You think everybody aims at the same happiness. What an idea! Your conception presupposes a sentimental turn of mind which is not ours, an unusual spirit, a special taste. You call your quirks virtue, or philosophy. But virtue and philosophy are not made for everybody. The few who can, have it; the few who can, keep it. Just imagine the universe philosophical and wise, and tell me if it would not be devilishly dull. Listen! I say hurrah for wisdom and philosophy — the wisdom of Solomon: to drink good wines, gorge on choice food, tumble pretty women, sleep in downy beds — outside of that, all is vanity.

MYSELF. What! And fighting for your country?

HE. Vanity! There are no countries left. All I see from pole to pole is tyrants and slaves.

MYSELF. What of helping your friends?

HE. Vanity! No one has any friends. And even if one had, should one risk making them ungrateful? Look close and you'll see that's all you get for being helpful. Gratitude is a burden and burdens are to be shuffled off.

MYSELF. To hold a position in society and discharge its duties?

HE. Vanity! What difference whether you hold a position or not, provided you have means, since you only seek a position in order to get wealth. Discharge one's duties — what does that bring you? — jealousy, worries, persecution. Is that the way to get on? Nonsense! Pay court, pay court, know the right people, flatter their tastes and fall in with their whims, serve their vices and second their misdeeds — there's the secret.

MYSELF. Watch over the education of one's children?

HE. Vanity! That's a tutor's business.

MYSELF. But if a tutor, imbued with your principles, neglects his duty, who will pay the penalty?

HE. Not I anyhow. Possibly, some day, my daughter's husband or my son's wife.

MYSELF. But suppose that either or both plunge into vice and debauchery?

HE. Then that is part of their social position.

MYSELF. If they disgrace themselves?

HE. It's impossible to disgrace yourself, no matter what you do, if you are rich.

### NOTES
1. Born under all the changeful stars there are.
2. These compliments are ironic. — TR.

# from *London*

## SAMUEL JOHNSON

By numbers here from shame or censure free,
All crimes are safe, but hated poverty.
This, only this the rigid law pursues,
This, only this provokes the snarling muse.
The sober trader at a tattered cloak
Wakes from his dream, and labours for a joke;
With brisker air the silken courtiers gaze,
And turn the varied taunt a thousand ways.
Of all the griefs that harass the distressed,
Sure the most bitter is a scornful jest;

Fate never wounds more deep the generous heart,
Than when a blockhead's insult points the dart.
Has Heaven reserved, in pity to the poor,
No pathless waste, or undiscovered shore?
No secret island in the boundless main?
No peaceful desert yet unclaimed by Spain?
Quick, let us rise, the happy seats explore,
And bear oppression's insolence no more.
This mournful truth is everywhere confest:
*Slow rises worth by poverty depressed.*

# from *The Deserted Village*

## OLIVER GOLDSMITH

Ill fares the land, to hastening ills a prey,
Where wealth accumulates, and men decay:
Princes and lords may flourish, or may fade;
A breath can make them, as a breath has made;
But a bold peasantry, their country's pride,
When once destroyed, can never be supplied.
    A time there was, ere England's griefs began,
When every rood of ground maintained its man;
For him light labour spread her wholesome store,
Just gave what life required, but gave no more:
His best companions, innocence and health;
And his best riches, ignorance of wealth.
    But times are altered; trade's unfeeling train
Usurp the land and dispossess the swain;
Along the lawn, where scattered hamlets rose,
Unwieldy wealth, and cumbrous pomp repose;
And every want to luxury allied,
And every pang that folly pays to pride.
These gentle hours that plenty bade to bloom,
Those calm desires that asked but little room,
Those healthful sports that graced the peaceful scene,
Lived in each look, and brightened all the green;

These far departing seek a kinder shore,
And rural mirth and manners are no more.


# from *Albion*

## WILLIAM BLAKE


Because of the Oppressors of Albion in every City & Village.
They mock at the Labourer's limbs: they mock at his starv'd Children.

All the marks remain of the slave's scourge and tyrant's Crown.
And of the Priest's o'ergorged Abdomen, & of the merchant's thin
Sinewy deception, & of the warrior's outbraving & thoughtlessness
In lineaments too extended & in bones too strait & long.
    They shew their wounds: they accuse.

# VIII

## Humanist Morality

*New concepts of morality, oriented toward man's liberation in a tolerant social order rather than toward the consciousness of sin and the hope of salvation, marked the Enlightenment. Before the century was over, the first steps had been taken to abolish slavery, imprisonment for debt, dungeon torture, persecution of "witches" and heretics, and other inhumanities to man. And in his* Supplement to Bougainville's "Voyage" *Diderot showed remarkable foresight into the evils of colonialism.*

# from *A Voyage to Lilliput*

## JONATHAN SWIFT

The first Request I made after I had obtained my Liberty, was, that I might have Licence to see *Mildendo*, the Metropolis; which the Emperor easily granted me, but with a special Charge to do no Hurt, either to the Inhabitants, or their Houses. The People had Notice by Proclamation of my Design to visit the Town. The Wall which encompassed it, is two Foot and an half high, and at least eleven Inches broad, so that a Coach and Horses may be driven very safely round it; and it is flanked with strong Towers at ten Foot Distance. I stept over the great *Western* Gate, and passed very gently, and sideling through the two principal Streets, only in my short Waistcoat, for fear of damaging the Roofs and Eves of the Houses with the Skirts of my Coat. I walked with the utmost Circumspection, to avoid treading on any Stragglers, who might remain in the Streets, although the Orders were very strict, that all People should keep in their Houses, at their own Peril. The Garret Windows and Tops of Houses were so crowded with Spectators, that I thought in all my Travels I had not seen a more populous Place. The City is an exact Square, each Side of the Wall being five Hundred Foot long. The two great Streets which run cross and divide it into four Quarters, are five Foot wide. The Lanes and Alleys which I could not enter, but only viewed them as I passed, are from Twelve to Eighteen Inches. The Town is capable of holding five Hundred Thousand Souls. The Houses are from three to five Stories. The Shops and Markets well provided.

THE Emperor's Palace is in the Center of the City, where the two great Streets meet. It is inclosed by a Wall of two Foot high, and Twenty Foot distant from the Buildings. I had his Majesty's Permission to step over this Wall; and the Space being so wide between that and the Palace, I could easily view it on every Side. The outward Court is a Square of Forty Foot, and includes two other Courts: In the inmost are the Royal Apartments, which I was very desirous to see, but found it extremely difficult; for the great Gates, from one Square into another, were but

Eighteen Inches high, and seven Inches wide. Now the Buildings of the outer Court were at least five Foot high; and it was impossible for me to stride over them, without infinite Damage to the Pile, although the Walls were strongly built of hewn Stone, and four Inches thick. At the same time, the Emperor had a great Desire that I should see the Magnificence of his Palace: But this I was not able to do till three Days after, which I spent in cutting down with my Knife some of the largest Trees in the Royal Park, about an Hundred Yards distant from the City. Of these Trees I made two Stools, each about three Foot high, and strong enough to bear my Weight. The People having received Notice a second time, I went again through the City to the Palace, with my two Stools in my Hands. When I came to the Side of the outer Court, I stood upon one Stool, and took the other in my Hand: This I lifted over the Roof, and gently set it down on the Space between the first and second Court, which was eight Foot wide. I then stept over the Buildings very conveniently from one Stool to the other, and drew up the first after me with a hooked Stick. By this Contrivance I got into the inmost Court; and lying down upon my Side, I applied my Face to the Windows of the middle Stories, which were left open on Purpose, and discovered the most splendid Apartments that can be imagined. There I saw the Empress, and the young Princess in their several Lodgings, with their chief Attendants about them. Her Imperial Majesty was pleased to smile very graciously upon me and gave me out of the Window her Hand to kiss.

But I shall not anticipate the Reader with farther Descriptions of this Kind, because I reserve them for a greater Work, which is now almost ready for the Press; containing a general Description of this Empire, from its first Erection, through a long Series of Princes, with a particular Account of their Wars and Politicks, Laws, Learning, and Religion; their Plants and Animals, their peculiar Manners and Customs, with other Matters very curious and useful; my chief Design at present being only to relate such Events and Transactions as happened to the Publick, or to my self, during a Residence of about nine Months in that Empire.

One Morning, about a fortnight after I had obtained my Liberty, *Reldresal,* Principal Secretary (as they style him) of private Affairs, came to my House, attended only by one Servant. He ordered his Coach to wait at a Distance, and desired I would give him an Hour's Audience; which I readily consented to, on Account of his Quality, and Personal Merits, as well as of the many good Offices he had done me during my Sollicitations at Court. I offered to lie down, that he might the more conveniently reach my Ear; but he chose rather to let me hold him in my Hand during our Conversation. He began with Compliments on my

Liberty; said, he might pretend to some Merit in it; but, however, added, that if it had not been for the present Situation of things at Court, perhaps I might not have obtained it so soon, For, *said he*, as flourishing a Condition as we appear to be in to Foreigners, we labour under two mighty Evils; a violent Faction at home, and the Danger of an Invasion by a most potent Enemy from abroad. As to the first, you are to understand, that for above seventy Moons past, there have been two struggling Parties in this Empire, under the Names of *Tramecksan,* and *Slamecksan,* from the high and low Heels on their Shoes, by which they distinguish themselves.

It is alledged indeed, that the high Heels are most agreeable to our ancient Constitution: But however this be, his Majesty hath determined to make use of only low Heels in the Administration of the Government, and all Offices in the Gift of the Crown; as you cannot but observe; and particularly, that his Majesty's Imperial Heels are lower at least by a *Drurr* than any of his Court; (*Drurr* is a Measure about the fourteenth Part of an Inch.) The Animosities between these two Parties run so high, that they will neither eat nor drink, nor talk with each other. We compute the *Tramecksan,* or High-Heels, to exceed us in Number; but the Power is wholly on our Side. We apprehend his Imperial Highness, the Heir to the Crown, to have some Tendency towards the High-Heels; at least we can plainly discover one of his Heels higher than the other; which gives him a Hobble in his Gait. Now, in the midst of these intestine Disquiets, we are threatened with an Invasion from the Island of *Blefuscu,* which is the other great Empire of the Universe, almost as large and powerful as this of his Majesty. For as to what we have heard you affirm, that there are other Kingdoms and States in the World, inhabited by human Creatures as large as your self, our Philosophers are in much Doubt; and would rather conjecture that you dropt from the Moon, or one of the Stars; because it is certain, that an hundred Mortals of your Bulk, would, in a short Time, destroy all the Fruits and Cattle of his Majesty's Dominions. Besides, our Histories of six Thousand Moons make no Mention of any other Regions, than the two great Empires of *Lilliput* and *Blefuscu.* Which two mighty Powers have, as I was going to tell you, been engaged in a most obstinate War for six and thirty Moons past. It began upon the following Occasion. It is allowed on all Hands, that the primitive Way of breaking Eggs before we eat them, was upon the larger End: But his present Majesty's Grand-father, while he was a Boy, going to eat an Egg, and breaking it according to the ancient Practice, happened to cut one of his Fingers. Whereupon the Emperor his Father, published an Edict, commanding all his Subjects, upon great Penalties, to break

43. Giovanni Battista Piranesi, *The Prisons, Plate XIV*. Etching. Piranesi's popular series of engravings, *The Prisons,* reflected the humanitarian trend of the Enlightenment.

the smaller End of their Eggs. The People so highly resented this Law, that our Histories tell us, there have been six Rebellions raised on that Account; wherein one Emperor lost his Life, and another his Crown. These civil Commotions were constantly fomented by the Monarchs of *Blefuscu;* and when they were quelled, the Exiles always fled for Refuge to that Empire. It is computed, that eleven Thousand Persons have, at several Times, suffered Death, rather than submit to break their Eggs at the smaller End. Many hundred large Volumes have been published upon this Controversy: But the Books of the *Big-Endians* have been long forbidden, and the whole Party rendred incapable by Law of holding Employments. During the Course of these Troubles, the Emperors of *Blefuscu* did frequently expostulate by their Ambassadors, accusing us of making a Schism in Religion, by offending against a fundamental Doctrine of our great Prophet *Lustrog,* in the fifty-fourth Chapter of the *Brundrecal,* (which is their *Alcoran.*) This, however, is thought to be a meer Strain upon the Text: For the Words are these; *That all true Believers shall break their Eggs at the convenient End:* and which is the convenient End, seems, in my humble Opinion, to be left to every Man's Conscience, or at least in the Power of the chief Magistrate to determine. Now the *Big-Endian* Exiles have found so much Credit in the Emperor of *Blefuscu's* Court; and so much private Assistance and Encouragement from their Party here at home, that a bloody War hath been carried on between the two Empires for six and thirty Moons with various Success; during which Time we have lost Forty Capital Ships, and a much greater Number of smaller Vessels, together with thirty thousand of our best Seamen and Soldiers; and the Damage received by the Enemy is reckoned to be somewhat greater than ours. However, they have now equipped a numerous Fleet, and are just preparing to make a Descent upon us: And his Imperial Majesty, placing great Confidence in your Valour and Strength, hath commanded me to lay this Account of his Affairs before you.

I DESIRED the Secretary to present my humble Duty to the Emperor, and to let him know, that I thought it would not become me, who was a Foreigner, to interfere with Parties; but I was ready, with the Hazard of my Life, to defend his Person and State against all Invaders.

# The Old Man's Farewell
### from *Supplement to Bougainville's "Voyage"*

## DENIS DIDEROT

He was the father of a numerous family. At the time of the Europeans' arrival, he cast upon them a look that was filled with scorn, though it revealed no surprise, no alarm and no curiosity. They approached him; he turned his back on them and retired into his hut. His thoughts were only too well revealed by his silence and his air of concern, for in the privacy of his thoughts he groaned inwardly over the happy days of his people, now gone forever. At the moment of Bougainville's departure, when all the natives ran swarming onto the beach, tugging at his clothing and throwing their arms around his companions and weeping, the old man stepped forward and solemnly spoke:

"Weep, wretched Tahitians, weep — but rather for the arrival than for the departure of these wicked and grasping men! The day will come when you will know them for what they are. Someday they will return, bearing in one hand that piece of wood you see suspended from this one's belt and in the other the piece of steel that hangs at the side of his companion. They will load you with chains, slit your throats and enslave you to their follies and vices. Someday you will be slaves to them, you will be as corrupt, as vile, as wretched as they are. But I have this consolation —

my life is drawing to its close, and I shall not see the calamity that I foretell. Oh Tahitians, Oh my friends! You have the means of warding off a terrible fate, but I would die before I would advise you to make use of it. Let them leave, and let them live."

Then, turning to Bougainville, he went on: "And you, leader of these brigands who obey you, take your vessel swiftly from our shores. We are innocent and happy, and you can only spoil our happiness. We follow the pure instinct of nature, and you have tried to efface her imprint from our hearts. Here all things are for all, and you have preached to us I know not what distinctions between mine and thine. Our women and girls we possess in common; you have shared this privilege with us, and your coming has awakened in them a frenzy they have never known before. They have become mad in your arms; you have become ferocious in theirs. They have begun to hate one another; you have cut one another's throats for them, and they have come home to us stained with your blood.

"We are free — but see where you have driven into our earth the symbol of our future servitude. You are neither a god nor a devil — by what right, then, do you enslave people? Orou! You who understand the speech of these men, tell every one of us, as you have told me, what they have written on that strip of metal — 'This land belongs to us.' This land belongs to you! And why? Because you set foot in it? If some day a Tahitian should land on your shores, and if he should engrave on one of your stones or on the bark of one of your trees: 'This land belongs to the people of Tahiti,' what would you think? You are stronger than we are! And what does that signify? When one of our lads carried off some of the miserable trinkets with which your ship is loaded, what an uproar you made, and what revenge you took! And at that very moment you were plotting, in the depths of your hearts, to steal a whole country! You are not slaves; you would suffer death rather than be enslaved, yet you want to make slaves of us! Do you believe, then, that the Tahitian does not know how to die in defense of his liberty? This Tahitian, whom you want to treat as a chattel, as a dumb animal — this Tahitian is your brother. You are both children of Nature — what right do you have over him that he does not have over you?

"You came; did we attack you? Did we plunder your vessel? Did we seize you and expose you to the arrows of our enemies? Did we force you to work in the fields alongside our beasts of burden? We respected our own image in you. Leave us our own customs, which are wiser and more decent than yours. We have no wish to barter what you call our ignorance for your useless knowledge. We possess already all that is good or necessary for our existence. Do we merit your scorn because we have not been

able to create superfluous wants for ourselves? When we are hungry, we
have something to eat; when we are cold, we have clothing to put on.
You have been in our huts — what is lacking there, in your opinion? You
are welcome to drive yourselves as hard as you please in pursuit of what
you call the comforts of life, but allow sensible people to stop when they
see they have nothing to gain but imaginary benefits from the continuation of their painful labors. If you persuade us to go beyond the bounds
of strict necessity, when shall we come to the end of our labor? When
shall we have time for enjoyment? We have reduced our daily and yearly
labors to the least possible amount, because to us nothing seemed more
desirable than leisure. Go and bestir yourselves in your own country;
there you may torment yourselves as much as you like; but leave us in
peace, and do not fill our heads with a hankering after your false needs
and imaginary virtues."

# An Address to the Public
# from an Anti-Slavery Society

## BENJAMIN FRANKLIN

It is with peculiar satisfaction we assure the friends of humanity,
that, in prosecuting the design of our association, our endeavors have
proved successful, far beyond our most sanguine expectations.

Encouraged by this success, and by the daily progress of that luminous
and benign spirit of liberty, which is diffusing itself throughout the
world, and humbly hoping for the continuance of the divine blessing on
our labours, we have ventured to make an important addition to our
original plan, and do therefore earnestly solicit the support and assistance
of all who can feel the tender emotions of sympathy and compassion, or
relish the exalted pleasure of beneficence.

Slavery is such an atrocious debasement of human nature, that its
very extirpation, if not performed with solicitous care, may sometimes
open a source of serious evils.

The unhappy man, who has long been treated as a brute animal, too
frequently sinks beneath the common standard of the human species.
The galling chains, that bind his body, do also fetter his intellectual

faculties, and impair the social affections of his heart. Accustomed to move like a mere machine, by the will of a master, reflection is suspended; he has not the power of choice; and reason and conscience have but little influence over his conduct, because he is chiefly governed by the passion of fear. He is poor and friendless; perhaps worn out by extreme labour, age, and disease.

Under such circumstances, freedom may often prove a misfortune to himself, and prejudical to society.

Attention to emancipated black people, it is therefore to be hoped, will become a branch of our national policy; but, as far as we contribute to promote this emancipation, so far that attention is evidently a serious duty incumbent on us, and which we mean to discharge to the best of our judgment and abilities.

To instruct, to advise, to qualify those, who have been restored to freedom, for the exercise and enjoyment of civil liberty, to promote in them habits of industry, to furnish them with employments suited to their age, sex, talents, and other circumstances, and to procure their children an education calculated for their future situation in life; these are the great outlines of the annexed plan, which we have adopted, and which we conceive will essentially promote the public good, and the happiness of these our hitherto too much neglected fellow-creatures.

A plan so extensive cannot be carried into execution without considerable pecuniary resources, beyond the present ordinary funds of the Society. We hope much from the generosity of enlightened and benevolent freemen, and will gratefully receive any donations or subscriptions for this purpose, which may be made to our treasurer, James Starr, or to James Pemberton, chairman of our committee of correspondence.

Signed, by order of the Society,

B. Franklin, *President.*

*Philadelphia, 9th of November, 1789.*

# On Slavery

## THOMAS JEFFERSON

The whole commerce between master and slave is a perpetual exercise of the most boisterous passions, the most unremitting despotism on the one part and degrading submissions on the other. . . . The man must be a prodigy who can retain his manners and morals undepraved by such circumstances. And with what execration should the statesman be loaded who, permitting one half the citizens thus to trample on the rights of the other, transforms those into despots and these into enemies, destroys the morals of the one part and the *amor patriae* of the other! For if a slave can have a country in this world, it must be any other in preference to that in which he is born to live and labor for another; . . . And can the liberties of a nation be thought secure when we have removed their only firm basis, a conviction in the minds of the people that these liberties are of the gift of God — that they are not to be violated but with His wrath? Indeed I tremble for my country when I reflect that God is just; that His justice cannot sleep forever; that, considering numbers, nature, and natural means only, a revolution of the wheel of fortune, an exchange of situation is among possible events; that it may become probable by supernatural interference! The Almighty has no attribute which can take side with us in such a contest.

.    .    .    .

I had for a long time ceased to read newspapers or pay any attention to public affairs, confident they were in good hands and content to be a passenger in our bark to the shore from which I am not distant. But this momentous question [whether Missouri was to be admitted to the Union as a slave state], like a fire bell in the night, awakened and filled me with terror. I considered it at once as the knell of the Union. It is hushed, indeed, for the moment. But this is a reprieve only, not a final sentence. A geographical line, coinciding with a marked principle, moral and political, once conceived and held up to the angry passions of men, will never be obliterated, and every new irritation will mark it deeper and deeper. I can say, with conscious truth, that there is not a man on earth who would sacrifice more than I would to relieve us from this heavy reproach in any *practicable* way. The cession of that kind of property (for so it is misnamed) is a bagatelle which would not cost me a second thought if, in that way, a general emancipation and *expatriation* could be effected; and gradually and with due sacrifices, I think it might be. But as it is, we have the wolf by the ears, and we can neither hold him nor safely let him go. Justice is in one scale and self-preservation in the other. . . .

# Treatise on Tolerance on the Occasion of the Death of Jean Calas

## VOLTAIRE

The murder of Jean Calas, committed in Toulouse with the sword of justice, the 9th of March, 1762, is one of the most singular events that calls for the attention of the present age and of posterity. We soon forget the crowd of victims who have fallen in the course of innumerable battles, not only because this is a destiny inevitable in war, but because those who thus fell might also have given death to their enemies, and did not lose their lives without defending themselves. Where the danger and the advantage are equal, our wonder ceases, and even pity itself is in some measure lessened; but where the father of an innocent family is delivered up to the hands of error, passion, or fanaticism; where the accused person has no other defense but his virtue; where the arbiters of his destiny have nothing to risk in putting him to death but their having been mistaken, and where they may murder with impunity by decree, then every one is ready to cry out, every one fears for himself, and sees that no person's life is secure in a court erected to watch over the lives of citizens, and every voice unites in demanding vengeance.

In this strange affair, we find religion, suicide, and parricide. The object of inquiry was, whether a father and a mother had murdered their own son in order to please God, and whether a brother had murdered his brother, or a friend his friend; or whether the judges had to reproach themselves with having broken on the wheel an innocent father, or with having acquitted a guilty mother, brother, and friend.

Jean Calas, a person of sixty-eight years of age, had followed the profession of a merchant in Toulouse for upwards of forty years, and was known by all as a good parent in his family. He was a Protestant, as was also his wife, and all his children, one son only excepted, who had abjured heresy, and to whom the father allowed a small annuity. Indeed, he appeared so far removed from that absurd fanaticism which destroys the bonds of society, that he even approved of the conversion of his son, Louis Calas, and he had for thirty years a maid-servant, who was a zealous Catholic, and who had brought up all his children.

Another of his sons, whose name was Marc-Antoine, was a man of letters, but, at the same time, of a restless, gloomy, and violent disposition. This young man finding that he could neither succeed nor enter into business as a merchant, for which indeed he was very unfit, nor be admitted to the bar as a lawyer, because he lacked the certificates of his being a Catholic, resolved to end his life, and gave some intimation of his design to one of his friends. He confirmed himself in his resolution by reading everything that had been written upon the subject of suicide.

At length, one day, having lost all his money in gambling, he chose that as a most proper opportunity for executing his design. A friend named Lavaisse, a young man of nineteen years of age, the son of a famous lawyer of Toulouse, and a youth esteemed by every one who knew him, happened to come from Bordeaux the evening before. He went by chance to dine with the Calas family at their house. Old Calas, his wife, Marc-Antoine, their eldest son, and Pierre their second son, all ate together that evening; after supper was over, they retired into another room, when Marc-Antoine suddenly disappeared. After some time, young Lavaisse took his leave, and Pierre Calas accompanied him downstairs; when they came near the store they saw Marc-Antoine hanging in his shirt behind the door, and his coat folded up and laid upon the counter. His shirt was not in the least rumpled, and his hair was well combed. There was no wound on his body, nor any other mark of violence.

We shall not here enter into all the minute circumstances with which the lawyers have filled their briefs; nor shall we describe the grief and despair of the unhappy parents; their cries were heard by the whole neighborhood. Lavaisse and Pierre Calas, almost beside themselves, ran, the one to fetch a surgeon, and the other an officer of justice.

While they were thus employed, and old Calas and his wife were sobbing in tears, the people of Toulouse gathered in crowds about the house. The Toulousians are a superstitious and headstrong people; they look upon their brothers who are not of the same religion as themselves, as monsters. It was at Toulouse that a solemn thanksgiving was ordered for the death of Henry III and that the inhabitants took an oath to murder the first person who should propose to acknowledge that great and good prince Henry IV for their sovereign. This same city still continues to solemnize, by an annual procession and bonfires, the day on which, about two hundred years ago, it ordered the massacre of four thousand of its citizens as heretics. In vain has the council issued six decrees prohibiting this detestable holiday. The Toulousians still continue to celebrate it as a high festival.

Some fanatic among the mob cried out that Jean Calas had hanged his own son; this cry, taken up, became in an instant unanimous; some persons added that the deceased was to have made his abjuration the next day; that his own family and young Lavaisse had murdered him out of hatred for the Catholic religion. No sooner was this opinion stated than it was fully believed by every one; and the whole town was persuaded that it is one of the articles of the Protestant religion for a father or mother to murder their own son, if he attempts to change his faith.

When minds are once aroused, they are not easily appeased. It was now imagined that all the Protestants of Languedoc had assembled together the preceding night, and had chosen by a plurality of voices one of their sect for an executioner; that the choice had fallen upon young Lavaisse; that this young man had, in less than four and twenty hours, received the news of his election, and had come from Bordeaux to assist Jean Calas, his wife, and their son Pierre, to murder a son, a brother, and a friend.

The Sieur David, magistrate of Toulouse, excited by these rumors, and desirous of bringing himself into notice by the ready execution of his office, took a step contrary to all the established rules and ordinances, by ordering the Calas family, together with their Catholic maid-servant and Lavaisse, to be put in irons.

After this a legal declaration was published which was no less vicious. Matters were carried still farther; Marc-Antoine Calas had died a Calvinist, and as such, if he had laid violent hands on himself, his body ought to have been dragged on a hurdle; he was buried with the greatest funeral pomp in the church of St. Stephen, in spite of the curate who entered his protest against this profanation of holy ground.

There are in Languedoc four orders of penitents, the white, the blue, the gray, and the black, who wear a long capuchin or hood, having a mask of cloth falling down over the face, in which are two holes to see through. These orders wanted the Duke of Fitz-James to become one of their body, but he refused. On the present occasion the white penitents performed a solemn service for Marc-Antoine Calas as for a martyr; nor was the festival of a martyr ever celebrated with greater pomp by any church: but then this pomp was truly terrible. Beneath a magnificent canopy was placed a skeleton which was made to move and which represented Marc-Antoine Calas, holding in one hand a branch of palm, and, in the other, the pen with which he was to sign his abjuration of heresy, and which in fact wrote the death-warrant of his father.

And now nothing more remained to be done for this wretch who had been his own murderer but the office of canonization; all the people looked on him as a saint; some invoked him, some went to pray at his tomb, some besought him to work miracles, while others gravely recounted those he had already performed: A monk pulled out one or two of his teeth, in order to have some lasting relics. An old woman, somewhat deaf, declared that she had heard the sound of bells; and a priest was cured of an apoplectic fit, after taking a stout emetic. Protocols were drawn up of these stupendous miracles, and the author of this account has in his possession an affidavit to prove that a young man of Toulouse went mad for having prayed several nights successively at the tomb of the new saint, without having been able to obtain the miracle he requested of him.

Among the order of the white penitents were some magistrates. The death of Jean Calas seemed then inevitable.

But what more particularly hastened his fate was the approach of that singular festival, which, as I have already observed, the Toulousians celebrate every year, in commemoration of the massacre of four thousand Huguenots; the year 1762 happened to be the *annum seculare* of this deed. The inhabitants were busied in making preparations for the solemnity; this circumstance added fresh fuel to the heated imagination of the people; every one cried out that a scaffold for the execution of the Calas family would be the greatest ornament of the ceremony; and that Providence itself seemed to have brought these victims to be sacrificed to our holy religion. Twenty persons heard these speeches, and others still more violent. And this, in the present age! this at a time when philosophy has made so great a progress! and while the pens of a hundred academies are employed in inspiring gentleness of manners. It should seem that enthusiasm enraged at the recent success of reason, fought under her standard with redoubled fury.

Thirteen judges met every day to try this cause; they had not, they could not, have any proof against this family; but mistaken religion took the place of proofs. Six of the judges persisted obstinate, resolved to sentence Jean Calas, his son, and Lavaisse, to be broken on the wheel, and his wife to be burned at the stake; the other seven judges, rather more moderate, were at least for having the accused examined. The debates were frequent and long. One of the judges, convinced in his mind of the innocence of the accused and of the impossibility of the crime, spoke warmly in their favor; he opposed the zeal of humanity to that of cruelty, and openly pleaded the cause of the Calas family in all the houses of Toulouse where misguided religion demanded with incessant cries the blood of these unfortunates. Another judge, well known for his violence, went about the town, raving with as much fury against the accused as his brother had been earnest in defending them. In short, the contest became so warm that both were obliged to enter protests against each other's proceedings, and retire into the country.

But by a strange fatality, the judge who had been on the favorable side had the delicacy to persist in his exceptions, and the other returned to give his vote against those on whom he could no longer sit as judge; and it was his single vote which carried the sentence to the wheel, there being eight voices against five, one of the six merciful judges being at last, after much contestation, brought over to the more rigorous side.

In my opinion, in cases of parricide, and where the head of a family is to be given over to the most dreadful punishment, the sentence ought to be unanimous, inasmuch as the proofs of so unheard of a crime ought to be of such a manner as to satisfy all the world: the least shadow of a doubt in a case of this nature should be sufficient to make the judge tremble who is about to pass sentence of death. The weakness of our reason, and the insufficiency of our laws, become every day more obvious; but surely there cannot be a greater example of this wretchedness than that a single vote should be sufficient to condemn a fellow-citizen to be broken alive on the wheel. The Athenians required at least fifty voices, over and above the majority of the judges, before they would dare to pronounce sentence of death. What does all this show? That we know, quite uselessly, that the Greeks were wiser and more humane than ourselves.

It appeared impossible that Jean Calas, who was an old man of sixty-eight, and had been long troubled with a swelling and weakness in his legs, should have been able by himself to have strangled his son and hanged him, a stout young fellow of eight and twenty, and more than commonly robust; therefore he must absolutely have been assisted in this act by his wife, his other son, Pierre Calas, Lavaisse, and by the servant-maid, and they had been together the whole night of this fatal adventure. But this supposition is altogether as absurd as the other; for can any one believe that a servant, who was a zealous Catholic, would have permitted Huguenots to murder a young man whom she herself had brought up, for his attachment to a religion to which she herself was devoted? That Lavaisse would have come purposely from Bordeaux to murder his friend, of whose pretended conversion he knew nothing? That an affectionate mother would have joined in laying violent hands on her own son? And lastly, how could they all together have been able to strangle a young man stronger than them all, without a long and violent struggle, or without his making such a noise as must have been heard by the whole neigh-

*44.* William Hogarth, *Gin Lane*.

borhood, without repeated blows passing between them, without any marks of violence, or without any of their clothes being torn.

It was evident that if this murder could have been committed, the accused persons were all equally guilty, because they did not leave each other's company an instant the whole night; but then it was equally evident that they were not guilty, and that the father alone could not be so, and yet, by the sentence of the judges, the father alone was condemned to expire on the rack.

The motive on which this sentence was passed was as unaccountable as all the rest of the proceeding. Those judges who had given their opinion for the execution of Jean Calas persuaded the others that this poor old man, unable to support the torments, would, under the blows of torturers, make a full confession of his crime and that of his accomplices. They were confounded, when the old man, dying on the wheel, called God as a witness of his innocence, and besought him to forgive his judges!

They were afterwards obliged to pass a second decree, which contradicted the first, namely to set at liberty the mother, her son Pierre, young Lavaisse, and the maid-servant; but one of the counsellors having made them aware that this latter decree contradicted the other, and that they condemned themselves, inasmuch as it was proved that all the accused parties had been constantly together during the whole time the murder was supposed to be committed, the setting at liberty of the survivors was an incontestable proof of the innocence of the master of the family whom they had ordered to be executed. They then determined to banish Pierre Calas, the son, which was an act as ill-grounded and absurd as any of the rest, for Pierre Calas was either guilty or not guilty of the murder; if he was guilty, he should have been broken on the wheel in the same manner as his father; if he was innocent, there was no reason for banishing him. But the judges, frightened by the punishment of the father, and by that tender piety with which he had died, thought to save their honor by making people believe that they showed mercy to the son; as if this was not a new degree of prevarication; and they thought that no bad consequences could arise from banishing this young man, who was poor and destitute of friends. His exile was not a great injustice after that which they had been already so unfortunate as to commit.

They began by threatening Pierre Calas in his prison cell that they would treat him as they had his father, if he would not abjure his religion. This the young man has declared on oath.

As Pierre was going out of the town, he was met by one of the abbés with a converting spirit, who made him return back to Toulouse, where he was shut up in a convent of Dominicans, and there compelled to perform all the functions of a convert to the Catholic religion; this was in part what his persecutors wanted; it was the price of his father's blood, and the religion they thought they were avenging seemed satisfied.

The daughters were taken from their mother, and shut up in a convent. This unhappy woman, who had been, as it were, sprinkled with the blood of her husband, who had held her eldest son lifeless within her arms, had seen the other banished, her daughters taken from her, herself stripped of her property, and left alone in the world destitute of bread, and bereft of hopes, was almost weighed down to the grave by the excess of her misfortunes. Some persons, who had maturely weighed all the circumstances of this horrible adventure, were so struck with them that they pressed Madame Calas, who now led a life of retirement and solitude, to exert herself, and go and demand justice at the foot of the throne. At this time she was scarcely able to sustain herself; besides, having been born in England and brought over to a distant province in France when very young, the very name of the city of Paris frightened her. She imagined that in the capital of the kingdom they must be still more savage than in Toulouse; at length, however, the duty of avenging the memory of her husband got the better of her weakness. She arrived in Paris half dead, and was surprised to find herself received with tenderness, sympathy, and offers of assistance.

In Paris reason always triumphs over fanaticism, however great, whereas in the provinces fanaticism almost always triumphs over reason.

M. de Beaumont, a famous lawyer of the Parliament of Paris, immediately took up her cause and drew up an opinion, which was signed by fifteen other lawyers. M. Loiseau, equally famous for his eloquence, likewise drew up a brief in favor of the family; and M. Mariette, solicitor to the council, drew up a formal statement of the case, which struck every one who read it with conviction.

These three generous defenders of the laws and of innocence made the widow a present of all the profits arising from the publication of these pleas, which filled not only Paris but all Europe with pity for this unfortunate woman, and every one cried aloud for justice to be done her. The public passed sentence on this affair long before it was determined by the council.

This pity made its way even to the Cabinet, notwithstanding the continual round of business, which often excludes pity and the familiarity of seeing unhappiness, which too frequently steels the heart even more. The daughters were restored to their mother, and all three in deep mourning, and in sobs, drew sympathetic tears from the eyes of their judges.

Nevertheless, this family had still some enemies for this was an affair of religion. Several persons, whom in France we call devout, declared publicly that it was much better to suffer an old Calvinist, though innocent, to be broken upon the wheel, than to force eight counsellors of Languedoc to admit that they had been mistaken; these people made use of this very expression: "That there were more magistrates than Calases"; by which they inferred that the Calas family ought to be sacrificed to the honor of the magistracy. They never reflected that the honor of a judge, like that of another man, consists in making reparation for his faults. In France no one believes that the pope, assisted by his cardinals, is infallible. One may also believe that eight judges of Toulouse are not. Every sensible and disinterested person declared that the decree of the court of Toulouse would be quashed anywhere in Europe, even though particular considerations might prevent it from being declared void by the council.

Such was the state of this surprising affair when it caused certain impartial, but sensible, persons to form the design of laying before the public a few reflections upon tolerance, indulgence, and commiseration, which the Abbé Houtteville in his bombastic and declamatory work, which is false in all the facts, calls a *monstrous dogma,* but which reason calls the *portion of human nature.*

Either the judges of Toulouse, carried away by the fanaticism of the mob, caused the innocent head of a family to be tortured to death, a thing which is without example; or this father and his wife murdered their eldest son, with the assistance of another son and a friend, which is altogether contrary to nature. In either case, the abuse of the most holy religion has produced a great crime. It is therefore to the interest of mankind to examine if religion should be charitable or savage.

# *Humanism*

## from *Persian Letters*

### MONTESQUIEU

I have often sought to find out which system of government was most in conformity with human reason. It seemed to me that the most perfect is that government which gets things done with the least expense, and that therefore the government that leads men in the manner most appropriate to their leanings and inclinations is the most perfect.

If under a gentle government, the nation is as submissive as under a strict government, then the first is preferable, since it is more in conformity with reason whereas severity is a motive foreign to it.

Be assured, my dear Rhedi, that in a state the degree of cruelty of punishment does not cause people to obey the laws more. In countries where punishment is moderate, the laws are respected just as well as in those where punishment is tyrannous and frightful.

Whether the government be gentle or cruel, punishment is always meted out by degree. A crime more or less serious calls for the infliction of a punishment more or less serious. One's imagination, of its own accord, conforms to the customs of the country where one is: a week of prison or a light fine impresses a European, brought up under a gentle government, as much as the loss of an arm frightens an Asiatic. They attach a certain degree of fear to a certain degree of punishment, and each man couples them in his own way. The despair of losing his reputation will literally torment a Frenchman sentenced to the selfsame punishment that would make a Turk lose scarcely a quarter hour's sleep.

Moreover, I cannot see that civil order, justice, and equity are better observed in Turkey, Persia, and among the Mongols than they are in the republics of Holland and Venice and even in England. I cannot see that fewer crimes are committed or that men, intimidated by the degree of punishment, are more submissive to the law.

On the contrary, I note a source of injustice and vexation at the center of these very states.

I find that even the prince, who is the law itself, is less master than anywhere else.

I can see that in times of stress there are always tumultuous movements when no one is the chief of state, and that once a cruel authority is scorned, no one retains enough authority to bring it back.

I observe that the despair of ever achieving impunity justifies disorder and makes it greater; that, in such states, there is never a minor revolt and never an interval between muttering and open sedition; that great events are not necessarily prepared by great causes. On the contrary, the least accident can produce a great revolution, often quite as unforeseen by those who make it as by those who suffer its consequences.

When Osman, emperor of the Turks, was dethroned, none of those who committed the overthrow planned to do so. They simply came as suppliants to demand justice on some complaint. A voice, never identified, rose from the crowd by chance, the name of Mustapha was spoken; and, suddenly, Mustapha was emperor.

# On the Morals of Jesus

## THOMAS JEFFERSON

Dear Sir, — In some of the delightful conversations with you, in the evenings of 1798–99, and which served as an anodyne to the afflictions of the crisis through which our country was then laboring, the Christian religion was sometimes our topic; and I then promised you, that one day or other, I would give you my views of it. They are the result of a life of inquiry and reflection, and very different from that anti-Christian system imputed to me by those who know nothing of my opinions. To the corruption of Christianity I am, indeed, opposed; but not to the genuine precepts of Jesus himself. I am a Christian, in the only sense in which he wished any one to be; sincerely attached to his doctrines, in preference to all others; ascribing to himself every *human* excellence; and believing he never claimed any other. At the short interval since these conversations, when I could justifiably abstract my mind from public affairs, the subject has been under my contemplation. But the more I considered it, the more it expanded beyond the measure of either my time or information. In the moment of my late departure from Monticello, I received from Dr. Priestley, his little treatise of "Socrates and Jesus Compared." This being a section of the general view I had taken of the field, it became a subject of reflection while on the road, and unoccupied otherwise. The result was, to arrange in my mind a syllabus, or outline of such an estimate of the comparative merits of Christianity, as I wished to see executed by some one of more leisure and information for the task, than myself. This I now send you, as the only discharge of my promise I can probably ever execute. . . .

## SYLLABUS OF AN ESTIMATE OF THE MERIT OF THE DOCTRINES OF JESUS, COMPARED WITH THOSE OF OTHERS

In a comparative view of the Ethics of the enlightened nations of antiquity, of the Jews and of Jesus, no notice should be taken of the corruptions of reason among the ancients, to wit, the idolatry and superstition of the vulgar, nor of the corruptions of Christianity by the learned among its professors.

Let a just view be taken of the moral principles inculcated by the most esteemed of the sects of ancient philosophy, or of their individuals; particularly Pythagoras, Socrates, Epicurus, Cicero, Epictetus, Seneca, Antoninus.

I. Philosophers. 1. Their precepts related chiefly to ourselves, and the government of those passions which, unrestrained, would disturb our tranquillity of mind. In this branch of philosophy they were really great.

2. In developing our duties to others, they were short and defective. They embraced, indeed, the circle of kindred and friends, and inculcated patriotism, or the love of our country in the aggregate, as a primary obligation: towards our neighbors and countrymen they taught justice, but scarcely viewed them as within the circle of benevolence. Still less have they inculcated peace, charity and love to our fellow men, or em-

braced with benevolence the whole family of mankind.

II. Jews. 1. Their system was Deism; that is, the belief in one only God. But their ideas of him and of his attributes were degrading and injurious.

2. Their Ethics were not only imperfect, but often irreconcilable with the sound dictates of reason and morality, as they respect intercourse with those around us; and repulsive and anti-social, as respecting other nations. They needed reformation, therefore, in an eminent degree.

III. Jesus. In this state of things among the Jews, Jesus appeared. His parentage was obscure; his condition poor; his education null; his natural endowments great; his life correct and innocent: he was meek, benevolent, patient, firm, disinterested, and of the sublimest eloquence.

The disadvantages under which his doctrines appear are remarkable.

1. Like Socrates and Epictetus, he wrote nothing himself.

2. But he had not, like them, a Xenophon or an Arrian to write for him. I name not Plato, who only used the name of Socrates to cover the whimsies of his own brain. On the contrary, all the learned of his country, entrenched in its power and riches, were opposed to him, lest his labors should undermine their advantages; and the committing to writing his life and doctrines fell on unlettered and ignorant men; who wrote, too, from memory, and not till long after the transactions had passed.

3. According to the ordinary fate of those who attempt to enlighten and reform mankind, he fell an early victim to the jealousy and combination of the altar and the throne, at about thirty-three years of age, his reason having not yet attained the *maximum* of its energy, nor the course of his preaching, which was but of three years at most, presented occasions for developing a complete system of morals.

4. Hence the doctrines which he really delivered were defective as a whole, and fragments only of what he did deliver have come to us mutilated, misstated, and often unintelligible.

5. They have been still more disfigured by the corruptions of schismatizing followers, who have found an interest in sophisticating and perverting the simple doctrines he taught, by engrafting on them the mysticisms of a Grecian sophist, frittering them into subtleties, and obscuring them with jargon, until they have caused good men to reject the whole in disgust, and to view Jesus himself as an impostor.

Notwithstanding these disadvantages, a system of morals is presented to us, which, if filled up in the style and spirit of the rich fragments he left us, would be the most perfect and sublime that has ever been taught by man.

The question of his being a member of the Godhead, or in direct com-

munication with it, claimed for him by some of his followers, and denied
by others, is foreign to the present view, which is merely an estimate of the
intrinsic merits of his doctrines.

1. He corrected the Deism of the Jews, confirming them in their belief
of one only God, and giving them juster notions of his attributes and
government.

2. His moral doctrines, relating to kindred and friends, were more
pure and perfect than those of the most correct of the philosophers, and
greatly more so than those of the Jews; and they went far beyond both in
inculcating universal philanthropy, not only to kindred and friends, to
neighbors and countrymen, but to all mankind, gathering all into one
family, under the bonds of love, charity, peace, common wants and common aids. A development of this head will evince the peculiar superiority
of the system of Jesus over all others.

3. The precepts of philosophy, and of the Hebrew code, laid hold of
actions only. He pushed his scrutinies into the heart of man; erected his
tribunal in the region of his thoughts, and purified the waters at the
fountain head.

4. He taught, emphatically, the doctrines of a future state, which was
either doubted, or disbelieved by the Jews; and wielded it with efficacy,
as an important incentive, supplementary to the other motives to moral
conduct.


# *The System of Nature*

## BARON D'HOLBACH

Every thing that has been advanced, evidently proves, that religious
morality is an infinite loser, when compared with the morality of nature,
with which it is found in perpetual contradiction. Nature invites man to
love himself, to preserve himself, to incessantly augment the sum of his
happiness: religion orders him to love only a formidable God, that deserves to be hated; to detest himself, to sacrifice to his frightful idol the
most pleasing and legitimate pleasures of his heart. Nature tells man to
consult reason, and to take it for his guide: religion teaches him that his
reason is corrupted, that it is only a treacherous guide, given by a deceitful God to lead his creatures astray. Nature tells man to enlighten him-

self, to search after truth, to instruct himself in his duties: religion enjoins him to examine nothing, to remain in ignorance, to fear truth; it persuades him, that there are no relations more important than those which subsist between him and a being of whom he will never have any knowledge. Nature tells the being who is in love with his welfare, to moderate his passions, to resist them when they are destructive to himself, to counterbalance them by real motives borrowed from experience: religion tells the sensible being to have no passions, to be an insensible mass, or to combat his propensities by motives borrowed from the imagination, and variable as itself. Nature tells man to be sociable, to love his fellow-creatures, to be just, peaceable, indulgent, and benevolent, to cause or suffer his associates to enjoy their opinions: religion counsels him to fly society, to detach himself from his fellow-creatures, to hate them, when their imagination does not procure them dreams conformable to his own, to break the most sacred bonds to please his God, to torment, to afflict, to persecute, and to massacre those who will not be mad after his own manner. Nature tells man in society to cherish glory, to labour to render himself estimable, to be active, courageous, and industrious: religion tells him to be humble, abject, pusillanimous, to live in obscurity, to occupy himself with prayers, with meditations, and with ceremonies; it says to him, be useful to thyself, and do nothing for others. Nature proposes to the citizen for a model, men endued with honest, noble, energetic souls, who have usefully served their fellow-citizens; religion commends to them abject souls, extols pious enthusiasts, frantic penitents, fanatics, who, for the most ridiculous opinions, have disturbed empires.

# from *On Crime and Punishment*

## MARCHESE DI BECCARIA

### CRIMES AND PENALTIES

The knowledge of the true relations between a sovereign and his subjects, and of those between different nations; the revival of commerce by the light of philosophical truths, diffused by printing; and the silent international war of industry, the most humane and the most worthy of rational men — these are the fruits which we owe to the enlightenment of this century. But how few have examined and combated the cruelty of punishments, and the irregularities of criminal procedures, a part of legislation so elementary and yet so neglected in almost the whole of Europe; and how few have sought, by a return to first principles, to dissipate the mistakes accumulated by many centuries, or to mitigate, with at least that force which belongs only to ascertained truths, the excessive caprice of ill-directed power, which has presented up to this time but one long example of lawful and cold-blooded atrocity! And yet the groans of the weak, sacrificed to the cruelty of the ignorant or to the indolence of the rich; the barbarous tortures, multiplied with a severity as useless as it is prodigal, for crimes either not proved or quite chimerical; the disgusting horrors of a prison, enhanced by that which is the cruelest executioner of the miserable — namely, uncertainty — these ought to startle those rulers whose function it is to guide the opinion of men's minds.

The immortal President, Montesquieu, has treated cursorily of this matter; and truth, which is indivisible, has forced me to follow the luminous footsteps of this great man; but thinking men, for whom I write, will be able to distinguish my steps from his. Happy shall I esteem myself if, like him, I shall succeed in obtaining the secret gratitude of the unknown and peaceable followers of reason, and if I shall inspire them with that pleasing thrill of emotion with which sensitive minds respond to the advocate of the interests of humanity.

To examine and distinguish all the different sorts of crimes and the manner of punishing them would now be our natural task, were it not that their nature, which varies with the different circumstances of times and places, would compel us to enter upon too vast and wearisome a mass of detail. But it will suffice to indicate the most general principles and the most pernicious and common errors, in order to undeceive no less those who, from a mistaken love of liberty, would introduce anarchy, than those who would be glad to reduce their fellow men to the uniform regularity of a convent.

What will be the penalty suitable for such and such crimes?

Is death a penalty really *useful and necessary* for the security and good order of society?

Are torture and torments *just,* and do they attain the *end* which the law aims at?

What is the best way of preventing crimes?

Are the same penalties equally useful in all times?

What influence have they on customs?

These problems deserve to be solved with such geometrical precision as shall suffice to prevail over the clouds of sophistication, over seductive eloquence, or timid doubt. Had I no other merit than that of having been the first to make clearer to Italy that which other nations have dared to write and are beginning to practise, I should deem myself fortunate; but if, in maintaining the rights of men and of invincible truth, I should contribute to rescue from the spasms and agonies of death any unfortunate victim of tyranny or ignorance, both so equally fatal, the blessings and tears of a single innocent man in the transports of his joy would console me for the contempt of mankind.

## OATHS

A contradiction between the laws and the natural feelings of mankind arises from the oaths which are required of an accused, to the effect that he will be a truthful man when it is his greatest interest to be false; as if a man could really swear to contribute to his own destruction, or as if religion would not be silent with most men when their interest spoke on the other side. The experience of all ages has shown that men have abused religion more than any other of the precious gifts of heaven; and for what reason should criminals respect it, when men esteemed as the wisest have often violated it? Too weak, because too far removed from the senses, are for the mass of people the motives which religion opposes to the tumult of fear and the love of life. The affairs of heaven are conducted by laws absolutely different from those which govern human affairs; so why compromise those by these? Why place men in the terrible dilemma of either sinning against God or concurring in their own ruin? The law, in fact, which enforces such an oath commands a man either to be a bad Christian or to be a martyr. The oath becomes gradually a mere formality, thus destroying the force of religious feelings, which for the majority of men are the only pledge of their honesty. How useless oaths are has been shown by experience, for every judge will bear me out when I say that no oath has ever yet made any criminal speak the truth; and the same thing is shown by reason, which declares all laws to be useless, and consequently injurious, which are opposed to the natural sentiments of man. Such laws incur the same fate as dams placed directly in the main stream of a river: either they are immediately thrown down and overwhelmed, or a whirlpool formed by themselves corrodes and undermines them imperceptibly.

## TORTURE

A cruelty consecrated among most nations by custom is the torture of the accused during his trial, on the pretext of compelling him to confess his crime, of clearing up contradictions in his statements, of discovering his accomplices, of purging him in some metaphysical and incomprehensible way from infamy, or finally of finding out other crimes of which he may possibly be guilty, but of which he is not accused.

A man cannot be called *guilty* before sentence has been passed on him by a judge, nor can society deprive him of its protection till it has been decided that he has broken the condition on which it was granted. What, then, is that right but one of mere might by which a judge is empowered to inflict a punishment on a citizen whilst his guilt or innocence are still undetermined? The following dilemma is no new one: either the crime is certain or uncertain; if certain, no other punishment is suitable for it than that affixed to it by law; and torture is useless, for the same reason that the criminal's confession is useless. If it is uncertain, it is wrong to torture an innocent person, such as the law adjudges him to be, whose crimes are not yet proved.

What is the political object of punishments? The intimidation of other men. But what shall we say of the secret and private tortures which the tyranny of custom exercises alike upon the guilty and the innocent? It is important, indeed, that no open crime shall pass unpunished; but the public exposure of a criminal whose crime was hidden in darkness is utterly useless. An evil that has been done and cannot be undone can only be punished by civil society insofar as it may affect others with the hope of impunity. If it be true that there are a greater number of men who either from fear or virtue respect the laws than of those who transgress them, the risk of torturing an innocent man should be estimated according to the probability that any man will have been more likely, other things being equal, to have respected than to have despised the laws.

But I say in addition: it is to seek to confound all the relations of things to require a man to be at the same time accuser and accused, to make pain the crucible of truth, as if the test of it lay in the muscles and sinews of an unfortunate wretch. The law which ordains the use of torture is a law which says to men: "Resist pain; and if Nature has created in you an inextinguishable self-love, if she has given you an inalienable right of self-defence, I create in you a totally contrary affection, namely, an heroic self-hatred, and I command you to accuse yourselves, and to speak the truth between the laceration of your muscles and the dislocation of your bones."

This infamous crucible of truth is a still-existing monument of that primitive and savage legal system which called trials by fire and boiling water, or the accidental decisions of combat, *judgments of God,* as if the rings of the eternal chain in the control of the First Cause must at every moment be disarranged and put out for the petty institutions of mankind.

The only difference between torture and the trial by fire and water is, that the result of the former seems to depend on the will of the accused, and that of the other two on a fact which is purely physical and extrinsic to the sufferer; but the difference is only apparent, not real. The avowal of truth under tortures and agonies is as little free as was in those times the prevention without fraud of the usual effects of fire and boiling water. Every act of our will is ever proportioned to the force of the sensible impression which causes it, and the sensibility of every man is limited. Hence the impression produced by pain may be so intense as to occupy a man's entire sensibility and leave him no other liberty than the choice of the shortest way of escape, for the present moment, from his penalty. Under such circumstances the answer of the accused is as inevitable as the impressions produced by fire and water; and the innocent man who is sensitive will declare himself guilty, when by so doing he hopes to bring his agonies to an end. All the difference between guilt and innocence is lost by virtue of the very means which they profess to employ for its discovery.

Torture is a certain method for the acquittal of robust villains and for the condemnation of innocent but feeble men. See the fatal drawbacks of this pretended test of truth — a test, indeed, that is worthy of cannibals; a test which the Romans, barbarous as they too were in many respects, reserved for slaves alone, the victims of their fierce and too highly lauded virtue. Of two men, equally innocent or equally guilty, the robust and courageous will be acquitted, the weak and the timid will be condemned, by virtue of the following exact train of reasoning on the part of the judge: "I as judge had to find you guilty of such and such a crime; you, A B, have by your physical strength been able to resist pain, and therefore I acquit you; you, C D, in your weakness have yielded to it; therefore I condemn you. I feel that a confession extorted amid torments can have no force, but I will torture you afresh unless you corroborate what you have now confessed."

The result, then, of torture is a matter of temperament, of calculation, which varies with each man according to his strength and sensibility; so that by this method a mathematician might solve better than a judge this problem: "Given the muscular force and the nervous sensibility of an innocent man, to find the degree of pain which will cause him to plead guilty to a given crime."

# IX

# Faith Without Dogma

*As the following selections will show, the Enlightenment did not abjure God. Rather, He was viewed as the "Prime Mover" in a universal dynamic order based on reason and manifested in the laws of Nature discovered by Newton and other great scientists. What may be called the religion of the philosophes was deism, faith in such a God, and only a handful of the Enlightenment thinkers could be termed atheists or agnostics. What the Enlightenment attacked in religion was what they held to be superstition, dogma, and persecution of the heretical.*

# Statute of Virginia for Religious Freedom

## THOMAS JEFFERSON

Well aware that the opinions and belief of men depend not on their own will but follow involuntarily the evidence proposed to their minds; that Almighty God has created the mind free and manifested His supreme will that free it shall remain by making it altogether insusceptible of restraint; that all attempts to influence it by temporal punishments, or burdens, or by civil incapacitations tend only to beget habits of hypocrisy and meanness and are a departure from the plan of the holy Author of our religion, who being Lord both of body and mind, yet chose not to propagate it by coercions on either, as was in His almighty power to do, but to extend it by its influence on reason alone; that the impious presumption of legislators and rulers, civil as well as ecclesiastical, who, being themselves but fallible and uninspired men, have assumed dominion over the faith of others, setting up their own opinions and modes of thinking as the only true and infallible, and as such endeavoring to impose them on others, has established and maintained false religions over the greatest part of the world and through all time; that to compel a man to furnish contributions of money for the propagation of opinions which he disbelieves and abhors is sinful and tyrannical; that even the forcing him to support this or that teacher of his own religious persuasion is depriving him of the comfortable liberty of giving his contributions to the particular pastor whose morals he would make his pattern and whose powers he feels most persuasive to righteousness, and is withdrawing from the ministry those temporal rewards which, proceeding from an approbation of their personal conduct, are an additional incitement to earnest and unremitting labors for the instruction of mankind; that our civil rights have no dependence on our religious opinions any more than our opinions in physics or geometry; that therefore the proscribing any citizen as unworthy the public confidence by laying upon

him an incapacity of being called to offices of trust and emolument
unless he profess or renounce this or that religious opinion is depriving
him injuriously of those privileges and advantages to which, in common
with his fellow citizens, he has a natural right; that it tends also to corrupt
the principles of that very religion it is meant to encourage, by bribing
with a monopoly of worldly honors and emoluments those who will ex-
ternally profess and conform to it; that though indeed these are criminal
who do not withstand such temptation, yet neither are those innocent
who lay the bait in their way; that the opinions of men are not the
object of civil government, nor under its jurisdiction; that to suffer the
civil magistrate to intrude his powers into the field of opinion and to
restrain the profession or propagation of principles on supposition of
their ill tendency is a dangerous fallacy which at once destroys all religious
liberty, because he, being of course judge of that tendency, will make his
opinions the rule of judgment and approve or condemn the sentiments
of others only as they shall square with or differ from his own; that it is
time enough, for the rightful purposes of civil government, for its officers
to interfere when principles break out into overt acts against peace and
good order; and, finally, that truth is great and will prevail if left to
herself; that she is the proper and sufficient antagonist to error and has
nothing to fear from the conflict unless by human interposition disarmed
of her natural weapons, free argument and debate; errors ceasing to be
dangerous when it is permitted freely to contradict them.

We, the General Assembly of Virginia, do enact that no man shall be
compelled to frequent or support any religious worship, place, or ministry
whatsoever, nor shall be enforced, restrained, molested, or burdened in
his body or goods, nor shall otherwise suffer on account of his religious
opinions or belief; but that all men shall be free to profess, and by argument to maintain, their opinions in matters of religion, and that the
same shall in no wise diminish, enlarge, or affect their civil capacities.

And though we well know that this Assembly, elected by the people
for the ordinary purposes of legislation only, have no power to restrain
the acts of succeeding Assemblies constituted with powers equal to our
own, and that therefore to declare this act irrevocable would be of no
effect in law; yet we are free to declare, and do declare, that the rights
hereby asserted are of the natural rights of mankind, and that, if any act
shall be hereafter passed to repeal the present resolution or to narrow its
operation, such act will be an infringement of natural right.

*45. Music Room, 20 Portman Square*, London. Copyright, *Country Life*, London.

*46. The Rooms of the Duc de Choiseul*, 1757. Miniature by Blarenberghe, painted on a snuffbox by A. Leferre.

# Religion

from *Persian Letters*

## MONTESQUIEU

The prohibition of divorce is not the sole cause of depopulation in Christian countries. The great number of eunuchs they keep is a no less considerable cause.

I am talking of the priests and dervishes, of both sexes, who vow themselves to eternal continence. With Christians, this is the virtue par excellence. And in this I cannot follow their reasoning, for I don't know what kind of a virtue is a virtue from which there results nothing.

I find that their learned doctors clearly contradict themselves when they say that marriage is sacred and that celibacy, which is the absolute opposite, is even more so. And this without mentioning that in the matter of precepts and fundamental dogmas the good is always the best.

The number of people professing celibacy is prodigious. In times past, fathers used to sentence their children to it from the cradle. Nowadays, they take vows themselves as early as the age of fourteen, which amounts to about the same thing.

This art or trade of continence has destroyed more men than pestilence and the bloodiest of wars. In every religious house there can be seen an eternal family in which nobody is born and which maintains itself at the expense of all the other families. These houses are always agape, like so many abysses where future races of men are buried.

This policy is quite different from that of the Romans, who established penal laws against those who refused to marry and chose to enjoy a freedom so contrary to the public utility.

I am speaking now only of Catholic countries. In the Protestant religion, everyone has the right to make children. This religion permits neither priests nor dervishes. If in its establishment, its founders, who brought everything back to primitive values, had not continually been accused of intemperance, there can be no doubt that, having made marriage a universal practice, they would have gone on to lighten the yoke still further and would thus have managed to remove the barrier that separates Nazarene and Moslem on this score.

However that may be, it is certain that religion gives Protestants an infinite advantage over Catholics.

I shall dare to put it thus: in the present state of Europe, it is impossible for the Catholic religion to last another five hundred years.

Prior to the humbling of Spanish power, the Catholics were much stronger than the Protestants. The latter have bit by bit managed to come to a position of equality. Protestants will continue to become richer and more powerful, and Catholics, weaker.

Protestant countries should be, and in reality, are more populous than Catholic countries. From which it follows, first, that taxes are more considerable since they increase along with the number of those who pay, and second, that the soil is better cultivated, and finally, that commerce flourishes to a greater extent because there are more people to make a fortune and because with more needs there are more resources for fulfilling them. When the number of people is only sufficient to till the soil, commerce must perish; and when the number is only enough to maintain commerce, the cultivation of the soil lags. That is to say, both decline at the same time, for you cannot concentrate on one except at the expense of the other.

As for Catholic countries, not only is cultivation of crops abandoned, but even industry is pernicious. It consists solely in learning five or six words in some dead language. As soon as a man has got that stock under his belt, he need no longer worry about his fortune. In the cloister, he will find a peaceful life, which would have cost him sweat and tears in the world.

That's not all. The dervishes hold almost all the wealth of the state. They are a society of greedy people, who always take and never give in return. They accumulate revenue continuously, in order to acquire capital. All this great wealth falls, so to speak, into paralysis: no more circulation of money, no more commerce, no more arts, no more manufactures.

There is no Protestant prince who fails to raise more taxes on his subjects than the Pope raises on his, and yet these latter are poor, and the former live in abundance. Commerce brings everything to the first; monasticism universally brings death to the others.

# Holy Willie's Prayer

## ROBERT BURNS

*And send the godly in a pet to pray.* — Pope

O Thou, that in the heavens dost dwell,
Wha, as it pleases best Tysel',
Sends ane to heaven an' ten to hell,
    A' for Thy glory,
And no for onie guid or ill
    They've done afore Thee!

I bless and praise Thy matchless might,
When thousands Thou hast left in night,
That I am here afore Thy sight,
    For gifts an' grace
A burning and a shining light
    To a' this place.

What was I, or my generation,
That I should get sic exaltation,
I wha deserv'd most just damnation
    For broken laws,
Sax thousand years ere my creation,
    Thro' Adam's cause.

When from my mither's womb I fell,
Thou might hae plung'd me deep in hell,
To gnash my gooms, and weep and wail,
    In burnin lakes,
Where damnéd devils roar and yell,
    Chain'd to their stakes.

Yet I am here a chosen sample,
To show Thy grace is great and ample;

I'm here a pillar o' Thy temple,
　　Strong as a rock,
A guide, a buckler, and example,
　　To a' Thy flock.

O Lord, Thou kens what zeal I bear,
When drinkers drink, an' swearers swear,
An' singing here, an' dancing there,
　　Wi' great and sma';
For I am keepit by Thy fear
　　Free frae them a'.

But yet, O Lord! confess I must,
At times I'm fash'd wi' fleshly lust:
An' sometimes, too, in warldly trust,
　　Vile self gets in;
But Thou remembers we are dust,
　　Defil'd wi' sin.

O Lord! yestreen, Thou kens, wi' Meg —
Thy pardon I sincerely beg;
O! may't ne'er be a livin plague
　　To my dishonour,
An' I'll ne'er lift a lawless leg
　　Again upon her.

Besides, I farther maun allow,
Wi' Leezie's lass, three time I trow —
But Lord, that Friday I was fou,
　　When I cam near her;
Or else, Thou kens, Thy servant true
　　Wad never steer her.

Maybe Thou lets this fleshly thorn
Buffet Thy servant e'en and morn,
Lest owre proud and high shou'd turn,
　　That he's sae gifted:
If sae, Thy han' maun e'en be borne,
　　Until Thou lift it.

Lord, bless Thy chosen in this place,
For here Thou has a chosen race:
But God confound their stubborn face
　　An' blast their name,

Wha bring Thy elders to disgrace
        An' public shame.

Lord, mind Gaw'n Hamilton's deserts;
He drinks, an' swears, an' plays at cartes,
Yet has sae mony takin arts,
        Wi' great and sma',
Frae God's ain priest the people's hearts
        He steals awa.

An' when we chasten'd him therefor,
Thou kens how he bred sic a splore,
An' set the warld in a roar
        O' laughing at us; —
Curse Thou his basket and his store,
        Kail an' potatoes.

Lord, hear my earnest cry and pray'r,
Against that Presbyt'ry o' Ayr;
Thy strong right hand, Lord, make it bare
        Upo' their heads;
Lord, visit them, an' dinna spare,
        For their misdeeds.

O Lord, my God! that glib-tongu'd Aiken,
My vera heart and flesh are quakin,
To think how we stood sweatin, shakin,
        An' p —— 'd wi' dread,
While he, wi' hingin lip an' snakin,
        Held up his head.

Lord, in Thy day o' vengeance try him,
Lord, visit them wha did employ him,
And pass not in Thy mercy by them,
        Nor hear their pray'r,
But for Thy people's sake destroy them,
        An' dinna spare.

But, Lord, remember me an' mine
Wi' mercies temporal and divine,
That I for grace and gear may shine,
        Excell'd by nane,
And a' the glory shall be Thine,
        Amen, Amen!

47. Michel Audran Gobelins, *The Memorable Judgment of Sancho Panza.* Tapestry.

48. Wedgwood porcelain vase designed by Flaxman, *The Apotheosis of Homer.* Victoria and Albert Museum. Crown Copyright.

# Prayer to God

## VOLTAIRE

No longer than do I address myself to men, but to you, God of all beings, of all worlds, and of all ages; if it may be permitted weak creatures lost in immensity and imperceptible to the rest of the universe, to dare to ask something of you, you who have given everything, and whose decrees are immutable as they are eternal. Deign to look with pity on the errors attached to our nature; let not these errors prove ruinous to us. You have not given us hearts to hate ourselves with, and hands to kill one another. Grant then that we may mutually aid each other to support the burden of a painful and transitory life; that the trifling differences in the garments that cover our frail bodies, in our insufficient languages, in our ridiculous customs, in our imperfect laws, in our idle opinions, in all our conditions so disproportionate in our eyes, and so equal in yours, that all the little variations that differentiate the atoms called *men* not be signs of hatred and persecution; that those who light candles in broad daylight to worship you bear with those who content themselves with the light of your sun; that those who dress themselves in a white robe to say that we must love you do not detest those who say the same thing in cloaks of black wool; that it may be all the same to adore you in a dialect formed from an ancient or a modern language; that those whose coat is colored red or violet, who rule over a little parcel of a little heap of mud of this world, and who possess a few round fragments of a certain metal, enjoy without pride what they call *grandeur* and *riches,* and may others look on them without envy: for you know that there is nothing in all these vanities to inspire envy or pride.

May all men remember that they are brothers! May they hold in horror tyranny exerted over souls, just as they do the violence which forcibly seizes the products of peaceful industry! And if the scourge of war is inevitable, let us not hate one another, let us not destroy one another in the midst of peace, and let us use the moment of our existence to bless, in a thousand different languages, from Siam to California, your goodness which has given us this moment.

# from *The Decline and Fall of the Roman Empire*

## EDWARD GIBBON

If we seriously consider the purity of the Christian religion, the sanctity of its moral precepts, and the innocent as well as austere lives of the greater number of those who during the first ages embraced the faith of the Gospel, we should naturally suppose that so benevolent a doctrine would have been received with due reverence even by the unbelieving world; that the learned and the polite, however they might deride the miracles, would have esteemed the virtues of the new sect; and that the magistrates, instead of persecuting, would have protected an order of men who yielded the most passive obedience to the laws, though they declined the active cares of war and government. If, on the other hand, we recollect the universal toleration of Polytheism, as it was invariably maintained by the faith of the people, the incredulity of philosophers, and the policy of the Roman senate and emperors, we are at a loss to discover what new offence the Christians had committed, what new provocation could exasperate the mild indifference of antiquity, and what new motives could urge the Roman princes, who beheld without concern a thousand forms of religion subsisting in peace under their gentle sway, to inflict a severe punishment on any part of their subjects who had chosen for themselves a singular but an inoffensive mode of faith and worship.

The religious policy of the ancient world seems to have assumed a more stern and intolerant character to oppose the progress of Christianity. About fourscore years after the death of Christ, his innocent disciples were punished with death by the sentence of a proconsul of the most amiable and philosophic character, and according to the laws of an emperor distinguished by the wisdom and justice of his general administration. The apologies which were repeatedly addressed to the successors of Trajan are filled with the most pathetic complaints that the Christians, who obeyed the dictates and solicited the liberty of conscience, were alone, among all the subjects of the Roman empire, excluded from the common benefits of their auspicious government. The deaths of a few eminent martyrs have been recorded with care; and from the time that Christianity was invested with the supreme power, the governors of the church have been no less diligently employed in displaying the cruelty, than in imitating the conduct, of their Pagan adversaries. To separate (if it be possible) a few authentic as well as interesting facts from an undigested mass of fiction and error, and to relate, in a clear and rational manner, the causes, the extent, the duration, and the most important circumstances of the persecutions to which the first Christians were exposed, is the design of the present chapter.

The sectaries of a persecuted religion, depressed by fear, animated with resentment, and perhaps heated by enthusiasm, are seldom in a proper temper of mind calmly to investigate, or candidly to appreciate, the motives of their enemies, which often escape the impartial and discerning view even of those who are placed at a secure distance from the flames of persecution. A reason has been assigned for the conduct of the emperors towards the primitive Christians, which may appear the more specious and probable as it is drawn from the acknowledged genius of Polytheism. It has already been observed that the religious concord of the world was principally supported by the implicit assent and reverence which the nations of antiquity expressed for their respective traditions and ceremonies. It might therefore be expected that they would unite with indignation against any sect or people which should separate itself from the communion of mankind, and, claiming the exclusive possession of divine knowledge, should disdain every form of worship except its own as impious and idolatrous. The rights of toleration were held by mutual indulgence: they were justly forfeited by a refusal of the accustomed tribute. As the payment of this tribute was inflexibly refused by the Jews, and by them alone, the consideration of the treatment which they experienced from the Roman magistrates will serve to explain how far these speculations are justified by facts, and will lead us to discover the true causes of the persecution of Christianity.

Without repeating what has been already mentioned of the reverence of the Roman princes and governors for the temple of Jerusalem, we shall only observe that the destruction of the temple and city was accompanied and followed by every circumstance that could exasperate the minds of the conquerors, and authorise religious persecutions by the most specious arguments of political justice and the public safety. From the reign of Nero to that of Antoninus Pius, the Jews discovered a fierce impatience of the dominion of Rome, which repeatedly broke out in the most furious massacres and insurrections. Humanity is shocked at the recital of the horrid cruelties which they committed in the cities of Egypt, of Cyprus, and of Cyrene, where they dwelt in treacherous friendship with the unsuspecting natives; and we are tempted to applaud the severe retaliation which was exercised by the arms of the legions against a race of fanatics whose dire and credulous superstition seemed to render them the implacable enemies not only of the Roman government, but of human kind. The enthusiasm of the Jews was supported by the opinion that it was unlawful for them to pay taxes to an idolatrous master, and by the flattering promise which they derived from their ancient oracles, that a conquering Messiah would soon arise, destined to break their fetters, and to invest the favourites of heaven with the empire of the earth. It was by announcing himself as their long-expected deliverer, and by calling on all the descendants of Abraham to assert the hope of Israel, that the famous Barchochebas collected a formidable army, with which he resisted during two years the power of the emperor Hadrian.

Notwithstanding these repeated provocations, the resentment of the Roman princes expired after the victory, nor were their apprehensions continued beyond the period of war and danger. By the general indulgence of Polytheism, and by the mild temper of Antoninus Pius, the Jews were restored to their ancient privileges, and once more obtained the permission of circumcising their children, with the easy restraint that they should never confer on any foreign proselyte that distinguishing mark of the Hebrew race. The numerous remains of that people, though they were still excluded from the precincts of Jerusalem, were permitted to form and to maintain considerable establishments both in Italy and in the provinces, to acquire the freedom of Rome, to enjoy municipal honours, and to obtain at the same time an exemption from the burdensome and expensive offices of society. The moderation or the contempt of the Romans gave a legal sanction to the form of ecclesiastical police which was instituted by the vanquished sect. The patriarch, who had fixed his residence at Tiberias, was empowered to appoint his subordinate ministers and apostles, to exercise a domestic jurisdiction, and to receive from his dispersed brethren an annual contribution. New synagogues were frequently erected in the principal cities of the empire; and the sabbaths, the fasts, and the festivals, which were either commanded by the Mosaic law or enjoined by the traditions of the Rabbis, were celebrated in the most solemn and public manner. Such gentle treatment insensibly assuaged the stern temper of the Jews. Awakened from their dream of prophecy and conquest, they assumed the behaviour of peaceable and industrious subjects. Their irreconcilable hatred of mankind, instead of flaming out in acts of blood and violence, evaporated in less dangerous gratifications. They embraced every opportunity of overreaching the idolaters in trade, and they pronounced secret and ambiguous imprecations against the haughty kingdom of Edom.

Since the Jews, who rejected with abhorrence the deities adored by their sovereign and by their fellow-subjects, enjoyed, however, the free exercise of their unsocial religion, there must have existed some other cause which exposed the disciples of Christ to those severities from which the posterity of Abraham was exempt. The difference between them is simple and obvious, but, according to the sentiments of antiquity, it was of the highest importance. The Jews were a *nation*, the Christians were a *sect:* and if it was natural for every community to respect the sacred institutions of their neighbours, it was incumbent on them to persevere in those of their ancestors. The voice of oracles, the precepts of philosophers, and the authority of the laws, unanimously enforced this national obligation. By their lofty claim of superior sanctity the Jews might provoke the Polytheists to consider them as an odious and impure race. By disdaining the intercourse of other nations they might deserve their contempt. The laws of Moses might be for the most part frivolous or absurd; yet, since they had been received during many ages by a large society, his followers were justified by the example of mankind, and it was universally acknowledged that they had a right to practise what it would have been criminal in them to neglect. But this principle, which protected the Jewish synagogue, afforded not any favour or security to the primitive church. By embracing the faith of the Gospel the Christians incurred the supposed guilt of an unnatural and unpardonable offence. They dissolved the sacred ties of custom and education, violated the religious institutions of their country, and presumptuously despised whatever their fathers had believed as true or had reverenced as sacred. Nor was this apostacy (if we may use the expression) merely of a partial or local kind; since the pious deserter who withdrew himself from the temples of Egypt or Syria would equally disdain to seek an asylum in those of Athens or Carthage. Every Christian rejected with contempt the superstitions of his family, his city, and his province. The whole body of Christians unanimously refused to hold any communion with the gods of Rome, of the empire, and of mankind. It was in vain that the oppressed believer asserted the inalienable rights of conscience and private judgment. Though his situation might excite the pity, his arguments could never reach the understanding, either of the philosophic or of the believing part of the Pagan world. To their apprehensions it was no less a matter of surprise that any individuals should entertain scruples against complying with the established mode of worship than if they had conceived a sudden abhorrence to the manners, the dress, or the language of their native country.

The surprise of the Pagans was soon succeeded by resentment, and the most pious of men were exposed to the unjust but dangerous imputation of impiety. Malice and prejudice concurred in representing the Christians as a society of atheists, who, by the most daring attack on the religious constitution of the empire, had merited the severest animadversion of the civil magistrate. They had separated themselves (they gloried in the confession) from every mode of superstition which was received in any part of the globe by the various temper of Polytheism: but it was not altogether so evident what deity, or what form of worship, they had substituted to the gods and temples of antiquity. The pure and sublime idea which they entertained of the Supreme Being escaped the gross conception of the Pagan multitude, who were at a loss to discover a spiritual and solitary God, that was neither represented under any corporeal figure or visible symbol, nor was adored with the accustomed pomp of libations and festivals, of altars and sacrifices. The sages of Greece and Rome, who had elevated their minds to the contemplation of the existence and attributes of the First Cause, were induced by reason or by vanity to reserve for themselves and their chosen disciples the privilege of this philosophical devotion. They were far from admitting the prejudices of mankind as the standard of truth, but they considered them as flowing from the original disposition of human nature; and they supposed that any popular mode of faith and worship which presumed to disclaim the assistance of the senses would, in proportion as it receded from superstition, find itself incapable of restraining the wonderings of the fancy and the visions of fanaticism. The careless glance which men of wit and learning condescended to cast on the Christian revelation served only to confirm their hasty opinion, and to persuade them that the principle, which they might have revered, of the Divine Unity, was defaced by the wild enthusiasm, and annihilated by the airy speculations, of the new sectaries. The author of a celebrated dialogue, which has been attributed to Lucian, whilst he affects to treat the mysterious subject of the Trinity in a style of ridicule and contempt, betrays his own ignorance of the weakness of human reason, and of the inscrutable nature of the Divine perfections.

It might appear less surprising that the founder of Christianity should not only be revered by his disciples as a sage and a prophet, but that he should be adored as a God. The Polytheists were disposed to adopt every article of faith which seemed to offer any resemblance, however distant or imperfect, with the popular mythology; and the legend of Bacchus, of

Hercules, and of Æsculapius had, in some measure, prepared their imagination for the appearance of the Son of God under a human form. But they were astonished that the Christians should abandon the temples of those ancient heroes who, in the infancy of the world, had invented arts, instituted laws, and vanquished the tyrants or monsters who infested the earth; in order to choose for the exclusive object of their religious worship an obscure teacher, who, in a recent age, and among a barbarous people, had fallen a sacrifice either to the malice of his own countrymen, or to the jealousy of the Roman government. The Pagan multitude, reserving their gratitude for temporal benefits alone, rejected the inestimable present of life and immortality which was offered to mankind by Jesus of Nazareth. His mild constancy in the midst of cruel and voluntary sufferings, his universal benevolence, and the sublime simplicity of his actions and character, were insufficient, in the opinion of those carnal men, to compensate for the want of fame, of empire, and of success; and whilst they refused to acknowledge his stupendous triumph over the powers of darkness and of the grave, they misrepresented, or they insulted, the equivocal birth, wandering life, and ignominious death, of the divine Author of Christianity.

The personal guilt which every Christian had contracted, in thus preferring his private sentiment to the national religion, was aggravated in a very high degree by the number and union of the criminals. It is well known, and has been already observed, that Roman policy viewed with the utmost jealousy and distrust any association among its subjects; and that the privileges of private corporations, though formed for the most harmless or beneficial purposes, were bestowed with a very sparing hand. The religious assemblies of the Christians, who had separated themselves from the public worship, appeared of a much less innocent nature: they were illegal in their principle, and in their consequences might become dangerous; nor were the emperors conscious that they violated the laws of justice, when, for the peace of society, they prohibited those secret and sometimes nocturnal meetings. The pious disobedience of the Christians made their conduct, or perhaps their designs, appear in a much more serious and criminal light; and the Roman princes, who might perhaps have suffered themselves to be disarmed by a ready submission, deeming their honour concerned in the execution of their commands, sometimes attempted, by rigorous punishments, to subdue this independent spirit, which boldly acknowledged an authority superior to that of the magistrate. The extent and duration of this spiritual conspiracy seemed to render it every day more deserving of his animadversion. We have already seen that the active and successful zeal of the Christians had insensibly diffused them through every province and almost every city of the empire. The new converts seemed to renounce their family and country, that they might connect themselves in an indissoluble band of union with a peculiar society, which everywhere assumed a different character from the rest of mankind. Their gloomy and austere aspect, their abhorrence of the common business and pleasures of life, and their frequent predictions of impending calamities, inspired the Pagans with the apprehension of some danger which would arise from the new sect, the more alarming as it was the more obscure. "Whatever," says Pliny, "may be the principle of their conduct, their inflexible obstinacy appeared deserving of punishment."

The precautions with which the disciples of Christ performed the offices of religion were at first dictated by fear and necessity; but they were continued from choice. By imitating the awful secrecy which reigned in the Eleusinian mysteries, the Christians had flattered themselves that they should render their sacred institutions more respectable in the eyes of the Pagan world. But the event, as it often happens to the operations of subtile policy, deceived their wishes and their expectations. It was concluded that they only concealed what they would have blushed to disclose. Their mistaken prudence afforded an opportunity for malice to invent, and for suspicious credulity to believe, the horrid tales which described the Christians as the most wicked of human kind, who practised in their dark recesses every abomination that a depraved fancy could suggest, and who solicited the favour of their unknown God by the sacrifice of every moral virtue. There were many who pretended to confess or to relate the ceremonies of this abhorred society. It was asserted, "that a new-born infant, entirely covered over with flour, was presented, like some mystic symbol of initiation, to the knife of the proselyte, who unknowingly inflicted many a secret and mortal wound on the innocent victim of his error; that as soon as the cruel deed was perpetrated, the sectaries drank up the blood, greedily tore asunder the quivering members, and pledged themselves to eternal secrecy, by a mutual consciousness of guilt. It was as confidently affirmed that this inhuman sacrifice was succeeded by a suitable entertainment, in which intemperance served as a provocative to brutal lust; till, at the appointed moment, the lights were suddenly extinguished, shame was banished, nature was forgotten; and, as accident might direct, the darkness of the night was polluted by the incestuous commerce of sisters and brothers, of sons and of mothers."

But the perusal of the ancient apologies was sufficient to remove even the slightest suspicion from the mind of a candid adversary. The Christians, with the intrepid security of innocence, appeal from the voice of rumour to the equity of the magistrates. They acknowledge that, if any proof can be produced of the crimes which calumny has imputed to them, they are worthy of the most severe punishment. They provoke the punishment, and they challenge the proof. At the same time they urge, with equal truth and propriety, that the charge is not less devoid of probability than it is destitute of evidence; they ask whether any one can seriously believe that the pure and holy precepts of the Gospel, which so frequently restrain the use of the most lawful enjoyments, should inculcate the practice of the most abominable crimes; that a large society should resolve to dishonour itself in the eyes of its own members; and that a great number of persons, of either sex, and every age and character, insensible to the fear of death or infamy, should consent to violate those principles which nature and education had imprinted most deeply in their minds. Nothing, it should seem, could weaken the force or destroy the effect of so unanswerable a justification, unless it were the injudicious conduct of the apologists themselves, who betrayed the common cause of religion, to gratify their devout hatred to the domestic enemies of the church. It was sometimes faintly insinuated, and sometimes boldly asserted, that the same bloody sacrifices, and the same incestuous festivals, which were so falsely ascribed to the orthodox believers, were in reality celebrated by the Marcionites, by the Carpocratians, and by several other sects of the Gnostics, who, notwithstanding they might deviate into the paths of heresy, were still actuated by the sentiments of men, and still governed by the precepts of Christianity. Accusations of a similar kind were retorted upon the church by the schismatics who had departed from its communion, and it was confessed on all sides that the most scandalous licentiousness of manners prevailed among great numbers of those who affected the name of Christians. A Pagan magistrate, who possessed neither leisure nor abilities to discern the almost imperceptible line which divides the orthodox faith from heretical pravity, might easily have imagined that their mutual animosity had extorted the discovery of their common guilt. It was fortunate for the repose, or at least for the reputation, of the first Christians, that the magistrates sometimes proceeded with more temper and moderation than is usually consistent with religious zeal, and that they reported, as the impartial result of their judicial inquiry, that the sectaries who had deserted the established worship appeared to them sincere in their professions and blameless in their manners, however they might incur, by their absurd and excessive superstition, the censure of the laws.

History, which undertakes to record the transactions of the past, for the instruction of future ages, would ill deserve that honourable office if she condescended to plead the cause of tyrants, or to justify the maxims of persecution. It must, however, be acknowledged that the conduct of the emperors who appeared the least favourable to the primitive church is by no means so criminal as that of modern sovereigns who have employed the arm of violence and terror against the religious opinions of any part of their subjects. From their reflections, or even from their own feelings, a Charles V. or a Louis XIV. might have acquired a just knowledge of the rights of conscience, of the obligation of faith, and of the innocence of error. But the princes and magistrates of ancient Rome were strangers to those principles which inspired and authorised the inflexible obstinacy of the Christians in the cause of truth, nor could they themselves discover in their own breasts any motive which would have prompted them to refuse a legal, and as it were a natural, submission to the sacred institutions of their country. The same reason which contributes to alleviate the guilt, must have tended to abate the rigour, of their persecutions. As they were actuated, not by the furious zeal of bigots, but by the temperate policy of legislators, contempt must often have relaxed, and humanity must frequently have suspended, the execution of those laws which they enacted against the humble and obscure followers of Christ. From the general view of their character and motives we might naturally conclude: I. That a considerable time elapsed before they considered the new sectaries as an object deserving of the attention of government. II. That in the conviction of any of their subjects who were accused of so very singular a crime, they proceeded with caution and reluctance. III. That they were moderate in the use of punishments; and IV. That the afflicted church enjoyed many intervals of peace and tranquillity.

.        .        .

We shall conclude this chapter by a melancholy truth which obtrudes itself on the reluctant mind; that, even admitting, without hesitation or inquiry, all that history has recorded, or devotion has feigned, on the subject of martyrdoms, it must still be acknowledged that the Christians, in the course of their intestine dissensions, have inflicted far greater severities on each other than they had experienced from the zeal of infidels. During the ages of ignorance which followed the subversion of the Roman empire in the West, the bishops of the Imperial city extended their dominion over the laity as well as clergy of the Latin church. The fabric of superstition which they had erected, and which might long have defied the feeble efforts of reason, was at length assaulted by a crowd of daring fanatics, who, from the twelfth to the sixteenth century, assumed the popular character of reformers. The church of Rome defended by violence the empire which she had acquired by fraud; a system of peace and benevolence was soon disgraced by the proscriptions, wars, massacres, and the institution of the holy office. And as the reformers were animated by the love of civil as well as of religious freedom, the Catholic princes connected their own interest with that of the clergy, and enforced by fire and the sword the terrors of spiritual censures. In the Netherlands alone more than one hundred thousand of the subjects of Charles V. are said to have suffered by the hand of the executioner; and this extraordinary number is attested by Grotius, a man of genius and learning, who preserved his moderation amidst the fury of contending sects, and who composed the annals of his own age and country at a time when the invention of printing had facilitated the means of intelligence and increased the danger of detection. If we are obliged to submit our belief to the authority of Grotius, it must be allowed that the number of Protestants who were executed in a single province and a single reign far exceeded that of the primitive martyrs in the space of three centuries and of the Roman empire. But if the improbability of the fact itself should prevail over the weight of evidence; if Grotius should be convicted of exaggerating the merit and sufferings of the reformers; we shall be naturally led to inquire what confidence can be placed in the doubtful and imperfect monuments of ancient credulity; what degree of credit can be assigned to a courtly bishop and a passionate declaimer, who, under the protection of Constantine, enjoyed the exclusive privilege of recording the persecutions inflicted on the Christians by the vanquished rivals or disregarded predecessors of their gracious sovereign.

# Credo

## THOMAS PAINE

It has been my intention for several years past to publish my thoughts upon Religion. I am well aware of the difficulties that attend the subject; and from that consideration had reserved it to a more advanced period of life. I intended it to be the last offering I should make to my fellow-citizens of all nations, and that at a time when the purity of the motive that induced me to it could not admit of a question, even by those who might disapprove the work.

The circumstance that has now taken place in France, of the total abolition of the whole national order of priesthood and of everything appertaining to compulsive systems of religion and compulsive articles of faith, has not only precipitated my intention, but rendered a work of this kind exceedingly necessary; lest, in the general wreck of superstition, of false systems of government, and false theology, we lose sight of morality, of humanity, and of the theology that is true.

As several of my colleagues, and others of my fellow-citizens of France, have given me the example of making their voluntary and individual profession of faith, I also will make mine; and I do this with all that sincerity and frankness with which the mind of man communicates with itself.

I believe in one God, and no more; and I hope for happiness beyond this life.

I believe in the equality of man, and I believe that religious duties consist in doing justice, loving mercy, and endeavoring to make our fellow-creatures happy.

But lest it should be supposed that I believe many other things in addition to these, I shall, in the progress of this work, declare the things I do not believe and my reasons for not believing them.

I do not believe in the creed professed by the Jewish church, by the Roman church, by the Greek church, by the Turkish church, by the Protestant church, nor by any church that I know of. My own mind is my own church.

All national institutions of churches — whether Jewish, Christian, or Turkish — appear to me no other than human inventions set up to terrify and enslave mankind and monopolize power and profit.

I do not mean by this declaration to condemn those who believe otherwise. They have the same right to their belief as I have to mine. But it is necessary to the happiness of man that he be mentally faithful to himself. Infidelity does not consist in believing or in disbelieving; it consists in professing to believe what he does not believe.

It is impossible to calculate the moral mischief, if I may so express it, that mental lying has produced in society. When a man has so far corrupted and prostituted the chastity of his mind as to subscribe his professional belief to things he does not believe, he has prepared himself for the commission of every other crime. He takes up the trade of a priest for the sake of gain, and, in order to *qualify* himself for that trade, he begins with a perjury. Can we conceive anything more destructive to morality than this?

Soon after I had published the pamphlet, COMMON SENSE, in America,

I saw the exceeding probability that a revolution in the system of government would be followed by a revolution in the system of religion. The adulterous connection of church and state, wherever it had taken place, whether Jewish, Christian, or Turkish, had so effectually prohibited, by pains and penalties, every discussion upon established creeds and upon first principles of religion, that until the system of government should be changed those subjects could not be brought fairly and openly before the world; but that whenever this should be done, a revolution in the system of religion would follow. Human inventions and priestcraft would be detected, and man would return to the pure, unmixed, and unadulterated belief of one God, and no more.

# On My Religion

## BENJAMIN FRANKLIN

You desire to know something of my Religion. It is the first time I have been questioned upon it. But I cannot take your Curiosity amiss, and shall endeavour in a few Words to gratify it. Here is my Creed. I believe in one God, Creator of the Universe. That he governs it by his Providence. That he ought to be worshipped. That the most acceptable Service we render to him is doing good to his other Children. That the soul of Man is immortal, and will be treated with Justice in another Life respecting its Conduct in this. These I take to be the fundamental Principles of all sound Religion, and I regard them as you do in whatever Sect I meet with them.

As to Jesus of Nazareth, my Opinion of whom you particularly desire, I think the System of Morals and his Religion, as he left them to us, the best the World ever saw or is likely to see; but I apprehend it has received various corrupting Changes, and I have, with most of the present Dissenters in England, some Doubts as to his Divinity; tho' it is a question I do not dogmatize upon, having never studied it, and think it needless to busy myself with it now, when I expect soon an Opportunity of knowing the Truth with less Trouble. I see no harm, however, in its being believed, if that Belief has the good Consequence, as probably it has, of making his Doctrines more respected and better observed; especially as I do not perceive, that the Supreme takes it amiss, by distinguishing the

49. *Corner cabinet* — black lacquer with Chinese scenes in gilt. An example of the Oriental influence, "chinoiserie," that was one of the trends of the Enlightenment.

50. *Bed,* period of Louis XVI.

Unbelievers in his Government of the World with any peculiar Marks of his Displeasure.

I shall only add, respecting myself, that, having experienced the Goodness of that Being in conducting me prosperously thro' a long life, I have no doubt of its Continuance in the next, though without the smallest Conceit of meriting such Goodness. My Sentiments on this Head you will see in the Copy of an old Letter enclosed, which I wrote in answer to one from a zealous Religionist, whom I had relieved in a paralytic case by electricity, and who, being afraid I should grow proud upon it, sent me his serious though rather impertinent Caution. . . .

P. S. Had not your College some Present of Books from the King of France? Please to let me know, if you had an Expectation given you of more, and the Nature of that Expectation? I have a Reason for the Enquiry.

I confide, that you will not expose me to Criticism and censure by publishing any part of this Communication to you. I have ever let others enjoy their religious Sentiments, without reflecting on them for those that appeared to me unsupportable and even absurd. All Sects here, and we have a great Variety, have experienced my good will in assisting them with Subscriptions for building their new Places of Worship; and, as I have never opposed any of their Doctrines, I hope to go out of the World in Peace with them all.

# from *Dialogues Concerning Natural Religion*

## DAVID HUME

Did I show you a house or palace where there was not one apartment convenient or agreeable, where the windows, doors, fires, passages, stairs, and the whole economy of the building were the source of noise, confusion, fatigue, darkness, and the extremes of heat and cold, you would certainly blame the contrivance, without any further examination. The architect would in vain display his subtility, and prove to you that, if this door or that window were altered, greater ills would ensue. What he says may be strictly true: the alteration of one particular, while the other parts of the building remain, may only augment the inconveniences.

But still you would assert in general that, if the architect had had skill and good intentions, he might have formed such a plan of the whole, and might have adjusted the parts in such a manner as would have remedied all or most of these inconveniences. His ignorance, or even your own ignorance of such a plan, will never convince you of the impossibility of it. If you find any inconveniences and deformities in the building, you will always, without entering into any detail, condemn the architect.

In short, I repeat the question: Is the world, considered in general and as it appears to us in this life, different from what a man or such a limited being would, *beforehand,* expect from a very powerful, wise, and benevolent Deity? It must be strange prejudice to assert the contrary. And from thence I conclude that, however consistent the world may be, allowing certain suppositions and conjectures with the idea of such a Deity, it can never afford us an inference concerning his existence. The consistency is not absolutely denied, only the inference. Conjectures, especially where infinity is excluded from the Divine attributes, may perhaps be sufficient to prove a consistency, but can never be foundations for any inference.

There seem to be *four* circumstances on which depend all or the greatest part of the ills that molest sensible creatures; and it is not impossible but all these circumstances may be necessary and unavoidable. We know so little beyond common life, or even of common life, that, with regard to the economy of a universe, there is no conjecture, however wild, which may not be just, nor any one, however plausible, which may not be erroneous. All that belongs to human understanding, in this deep ignorance and obscurity, is to be sceptical or at least cautious, and not to admit of any hypothesis whatever, much less of any which is supported by no appearance of probability. Now this I assert to be the case with regard to all the causes of evil and the circumstances on which it depends. None of them appear to human reason in the least degree necessary or unavoidable, nor can we suppose them such, without the utmost license of imagination.

The *first* circumstance which introduces evil is that contrivance or economy of the animal creation by which pains, as well as pleasures, are employed to excite all creatures to action, and make them vigilant in the great work of self-preservation. Now pleasure alone, in its various degrees, seems to human understanding sufficient for this purpose. All animals might be constantly in a state of enjoyment; but when urged by any of the necessities of nature, such as thirst, hunger, weariness, instead of pain, they might feel a diminution of pleasure by which they might be prompted to seek that object which is necessary to their subsistence. Men pursue pleasure as eagerly as they avoid pain; at least, they might have been so constituted. It seems, therefore, plainly possible to carry on the business of life without any pain. Why then is any animal ever rendered susceptible of such a sensation? If animals can be free from it an hour, they might enjoy a perpetual exemption from it, and it required as particular a contrivance of their organs to produce that feeling as to endow them with sight, hearing, or any of the senses. Shall we conjecture that such a contrivance was necessary, without any appearance of reason, and shall we build on that conjecture as on the most certain truth?

But a capacity of pain would not alone produce pain were it not for the *second* circumstance, viz., the conducting of the world by general laws; and this seems nowise necessary to a very perfect Being. It is true, if everything were conducted by particular volitions, the course of nature would be perpetually broken, and no man could employ his reason in the conduct of life. But might not other particular volitions remedy this inconvenience? In short, might not the Deity exterminate all ill, wherever it were to be found, and produce all good, without any preparation or long progress of causes and effects?

Besides, we must consider that, according to the present economy of the world, the course of nature, though supposed exactly regular, yet to us appears not so, and many events are uncertain, and many disappoint our expectations. Health and sickness, calm and tempest, with an infinite number of other accidents whose causes are unknown and variable, have a great influence both on the fortunes of particular persons and on the prosperity of public societies; and indeed all human life, in a manner, depends on such accidents. A being, therefore, who knows the secret springs of the universe might easily, by particular volitions, turn all these accidents to the good of mankind and render the whole world happy, without discovering himself in any operation. A fleet whose purposes were salutary to society might always meet with a fair wind. Good princes enjoy sound health and long life. Persons born to power and authority be framed with good tempers and virtuous dispositions. A few such events as these, regularly and wisely conducted, would change the face of the world, and yet would no more seem to disturb the course of nature or confound human conduct than the present economy of things where the causes are secret and variable and compounded. Some small touches given to Caligula's brain in his infancy might have converted him into a Trajan. One wave, a little higher than the rest, by burying Caesar and his fortune in the bottom of the ocean, might have restored liberty to a considerable part of mankind. There may, for aught we know, be good reasons why Providence interposes not in this manner, but they are unknown to us; and, though the mere supposition that such reasons exist may be sufficient to *save* the conclusion concerning the Divine attributes, yet surely it can never be sufficient to *establish* that conclusion.

If everything in the universe be conducted by general laws, and if animals be rendered susceptible of pain, it scarcely seems possible but some ill must arise in the various shocks of matter and the various concurrence and opposition of general laws; but this ill would be very rare were it not for the *third* circumstance which I proposed to mention, viz., the great frugality with which all powers and faculties are distributed to every particular being. So well adjusted are the organs and capacities of all animals, and so well fitted to their preservation, that, as far as history or tradition reaches, there appears not to be any single species which has yet been extinguished in the universe. Every animal has the requisite endowments, but these endowments are bestowed with so scrupulous an economy that any considerable diminution must entirely destroy the creature. Wherever one power is increased, there is a proportional abatement in the others. Animals which excel in swiftness are commonly defective in force. Those which possess both are either imperfect in some of their senses or are oppressed with the most craving wants. The human species, whose chief excellence is reason and sagacity, is of all others the most necessitous, and the most deficient in bodily advantages, without clothes, without arms, without food, without lodging, without any convenience of life, except what they owe to their own skill and industry. In short, nature seems to have formed an exact calculation of the necessities of her creatures, and, like a *rigid master,* has afforded them little more powers or endowments than what are strictly sufficient to supply those necessities. An *indulgent parent* would have bestowed a large stock in order to guard against accidents, and secure the happiness and welfare of the creature in the most unfortunate concurrence of circumstances. Every course of life would not have been so surrounded with precipices that the least departure from the true path, by mistake or necessity, must involve us in misery and ruin. Some reserve, some fund, would have been provided to ensure happiness, nor would the powers and the necessities have been adjusted with so rigid an economy. The Author of nature is inconceivably powerful; his force is supposed great, if not altogether inexhaustible, nor is there any reason, as far as we can judge, to make him observe this strict frugality in his dealings with his creatures. It would have been better, were his power extremely limited, to have created fewer animals, and to have endowed these with more faculties for their happiness and preservation. A builder is never esteemed prudent who undertakes a plan beyond what his stock will enable him to finish.

In order to cure most of the ills of human life, I require not that man should have the wings of the eagle, the swiftness of the stag, the force of the ox, the arms of the lion, the scales of the crocodile or rhinoceros; much less do I demand the sagacity of an angel or cherubim. I am contented to take an increase in one single power or faculty of his soul. Let him be endowed with a greater propensity to industry and labour, a more vigorous spring and activity of mind, a more constant bent to business and application. Let the whole species possess naturally an equal diligence with that which many individuals are able to attain by habit and reflection, and the most beneficial consequences, without any allay of ill, is the immediate and necessary result of this endowment. Almost all the moral as well as natural evils of human life arise from idleness; and were our species, by the original constitution of their frame, exempt from this vice or infirmity, the perfect cultivation of land, the improvement of arts and manufactures, the exact execution of every office and duty, immediately follow; and men at once may fully reach that state of society which is so imperfectly attained by the best regulated government. But as industry is a power, and the most valuable of any, nature seems determined, suitably to her usual maxims, to bestow it on men with a very sparing hand, and rather to punish him severely for his deficiency in it than to reward him for his attainments. She has so contrived his frame that nothing but the most violent necessity can oblige him to labour; and she employs all his other wants to overcome, at least in part, the want of diligence, and to endow him with some share of a faculty of which she has thought fit naturally to bereave him. Here our demands may be allowed very humble, and therefore the more reasonable. If we required the endowments of superior penetration and judgment, of a more delicate taste of beauty, of a nicer sensibility to benevolence and friendship, we might be told that we impiously pretend to break the order of nature, that we want to exalt ourselves into a higher rank of being, that the presents which we require, not being suitable to our state and condition, would only be pernicious to us. But it is hard, I dare to repeat it, it is hard that, being placed in a world so full of wants and necessities, where almost every being and element is either our foe or refuses its assistance . . . we should also have our own temper to struggle with, and should be deprived of that faculty which can alone fence against these multiplied evils.

The *fourth* circumstance whence arises the misery and ill of the universe is the inaccurate workmanship of all the springs and principles of the great machine of nature. It must be acknowledged that there are few parts of the universe which seem not to serve some purpose, and whose removal would not produce a visible defect and disorder in the whole. The parts hang all together, nor can one be touched without affecting the rest, in a greater or less degree. But at the same time, it must be observed that none of these parts or principles, however useful, are so accurately adjusted as to keep precisely within those bounds in which their utility consists; but they are, all of them, apt, on every occasion, to run into the one extreme or the other. One would imagine that this grand production had not received the last hand of the maker — so little finished is every part, and so coarse are the strokes with which it is executed. Thus the winds are requisite to convey the vapours along the surface of the globe, and to assist men in navigation; but how often, rising up to tempests and hurricanes, do they become pernicious? Rains are necessary to nourish all the plants and animals of the earth; but how often are they defective? how often excessive? Heat is requisite to all life and vegetation, but is not always found in the due proportion. On the mixture and secretion of the humours and juices of the body depend the health and prosperity of the animal; but the parts perform not regularly their proper function. What more useful than all the passions of the mind, ambition, vanity, love, anger? But how often do they break their bounds and cause the greatest convulsions in society? There is nothing so advantageous in the universe but what frequently becomes pernicious, by its excess or defect; nor has nature guarded, with the requisite accuracy, against all disorder or confusion. The irregularity is never perhaps so great as to destroy any species, but is often sufficient to involve the individuals in ruin and misery.

On the concurrence, then, of these *four* circumstances does all or the greatest part of natural evil depend. Were all living creatures incapable of pain, or were the world administered by particular volitions, evil never could have found access into the universe; and were animals endowed with a large stock of powers and faculties, beyond what strict necessity requires, or were the several springs and principles of the universe so accurately framed as to preserve always the just temperament and medium, there must have been very little ill in comparison of what we feel at present. What then shall we pronounce on this occasion? Shall we say that these circumstances are not necessary, and that they might easily have been altered in the contrivance of the universe? This decision seems too presumptuous for creatures so blind and ignorant. Let us be more modest in our conclusions. Let us allow that, if the

*51. Eighteenth-Century Room,* period of Louis XVI.

goodness of the Deity (I mean a goodness like the human) could be established on any tolerable reasons *a priori,* these phenomena, however untoward, would not be sufficient to subvert that principle, but might easily, in some unknown manner, be reconcilable to it. But let us still assert that, as this goodness is not antecedently established but must be inferred from the phenomena, there can be no grounds for such an inference while there are so many ills in the universe, and while these ills might so easily have been remedied, as far as human understanding can be allowed to judge on such a subject. I am sceptic enough to allow that the bad appearances, notwithstanding all my reasonings, may be compatible with such attributes as you suppose, but surely they can never prove these attributes. Such a conclusion cannot result from scepticism, but must arise from the phenomena, and from our confidence in the reasonings which we deduce from these phenomena.

Look round this universe. What an immense profusion of beings, animated and organized, sensible and active! You admire this prodigious variety and fecundity. But inspect a little more narrowly these living existences, the only beings worth regarding. How hostile and destructive to each other! How insufficient all of them for their own happiness! How contemptible or odious to the spectator! The whole presents nothing but the idea of a blind nature, impregnated by a great vivifying principle, and pouring forth from her lap, without discernment or parental care, her maimed and abortive children!

Here the Manichaean system occurs as a proper hypothesis to solve the difficulty; and, no doubt, in some respects it is very specious and has more probability than the common hypothesis, by giving a plausible account of the strange mixture of good and ill which appears in life. But if we consider, on the other hand, the perfect uniformity and agreement of the parts of the universe, we shall not discover in it any marks of the combat of a malevolent with a benevolent being. There is indeed an opposition of pains and pleasures in the feelings of sensible creatures; but are not all the operations of nature carried on by an opposition of principles, of hot and cold, moist and dry, light and heavy? The true conclusion is that the original Source of all things is entirely indifferent to all these principles, and has no more regard to good above ill than to heat above cold, or to drought above moisture, or to light above heavy.

There may *four* hypotheses be framed concerning the first causes of the universe: that they are endowed with perfect goodness; that they have perfect malice; that they are opposite and have both goodness and malice; that they have neither goodness nor malice. Mixed phenomena can never prove the two former unmixed principles; and the uniformity and steadiness of general laws seem to oppose the third. The fourth, therefore, seems by far the most probable.

What I have said concerning natural evil will apply to moral with little or no variation; and we have no more reason to infer that the rectitude of the Supreme Being resembles human rectitude than that his benevolence resembles the human. Nay, it will be thought that we have still greater cause to exclude from him moral sentiments, such as we feel them, since moral evil, in the opinion of many, is much more predominant above moral good than natural evil above natural good.

# Coda:
# The Romantic Counterthrust

*An age so committed to Nature could not escape conflict between reason and instinct, felt as the bidding of Nature. Some of the men of the Enlightenment moved into romanticism merely through intensification of their faith in Nature. With others it was a conscious withdrawal from reason, with its restraints, into the freer realm of emotion. For Rousseau rationalism was, from the beginning, the destroyer's mark of civilization, which he conceived of as the corruption of Nature. Before the end of the Enlightenment, romanticism had already attained the ascendancy which it was to hold through the first decades of the following century.*

# from *The Discourses on Art*

## JOSHUA REYNOLDS

I observe, as a fundamental ground, common to all the Arts with which we have any concern in this discourse, that they address themselves only to two faculties of the mind, its imagination and its sensibility.

All theories which attempt to direct or to control the Art, upon any principles falsely called rational, which we form to ourselves upon a supposition of what ought in reason to be the end or means of Art, independent of the known first effect produced by subjects on the imagination, must be false and delusive. For though it may appear bold to say it, the imagination is here the residence of truth. If imagination be affected, the conclusion is fairly drawn; if it be not affected, the reasoning is erroneous, because the end is not obtained; the effect itself being the test, and the only test, of the truth and efficacy of the means.

There is in the commerce of life, as in Art, a sagacity which is far from being contradictory to right reason, and is superior to any occasional exercise of that faculty; which supersedes it; and does not wait for the slow progress of deduction, but goes at once, by what appears a kind of intuition, to the conclusion. A man endowed with this faculty, feels and acknowledges the truth, though it is not always in his power, perhaps, to give a reason for it; because he cannot recollect and bring before him all the materials that gave birth to his opinion; for very many and very intricate considerations may unite to form the principle, even of small and minute parts, involved in, or dependent on, a great system of things: though these in process of time are forgotten, the right impression remains fixed in his mind.

This impression is the result of the accumulated experience of our whole life, and has been collected, we do not always know how or when. But this mass of collective observation, however acquired, ought to prevail over that reason, which however powerfully exerted on any particular occasion, will probably comprehend but a partial view of the subject; and our conduct in life as well as in the Arts, is, or ought to be, generally governed by this habitual reason: it is our happiness that we are enabled to draw on such funds. If we were obliged to enter into a theoretical deliberation on every occasion, before we act, life would be at a stand, and Art would be impracticable.

It appears to me therefore, that our first thoughts, that is, the effect which any thing produces on our minds on its first appearance, is never to be forgotten; and it demands for that reason, because it is the first, to be laid up with care. If this be not done, the Artist may happen to impose on himself by partial reasoning; by a cold consideration of those animated thoughts which proceed, not perhaps from caprice or rashness (as he may afterwards conceit), but from the fullness of his mind, enriched with the copious stores of all the various inventions which he had ever seen, or had ever passed in his mind. These ideas are infused into his design, without any conscious effort; but if he be not on his guard, he may reconsider and correct them, till the whole matter is reduced to a common-place invention.

This is sometimes the effect of what I mean to caution you against; that is to say, an unfounded distrust of the imagination and feeling, in favour of narrow, partial, confined, argumentative theories; and of principles that seem to apply to the design in hand; without considering those general impressions on the fancy in which real principles of *sound reason,* and of much more weight and importance, are involved, and, as it were, lie hid, under the appearance of a sort of vulgar sentiment.

# from *The Disciples at Saïs*

## NOVALIS

A merry playfellow, his temples decked with roses and convolvulus came running by and saw the Disciple sitting absorbed in himself. "Dreamer!" he cried, "thou art quite on the wrong road. In such a way thou wilt make no great progress. The mood's the best of all things. Is that indeed a mood of Nature? Thou art still young, and dost thou not feel the dictates of youth in every vein? Do not Love and Longing fill thy breast? How canst thou sit in solitude? Does Nature sit solitary? Joy and desire flee from the solitary; and what use is Nature to thee without desire? Only with men is she at home, this Spirit who crowds all the senses with a thousand different colours, who surrounds thee like an invisible Lover. At our Feasts her tongue is loosed; she sits aloft and carols songs of gladdest life. Thou hast never yet loved, poor fellow; at the first kiss a new world will open to thee and life will penetrate thy ravished heart with its thousand rays. I will tell thee a tale. Listen! There lived once upon a time in the land of the setting sun a young man. He was very good, but above the ordinary, extraordinary. He fretted himself incessantly about nothing and yet again nothing, went quietly about on his own account when others played together and were merry, and indulged in strange things. Caves and woods were his favorite haunts; he talked continually with quadrupeds and birds, with trees and rocks; of course in no sensible words, but only in such foolish twaddle as would make one die of laughing. But he ever remained morose and solemn notwithstanding that the squirrels and monkeys, the parrots and bullfinches gave themselves all the trouble in the world to distract him and put him in the right path again. The goose told him tales, the stream rippled a roundelay, a great heavy stone made comic leaps and a rose crept round him amicably and twined herself in his locks, while the ivy caressed his thoughtful brow. But his solemnity and depression were stubborn. His parents were very grieved; they knew not what they ought to do. He was healthy and eat well; they had never crossed him. Only a few years back he was cheerful and blithe as anyone, first in all games, and approved by every maiden. He was really beautiful, looked like a picture and danced like an angel. Amongst the maidens there was one, a precious, exquisite child; she seemed to be of wax, her hair was like gold silk, her lips were cherry red like a doll's, her eyes burning black. Who saw her might have thought to perish of it, so lovely was she. At that time Rosenblütchen, for so she was called, was dear to the beautiful Hyacinth, for that was his name, and in fact he loved her to the point of death. The other children knew nothing about it. The violet had whispered it to them first. The house kittens had noticed it, for the houses of their parents lay close together. When at night Hyacinth stood at his window and Rosenblütchen at hers, and the little cats passed by on their mouse-hunt and saw the two there they laughed and giggled so loud that it made the lovers quite cross. The violet had told it in confidence to the strawberry, who told it to her friend the gooseberry, who did not omit to scratch Hyacinth as he came along. So very soon the whole garden and wood knew all about it, and when Hyacinth went out there rang from all sides: "Little Rosenblütchen is my darling!" Then Hyacinth was annoyed, but he had to laugh with all his heart when a little lizard came gliding past, sat himself on a warm stone, and waving his little tail, sang:

Rosenblütchen, little pet,
Once upon a time went blind,
So when Hyacinth she met
She embraced him. Being blind
She just thought he was her mother,
When she found it was another
Did she mind? no not a bit,
Only kissed him as before.
Was she frightened? not a whit,
Merely kissed him more and more.

Alas, how soon this glorious time was over. There came a man from foreign parts who had travelled astonishingly far, who had a long beard, deep eyes, fearsome eyebrows, and who wore a marvellous robe of many folds with strange figures woven into it. He sat himself down before the house belonging to Hyacinth's parents. Hyacinth was filled with curiosity, and went out to him and brought him bread and wine. He parted his white beard, and told his story far on into the night. Hyacinth kept awake and did not fidget nor grow tired of listening. From what transpired afterwards he told a great deal about strange lands, of unexplored regions, of amazing extraordinary things. He stayed there three days and descended with Hyacinth into profound depths. Rosenblütchen heartily cursed the old warlock, for Hyacinth became quite possessed by his discourse, and concerned himself with nothing else. He would scarcely take his food. At last the old man went away, but he left with Hyacinth a little book in which no one could read. Hyacinth gave him more fruit, bread and wine, and accompanied him far upon his way. He returned pensive and from thenceforward began a new way of life. Rosenblütchen certainly had a right to be pitied, for from that time he made little enough of her, and was always self-engrossed. Now it happened that one day he came home, and was as though new born. He fell on the necks of his parents and wept. "I must away into strange lands," he said; "the old Sibyl in the forest has told me how I am to become whole; she threw the book into the fire, and bade me come to you and ask your blessing. Perhaps I may return soon, perhaps never. Greet little Rosenblütchen; I would willingly have spoken with her. I know not how it is with me; something urges me away. If I try to think of the old days, mightier thoughts intervene. Peace is fled together with heart and love. I must go seek them. I would like to tell you whither, but I do not know. Thither where the Mother of All Things lives, the Veiled Virgin. My desire is aflame for Her. Farewell." He tore himself away

from them and departed. His parents lamented and shed tears. Rosenblütchen stayed in her chamber and wept bitterly. Hyacinth hastened
through valleys and deserts, over mountains and streams, towards the
Mysterious Land. He questioned men and animals, rocks and trees concerning Isis, the sacred Goddess. Many laughed, many kept silence, from
none did he receive the information he sought. At first he passed through
a rude wild country; mists and clouds intercepted his passage and never-
ceasing storms. Then he passed through interminable deserts of sand
and fiery dust, and as he wandered his humour also was changed. The
time seemed long to him; the inward tumult was appeased, he grew
more gentle and the mighty urgence was gradually reduced to a quiet '
but intense aspiration in which his whole spirit was melted. It was as
though many years had passed over him. The country became at the
same time richer and more varied, the air warm and azure, the road
more level. Green bushes allured him with pleasant shade. But he did
not understand their speech. Besides they did not seem to speak while
yet they filled his heart with green colours and a cool still perfume. That
sweet longing waxed higher and higher in him, and the leaves expanded
with sap; birds and beasts were noisier and more joyous, the fruits more
aromatic, the heavens a deeper blue, the air milder, his love warmer,
time went faster as if it saw itself nearing the goal. One day he lighted
on a crystal brook, and on a cloud of flowers that came tripping down
the valley between black mountain peaks as high as heaven. They
greeted him kindly, with familiar words. "Dear country folk," he said,
"where can I really find the sacred dwelling-place of Isis? It must
needs be somewhere near here, and you are perhaps more at home
than I." "We are only passing through," answered the flowers; "a
family of spirits is travelling abroad, and we prepare their way and
resting-place. Yet we have but just come through a place where we heard
your name. Only go upwards whence we came, and you will learn more."
The flowers and the brook laughed as they said this, offered him a re-
freshing draught, and went on their way. He followed their advice, asked
again and again, and finally came to that long-sought dwelling that lay
hidden beneath palms and other rare trees. His heart beat with an
infinite yearning, and the sweetest shyness overcame him in this habitation of the eternal centuries. He slumbered enveloped by heavenly per-
fumes, for it was only a dream that could lead him to the Holy of Holies.
Mysteriously his dream led him to the sound of loud, delicious music
and alternating harmonies through endless halls full of curious things.
It all seemed to him so familiar, and yet of an hitherto unrecognised
splendour. Then the last vestiges of earthliness disappeared as though

consumed in air, and he stood before the Celestial Virgin. He raised
the diaphanous glistening veil, and Rosenblütchen sank into his arms.
A distant music encompassed the secrets of the lovers' meeting, and the
effusions of their love, and shut away everything inharmonious from this
abode of rapture. Hyacinth lived ever after with Rosenblütchen, among
his glad parents and his playfellows, and innumerable grandchildren
thanked the old Sibyl for her counsel and her fire, for at that time people
had as many children as they wished for.

# from *Faust*

## JOHANN  WOLFGANG  VON  GOETHE

Out on't! I've searched philosophy,
Medicine and Law I've sifted in vain,
And (God above!) to Theology
I've given the best of heart and brain.
Pitiful fool! I ponder and pore
And grow no wiser than before.
Ah, but I wear the master's gown,
The doctor's scarlet; up and down
These ten years past with cons and pros
I've led my scholars by the nose.
I see that knowledge exceeds man's art;
That's a fire consumes my heart.
It's true I have more sense than your lettered
Triflers, your coxcombs, laic and priest,
Penman and schoolman; I'm not fettered
By their nice scruples — not the least
Elusive grain of a misgiving.
Hell and the Devil don't frighten me;
But I've paid for that a ruinous fee,
No less than the loss of all joy in living,
Of the dream that knowledge was mine to reach,
The dream that by something I could teach
Men might be profited or bettered.
Silver and gold, God wot, I've none,
And little honour under the sun.
A dog would scorn the life dealt me;

So my days are given to sorcery.
If mind can solve and tongue rehearse
The secrets of the universe —
That then no more my sour sweat flow
As I grind out my dry harangue,
Talking of what I do not know;
But peradventure I may sound
What's clapped within the world's great round;
Behold all procreant powers at work;
And quit at last of quibble and quirk
Let all the peddling truck go hang.

O, full, round moon, that thou might'st look
Thy last on so much toil and pain,
That kept me bending o'er my book,
While slow the midnight hours would wane!
Sad mistress, then thou shon'st above
Crabbed script and ponderous tome,
But, oh, among the hills to roam,
Companioned by the light I love!
To float with spirits by mountain-caves
And over the meadows by thy white beams;
To find the peace that my heart craves,
Bathed in the dew of thy healing streams!

Why should I mope in this stony gaol —
Accurséd den of damp and mould,
Where the very heaven's sweet light looks pale
Through painted windows, dusk and old?
Penned in this close, blind, bookish stye
Where the worm gnaws and the dust lies thick,
With smoky manuscripts heaped high
As the gaunt, ribbed roof of blackened brick.
Beakers and boxes, stacked and shelved,
Crucibles, calipers, balances fine —
All the old lumber since Adam delved —
If you call that a world, you may call it mine!

And would'st thou learn why thy heart sinks,
Held in the iron vice of woe!
What incommunicable throe
Thy life-blood's genial current shrinks?

For Nature, warm with living hues,
Where God set man, I taste the breath
Of chymic vapours, charnel dews,
Men's skulls, beast's ribs — the bones of death!

Take wings! Mount, mount, o'er the wide land!
Is not this volume's deep presage,
From Nostradamus' very hand,
Thine all-sufficient equipage?
The stars shall tell thee of their path,
Nature's sweet wisdom make thee whole;
Strong in all strength that Spirit hath
Thy soul shall commune with her soul.
In vain this adust thought would read
The holy symbols: Spirits of air
That hover near me, in my need
Answer, — if ye have heard my prayer!

(He [Faust] opens the book and looks at the<br>Sign of the Macrocosm.)

Ha! At a glance what instantaneous rapture fills
Each pulse, each vein and every part of me!
Joy, sacred Joy, through youth rekindled, thrills,
And makes each nerve a tingling ecstasy!
Was it a God that drew these magic lines
Of might to make my soul's wild storm relent,
And brim me with a measureless content,
When by supreme compulsion of these signs,
The powers unveil that hide sky, sea, and firmament?

Am I a God? Such light breaks through the murk
In these pure contours to the soul's sense lies
All Nature, visibly at work.
Ah, now I grasp the saying of the wise:
"The world of spirits is not shut away:
Thy heart is dead, thy body's bolts fast drawn;
Up, Student, up, and bathe that breast of clay
In the empyreal crimson of the dawn."

(He gazes at the Sign.)

All weaves one fabric; all things give
Power unto all to work and live!
Above, below, the star-throng burns,
Still handing on their golden urns,

With benediction in their wings:
Heaven stoops to earth! To heaven earth clings,
And through the vast one harmony rings.

A vision, but no more! O Nature, tell me where
I may possess thee, measurelessly fair?
Where are the breasts, the founts where life is nursed?
On you heaven hangs and earth; towards you we press
Our own, run dry or brimmed with bitterness!
Ye flow, ye brim for me, — and yet I thirst!

# from *Elective Affinities*

## JOHANN WOLFGANG VON GOETHE

Two children of neighboring families, a boy and a girl, of an age which would suit well for them at some future time to marry, were brought up together with this agreeable prospect, and the parents on both sides, who were people of some position in the world, looked forward with pleasure to their future union.

It was too soon observed, however, that the purpose seemed likely to fail; the dispositions of both children promised everything which was good, but there was an unaccountable antipathy between them. Perhaps they were too much like each other. Both were thoughtful, clear in their wills, and firm in their purposes. Each separately was beloved and respected by his or her companions, but whenever they were together they were always antagonists. Forming separate plans for themselves, they only met mutually to cross and thwart one another; never emulating each other in pursuit of one aim, but always fighting for a single object. Good natured and amiable everywhere else, they were spiteful and even malicious whenever they came in contact.

This singular relation first showed itself in their childish games, and it continued with their advancing years. The boys used to play at soldiers, divide into parties, and give each other battle, and the fierce haughty young lady set herself at once at the head of one of the armies, and fought against the other with such animosity and bitterness that the latter would have been put to a shameful flight, except for the desperate bravery of her own particular rival, who at last disarmed his antagonist and took her prisoner; and even then she defended herself with so much fury that to save his eyes from being torn out, and at the same time not to injure his enemy, he had been obliged to take off his silk handkerchief and tie her hands with it behind her back.

This she never forgave him: she made so many attempts, she laid so many plans to injure him, that the parents, who had been long watching these singular passions, came to an understanding together and resolved to separate these two hostile creatures, and sacrifice their favorite hopes.

The boy shot rapidly forward in the new situation in which he was placed. He mastered every subject which he was taught. His friends and his own inclination chose the army for his profession, and everywhere, let him be where he would, he was looked up to and beloved. His disposition seemed formed to labor for the well-being and the pleasure of others; and he himself, without being clearly conscious of it, was in himself happy at having got rid of the only antagonist which nature had assigned to him.

The girl, on the other hand, became at once an altered creature. Her growing age, the progress of her education, above all, her own inward feelings, drew her away from the boisterous games with boys in which she had hitherto delighted. Altogether she seemed to want something; there was nothing anywhere about her which could deserve to excite her hatred, and she had never found any one whom she could think worthy of her love.

A young man, somewhat older than her previous neighbor-antagonist, of rank, property, and consequence, beloved in society, and much sought after by women, bestowed his affections upon her. It was the first time that friend, lover, or servant had displayed any interest in her. The preference which he showed for her above others who were older, more cultivated, and of more brilliant pretensions than herself, was naturally gratifying; the constancy of his attention, which was never obtrusive, his standing by her faithfully through a number of unpleasant incidents, his quiet suit, which was declared indeed to her parents, but which as she was still very young he did not press, only asking to be allowed to hope; all this engaged him to her, and custom and the assumption in the world that the thing was already settled, carried her along with it. She had so often been called his bride that at last she began to consider herself so, and neither she nor any one else ever thought any further trial could be necessary before she exchanged rings with the person who for so long a time had passed for her bridegroom.

The peaceful course which the affair had all along followed was not at

52.  Henry Fuseli, *The Nightmare*. One of the eighteenth-century paintings reflecting the romantic trend.

all precipitated by the betrothal. Things were allowed to go on both sides just as they were; they were happy in being together, and they could enjoy to the end the fair season of the year as the spring of their future more serious life.

The absent youth had meanwhile grown up into everything which was most admirable. He had obtained a well-deserved rank in his profession, and came home on leave to visit his family. Towards his fair neighbor he found himself again in a natural but singular position. For some time past she had been nourishing in herself such affectionate family feelings as suited her position as a bride; she was in harmony with everything about her; she believed that she was happy, and in a certain sense she was so. Now first for a long time something again stood in her way. It was not to be hated — she had become incapable of hatred. Indeed the childish hatred, which had in fact been nothing more than an obscure recognition of inward worth, expressed itself now in a happy astonishment, in pleasure at meeting, in ready acknowledgments, in a half willing, half unwilling, and yet irresistible attraction; and all this was mutual. Their long separation gave occasion for longer conversations; even their old childish foolishness served, now that they had grown wiser, to amuse them as they looked back; and they felt as if at least they were bound to make good their petulant hatred by friendliness and attention to each other — as if their first violent injustice to each other ought not to be left without open acknowledgment.

On his side it all remained in a sensible, desirable moderation. His position, his circumstances, his efforts, his ambition, found him so abundant an occupation, that the friendliness of this pretty bride he received as a very thankworthy present; but without, therefore, even so much as thinking of her in connection with himself, or entertaining the slightest jealousy of the bridegroom, with whom he stood on the best possible terms.

With her, however, it was altogether different. She seemed to herself as if she had awakened out of a dream. Her fightings with her young neighbor had been the beginnings of an affection; and this violent antagonism was no more than an equally violent innate passion for him, first showing under the form of opposition. She could remember nothing else than that she had always loved him. She laughed over her martial encounter with him with weapons in her hand; she dwelt upon the delight of her feelings when he disarmed her. She imagined that it had given her the greatest happiness when he bound her; and whatever she had done afterwards to injure him, or to vex him, presented itself to her as only an innocent means of attracting his attention. She cursed their separation. She bewailed the sleepy state into which she had fallen. She execrated the insidious lazy routine which had betrayed her into accepting so insignificant a bridegroom. She was transformed — doubly transformed, forwards or backwards, which ever way we like to take it.

She kept her feelings entirely to herself; but if any one could have divined them and shared them with her, he could not have blamed her; for indeed the bridegroom could not sustain a comparison with the other as soon as they were seen together. If a sort of regard to the one could not be refused, the other excited the fullest trust and confidence. If one made an agreeable acquaintance, the other we should desire for a companion; and in extraordinary cases, where higher demands might have to be made on them, the bridegroom was a person to be utterly despaired of, while the other would give the feeling of perfect security.

There is a peculiar innate tact in women which discovers to them dif-

ferences of this kind; and they have cause as well as occasion to cultivate it.

The more the fair bride was nourishing all these feelings in secret, the
less opportunity there was for any one to speak a word which could tell
in favor of her bridegroom, to remind her of what her duty and their
relative position advised and commanded — indeed, what an unalterable
necessity seemed now irrevocably to require; the poor heart gave itself
up entirely to its passion.

On one side she was bound inextricably to the bridegroom by the
world, by her family, and by her own promise; on the other, the ambitious young man made no secret of what he was thinking and planning
for himself, conducting himself, towards her no more than a kind but
not at all a tender brother, and speaking of his departure as immediately
impending; and now it seemed as if her early childish spirit woke up
again in her with all its spleen and violence, and was preparing itself
in its distemper, on this higher stage of life, to work more effectively and
destructively. She determined that she would die to punish the once
hated, and now so passionately loved, youth for his want of interest in
her; and as she could not possess himself, at least she would wed herself
for ever to his imagination and to his repentance. Her dead image should
cling to him, and he should never be free from it. He should never cease
to reproach himself for not having understood, not examined, not valued
her feelings toward him.

This singular insanity accompanied her wherever she went. She kept
it concealed under all sorts of forms; and although people thought her
very odd, no one was observant enough or clever enough to discover the
real inward reason.

In the mean time, friends, relations, acquaintances had exhausted
themselves in contrivances for pleasure parties. Scarcely a day had passed,
but something new and unexpected was set on foot. There was hardly a
pretty spot in the country round which had not been decked out and prepared for the reception of some merry party. And now our young visitor
before departing wished to do his part as well, and invited the young
couple, with a small family circle, to an expedition on the water. They
went on board a large beautiful vessel dressed out in all its colors, — one
of the yachts which had a small saloon and a cabin or two besides, and
are intended to carry with them upon the water the comfort and conveniences of land.

They set out upon the broad river with music playing. The party had
collected in the cabin, below deck, during the heat of the day, and were

amusing themselves with games. Their young host, who could never remain without doing something, had taken charge of the helm, to relieve the old master of the vessel, and the latter had lain down and was fast asleep. It was a moment when the steerer required all his circumspectness, as the vessel was nearing a spot where two islands narrowed the channel of the river, while shallow banks of shingle stretching off, first on one side and then on the other, made the navigation difficult and dangerous. Prudent and sharp-sighted as he was, he thought for a moment that it would be better to wake the master; but he felt confident in himself, and he thought he would venture and make straight for the narrows. At this moment his fair enemy appeared upon deck with a wreath of flowers in her hair. "Take this to remember me by," she cried out. She took it off and threw it to the steerer. "Don't disturb me," he answered quickly, as he caught the wreath; "I require all my powers and all my attention now." "You will never be disturbed by me any more," she cried; "you will never see me again." As she spoke, she rushed to the forward part of the vessel, and from thence she sprang into the water. Voice upon voice called out, "Save her, save her, she is sinking!" He was in the most terrible difficulty. In the confusion the old ship-master woke, and tried to catch the rudder, which the young man bid him take. But there was no time to change hands. The vessel stranded; and at the same moment, flinging off the heaviest of his upper garments, he sprang into the water and swam towards his beautiful enemy. The water is a friendly element to a man who is at home in it, and who knows how to deal with it; it buoyed him up, and acknowledged the strong swimmer as its master. He soon overtook the beautiful girl, who had been swept away before him; he caught hold of her, raised her and supported her, and both of them were carried violently down by the current, till the shoals and islands were left far behind, and the river was again open and running smoothly. He now began to collect himself; they had passed the first immediate danger, in which he had been obliged to act mechanically without time to think; he raised his head as high as he could to look about him; and then swam with all his might to a low bushy point, which ran out conveniently into the stream. There he brought his fair burden to dry land, but he could find no signs of life in her; he was in despair, when he caught sight of a trodden path leading among the bushes. Again he caught her up in his arms, hurried forward, and presently reached a solitary cottage. There he found kind, good people — a young married couple; the misfortunes and the dangers explained themselves instantly; every remedy he could think of was instantly applied; a bright fire blazed up: woollen blankets were spread on a bed, counterpane, cloaks, skins, whatever there was at hand which would serve for warmth, were heaped over her as fast as possible. The desire to save life overpowered, for the present, every other consideration. Nothing was left undone to bring back to life the beautiful half-torpid, naked body. It succeeded; she opened her eyes! her friend was before her; she threw her heavenly arms about his neck. In this position she remained for a time; and then a stream of tears burst out and completed her recovery. "Will you forsake me," she cried, "now when I find you again thus?" "Never," he answered, "never," hardly knowing what he said or did. "Only consider yourself," she added; "take care of yourself, for your sake and for mine."

She now began to collect herself, and for the first time recollected the state in which she was; she could not be ashamed before her darling, before her preserver; but she gladly allowed him to go, that he might take care of himself; for the clothes which he still wore were wet and dripping.

Their young hosts considered what could be done. The husband offered the young man, and the wife offered the fair lady, the dresses in which they had been married, which were hanging up in full perfection, and sufficient for a complete suit, inside and out, for two people. In a short time our pair of adventurers were not only equipped, but in full costume. They looked most charming, gazed at one another, when they met, with admiration, and then with infinite affection, half laughing at the same time at the quaintness of their appearance, they fell into each other's arms.

The power of youth and the quickening spirit of love in a few moments completely restored them; and there was nothing wanted but music to have set them both off dancing.

To have found themselves brought from the water on dry land, from death into life, from the circle of their families into a wilderness, from despair into rapture, from indifference to affection and to love, all in a moment: the head was not strong enough to bear it; it must either burst, or go distracted; or if so distressing an alternative were to be escaped, the heart must put out all its efforts.

Lost wholly in each other, it was long before they recollected the alarm and anxiety of those who had been left behind; and they themselves, indeed, could not well think, without alarm and anxiety, how they were again to encounter them. "Shall we run away? shall we hide ourselves?" said the young man. "We will remain together," she said, as she clung about his neck.

The peasant having heard them say that a party was aground on the shoal, had hurried down, without stopping to ask another question, to the shore. When he arrived there, he saw the vessel coming safely down the stream. After much labor it had been got off; and they were now going on in uncertainty, hoping to find their lost ones again somewhere. The peasant shouted and made signs to them, and at last caught the attention of those on board; then he ran to a spot where there was a convenient place for landing, and went on signalling and shouting till the vessel's head was turned toward the shore; and what a scene there was for them when they landed. The parents of the two betrothed first pressed on the banks; the poor loving bridegroom had almost lost his senses. They had scarcely learnt that their dear children had been saved, when in their strange disguise the latter came forward out of the bushes to meet them. No one recognized them till they were come quite close. "Who do I see?" cried the mothers. "What do I see?" cried the fathers. The preserved ones flung themselves on the ground before them. "Your children," they called out; "a pair." "Forgive us!" cried the maiden. "Give us your blessing!" cried the young man. "Give us your blessing!" they cried both, as all the world stood still in wonder. Your blessing! was repeated the third time; and who would have been able to refuse it?

# from *The Confessions*

## JEAN-JACQUES ROUSSEAU

I am commencing an undertaking, hitherto without precedent, and which will never find an imitator. I desire to set before my fellows the likeness of a man in all the truth of nature, and that man myself.

I alone. I know my heart, and I know men. I am not made like any of those I have seen; I dare to believe that I am not made like any of those who are in existence. If I am not better, at least I am different. Whether Nature has acted rightly or wrongly in destroying the mould in which she cast me, can only be decided after I have been read.

Let the trumpet of the Day of Judgment sound when it will, I will present myself before the Sovereign Judge with this book in my hand. I will say boldly: "This is what I have done, what I have thought, what I was. I have told the good and the bad with equal frankness. I have neither omitted anything bad, nor interpolated anything good. If I have occasionally made use of some immaterial embellishments, this has only been in order to fill a gap caused by lack of memory. I may have assumed the truth of that which I knew might have been true, never of that which I knew to be false. I have shown myself as I was: mean and contemptible, good, high-minded and sublime, according as I was one or the other. I have unveiled my inmost self even as Thou hast seen it, O Eternal Being. Gather round me the countless host of my fellow-men; let them hear my confessions, lament for my unworthiness, and blush for my imperfections. Then let each of them in turn reveal, with the same frankness, the secrets of his heart at the foot of the Throne, and say, if he dare, '*I was better than that man!*' "

I was born at Geneva, in the year 1712, and was the son of Isaac Rousseau and Susanne Bernard, citizens. The distribution of a very moderate inheritance amongst fifteen children had reduced my father's portion almost to nothing; and his only means of livelihood was his trade of watchmaker, at which he was really very clever. My mother, a daughter of the Protestant minister Bernard, was better off. She was clever and beautiful, and my father had found difficulty in obtaining her hand. Their affection for each other had begun almost as soon as they were born. When only eight years old, they walked every evening upon the Treille; at ten, they were inseparable. Sympathy and union of soul strengthened in them the feeling produced by intimacy. Both, naturally full of tender sensibility, only waited for the moment when they should find the same disposition in another — or, rather, this moment waited for them, and each abandoned his heart to the first which opened to receive it. Destiny, which appeared to oppose their passion, only encouraged it. The young lover, unable to obtain possession of his mistress, was consumed by grief. She advised him to travel, and endeavour to forget her. He travelled, but without result, and returned more in love than ever. He found her whom he loved still faithful and true. After this trial of affection, nothing was left for them but to love each other all their lives. This they swore to do, and Heaven blessed their oath.

Gabriel Bernard, my mother's brother, fell in love with one of my father's sisters, who only consented to accept the hand of the brother, on condition that her own brother married the sister. Love arranged everything, and the two marriages took place on the same day. Thus my uncle became the husband of my aunt, and their children were doubly my first cousins. At the end of a year, a child was born to both, after which they were again obliged to separate.

My uncle Bernard was an engineer. He took service in the Empire and in Hungary, under Prince Eugène. He distinguished himself at the siege and battle of Belgrade. My father, after the birth of my only brother, set out for Constantinople, whither he was summoned to undertake the post of watchmaker to the Sultan. During his absence, my mother's beauty, intellect and talents gained for her the devotion of numerous admirers. M. de la Closure, the French Resident, was one of the most eager to offer his. His passion must have been great, for, thirty years later, I saw him greatly affected when speaking to me of her. To enable her to resist such advances, my mother had more than her virtue: she loved her husband tenderly. She pressed him to return; he left all, and returned. I was the unhappy fruit of this return. Ten months later I was born, a weak and ailing child; I cost my mother her life, and my birth was the first of my misfortunes.

I have never heard how my father bore this loss, but I know that he was inconsolable. He believed that he saw his wife again in me, without being able to forget that it was I who had robbed him of her; he never embraced me without my perceiving, by his sighs and the convulsive manner in which he clasped me to his breast, that a bitter regret was mingled with his caresses, which were on that account only the more tender. When he said to me, "Jean-Jacques, let us talk of your mother," I used to answer, "Well, then, my father, we will weep!" — and this word alone was sufficient to move him to tears. "Ah!" said he, with a sigh, "give her back to me, console me for her loss, fill the void which she has left in my soul. Should I love you as I do, if you were only my son?" Forty years after he had lost her, he died in the arms of a second wife, but the name of the first was on his lips and her image at the bottom of his heart.

Such were the authors of my existence. Of all the gifts which Heaven had bestowed upon them, a sensitive heart is the only one they bequeathed to me; it had been the source of their happiness, but for me it proved the source of all the misfortunes of my life.

I was brought into the world in an almost dying condition; little hope was entertained of saving my life. I carried within me the germs of a complaint which the course of time has strengthened, and which at times allows me a respite only to make me suffer more cruelly in another manner. One of my father's sisters, an amiable and virtuous young woman, took such care of me that she saved my life. At this moment, while I am writing, she is still alive, at the age of eighty, nursing a husband younger than herself, but exhausted by excessive drinking. Dear aunt, I forgive you for having preserved my life; and I deeply regret that, at the end of your days, I am unable to repay the tender care which you lavished upon me at the beginning of my own. My dear old nurse Jacqueline is also still alive, healthy and robust. The hands which opened my eyes at my birth will be able to close them for me at my death.

I felt before I thought: this is the common lot of humanity. I experienced it more than others. I do not know what I did until I was five or six years old. I do not know how I learned to read; I only remember my earliest reading, and the effect it had upon me; from that time I date my uninterrupted self-consciousness. My mother had left some romances behind her, which my father and I began to read after supper. At first it was only a question of practising me in reading by the aid of amusing books; but soon the interest became so lively, that we used to read in turn without stopping, and spent whole nights in this occupation. We were unable to leave off until the volume was finished. Sometimes, my father, hearing the swallows begin to twitter in the early morning, would say, quite ashamed, "Let us go to bed; I am more of a child than yourself."

In a short time I acquired, by this dangerous method, not only extreme facility in reading and understanding what I read, but a knowledge of the passions that was unique in a child of my age. I had no idea of things in themselves, although all the feelings of actual life were already known to me. I had conceived nothing, but felt everything. These confused emotions which I felt one after the other, certainly did not warp the reasoning powers which I did not as yet possess; but they shaped them in me of a peculiar stamp, and gave me odd and romantic notions of human life, of which experience and reflection have never been able wholly to cure me.

[1719–1723.] — The romances came to an end in the summer of 1719. The following winter brought us something different. My mother's library being exhausted, we had recourse to the share of her father's which had fallen to us. Luckily, there were some good books in it; in fact, it could hardly have been otherwise, for the library had been collected by a minister, who was even a learned man according to the fashion of the day, and was at the same time a man of taste and intellect. The "History of the Empire and the Church," by Le Sueur; Bossuet's "Treatise upon Universal History"; Plutarch's "Lives of Famous Men"; Nani's "History of Venice"; Ovid's "Metamorphoses"; La Bruyère; Fontenelle's "Worlds"; his "Dialogues of the Dead"; and some volumes of Molière — all these were brought over into my father's room, and I read to him out of them while he worked. I conceived a taste for them that was rare and perhaps unique at my age. Plutarch, especially, became my favourite author. The pleasure I took in reading him over and over again cured me a little of my taste for romance, and I soon preferred Agesilaus, Brutus, and Aristides to Orondates, Artamenes, and Juba. This interesting reading, and the conversations between my father and myself to which it gave rise, formed in me the free and republican spirit, the proud and indomitable character unable to endure slavery or servitude, which has tormented me throughout my life in situations the least fitted to afford it scope. Unceasingly occupied with thoughts of Rome and Athens, living as it were amongst their great men, myself by birth the citizen of a republic and the son of a father whose patriotism was his strongest passion, I was fired by his example; I believed myself a Greek or a Roman; I lost my identity in that of the individual whose life I was reading; the recitals of the qualities of endurance and intrepidity which arrested my attention made my eyes glisten and strengthened my voice. One day, while I was relating the history of Scaevola at table, those present were alarmed to see me come forward and hold my hand over a chafing-dish, to illustrate his action.

I had a brother seven years older than myself, who was learning my father's trade. The excessive affection which was lavished upon myself caused him to be somewhat neglected, which treatment I cannot approve of. His education felt the consequences of this neglect. He took to evil courses before he was old enough to be a regular profligate. He was put with another master, from whom he was continually running away, as he had done from home. I hardly ever saw him; I can scarcely say that I knew him; but I never ceased to love him tenderly, and he loved me as much as a vagabond can love anything. I remember that, on one occasion, when my father was chastising him harshly and in anger, I threw myself impetuously between them and embraced him closely. In this manner I covered his body with mine, and received the blows which were aimed at him; I so obstinately maintained my position that at last my father was obliged to leave off, being either disarmed by my cries and tears, or afraid of hurting me more than him. At last, my brother turned out so badly that he ran away and disappeared altogether. Sometime afterwards we heard that he was in Germany. He never once wrote to us. From that time nothing more has been heard of him, and thus I have remained an only son.

If this poor boy was carelessly brought up, this was not the case with his brother; the children of kings could not be more carefully looked after than I was during my early years — worshipped by all around me, and, which is far less common, treated as a beloved, never as a spoiled child. Till I left my father's house, I was never once allowed to run about the streets by myself with the other children; in my case no one ever had to satisfy or check any of those fantastic whims which are attributed to Nature, but are all in reality the result of education. I had the faults of my age: I was a chatterbox, a glutton, and, sometimes, a liar. I would have stolen fruits, bonbons, or eatables; but I have never found pleasure in doing harm or damage, in accusing others, or in tormenting poor dumb animals. I remember, however, that I once urinated in a saucepan belonging to one of our neighbours, Madame Clot, while she was at church. I declare that, even now, the recollection of this makes me laugh, because Madame Clot, a good woman in other respects, was the most confirmed old grumbler I have ever known. Such is the brief and true story of all my childish offences.

How could I become wicked, when I had nothing but examples of gentleness before my eyes, and none around me but the best people in the world? My father, my aunt, my nurse, my relations, our friends, our neighbours, all who surrounded me, did not, it is true, obey me, but they loved me; and I loved them in return. My wishes were so little excited and so little opposed, that it did not occur to me to have any. I can swear that, until I served under a master, I never knew what a fancy was.

[When his father was exiled in Geneva, Jean-Jacques was sent to board with the Pastor Lambercier and his sister. The following passage is famous for its acknowledgment of masochistic impulses. He was then eight years old.]

As Mademoiselle Lambercier had the affection of a mother for us, she also exercised the authority of one, and sometimes carried it so far as to inflict upon us the punishment of children when we had deserved it. For some time she was content with threats, and this threat of a punishment that was quite new to me appeared very terrible; but, after it had been carried out, I found the reality less terrible than the expectation; and, what was still more strange, this chastisement made me still more devoted to her who had inflicted it. It needed all the strength of this devotion and all my natural docility to keep myself from doing something which would have deservedly brought upon me a repetition of it; for I had found in the pain, even in the disgrace, a mixture of sensuality which had left me less afraid than desirous of experiencing it again from the same hand. No doubt some precocious sexual instinct was mingled with this feeling, for the same chastisement inflicted by her brother would not have seemed to me at all pleasant. But, considering his disposition, there was little cause to fear the substitution; and if I kept myself from deserving punishment, if was solely for fear of displeasing Mademoiselle Lambercier; for, so great is the power exercised over me by kindness, even by that which is due to the senses, that it has always controlled the latter in my heart.

The repetition of the offence, which I avoided without being afraid of it, occurred without any fault of mine, that is to say, of my will, and I may say that I profited by it without any qualm of conscience. But this second time was also the last; for Mademoiselle Lambercier, who had no doubt noticed something which convinced her that the punishment did not have the desired effect, declared that it tired her too much, and that she would abandon it. Until then we had slept in her room, sometimes even in her bed during the winter. Two days afterwards we were put to sleep in another room, and from that time I had the honour, which I would gladly have dispensed with, of being treated by her as a big boy.

Who would believe that this childish punishment, inflicted upon me when only eight years old by a young woman of thirty, disposed of my tastes, my desires, my passions, and my own self for the remainder of my life, and that in a manner exactly contrary to that which should have been the natural result? When my feelings were once inflamed, my desires so went astray that, limited to what I had already felt, they did not trouble themselves to look for anything else. In spite of my hot blood, which has been inflamed with sensuality almost from my birth, I kept myself free from every taint until the age when the coldest and most sluggish temperaments begin to develop. In torments for a long time, without knowing why, I devoured with burning glances all the pretty women I met; my imagination unceasingly recalled them to me, only to make use of them in my own fashion, and to make of them so many Mlles. Lambercier.

Even after I had reached years of maturity, this curious taste, always abiding with me and carried to depravity and even frenzy, preserved my morality, which it might naturally have been expected to destroy. If ever a bringing-up was chaste and modest, assuredly mine was. My three aunts were not only models of propriety, but reserved to a degree which has long since been unknown amongst women. My father, a man of pleasure, but a gallant of the old school, never said a word, even in the presence of women whom he loved more than others, which would have brought a blush to a maiden's cheek; and the respect due to children has never been so much insisted upon as in my family and in my presence. In this respect I found M. Lambercier equally careful; and an excellent servant was dismissed for having used a somewhat too free expression in our presence. Until I was a young man, I not only had no distinct idea of the union of the sexes, but the confused notion which I had regarding it never presented itself to me except in a hateful and disgusting form. For common prostitutes I felt a loathing which has never been effaced: the sight of a profligate always filled me with contempt, even with affright. My horror of debauchery became thus pronounced ever since the day when, walking to Little Sacconex by a hollow way, I saw on both sides holes in the ground, where I was told that these creatures carried on their intercourse. The thought of the one always brought back to my mind

the copulation of dogs, and the bare recollection was sufficient to disgust me.

This tendency of my bringing-up, in itself adapted to delay the first outbreaks of an inflammable temperament, was assisted, as I have already said, by the direction which the first indications of sensuality took in my case. Busying my imagination solely with what I had actually felt, in spite of most uncomfortable effervescence of blood, I knew how to turn my desires only in the direction of that kind of pleasure with which I was acquainted, without ever going as far as that which had been made hateful to me, and which, without my having the least suspicion of it, was so closely related to the other. In my foolish fancies, in my erotic frenzies, in the extravagant acts to which they sometimes led me, I had recourse in my imagination to the assistance of the other sex, without ever thinking that it was serviceable for any purpose than that for which I was burning to make use of it.

In this manner, then, in spite of an ardent, lascivious and precocious temperament, I passed the age of puberty without desiring, even without knowing of any other sensual pleasures than those of which Mademoiselle Lambercier had most innocently given me the idea; and when, in course of time, I became a man, that which should have destroyed me again preserved me. My old childish taste, instead of disappearing, became so associated with the other, that I could never banish it from the desires kindled by my senses. This madness, joined to my natural shyness, has always made me very unenterprising with women, for want of courage to say all or power to do all, inasmuch as the kind of enjoyment, of which the other was only for me the final consummation could neither be appropriated by him who longed for it, nor guessed by her who was able to bestow it. Thus I have spent my life in idle longing, without saying a word, in the presence of those whom I loved most. Too bashful to declare my taste, I at least satisfied it in situations which had reference to it and kept up the idea of it. To lie at the feet of an imperious mistress, to obey her commands, to ask her forgiveness — this was for me a sweet enjoyment; and, the more my lively imagination heated my blood, the more I presented the appearance of a bashful lover. It may be easily imagined that this manner of making love does not lead to very speedy results, and is not very dangerous to the virtue of those who are its object. For this reason I have rarely possessed, but have none the less enjoyed myself in my own way — that is to say, in imagination. Thus it has happened that my senses, in harmony with my timid disposition and my romantic spirit, have kept my sentiments pure and my morals blameless, owing to the very tastes which, combined with a little more impudence, might have plunged me into the most brutal sensuality.

I have taken the first and most difficult step in the dark and dirty labyrinth of my confessions. It is easier to admit that which is criminal than that which is ridiculous and makes a man feel ashamed. Henceforth I am sure of myself; after having ventured to say so much, I can shrink from nothing. One may judge what such confessions have cost me, from the fact that, during the whole course of my life, I have never dared to declare my folly to those whom I loved with the frenzy of a passion which deprived me of sight and hearing, which robbed me of my senses and caused me to tremble all over with a convulsive movement. I have never brought myself, even when on most intimate terms, to ask women to grant me the only favour of all which was wanting. This never happened to me but once — in my childhood, with a girl of my own age; even then, it was she who first proposed it.

While thus going back to the first traces of my inner life, I find elements which sometimes appear incompatible, and yet have united in order to produce with vigour a simple and uniform effect; and I find others which, although apparently the same, have formed combinations so different, owing to the co-operation of certain circumstances, that one would never imagine that these elements were in any way connected. Who, for instance, would believe that one of the most powerful movements of my soul was tempered in the same spring from which a stream of sensuality and softness has entered my blood? Without leaving the subject of which I have just spoken, I shall produce by means of it a very different impression.

One day I was learning my lesson by myself in the room next to the kitchen. The servant had put Mademoiselle Lambercier's combs in front of the fire-place to dry. When she came back to fetch them, she found one with a whole row of teeth broken. Who was to blame for the damage? No one except myself had entered the room. On being questioned, I denied that I had touched the comb. M. and Mademoiselle Lambercier both began to admonish, to press, and to threaten me; I obstinately persisted in my denial; but the evidence was too strong, and outweighed all my protestations, although it was the first time that I had been found to lie so boldly. The matter was regarded as serious, as in fact it deserved to be. The mischievousness, the falsehood, the obstinacy appeared equally deserving of punishment; but this time it was not by Mademoiselle Lambercier that chastisement was inflicted. My uncle Bernard was written to, and he came. My poor cousin was accused of another equally grave offence; we were involved in the same punishment. It was terrible. Had they wished to look for the remedy in the evil itself and to deaden forever my depraved senses, they could not have set to work better, and for a long time my senses left me undisturbed.

They could not draw from me the desired confession. Although I was several times brought up before them and reduced to a pitiable condition, I remained unshaken. I would have endured death, and made up my mind to do so. Force was obliged to yield to the diabolical obstinacy of a child — as they called my firmness. At last I emerged from this cruel trial, utterly broken, but triumphant.

It is now nearly fifty years since this incident took place, and I have no fear of being punished again for the same thing. Well, then, I declare in the sight of heaven that I was innocent of the offence, that I neither broke nor touched the comb, that I never went near the fire-place, and had never even thought of doing so. It would be useless to ask me how the damage was done: I do not know, and I cannot understand; all that I know for certain is, that I had nothing to do with it.

Imagine a child, shy and obedient in ordinary life, but fiery, proud, and unruly in his passions: a child who had always been led by the voice of reason and always treated with gentleness, justice, and consideration, who had not even a notion of injustice, and who for the first time becomes acquainted with so terrible an example of it on the part of the very people whom he most loves and respects! What an upset of ideas! what a disturbance of feelings! what revolution in his heart, in his brain, in the whole of his little intellectual and moral being! Imagine all this, I say, if possible. As for myself, I feel incapable of disentangling and following up the least trace of what then took place within me.

I had not yet sense enough to feel how much appearances were against me, and to put myself in the place of the others. I kept to my own place, and all that I felt was the harshness of a frightful punishment for an offence which I had not committed. The bodily pain, although severe, I felt but little: all I felt was indignation, rage, despair. My cousin, whose case was almost the same, and who had been punished for an involuntary mistake as if it had been a premeditated act, following my example, flew into a rage, and worked himself up to the same pitch of excitement as myself. Both in the same bed, we embraced each other with convulsive transports: we felt suffocated; and when at length our young hearts, somewhat relieved, were able to vent their wrath, we sat upright in bed and began to shout, times without number, with all our might: *Carnifex! carnifex! carnifex!* [executioner]

While I write these words, I feel that my pulse beats faster; those moments will always be present to me though I should live a hundred thousand years. That first feeling of violence and injustice has remained so deeply graven on my soul, that all the ideas connected with it bring back to me my first emotion; and this feeling, which, in its origin, had reference only to myself, has become so strong in itself and so completely detached from all personal interest, that, when I see or hear of any act of injustice — whoever is the victim of it, and wherever it is committed — my heart kindles with rage, as if the effect of it recoiled upon myself. When I read of the cruelties of a ferocious tyrant, the crafty atrocities of a rascally priest, I would gladly set out to plunge a dagger into the heart of such wretches, although I had to die for it a hundred times. I have often put myself in a perspiration, pursuing or stoning a cock, a cow, a dog, or any animal which I saw tormenting another merely because it felt itself the stronger. This impulse may be natural to me, and I believe that it is; but the profound impression left upon me by the first injustice I suffered was too long and too strongly connected with it, not to have greatly strengthened it.

With the above incident the tranquillity of my childish life was over.

From that moment I ceased to enjoy a pure happiness, and even at the present day I feel that the recollection of the charms of my childhood ceases there. We remained a few months longer at Bossey. We were there, as the first man is represented to us — still in the earthly paradise, but we no longer enjoyed it; in appearance our condition was the same, in reality it was quite a different manner of existence. Attachment, respect, intimacy, and confidence no longer united pupils and guides: we no longer regarded them as gods, who were able to read in our hearts; we became less ashamed of doing wrong and more afraid of being accused; we began to dissemble, to be insubordinate, to lie. All the vices of our age corrupted our innocence and threw a veil of ugliness over our amusements. Even the country lost in our eyes that charm of gentleness and simplicity which goes to the heart. It appeared to us lonely and sombre: it seemed as if it were covered with a veil which concealed its beauties from our eyes. We ceased to cultivate our little gardens, our plants, our flowers. We no longer scratched up the ground gently, or cried with joy when we saw the seed which we had sown beginning to sprout. We were disgusted with the life, and the others were disgusted with us; my uncle took us away, and we separated from M. and Mademoiselle Lambercier, having had enough of each other, and feeling but little regret at the separation.

# from *Paul and Virginia*

## BERNARDIN DE SAINT-PIERRE

You Europeans, whose minds are imbued from infancy with prejudices at variance with happiness, cannot imagine all the instruction and pleasure to be derived from nature. Your souls, confined to a small sphere of intelligence, soon reach the limit of its artificial enjoyments; but nature and the heart are inexhaustible. Paul and Virginia had neither clock, nor almanack, nor books of chronology, history, or philosophy. The periods of their lives were regulated by those of the operations of nature, and their familiar conversation had a constant reference to the changes of the seasons. They knew the time of day by the shadows of the trees; the seasons, by the times when these trees bore flowers or fruit; and the years, by the number of their harvests. These soothing images diffused an inexpressible charm over their conversation. "It is time to dine," said Virginia, "the shadows of the plantain trees are at their roots"; or, "Night approaches; the tamarinds are closing their leaves." "When will you come and see us?" inquired some of her companions in the neighbourhood. "At the time of the sugarcanes," answered Virginia. "Your visit will be then still more delightful," resumed her young acquaintances. When she was asked what was her own age, and that of Paul — "My brother," said she, "is as old as the great cocoa tree of the fountain; and I am as old as the little one: the mangoes have borne fruit twelve times, and the orange trees have flowered four-and-twenty times, since I came into the world."

Their lives seemed linked to that of the trees, like those of fauns or dryads. They knew no other historical epochs than those of the lives of their mothers, no other chronology than that of their orchards, and no other philosophy than that of doing good, and resigning themselves to the will of Heaven.

What need, indeed, had these young people of riches or learning such as ours? Even their necessities and their ignorance increased their happiness. No day passed in which they were not of some service to one another, or in which they did not mutually impart some instruction. Yes, instruction; for if errors mingled with it, they were, at least, not of a dangerous character. A pure-minded being has none of that description to fear. Thus grew these children of nature. No care had troubled their peace, no intemperance had corrupted their blood, no misplaced passion had depraved their hearts. Love, innocence, and piety possessed their souls; and those intellectual graces were unfolding daily in their features, their attitudes, and their movements. Still in the morning of life, they had all its blooming freshness; and surely such in the Garden of Eden appeared our first parents, when, coming from the hands of God, they first saw and approached each other, and conversed together, like brother and sister. Virginia was gentle, modest, and confiding as Eve; and Paul, like Adam, united the stature of manhood with the simplicity of a child.

# from *The Commonplace Book*

## WILLIAM BLAKE

Mock on, Mock on Voltaire, Rousseau:
Mock on, Mock on: 'tis all in vain!
You throw the sand against the wind,
And the wind blows it back again.
  And every sand becomes a Gem
Reflected in the beams divine;
Blown back they blind the mocking Eye,
But still in Israel's paths they shine.
  The Atoms of Democritus
And Newton's Particles of light
Are sands upon the Red sea shore,
Where Israel's tents do shine so bright.

# BIBLIOGRAPHY

Many books were consulted in the preparation of this anthology. These included encyclopedia entries and works on cultural history that provided summaries and judgments on the eighteenth century. Except for minor differences of emphasis, there was too little variation to warrant singling out any number of them. I therefore am limiting my list here to books that I found particularly readable or distinctive in their approach and to a number of related anthologies whose introductions and editorial commentary proved informative and stimulating.

Becker, Carl L.: *The Heavenly City,* Yale University Press, New Haven, Conn.

Berlin, Isaiah: *The Age of Enlightenment,* George Braziller, Inc., New York.

Brinton, Crane (ed.): *The Portable Age of Reason Reader,* Viking Press, New York.

Bronowski, J., and Mazlish, Bruce: *The Western Intellectual Tradition,* Harper & Row, Publishers, Inc., New York.

Clapp, James G., and others (eds.): *The Foundations of Western Thought,* Alfred A. Knopf, Inc., New York.

Cobban, Alfred: *In Search of Humanity,* George Braziller, Inc., New York.

Havens, George R.: *Age of Ideas,* Holt, Rinehart and Winston, Inc., New York.

Hugo, Howard E. (ed.): *The Portable Romantic Reader,* Viking Press, New York.

Snyder, Louis (ed.): *The Age of Reason,* D. Van Nostrand Co., Inc., Princeton, N.J.

# BIOGRAPHICAL NOTES

*Beaumarchais, Pierre Augustin Caron de.* 1732–1799. French playwright, financial promoter, and libertarian. Helped to supply the American revolutionary army. His satirical comedies *The Barber of Seville* and *The Marriage of Figaro* expressed equalitarian ideas, for which they were, for a time, banned.

*Beccaria, Marchese di Cesare Bonesana.* 1738–1794. Italian jurist, statesman, and economist, best known for his book *On Crime and Punishment,* which is regarded as the foundation of modern penology.

*Berkeley, George.* 1685–1753. British philosopher and cleric. Lived for three years in America, whose future as a great power he foresaw.

*Bernardin de Saint-Pierre, Jacques Henri.* 1737–1814. One of the initiators of the romantic movement. Best known for his idyllic romance *Paul and Virginia.*

*Blake, William.* 1757–1827. British poet, artist, and mystic. One of the first to recognize the dehumanization of man in the early stages of the Industrial Revolution.

*Buffon, Comte Georges Louis Leclerc de.* 1707–1788. French naturalist whose work in taxonomy ranks with that of Linnaeus and whose multivolume *Natural History* is a classic of scientific popularization.

*Burns, Robert.* 1759–1796. Scottish poet noted for his democratic views and his satires on pharisaical religiosity.

*Condorcet, Marie Jean Antoine Nicholas de Caritat, Marquis de.* 1743–1794. French philosophe, mathematician, and politician. A Girondist, he was arrested during the Terror and died in prison. His faith in reason and progress remained unshaken, and his last work, finished in his prison cell, upheld that faith.

*Defoe, Daniel.* 1659?–1731. English journalist and pamphleteer whose stormy career included imprisonment, pillory, and espionage. Turning to fiction in his sixties, Defoe, with his masterpiece, *The Adventures of Robinson Crusoe,* achieved world renown and has special importance as an expression of the ways and interests of the rising middle class.

*Diderot, Denis.* 1713–1784. French philosophe and chief editor of the Encyclopedia. For commentary on and summary of his career see Introduction.

*Fielding, Henry.* British novelist and playwright, most famous for his novel, *Tom Jones,* a classic of English literature.

*Fontenelle, Bernard Le Bovier de.* 1657–1757. Poet, dramatist and essayist. Famous for his popularizations of science, particularly of the astronomical theories of Descartes. Among other works were a *History of Oracles* attacking superstitious religious beliefs, a comparison between the "ancients and the moderns" pointing out that the moderns were necessarily in advance since they could proceed from the points reached by the ancients, and *Dialogues of the Dead* in which great personages of the past turned the light of reason on human experience.

*Franklin, Benjamin.* 1706–1790. American statesman, diplomat, scientist, philosopher, publisher, and inventor. Aphorisms from his *Poor Richard's Almanack* have become part of the world's store of proverbs. His autobiography has become a classic.

*Gibbon, Edward.* 1737–1794. British historian, whose *Decline and Fall of the Roman Empire* was one of the major productions of the eighteenth century and remains a classic of historical literature.

*Gluck, Christoph Willibald von.* 1714–1787. German composer who wrote for the Parisian public. He initiated a reforming style in opera in which music served a more expressive and dramatic function than before.

*Goethe, Johann Wolfgang von.* 1749–1832. Regarded as Germany's greatest writer. Gave impetus to the romantic movement by his tragic drama *Goetz von Berlichingen* and his novel *The Sorrows of Werther.* Now best-known for his epic drama *Faust.*

*Goldsmith, Oliver.* 1728–1774. British playwright, poet, essayist, and novelist. His *The Citizen of the World* was modeled on Montesquieu's *Persian Letters.* Among his best-known poems is *The Deserted Village,* describing the ravages of the Industrial Revolution.

*Gray, Thomas.* 1716–1771. British poet whose *Elegy Written in a Country Churchyard* fostered the taste for the simple and natural.

*Handel, George Frederick.* 1685–1759. German-born composer who wrote chiefly for the London public. Ranks among the greatest composers of what is now regarded as the classical age of music.·

*Helvétius, Claude-Adrien.* 1715–1771. A man of great wealth and influence whose house was used by the Encyclopedists as their meeting place. His equalitarian views were too extreme even for Diderot. His chief work, *De l'Esprit,* was condemned and publicly burned.

*Holbach, Baron Paul Henri Dietrich d'.* 1723–1789. German-born nobleman who assumed French citizenship. One of the Encylopedists, but went further than the rest in his atheistic views.

*Hume, David.* 1711–1776. British philosopher and historian. An empiricist chiefly known for his skeptical views: "I have discovered but one truth, that there is no truth." Derived all knowledge from experience and sense impressions which could never be conclusively validated. Influenced by Rousseau, he gave priority to the emotions ("passions") over the powers of the intellect.

*Jefferson, Thomas.* 1743–1826. Third President of the United States, author of the American Declaration of Independence and largely responsible for the Bill of Rights amendments in the Constitution. Inventor, architect, naturalist, statesman, and philosopher and, to the end of his life, a vigorous upholder of democracy.

*Johnson, Samuel.* 1709–1784. British essayist, critic, dramatist, poet, biographer, and lexicographer. His *Lives of the Poets* remains a classic, and his pathbreaking dictionary helped to systematize English usage. Though a Tory in politics, his works reflect his own early poverty and show awareness of social conditioning.

*Kant, Immanuel.* 1724–1804. German philosopher with democratic sympathies and liberal religious views. Influenced by Hume and Rousseau. In his philosophy he sought to determine the laws and limits of knowledge, avoiding dogmatism and overestimation, and skepticism and underestimation of the role of reason.

*Laclos, Pierre Ambroise François Choderlos de.* 1741–1803. Served with the French revolutionary army. In his novel *Dangerous Acquaintances* he portrayed the heartlessness of upper-class love intrigues.

*Locke, John.* 1632–1704. English philosopher. Although most of his work was done in the previous century, Locke exerted his chief influence in the eighteenth. The French philosophes venerated him, and both the American constitution and the first French republican constitution were largely shaped after his ideas.

*Montesquieu, Baron de La Brède et de. Charles de Secondat.* 1689–1755. One of the leading Encyclopedists. For commentary on and summary of his career see Introduction.

*Novalis,* pseudonym of *Baron Friedrich von Hardenberg.* 1772–1801. German lyric poet and one of the founders of the romantic movement.

*Paine, Thomas.* 1737–1809. Born in England, emigrated to America, and had a brief political career in Paris during the Revolution, barely escaping the guillotine. One of the greatest of the eighteenth-century pamphleteers. Among his best-known works are *Common Sense, The Rights of Man,* and *The Age of Reason.*

*Pope, Alexander.* 1688–1744. British poet and satirist. His *Essay on Man,* which is virtually a versification of the ideas of the Earl of Shaftesbury, ranks among the great philosophical poems of literature and was influential in spreading the concepts of the Enlightenment. Many of its lines or couplets have become standard quotations.

*Rameau, Jean Philippe.* 1683–1764. One of the greatest of the French composers. Himself a philosophe, he held that music was consciously or intuitively constructed on mathematical principles.

*Reynolds, Sir Joshua.* 1723–1792. British portrait painter famous also for his literary associations — he was a member of the Samuel Johnson circle — and, of course, for his formulations of theories of aesthetic individualism.

*Rousseau, Jean-Jacques.* 1712–1778. Swiss-born French philosophe. For commentary on and summary of his career see Introduction.

*Schiller, Johann Christoph Friedrich von.* 1759–1805. German poet and playwright, an associate of Goethe, and influential in spreading the ideas of both the Enlightenment and romanticism.

*Shaftesbury, Third Earl of. Anthony Ashley Cooper.* 1671–1713. British moral philosopher, now best known as Pope's mentor. His chief work was *Characteristics of Men, Manners, Opinions, Times.*

*Smith, Adam.* 1723–1790. British political economist. In a long residence in France absorbed the ideas of the French physiocrats. His *The Wealth of Nations* remains a classic and was a powerful influence in supplanting mercantilism by free trade.

*Sterne, Laurence.* 1713–1768. British novelist who was much influenced by Locke, especially his theory of associations, and whose whimsical style is largely dependent on association of ideas.

*Swift, Jonathan.* 1667–1745. British satirist, poet, and pamphleteer. His best-known work is the classic *Gulliver's Travels.*

*Voltaire,* assumed name of *François Marie Arouet.* 1694–1778. Greatest and most influential of the philosophes. For commentary on and summary of his career see Introduction.

*White, Gilbert.* 1720–1793. British naturalist and curate of Selborne, where he made the observations on which his classic *The Natural History of Selborne* was based.

*Winckelmann, Johann Joachim.* 1717–1768. German-born archaeologist who converted to Catholicism to facilitate his classical studies in Italy. Influential in promoting the classical revival in the late eighteenth century.

## DATE DUE

|  |  |  |  |
|---|---|---|---|
|  |  |  |  |
|  |  |  |  |
|  |  |  |  |
|  |  |  |  |
|  |  |  |  |
|  |  |  |  |
|  |  |  |  |
|  |  |  |  |
|  |  |  |  |
|  |  |  |  |
|  |  |  |  |
|  |  |  |  |
|  |  |  |  |
|  |  |  |  |
|  |  |  |  |
|  |  |  |  |
|  |  |  |  |
|  |  |  |  |

PRINTED IN U.S.A.